Hollywood Independent

Harold Mirisch, William Wyler, Shirley MacLaine and Walter Mirisch (left to right) discussing *The Children's Hour*.

Hollywood Independent

How the Mirisch Company Changed Cinema

Paul Kerr

BLOOMSBURY ACADEMIC
NEW YORK • LONDON • OXFORD • NEW DELHI • SYDNEY

BLOOMSBURY ACADEMIC
Bloomsbury Publishing Inc
1385 Broadway, New York, NY 10018, USA
50 Bedford Square, London, WC1B 3DP, UK
29 Earlsfort Terrace, Dublin 2, Ireland

BLOOMSBURY, BLOOMSBURY ACADEMIC and the Diana logo are trademarks of
Bloomsbury Publishing Plc

First published in the United States of America 2023
Paperback edition published 2024

Copyright © Paul Kerr, 2023

For legal purposes the Acknowledgements on p. vii constitute an extension of this copyright page.

Cover design by Eleanor Rose

Cover image: *Some Like it Hot*, 1959, Dir. Billy Wilder © Mirisch Corporation / RNB / Collection Christophel / ArenaPAL www.arenapal.com

All rights reserved. No part of this publication may be reproduced or transmitted in any form or by any means, electronic or mechanical, including photocopying, recording, or any information storage or retrieval system, without prior permission in writing from the publishers.

Bloomsbury Publishing Inc does not have any control over, or responsibility for, any third-party websites referred to or in this book. All internet addresses given in this book were correct at the time of going to press. The author and publisher regret any inconvenience caused if addresses have changed or sites have ceased to exist, but can accept no responsibility for any such changes.

Library of Congress Cataloging-in-Publication Data
Names: Kerr, Paul, author.
Title: Hollywood independent : how the Mirisch Company changed cinema / Paul Kerr.
Description: New York : Bloomsbury Academic, 2023. | Includes bibliographical references and index. | Summary: "Explains how a new kind of independent production company, The Mirisch Company, remade Hollywood in the decade between the end of the studio system in the mid-50s and the emergence of the so-called "Movie Brats" (Spielberg, Scorsese, Coppola and Lucas) some 15 years later"– Provided by publisher.
Identifiers: LCCN 2022043121 (print) | LCCN 2022043122 (ebook) | ISBN 9781501336751 (hardback) | ISBN 9798765103746 (paperback) | ISBN 9781501336768 (epub) | ISBN 9781501336775 (pdf) | ISBN 9781501336782 (ebook other)
Subjects: LCSH: Mirisch Company. | Motion picture studios–California–Los Angeles–History. | Motion picture industry–California–Los Angeles–History.
Classification: LCC PN1999.M58 K47 2023 (print) | LCC PN1999.M58 (ebook) | DDC 384/.806579493–dc23/eng/20221123
LC record available at https://lccn.loc.gov/2022043121
LC ebook record available at https://lccn.loc.gov/2022043122

ISBN: HB: 978-1-5013-3675-1
PB: 979-8-7651-0374-6
ePDF: 978-1-5013-3677-5
eBook: 978-1-5013-3676-8

Typeset by Deanta Global Publishing Services, Chennai, India

To find out more about our authors and books visit www.bloomsbury.com and sign up for our newsletters.

Contents

List of figures		vi
Acknowledgements		vii
Introduction		1
1	Prequel: What did you do in the war, daddy? The Mirisch brothers before entering production	19
2	Prequel: The first time: The Mirisches at Monogram, Allied Artists and Moulin Productions	43
3	How to succeed in business without really trying: Towards a corporate history of the Mirisch companies	79
4	The organization: Corporate culture and the Mirisch Company as 'author'	105
5	'This book is all that I need': Adaptation as aesthetic and business strategy at the Mirisch Company	137
6	Same time next year *or* the return of the seven: The Mirisch Company's sequels and series for cinema and television	155
7	'You can't kill a squadron': The Mirisch Second World War film cycle	179
8	The border jumpers: 'Lend lease in reverse' – The Mirisch Company and transnational cinema	201
9	The children's hour – Why the Mirisch brothers never worked with the movie brats	215
10	Midway: Between blockbusters and television – The Mirisch Company after United Artists	251
11	Conclusion – Cast a giant shadow	265
Mirisch Company filmography		271
Bibliography		283
Index		299

Figures

Frontispiece	Harold Mirisch, William Wyler, Shirley MacLaine and Walter Mirisch (left to right) discussing *The Children's Hour*	ii
1	The fictional director and producer, in the opening scene of *The Party*	8
2	Alfred Hitchcock, Producer, and Harold Mirisch, RKO Theaters Executive, in New York where the producer is testing Broadway stars for his next RKO picture, *Notorious*	29
3	The Bijou cinema in *Fall Guy*	48
4	Tribute to Harold Mirisch, Motion Picture Pioneer of the Year, 1964	86
5	Joe and Jerry visit MCA's Chicago office in *Some Like It Hot*	122
6	The anonymous corporate office in *The Apartment*, antithesis of the small family business that was the Mirisch Company	133
7	Thomas Crown (Steve McQueen) signs a contract in the opening scenes of *The Thomas Crown Affair*	135
8	*Hawaii* poster	141
9	*Return of the Seven* poster	158
10	The thousand plane raid plan being 'pitched' to top brass in *The 1000 Planes Raid*	193
11	*Avanti* poster	205
12	The slap, from *In the Heat of the Night*	217
13	The submarine crew watching *Jaws* in *Grey Lady Down*	257
14	Leonardo DiCaprio as 'Rick Dalton' as *The Great Escape*'s 'Hilts', in *Once Upon a Time . . . in Hollywood*	267

Acknowledgements

This book is the belated product of three professions and countless collaborations. My first professional job was at the British Film Institute, where I began to write seriously about film and television. The earliest extended article I published was about the industrial determinants of film noir.[1] I followed this up with an essay about the B movie director Joseph H. Lewis.[2] Both pieces foregrounded the film industry, not only as a constraint on but also as a condition for certain kinds of creative work. And both mentioned Monogram and Allied Artists, where, coincidentally, the Mirisch brothers first worked in production. In this period, I also edited an anthology about the American movie business *The Hollywood Film Industry*,[3] and co-edited and co-wrote a collection of new work on an American independent television production company, *MTM: Quality Television*.[4] The Mirisch Company and independent production constitute what would once have been called a structuring absence in the former volume, while Mirisch-Rich provided an unsuccessful precedent as TV independent for the subject and strategy of the latter.

That second book's publication prompted my accidental entry into another career, television, as a researcher on *The Cat Factory* (C4 1984), a documentary about MTM for the UK's then-new Channel Four. Indeed, that channel was pioneering the commissioning of an increasing proportion of its programming from equally new independent production companies, one of which, Illuminations, was the producer of that very documentary. My subsequent twenty-plus year career as a TV producer included two brief stints working inside the BBC and contracts of various lengths at five very distinct independent production companies, making programmes for both the BBC and C4. The dozens of programmes I produced in this period include *Who's Crying Now?* (BBC2 1993), a documentary directed by Saskia Baron about the rise and fall of the British independent film production company Palace Pictures, and two 'making-of' documentaries about Mirisch Company classics – *Guns for Hire* (C4 2000), about the production of *The Magnificent Seven* (Sturges, 1960), directed by Louis Heaton, and *Nobody's Perfect* (BBC2 2001), about the making of *Some Like It Hot* (Wilder, 1959) which I directed myself. From all my colleagues on these programmes and at those companies, I learnt a great deal about independent production. I want to thank all my collaborators on – and interviewees for – those programmes, including

---

[1] Paul Kerr, "Out of What Past?' Notes on the "B" Film Noir', *Screen Education* vol 32–3, Autumn–Winter 1979–80: 45–65.
[2] Paul Kerr, 'My Name Is Joseph H. Lewis', *Screen* vol 24 no 4–5, July–October 1983: 48–67.
[3] Paul Kerr (ed), *The Hollywood Film Industry*, London: RKP, 1986.
[4] Jane Feuer, Paul Kerr and Tise Vahimagi (eds), *MTM: 'Quality Television'*, London: BFI, 1984.

Walter Mirisch himself, for further widening my interest in and, I hope, understanding of independent production.

Eventually, my luck as a freelance producer ran out, and, scrabbling for a third career, I found myself teaching, first at London Metropolitan University and subsequently at Middlesex University. This new professional identity both required and facilitated some sustained thinking about film and television of the kind that I had had little time for over the previous two and a half decades. Among a number of articles I published was a production study of the last TV documentary I worked on, *The Last Slave* (C4 2007),[5] made at another independent production company, October Films, an article for a Billy Wilder anthology about the corporate authorship of *Some Like It Hot*,[6] and an analysis of the impact on the world cinema series I produced for BBC2, *Moving Pictures (1990–96)*, of its shift from being a BBC in-house production to being made by an independent company.[7] I was also a co-investigator on a major, AHRC-funded, research project on British television documentary and the independent sector.[8] Clearly, independent production was very much on my mind, with well over two decades' experience inside just such companies to temper any tempting academic generalizations.

In the academic sphere, I am pleased to be able to thank the following libraries and librarians: Sue Nolan and the staff at Middlesex University Shepherd Library, Clarissa Yingling and her colleagues at Baker Library Special Collections, Harvard Business School, Susan Kreuger and her colleagues at the Wisconsin Historical Society, which holds the collection of the Wisconsin Center for Film and Theater Research (including the United Artists Collection Addition and the Walter Mirisch Papers), whose assistant director, Mary K. Huelsbeck, and her colleagues were a huge help, the staff of the British Library, the Margaret Herrick Library (visited briefly during the pre-production research for the *Some Like It Hot* documentary) and the British Film Institute library. The University of Wisconsin is also the base of the invaluable 'Media History Digital Library' (https://mediahistoryproject.org/) which facilitated far more name and title searches than I could ever have managed manually. Support from Middlesex's Faculty of Arts and Creative Industries allowed me to visit Madison for a week in 2018. Middlesex also subscribed to *Variety*'s digital archive, to enable me to further research Mirisch's activities. Early drafts of several of the following chapters were presented, with Middlesex support, at conferences, too numerous to mention, at which I tested some of the ideas and rehearsed some of the arguments developed

---

[5] Paul Kerr, 'The Last Slave (2007): The Genealogy of a British Television History Programme', *Historical Journal of Film, Radio and Television* vol 29 no 3, 2009: 381–97.
[6] Paul Kerr, '"A Small, Effective Organization": The Mirisch Company, the Package-Unit System and the Production of Some Like It Hot', in Karen McNally (ed), *Billy Wilder, Movie-Maker: Critical Essays on the Films*, McFarland & Company, 2011.
[7] Paul Kerr, 'Making Film Programmes for the BBC and Channel 4: The Shift from In-house "Producer Unit" to Independent "Package-Unit" Production', *Historical Journal for Film, Radio and Television* vol 33 no 3, September 2013: 434–53.
[8] James Bennett, Niki Strange, Paul Kerr and Andrea Medrado, *Multiplatforming Public Service Broadcasting: The Economic and Cultural Role of UK TV and Digital Independents*, Royal Holloway, University of London, University of Sussex and London Metropolitan University, 2012.

here. I have recently published articles about the company and its films in books about United Artists, Westerns and seriality and some of what follows first appeared in part, in draft form in those collections.[9] The chapters in this volume owe a debt to the editors of those volumes, and thanks are particularly due to Yannis Tzioumakis, Tino Balio and Lee Broughton.

Acknowledgements in books like this are usually kept to academic colleagues, friends and family. And, of course, I owe a great deal to colleagues at London Metropolitan and particularly Middlesex Universities, specifically Basil Glynn, Deborah Klika, Tom McGorrian and Paul Cobley. But I also owe a debt of gratitude to the dozens of programme-makers I worked with over almost twenty-five years, of which a handful of names with whom I worked closely and from whom I learnt hugely will have to stand in for the rest: John Wyver and Linda Zuck at Illuminations, Michael Jackson, then of Beat Ltd, Alex Graham and Jane Root then at Wall to Wall Television, Saskia Baron, Louis Heaton and Daniel Wolf, then at Barraclough Carey Productions and Jane Manning, Denman Rooke and Adam Bullmore at October Films. Thanks also to Sharmila Mary and Venkat Perla Ramesh, project managers at Deanta, and Amy Brownbridge, production editor at Bloomsbury. Then there are the patient and painstaking staff at Bloomsbury Academic, my editor Katie Gallof and editorial assistant Stephanie Grace-Petinos and the anonymous reviewer whose detailed feedback was extremely helpful. Finally, I want to thank my mother, whose love of old Hollywood remains undimmed at ninety-eight, and my son, Sammy, who sat through more Mirisch films than is probably sensible for anyone not writing a book about them.

None of this would have been possible, however, without the patience, love, support and critical encouragement of Ruth Baumgarten, to whom this book is dedicated.

---

[9] Paul Kerr, 'The Magnificent Seven Mirisch Companies: Competitive Strategy and Corporate Authorship', in Peter Krämer, Gary Needham, Yannis Tzioumakis and Tino Balio (eds), *United Artists*, London, New York: Routledge, 2020, 112–31; '"It Seemed Like a Good Idea at the Time": Hollywood, Homology and Hired Guns – The Making of The Magnificent Seven', in Lee Broughton (ed), *Reframing Cult Westerns: From The Magnificent Seven to the Hateful Eight*. New York: Bloomsbury Academic, 2020; Paul Kerr, 'A Forgotten Episode in the History of Hollywood Cinema, Television and Seriality: The Case of the Mirisch Company', in Ariane Hudelet and Anne Cremieux (eds), *Exploring Seriality on Screen: Audiovisual Narratives in Film and Television*, Abingdon: Routledge, 2021. These four essays were early drafts of sections of Chapters 3, 4 and 6.

Introduction

The Mirisch Company, in its multiple manifestations, was the most commercially and critically successful independent production company in Hollywood from the late 1950s to the mid-1970s. Its films won the Best Picture Oscar three times between 1960 and 1967, a record that remained unequalled among small independents until Miramax's success in the 1990s, while supplying United Artists with five of its ten most profitable films between 1957 and 1969. Mirisch productions include several of the most celebrated and successful films in the history of Hollywood: *The Apartment* (Wilder, 1960), *Fiddler on the Roof* (Jewison, 1971), *The Great Escape* (Sturges, 1963), *In the Heat of the Night* (Jewison, 1967), *The Magnificent Seven, Man of the West* (Mann, 1958), *The Pink Panther* (Edwards, 1964), *Some Like It Hot, The Thomas Crown Affair* (Jewison, 1968) and *West Side Story* (Wise/Robbins, 1961) are all hugely iconic and influential titles in Hollywood's postwar history. Yet despite, or perhaps because of, the familiarity of their films, the company that produced them remains all but unknown. Founded by three brothers in 1957, Mirisch produced sixty-eight films for UA, making an average of four films annually for that company, before the relationship ended in 1974, and then made another five for Universal, as well as several TV movies and series, before producing one final feature for UA. Subsequently, the surviving brother, Walter Mirisch, has been credited as executive producer on seven TV movies, three further TV series and a feature film.

However, despite an excellent chapter in Tino Balio's second volume on the history of United Artists (Balio, 1987 and 2009), complemented by Walter Mirisch's recent, anecdotal, autobiography (Mirisch, 2008) there has, until now, been no book-length study of the Mirisch Company.[1] And yet many of its productions remain not only very visible in the cinematic culture but also extremely 'viable' as sources of plots and characters, dialogue and iconography, series and sequels, remakes and reboots. Most recently, the announcement of the acquisition, in May 2021, of MGM by Amazon was explained by Amazon's Jeff Bezos in terms of IP. 'MGM has a vast, deep catalogue of much beloved intellectual property. With the talent at Amazon and MGM Studios, we can reimagine and develop that IP for the 21st Century.' Reports of the acquisition in the trade press cited Mirisch's *The Magnificent Seven* and *The Pink Panther* among the examples of this evergreen IP.[2]

---

[1] Tino Balio, *United Artists: The Company that Changed the Film Industry*, University of Wisconsin Press, 1987 and 2009; Walter Mirisch, *I Thought We Were Making Movies, Not History*, University of Wisconsin Press, 2008.
[2] 'Amazon to "Reimagine and Develop" MGM Shows After $8.45bn Deal', *Television Business International* https://tbivision.com/2021/05/27/amazon-to-reimagine-develop-mgm-shows-after-8-45bn-deal/MGM had acquired UA's library.

The continuing *visibility* of Mirisch movies is revealed in the compilation *Precious Images* (Workman, 1986), commissioned by the Directors Guild to celebrate its fiftieth anniversary. Of ninety-one iconic extracts included from films made between 1959 and 1971, for instance, a magnificent eight are from Mirisch productions – *Some Like It Hot, The Apartment, The Magnificent Seven, West Side Story, The Great Escape, The Pink Panther, In the Heat of the Night* and *The Fiddler on the Roof.* Recent remakes of *Pink Panther, Magnificent Seven, West Side Story* and *Midway* (Smight, 1976) suggest it is often 'twice upon a time in Hollywood', as Mirisch movies are variously plundered, pastiched, recycled and referenced, always already familiar. And yet, neither the successive Mirisch companies which produced them nor the three Mirisch brothers who founded and ran them receive even a mention in David Thomson's *New Biographical Dictionary of Film.*[3] Walter Mirisch is included in Ephraim Katz's *Film Encyclopaedia*, but neither his brothers nor their companies merit an entry of their own.[4] *Movie History: A Survey* does refer to the company but manages to misspell its name not once but twice, and then omits it entirely from the index.[5]

Even Neal Gabler's *An Empire of Their Own*, a book-length study of how the Jewish moguls ran Hollywood, excludes them, as it only deals with the studio era.[6] Louis B. Mayer died in 1957, while Harry Cohn and Harry Warner passed away the following year. Sam Goldwyn, born in Poland, like the Mirisch's father, survived longer. (As the Hollywood saying goes, 'From Poland to Polo in one generation'.) When the brothers rented offices at Samuel Goldwyn Studio, they were entirely conscious of continuing a tradition of Jewish movie moguls. (United Artists' Los Angeles HQ was also at 1041 North Formosa Avenue.) Indeed, Samuel Goldwyn was one of the speakers when Harold was named Movie Pioneer of the Year, in November 1964.[7] Walter records in his autobiography lunching with Goldwyn regularly, while Marvin was one of the latter's last callers.

Like their Jewish movie mogul predecessors, the brothers began in exhibition and distribution before moving into production, which was precisely how the vertical integration of the industry itself occurred. This volume, however, is not about Mirisch across 'the film industry', which includes not only production but also distribution and exhibition and focuses almost exclusively on production, as it was United Artists, not Mirisch, which was responsible for the distribution and exhibition of almost all Mirisch Pictures. Nevertheless, the company was intimately involved in both the marketing and distribution strategies of their productions. However, despite similarities with their celebrated predecessors, the brothers were never publicity-seekers, but hid in plain sight – and Balio's study notwithstanding, apparently, their company continues to do so – from film history.

---

[3] David Thomson, *The New Biographical Dictionary of Film*, London: Little, Brown, 2002.
[4] Ephraim Katz, *The Film Encyclopaedia* (3rd edition), Harper Perennial, 1998.
[5] Douglas Gomery and Clara Pafort-Overdun, *Movie History: A Survey* (2nd edition), New York and London: Routledge, 2011.
[6] Neal Gabler, *An Empire of Their Own: How the Jews Invented Hollywood*, Random House, 1998.
[7] 'Colleagues Cite Harold Mirisch as Movie Pioneer of the Year', *New York Times*, 24.11.64.

Tarantino and Mirisch

One of the conceits in Quentin Tarantino's recent 'novelization' of his latest film, *Once Upon a Time in Hollywood* (2021),[8] is that his actor hero, Rick Dalton, was on a shortlist for the role of the 'Cooler King' in *The Great Escape*, the part played in the latter film by Steve McQueen. Tarantino's film makes much of this, constructing a sequence in which Leonardo DiCaprio (Dalton) was shot against a green screen, wearing McQueen's iconic costume, with VFX technology deployed to replace McQueen with Dalton in a key scene from the original film. But the novel is also peppered with movie references, including numerous explicit and implicit references to Mirisch productions, creating a credible context for Dalton's fictional film and TV career. Furthermore, in a book published in 2021, Walter Mirisch's 100th year, it is striking to discover four mentions of the Mirisch Company (on pages 113, 114 and twice on page 376), and another of the Mirisch Bros (also 376).

Tarantino's narrator also informs us that, director Paul

> Wendkos was preparing a film for a small British production company called Oakmont Productions which had an international distribution deal through MGM. Oakmont specialized in modestly budgeted World War Two action-adventure vehicles featuring British casts, except for the lead, who was usually an American actor known from television. Some examples were Boris Sagal's The Thousand Plane Raid starring Christopher (Rat Patrol) George; Mosquito Squadron starring David (Man From Uncle) McCallum; Billy Graham's Submarine X-1 starring a pre-Godfather, post-El Dorado James Caan; Walter Grauman's The Last Escape starring Stuart (Cimarron Strip) Whitman; and Wendkos's Attack on the Iron Coast, starring Lloyd (Sea Hunt) Bridges. Wendkos was gearing up to do one more, a Navy-based adventure with the pulpy title Hell Boats.[9]

Tarantino's reinvention of the latter's production history has the film's actual star, James Franciscus, unavailable and Rick Dalton having to step in. But Tarantino's Wendkos offers Rick the part in March 1970, when the actual film was shot in late summer 1968 and then left on the shelf for over a year. Of course, Tarantino's novelization is an alternative, counterfactual, 'hypothetical' history, semi-dependent on its readers being oblivious to the actual, factual history of Hollywood. Nevertheless, the author fails to note, or perhaps even know, that Oakmont Productions was not a British company at all, but a subsidiary of the Mirisch Company. Nor that it was United Artists, not MGM, which released Oakmont films. (MGM only assumed ownership when it acquired UA much later.) Nor does Tarantino add that *Rat Patrol* (ABC 1966–8) was itself a Mirisch production (more specifically, a Mirisch-Rich Production).

---

[8] Quentin Tarantino, *Once Upon a Time in Hollywood*, London: Weidenfeld and Nicholson, 2021.
[9] Ibid, 112–13.

As Tarantino sums them up, 'All the Oakmont Productions were pretty much the same, with Mosquito Squadron and Attack on the Iron Coast being the pick of the litter. But for what they were, they weren't bad. They were pretty entertaining if unmemorable potboilers.'[10] Tarantino then invents an attempted Wendkos/Dalton collaboration on *Guns of the Magnificent Seven* (Wendkos, 1969), the third film in the series, 'a few years earlier' (though in fact the latter was made at the same time as the Oakmont films) for which Dalton proved unavailable. Nevertheless, 'Wendkos did such a good job with that assignment, the Mirisch Company offered Paul the fourth film in the series, at the time titled Cannons for the Magnificent Seven.'[11] And the novel provides a convincing, albeit fictional, pre-production history of what became Mirisch's *Cannon for Cordoba* (Wendkos, 1970) – which did not, in fact, originate as an intended *Magnificent Seven* sequel.

In another film historical aside, this time about Lee Marvin, Tarantino's narrator explains that

> As Marvin got older, he seemed more and more haunted by the ghosts of the soldiers he killed on the battlefield. During the climax of his 1974 western, The Spikes Gang, when Marvin is supposed to shoot his young co-star Gary Grimes (the young lad from The Summer of '42) apparently Grimes's look or age or both brought to mind a young soldier Marvin killed during the war. The Oscar-winning tough guy sat in his trailer and drank himself into a stupor. . . . The rest of The Spikes Gang is an okay seventies western. Enjoyable enough to watch, but not memorable enough to stay in the mind. Except for that climactic violent shoot-out and the vicious expression on Marvin's totem-pole face.[12]

The Spikes Gang (Fleischer, 1974) was yet another Mirisch production.

Finally, on the 'questionable' shortlist which Dalton cites about the casting of the 'Cooler King' in *The Great Escape*, Tarantino has his hero tick off a series of explanations for why he, Rick Dalton, would never have got the part. Because McQueen would never have turned it down. Because 'the three Georges' – Peppard, Maharis and Chakiris – were all ahead of him on that list. And more specifically, because 'two years later, Sturges cast Maharis in the lead in a thriller called The Satan Bug – which suggests he's partial to Maharis'. Of course, Sturges was on a multi-picture deal with the Mirisch Company and *The Satan Bug* (Sturges, 1965) was also a Mirisch film. As for Chakiris,

> One, there is that inexplicable Oscar he'd got . . . Two, The Great Escape was produced by the Mirisch Brothers for the Mirisch Company . . . George Chakiris has a deal with the Mirisch Company. He made the 633 Squadron with 'em. He made Diamond Head with 'em. He made that goofy Aztec movie with 'em. So not only do they like him – he's under fucking contract with 'em.[13]

---

[10] Ibid, 113.
[11] Ibid, 114.
[12] Ibid, 309–10.
[13] Ibid, 375–6.

In fact, while the 'goofy Aztec movie' *Kings of the Sun* (Lee Thompson, 1963), *The Satan Bug* and *633 Squadron* (Grauman, 1964) were indeed all Mirisch productions, *Diamond Head* (Green, 1962) was not. But whether these historical errors are intentional or not remains impossible to tell. Meanwhile, for Dalton, Peppard, inevitably top of any such list, would never have turned it down, even if McQueen had. Dalton's relegation to the bottom of this list is doubly ironic in that Dalton's fictional TV series, *Bounty Law*, was partly based on McQueen's *Wanted: Dead or Alive* (CBS, 1958–61).

By my count, that makes fifteen of the fifty or so Mirisch films made by 1969, the year in which both film and book are set, which are either explicitly name-checked or implicitly referenced in the novel. *The Great Escape, The Satan Bug, Cannon for Cordoba, The Magnificent Seven, Guns of the Magnificent Seven, 633 Squadron, The Spikes Gang, Kings of the Sun, West Side Story* (that 'inexplicable' Oscar-winner), plus the six Oakmont films. (Not to mention *Massacre Harbor* (Peyser, 1968), the movie quickly compiled from three episodes of *Rat Patrol*, the TV series Tarantino also cites in passing. Indeed, it is ironically appropriate that Tarantino refers to *Rat Patrol*, since it, too, recycled shots from *The Great Escape*.) That amounts to an astonishing 30 per cent of Mirisch's output in the period. The company's movies clearly loom large in Tarantino's cinematic imaginary. But as Tarantino's narrator puts it, many of them were 'unmemorable', indeed all but forgotten. Which is, of course, what licensed this jeu d'esprit in the first place.

Forgetting and remembering

Ironically, the protagonist of Walter Mirisch's first-ever film as a producer at Monogram, *Fall Guy* (Le Borg, 1947), is himself forgetful, resulting from a drug-induced form of amnesia. Two decades later, in *Mosquito Squadron* (Sagal, 1969) RAF Squadron Leader David Scott loses his memory when his plane is shot down. In *Return from the Ashes* (Lee Thompson, 1965) Pilgrin (Maximilian Schell) fails to recognize his wife, Michelle, (Ingrid Thulin) on her return from a concentration camp after the war. Like amnesia, blindness is a familiar film trope. In *Stolen Hours* (Petrie, 1963), Susan Hayward suffers loss of vision and blinding headaches, intimations of her fatal illness. In *The Great Escape* Donald Pleasance goes blind forging passports in a prisoner-of-war camp. In *The Hallelujah Trail* (Sturges, 1966), reprising that disability, Pleasance's Oracle is a 'blind-drunk seer'. In *633 Squadron*, Bissell is blinded in a crash-landing. In *Attack on the Iron Coast* (Wendkos, 1968), Kimberly is blinded in a training accident. The ubiquity of the device in plots and characters may seem like a lack of originality, a shortcut to individuating characterization, at the Mirisch Company, which produced all those films. And indeed, such shortcuts were no stranger to Mirisch productions. But there can be a kind of blindness and forgetfulness in film history too. Film scholarship deploys selective lenses, privileging particular perspectives, like auteurism (which Harvard referencing rules reinforce), while obscuring others. While respectful mentions of auteur classics *Magnificent Obsession* (Sirk, 1954) and *The Magnificent Ambersons* (Welles, 1942) grace almost every film history textbook, an arguably more influential movie, *The Magnificent Seven*, remains relatively rarely cited. This book, then, addresses one such blindspot in studies of Hollywood, an independent production company which was responsible for a disproportionate percentage of popular 'classic', if not necessarily 'canonical', Hollywood productions, many of them hugely influential both at the time and since.

In fact, without knowing it, I grew up watching Mirisch movies. *The Magnificent Seven*, *The Great Escape*, *633 Squadron* and *The Pink Panther* were among the first films I ever saw at the cinema. In my teens, *The Thomas Crown Affair* and *In the Heat of the Night* loomed large, the former for its sexy 'stylishness', split screen and that spinning, 360-degree kiss, the latter for its radical, racial 'content'. I can still see and hear Sidney Poitier's detective slapping that white planter – and the instant intake of breath in the stalls. Later, at University, I caught up with *The Apartment* and *Man of the West*. People often reminisce about pop and rock music having provided the soundtrack to their youth, but for me Elmer Bernstein's ubiquitous scores for *The Magnificent Seven* and *The Great Escape*, Ron Goodwin's music for *633 Squadron* and Henry Mancini's *Pink Panther* theme are all equally unforgettable, as, less happily, is the earworm of *Windmills of My Mind*, from *The Thomas Crown Affair*. But Mirisch also laid an image track, a greenscreen backdrop to my adolescence, the iconic residue of hours spent in the cinema and in front of the small screen too, including *Some Like It Hot*, transmitted on BBC1 on Xmas Day 1968 and the controversial TV series *Rat Patrol*, bought and then virtually banned by the BBC after only six episodes in 1967. Meanwhile, *633 Squadron* (BBC1 17.11.70, with an audience of 20.5 million) and *The Great Escape* (BBC1 28.12.71, with an audience of 21.5 million) were the first two films to rate over 20 million viewers on British TV in the 1970s.[14] Even the first academic film book I read, V. F. Perkins' *Film as Film*, ends with a critique of two Mirisch-connected productions, *Moulin Rouge* (Huston, 1952), a prestige-heavy international biopic *and The Loudest Whisper* (aka *The Children's Hour*) (Wyler, 1961), a stage adaptation, a critique which relates to the brothers' alleged (over-) reliance on artistic pretexts with a prior cultural capital in legitimating and licensing their projects.[15]

If my early viewing coincided with several Mirisch classics, my own twenty-year career as a TV producer, such as it was, has reinforced my interest in and perhaps partisanship for the contribution of creative producers. In Hollywood cinema, the prestige of the producer has fallen in proportion to the rise of that of the auteur director and while some studio-era producers' names have been celebrated, those of the post-Paramount Decree independent era remain lesser known, particularly those operating in the interregnum between the mid-1950s and the American New Wave, which is customarily dated from just over a decade later. In this sense, the producer is, implicitly and sometimes explicitly, the default fall guy of the auteur theory, making the title of Walter Mirisch's first film as producer ironic.

---

[14] Sheldon Hall, 'Feature Films on British Television in the 1970s' http://bufvc.ac.uk/articles/feature-films-on-british-television-in-the-1970s/8.

[15] V. F. Perkins, *Film as Film*, London: Penguin, 1972, 122–4, 125–7, 130, 192.

The Mirisch Company as 'author'

In what follows, I make two arguments. First, the Mirisch Company and its successors provide a missing link between the end of studio-era Hollywood, brought about by antitrust legislation, blacklisting, the rise of television and talent agencies and demographic change and the beginning of what is variously known as the New Hollywood/New American Cinema/American Renaissance. The Mirisch's package-unit system as an independent provided a blueprint for Hollywood's mode of production after the end of vertical integration, while their movies themselves built a bridge between studio-era 'family films' and the indie cinema/blockbuster duality that followed. In the late 1950s and 1960s Hollywood, Mirisch created a hybrid between residual classical cinema norms and forms and the emerging franchise era, helping to re-popularize cinematic sequels, a strategy which was later legitimated by Coppola's *The Godfather* (1972) Spielberg's *Jaws* (1975) and Lucas's *Star Wars* (1977). But if the movie brats were the first generation of Hollywood filmmakers to see themselves as artists rather than artisans, Mirisch had already deployed the very studio-era veterans who had been hailed by the auteurists, directors like Ford, Mann, Wilder and Wyler, while also offering contracts to a younger generation of successful if less-signature filmmakers, including Blake Edwards, Norman Jewison and George Roy Hill. The Mirisch Company was also among the pioneers of co-productions, runaway production and the exploitation of frozen cash and foreign subsidies, cross-collateralization, media convergence, merchandizing, saturation release strategies and many more industry innovations of the period. The brothers' films, individually and corporately, were the recipients of eighty-four Academy Award nominations and twenty-eight Oscars, including three for Best Picture – for *The Apartment*, *West Side Story* and *In the Heat of the Night*. Walter served three terms as the president of the Producers Guild of America and four terms as the president of the Academy of Motion Picture Arts and Sciences as well as being awarded the Academy's two highest honours, the Irving G. Thalberg Memorial Award and the Jean Hersholt Humanitarian Award (in 1978 and 1983 respectively).

The second argument this volume makes is about Mirisch as a corporate author of its films. This study seeks to avoid demoting the director as an auteur only to replace her with the producer but instead attempts to identify the specific structures and strategies deployed by the Mirisch companies. Indeed, focusing neither on one of the five majors (MGM, Warner Bros, 20th Century Fox, Paramount or RKO) nor the so-called little three (Columbia, Universal or United Artists) nor yet on auteur filmmakers, it concentrates on one specific production company – and its particular corporate culture – identifying that distinct and distinctive independent and its package-unit system as a key determinant of its films. But can a production company be considered an author? It is a counterintuitive proposition, in that the auteur theory was built on the explicit assumption that an auteur director was inherently in conflict with and constrained by a producing organization. As Andrew Sarris put it 'the auteur theory values the personality of a director precisely because of the barriers to its expression' and that work with an auteur's fingerprints on it was 'almost miraculously extracted

Figure 1 The fictional director and producer, in the opening scene of *The Party*.

from his money-oriented environment'.[16] And the professional most closely identified with such an environment historically is the Hollywood producer, the personification of the company, characterized by an obsession with schedules, budgets and bankability. And yet, counterintuitively, it was Norman Jewison who expressed concern about the escalating budget of *Gaily Gaily* (Jewison, 1969) in a letter to Harold Mirisch (24.1.68) while Marvin Mirisch insisted that he should go-ahead with or without the insurance of big-name stars (Jewison wanted someone like Sophia Loren).[17] Thus this volume combines the case for the company as a vital bridge between the so-called 'classical' studio era and the New Hollywood era with a second thrust, arguing that the Mirisch Company can itself be considered as an author (Figure 1).

The book

It may also be helpful, at this point, to clarify what this book is not. It is not a biography of the three Mirisch brothers, Harold and his half-brothers Marvin and Walter, despite its attention to their formative careers in the film industry before launching their own independent production company. Nor does it deal, in comparable detail, with Walter and Marvin Mirisch's work in Hollywood (Harold died in 1968) after the 1970s. It is not a compilation of production studies of all the features, TV series and TV movies which the company produced. Several studies of specific Mirisch productions already exist. There are also numerous 'making-of' documentaries, indeed I produced a couple myself. And, of course, the major directors who worked for Mirisch themselves wrote autobiographies and/or have been the subject of biographies and critical studies, as have several of their screenwriters and stars. I do not discuss in detail the TV series Mirisch made, nor the many animations, both

[16] Andrew Sarris, *The American Cinema: Directors and Directions, 1929–1968*, New York: EP Dutton, 1968, 31, 37.
[17] Norman Jewison and Marvin Mirisch letters, United Artists Collection Addition, Box 5, File 18.

televisual and theatrical, that Mirisch was credited with, in conjunction with the animation company, DePatie-Freleng.

What follows therefore is neither an exhaustive business nor forensic financial history of the many corporate entities that bore the brothers' family name – The Mirisch Company, the Mirisch Corporation, Mirisch Films, Mirisch Productions, Mirisch Pictures and Mirisch-Rich Television, let alone Ashton Productions or Oakmont Productions. The Mirisch papers housed at UCLA remain closed until the death of the surviving brother, Walter (whose personal papers, however, are held at The Center for Film and Theater Research by the Wisconsin Historical Society in Madison, Wisconsin) and such a publication must await access to that collection. Furthermore, the Samuel Goldwyn Studio was almost destroyed by a fire in May 1974 in which much of the company's business records were lost. It is not an analysis of every one of their features, TV movies and series nor an exhaustive chronology of their activities over some seven decades in the film and television industries. My focus is primarily on less than twenty years, when the brothers negotiated a series of successful deals with the financier-distributor, United Artists, for whom they produced sixty-eight feature films and several TV series. The focus here is on the Mirisch mode of production, its corporate culture, its specific strategies for assigning roles and responsibilities, its hiring policies and hierarchies of labour – and how those things sometimes reveal themselves in the films the company produced.

The evidence examined includes not only archive documents recording the company's production practices, trade publications reporting on Mirisch's activities and on those of their peers and the personal recollections of the people who worked there, but also the films themselves. Regarding the latter, rather than taking a sample, either randomly generated or comprised of the best-known productions, my methodology has been to watch every film the company produced as well as multiple examples of every TV series it made during the contractual relationship with United Artists. This strategy allows the analysis to avoid auteurism, and incorporate more than just the classics, while acknowledging that some of those productions were more influential, including inside the company, than others. Of course, on occasion, the brothers employed filmmakers who took the company in fresh directions, in terms of subject matter or style, and inevitably such filmmakers proved influential too. But always within and against the Mirisch corporate culture, the strategic priorities and personal predispositions of the three brothers who founded and ran the company. At the Mirisch Company, the imperatives of corporate custom, the structural opportunities furnished by the family firm itself, and the intentions of three key individuals arguably combine to provide the best and most relevant explanations of why they produced the films they did – and why those films took the forms they did.

This volume is thus a contribution to a comparatively under-researched period in Hollywood history, through a comparatively under-deployed lens, that of a single independent production company. This period roughly corresponds with the years between the last major studio's divorce in 1955, following the 1948 Paramount Decree, and the ascent of the movie brats – and the blockbuster era – with *Jaws* in 1975. Independent production remains a contested term, though Janet Staiger usefully defines an independent as 'a firm which was not owned by nor owned a distribution organization'.[18] Staiger argues that most independents, before divorcement, followed either the director-unit, central producer or producer-unit system of management, which she exemplifies with Chaplin, Monogram and Selznick respectively.[19] Warner Brothers, where Harold began his career, employed a producer-unit system, while RKO had both in-house, director-unit and producer-unit systems in place when he arrived. When Charles Koerner replaced George Schaefer in charge at the company in 1942, RKO returned to renting space to independents, which they shared with in-house staff producer units. The Samuel Goldwyn Studio, where the Mirisch Company was based for almost twenty years, had itself deployed the producer-unit system during the studio era.

The package-unit system

The Mirisch Company, on the other hand, used the 'package-unit' system of production, whereby, according to Staiger, the film, not the firm, was the organizing principle.[20] In fact, the Mirisch Company deployed characteristics of both the producer-unit and the package-unit systems, since while the means of production were hired or rented specifically for each production, alongside the package itself – usually comprising story, stars and director – there was continuity of employment for at least a minimal staff and, at least on occasion, continuity of production from one film to another – specifically in the company's seven film Second World War cycle, its *Magnificent Seven*, *Pink Panther* and *In the Heat of the Night* sequels, and its multiple picture deals with stars and directors. Such multi-film commitments mitigated against the one-film-at-a-time logic of the film rather than firm-centred approach of the average independent. Matthew Bernstein, in his work on Walter Wanger, is at pains to argue that in Hollywood such independence was only ever semi-independent, a relative autonomy.[21] Balio, meanwhile, describes Mirisch as an 'umbrella' company, 'managers' or 'packagers', on whom other producer-director units or independents could rely, to handle everything from pre-production logistics to post-production merchandizing arrangements.[22] I hope to provide evidence here that Mirisch's contribution to the films which bear the company name was far more than such simple 'management' implies. Their fingerprints are, I will argue, visible in the choice of material, the appointment of the key crew and cast, and in making creative decisions about style, setting and subject matter.

---

[18] David Bordwell, Janet Staiger and Kristin Thompson, *The Classical Hollywood Cinema: Film Style & Mode of Production to 1960*, London: Routledge, 1985, 330.
[19] Ibid, 318.
[20] Ibid, 330.
[21] Matthew Bernstein, *Walter Wanger: Hollywood Independent*, University of California Press, 1994.
[22] Balio, 2009: 161.

Staiger identifies several strategies deployed by independent production companies using the package-unit system – differentiation on the basis of its innovations, story, stars and director; targeting specific demographics or audiences rather than a single homogenous mass audience; runaway production; profit-sharing; and the rise of the hyphenate talent, like producer-director-writer Billy Wilder.[23] Balio adds to this list a big picture strategy and the rise of the blockbuster; differentiation from TV through Cinemascope and Panavision as well as 3D; and the exploitation of sex and violence and 'adult' themes, particularly in response to a shift in audience tastes beginning in about 1967 to target the youth market.[24]

The Mirisch Company was far from being the only independent in Hollywood at the time. In 1949 one-fifth of the movies released by the majors were made by indies. Less than a decade later, in 1957, this had risen to 58 per cent.[25] Precise percentages and production figures vary slightly according to source – and definition – but there had certainly been a steady rise in the number of independent producers from forty in 1945, to ninety-three in 1947 to 165 in 1957.[26] By the late 1950s, only Universal refused to work with indies. Maltby, like Bernstein, refers to such companies as 'semi-independent' because of their reliance on studio distribution deals and finance. Nevertheless, 'By 1960 more than half the pictures the studios distributed were made by independents.'[27] By 1967 UA, which pioneered this approach, had become the leading distributor in Hollywood. As in-house production companies, the major studios were becoming unsustainable. In 1958 *Variety* reported that 'it is generally believed that the entire theatrical output of Hollywood can now be made in one studio' – production had declined to such an extent.[28]

Exhibition and publicity

Nor was this simply about shifts in production. In exhibition, too, the paradigm was shifting dramatically. Between 1947 and 1963 48 per cent of four-walled cinemas closed, at the rate of two a day. In 1956 of 19,000 cinemas operating in the United States, 5,200 were running at a loss and another 5,700 only breaking even.[29] Marketing became increasingly important, not least through the new competitor medium of TV. Release patterns were radically revamped. According to Giovacchini, 'Saturation release' was first coined as a term by *Variety* 20 years before *Jaws*, for the release of *Godzilla, King of the Monsters* (Morse/Honda, 1956).[30] In fact, four years earlier, the trade press reported

---

[23] Bordwell, Staiger, Thompson, 1985: 332–4.
[24] Balio, 2009: 161–96.
[25] Ibid, 87.
[26] Richard Maltby, *Hollywood Cinema* (2nd edition), Blackwell Publishing, 2003, 170.
[27] Saverio Giovacchini, 'Postwar Hollywood, 1947–1967', in Jon Lewis (ed), *Producing*, London: I.B. Tauris, 2016, 83.
[28] 'Studio O'Head: What to Do?' *Variety*, 12.3.58: 5.
[29] Maltby, 2003: 163.
[30] Giovacchini, 2016: 78.

that 'A five-day advance of dates for national "Monogram Drive-In Week" May 24th-30th will coincide with a planned national saturation booking of the Walter Mirisch Cinecolor production, Wild Stallion, which stars Ben Johnson!'[31]

A 1957 survey found that only 15 per cent of the American public attended the cinema as often as once a week and that three-quarters of those frequent attendees were under the age of thirty. This age group already accounted for nearly two-thirds of all cinema admissions at the time.[32] By 1958 one-third of cinemas in the United States were drive-ins. But this was the very cinema the Mirisches left behind – or hoped to – by quitting Allied Artists and setting up on their own. Allied Artists and AIP, among others, were competing to supply double bills for the 8,000 cinemas that still ran them in the mid-1950s, but this was precisely the low-lying market (and demographic) Mirisch had consciously decided to abandon, for cinematic higher ground. By 1962, cinema admissions had fallen to 25 per cent of their 1946 level.[33]

At the other end of the spectrum from drive-ins were Roadshows, which, for prestige productions, replaced the exhibition practice of continuous performances with a limited number of screenings (usually two a day), reserved seats (hard tickets), higher than normal admission prices and long engagements, rather than one-week runs or less. In 1968 of the twenty-five movies that had earned over $15 million, seventeen had 'hard ticket' premieres. A 1972 *Variety* analysis revealed that in 1971, 52 per cent of total US box office income had been earned by only fourteen movies. Meanwhile, only a third of the 185 films released that year had broken even.[34] And yet the Mirisch Company persevered with producing mid-range features, essentially avoiding putting all their cinematic eggs in the single basket of a would-be blockbuster, (perhaps *Hawaii* (Roy Hill, 1966) is the sole example of Mirisch's attempt at one) by continuing to produce an average of four films a year throughout their contract with UA.

Mirisch deployed specific business and aesthetic practices, enabling it to maintain and sustain studio-era Hollywood's distinct film forms and norms, memes and themes, but at the same time carve out a recognizable corporate style all its own, not only as a company but also in its creative output. It thus built a bridge into the future of filmmaking in America: sometimes independent, realistic, controversial and candid, but at others formulaic, franchise-friendly, and, increasingly set in the past. This duality was, for well over a decade, key to the company's success and survival but was ultimately to prove its undoing.

Mirisch, authorship and genre

It is a curious coincidence that the formation of the Mirisch Company, in 1957, coincided with the auteur theory. The auteur theory (or 'la Politique des Auteurs')

[31] 'News in Brief', *Motion Picture Daily*, 12.3.52: 7.
[32] Maltby, 2003: 159–60.
[33] Ibid, 161–4.
[34] 'Hits Few: Beasts of Burden: Analysis of 1971 Boom-Bust Biz', *Variety*, 30.11.72: 5–6.

can be dated back to an article by François Truffaut entitled 'Une certaine tendance du cinema français' published in January 1954.³⁵ I am not, here, suggesting that the Mirisch brothers were paid up subscribers to either *Cahiers* itself or, indeed, its politique. But it is striking that both that politique and the company emerged at the same time, both symptoms of other post-war changes. André Bazin's subsequent article 'La politique des auteur', singled out John Ford and Anthony Mann as exemplary Western directors, whose mastery of their material could be measured against the classical conventions of the Western genre in which much of their best work was done.³⁶ (This was the article in which Bazin famously lauded what he called 'the genius of the system', not just celebrating individual auteurs but also the studio and cinematic system which employed them.) Both 'auteurs' were working for Mirisch within months of that article.

Five of Mirisch's first seven films were Westerns – two of which, *The Horse Soldiers* (Ford, 1959) and *Man of the West* were directed by John Ford and Anthony Mann respectively. Like Bazin, Jean-Luc Godard was a huge admirer of Anthony Mann, specifically of *Man of the West*, which he called a 'reinvention of the Western' and 'an admirable lesson in cinema – in modern cinema'.³⁷ *Cahiers* also dedicated an article to one of Walter Mirisch's productions at Allied Artists, *Wichita*, (Tourneur, 1955) – a key moment in the journal's recalibration of its role.³⁸ Typically, *Wichita* is also discussed exclusively in terms of its director, Jacques Tourneur. Godard dedicated his first feature, *A Bout de Souffle* (*Breathless*) (1960) to Monogram. The common denominator of those two enthusiasms is Mirisch, as all three brothers had been Monogram executives in the 1950s, with Harold as vice president and Walter as head of production. The latter, indeed, not only greenlit the films Godard acknowledged with his dedication, but also personally produced *Man of the West*. And yet it seems likely the Mirisch brothers were as oblivious to the affection with which their films were held by the young Turks of the avant-garde as Godard was about Mirisch.

Asked later about that dedication Godard replied, 'I did it to prove that you can do pictures that are both interesting and cheap. In America a cheap picture is not considered interesting, and I said "Why not?" because actually there are many American directors who do B and C pictures who are very interesting.'³⁹ Ironically, while many Monogram and Allied Artists pictures, while cheap, remain interesting, several of their more 'ambitious projects' failed to live up to expectations; the Mirisch Company's own productions often echoed that binary, with an implicit assumption that the higher budgeted projects were inherently more interesting than the low-budget ones. In fact, however, the bigger budget films Mirisch produced were only marginally more likely to be successful critically, or indeed commercially, than the low-budget movies.

---

[35] Francois Truffaut, 'Une certaine tendance du cinema français', *Cahiers du Cinéma* 31, January 1954.
[36] Andre Bazin, 'La politique des auteur', *Cahiers du Cinéma* 70, April 1957.
[37] Jean-Luc Godard, 'Supermann: Man of the West', *Cahiers du Cinema* 92, February 1959.
[38] Jean-Claude Biette, 'Rewatching *Wichita*', *Cahiers* 281, October 1977.
[39] 'An Interview with Jean-Luc Godard', *Film Quarterly* vol 17 no 3, Spring 1964: 8.

Walter Mirisch himself, in his autobiography, discussing the role of the Screen Producers Guild, which he joined in 1951, recalls:

> Unfortunately, a great deal of what was achieved by the Producers Guild in those early days has been lost, either by default or from pressure by the Directors Guild, which clearly had a great deal more power with the studios. If directors go on strike, they can stop productions. If producers go on strike, substitutes, at least on a temporary basis, are readily available.[40]

Jon Lewis, in his book on Hollywood producers, echoes this disappointment.

> The role of the producer during Hollywood's so-called transition era (1947-1967) changed yet again as the studio system unravelled in the wake of two significant destabilizing events: the Blacklist and the Paramount Decision. . . . The following decade saw a sea change in the public image of the producer as the industry briefly embraced the auteur theory. . . . As directors gained in prestige and power, studio producers appeared to take a back seat. As the industry entered the blockbuster era, and as high-concept, pre-sold properties remade Hollywood into a producer's industry once again, the producer him or herself became an auteur of sorts.[41]

The Mirisch Company occupied precisely this all but invisible interregnum between studio-era producers and those so-called auteur producers who emerged in the 1980s to handle high-concept blockbusters or run auteur indies.

Walter Mirisch, for instance, originated the ideas for many of his productions, developed them, often from presold properties, selected the screenwriters and directors, hired crews and casts, supervised production and post-production and oversaw release strategies. But until relatively recently few recognized the role of such producers.

The genius of the Mirisch system

Thomas Schatz's *The Genius of the System*, taking its title from Bazin's remark, is an analysis of the extent to which production executives were decisive in the studio era. Schatz argues that more than any single individual, movies from the Hollywood system were the result of

> a melding of institutional forces [where] the style of a writer, director, star, – or even a cinematographer, art director, or costume designer – fused with the studio's production operations and management structure, its resources and talent pool,

---

[40] Mirisch, 2008, 63.
[41] Lewis, 2016, 6.

its narrative traditions and market strategy. And ultimately, any individual's style was no more than an inflection of an established studio style.[42]

And, he suggests, that style derived from and was determined by the decisions of a group of production executives.

> these men – and they were always men – translated an annual budget . . . coordinated the operations of the entire plant, conducted contract negotiations, developed stories and scripts, screened 'dailies' as pictures were being shot, and supervised editing until a picture was ready for shipment to New York for release.[43]

But even if this was true during the studio era, can a comparable case be made for the executives of independent production companies – like Mirisch – in the period that followed the end of vertical integration and the transformation of the majors from being production studios with their own distribution and exhibition arms, into what were largely financing institutions? Schatz's study ends in the 1960s. Balio's focus, on the other hand, implies that a major distributor-financier, like United Artists, proved far more influential than those small independents they funded and whose pictures they distributed. This volume attempts to make the case for Mirisch.

The specific business strategies the brothers adopted and adapted at the Mirisch Company followed a fluctuating series of criteria over the course of two decades. In pre-production, there was a distinct predilection for prioritizing pretexts, whether literary, theatrical or cinematic (or, indeed, historical); such pretexts functioned negatively as risk avoidance strategies and positively as amortizable assets, an investment in IP written off as early marketing. Thus, of the sixty-eight films which Mirisch produced for United Artists, thirty-eight were adaptations of prior works. (Alongside adaptations of page and stage, as well as remakes of films, there were another five features based on or inspired by actual historical events and/or characters.) Lewis credits Paramount's Robert Evans as having 'promoted films as "pre-sold properties" movies based on source material familiar to the mass audience before the term or the strategy became a marketing cliché in the industry'.[44] But the Mirisches did precisely that, well over a decade before Evans.

The selection of such pretexts was made on a range of additional grounds including generic familiarity, sociopolitical issues raised, rights costs, capacity for controversy and viability as star vehicles. In production terms, additional criteria come into play including the economics of foreign filming and subsequent savings in location and labour costs, the availability of local subsidies and/or frozen funds as well as the box office benefits of international backdrops, subject matter and stars. Thus, of those sixty-eight films, thirty were so-called 'runaway productions'. If one criterion for selection

---

[42] Thomas Schatz, *The Genius of the System: Hollywood Filmmaking in the Studio Era*, Pantheon, 1988, 525.
[43] Ibid, 526.
[44] Jon Lewis, 'The Auteur Renaissance 1968–1980', in Lewis (ed), *Producing*, I. B. Tauris, 2016, 88.

for production was a project's uniqueness, often achieved, ironically, via its pre-existing profile – its visibility, and indeed viability, in other media – another, alternative criterion was a film's future reproducibility, its potential as a blueprint, or cinematic pilot, for sequels and/or series in both cinema and television. Of the sixty-eight, in fact, only eleven were neither adaptations nor runaways, nor begetters of sequels or sequels themselves nor, indeed, models for or members of a cinematic cycle. Three of those sixty-eight features launched seven sequels between them, and another spawned a cycle of six very similar successors.

The book's structure

The structure of the book is as follows – the first three chapters and the penultimate one are all essentially chronological, tracing the brothers' careers before, during and after the creation of their own production companies. The rest are more broadly thematic, looking at a range of both business and aesthetic strategies those companies deployed to minimize risk and maximize profitability but also, as and when appropriate, to generate quality. Those first two chapters discuss the backgrounds of the brothers and how their various careers, in industry and retail, in film production, distribution and exhibition, before founding the Mirisch Company, contributed both to their business and cinematic strategies and priorities. Chapter 3 provides an account of the company's business history and managerial decisions over the course of its seventeen-year contract period with United Artists. Chapter 4 explores the ways in which – and the extent to which – an independent production company can be considered a corporate author, whose productions might be sometimes seen as a species of 'autobiographical allegory'. Chapter 5 discusses Mirisch's propensity for adaptations of existing texts, of presold material. Chapter 6 considers Mirisch as a pioneer of transnational or runaway production, both as a cost-cutting strategy, a means of freeing frozen funds in foreign markets, and a way of distinguishing its output from more domestic (and televisual) fare, not only for American audiences but also for the increasingly important international market. Chapter 7 identifies another Mirisch strategy – its seven sequels – and discusses them as a forerunner of the film franchises which characterize much of today's Hollywood. It locates the model for this initiative firmly in the company's TV output, both as a means of sustaining continuous production when the package-unit system was prioritizing a single film and as a bi-media business strategy in which film and television might sweat each other's assets. Chapter 8 analyses the film cycle which the Mirisch Company produced, six Second World War films made in swift succession in response to the success of *633 Squadron*, exploiting the subsidies of Britain's Eady Levy as well as other national discounts and incentives. Chapter 9 asks why the movie brats never worked with the Mirisches and addresses the latter's demographic and aesthetic distance from both these young filmmakers and the young audiences increasingly dominating cinemagoing – and thus provides a post-mortem on the company's eventual fall from critical and commercial grace. The tenth chapter examines Mirisch's strategy after the end of the UA deal, and a brief final chapter examines the company's extraordinary legacy in – and impact on – Hollywood and cinema today.

Mirisch and classical cinema

In the early 1970s, just as Mirisch's contractual relationship with UA came to an end, film scholars on both sides of the Atlantic began to talk about Hollywood studio filmmaking as a 'classical' cinema, mostly under the influence of French film theory. At the end of that decade David Bordwell, Janet Staiger and Kristin Thompson began work on their seminal study, *The Classical Hollywood Cinema*.[45] That study stops in 1960, when the vertically integrated studios were literally history, but classical filmmaking did not simply cease there and then. Quite how it was sustained and indeed how it has been challenged and/or reinvented, revised and refined, if not entirely rebooted, is, in part, the story of the very production company which is the subject of this volume. That classicism in style, if not always in subject matter, can be illuminated by reference to one brief exchange in *The Apartment*. Jack Lemmon's 'Bud' remarks, 'The mirror, it's broken' to which Shirley MacLaine's Fran replies, 'Yes, I know. Makes me look the way I feel.' The style of Mirisch movies rarely looks the way the characters or indeed the stories 'feel'. It is a classical style, restrained and realist and occasionally veering towards naturalism – in Mirisch's early 1960s black and white films *The Apartment*, *Two for the Seesaw* (Wise, 1962) and *Town Without Pity* (Reinhardt, 1961), or uncomfortably flirting with excess on the other – in the speeded up, but overlong 'comic' chases of *The Hallelujah Trail*, the slow motion imaginary reunion of father and son in *The Spikes Gang*, the indulgent silent cinema 'improv' of *The Party (Edwards, 1968)*, the redundant addition of 'hilarious' musical cues in *Irma La Douce* (Wilder, 1963), while late exceptions like the split screen of *The Thomas Crown Affair* or the fractured linearity of *The Landlord* (Ashby, 1970) stand out as dramatically as the breathtaking landscape compositions in *The Horse Soldiers* and *Man of the West*.

While individual talents and national and international events no doubt contribute hugely to the shape of films, the imperatives of corporate custom and practice, the structural opportunities furnished by specific companies and their corporate cultures, and the conscious and unconscious intentions of less celebrated individuals often provide the most proximate and precise explanations for deciding which films were greenlit, the way they were made and how they turned out. That mutually reinforcing interdependence of aesthetic and industrial processes and practices, captured in Bordwell et al's concept of a 'mode of film practice' and its continuation, into the 1960s and beyond, is at the heart of what I am attempting to investigate here.

Finally, a note on the title of this volume, *Hollywood Independent: How the Mirisch Company Changed Cinema*. Not entirely inadvertently, the title is reminiscent of several

---

[45] Bordwell, Staiger, Thompson, 1985.

other influential volumes. Like the book's content itself, it owes a great deal to the work of other scholars. Matthew Bernstein's invaluable study of another producer, Walter Wanger, deploys the phrase Hollywood Independent in its subtitle, while Denise Mann's book on post-war independents uses the plural as its title.[46] The current volume focuses on a period which began in the mid-1940s and specifically on a production company which, for most of its existence, was in a contractual relationship with United Artists. By echoing the titles of Tino Balio's *United Artists: The Company That Changed the Film Industry* and David Bordwell's *Reinventing Hollywood: How 1940s Filmmakers Changed Movie Storytelling*, respectively, I am proposing an analogous *change*, exemplified and in some senses initiated by the Mirisch Company, both at the level of industry and cinema, of business strategy but also of style and storytelling, which that company, as I hope to demonstrate, was both paradigm and often pioneer.[47] Walter Mirisch, the youngest of the four Mirisch brothers, died aged 101 in February 2023, as this book was going to print.

---

[46] Matthew Bernstein, *Walter Wanger: Hollywood Independent*, University of Minnesota Press, 2000; Denise Mann, *Hollywood Independents: The Postwar Talent Takeover*, University of Minnesota Press, 2008.

[47] Balio, 1987; David Bordwell, *Reinventing Hollywood: How 1940s Filmmakers Changed Movie Storytelling*, University of Chicago Press, 2017.

1

Prequel

What did you do in the war, daddy? The Mirisch brothers before entering production

Beginnings

The three siblings who formed the Mirisch Company – there were four brothers in all – were half-brothers. Their father, Max Mirisch, was born Mendel Mirosz in March 1873 to a Jewish family in Juden Gasse (Jew Street) in Kazimierz, the Jewish district of Krakow. By the end of the nineteenth-century Jews made up 25 per cent of the population in southern Poland, then officially known as Galicia. In 1891, Max emigrated to America, aged only seventeen and worked as a tailor in New York. He was far from alone – not only had one of his sisters, Anna, already made the journey, but between 1880 and 1914 some 2 million East European Jews also emigrated to the United States. Before the First World War there were an estimated 60,000 Jews from Galicia in New York alone. Most Jewish migrants were artisans, while the poor and the wealthy tended to stay behind. Max married Flora Glashut (born 1874), herself the daughter of immigrants, in June 1903 and they had two sons – Irving, born on 18 March 1904, and Harold, born on 4 May 1907. Flora died of cancer in March 1916 and the following year Max married Josephine Urbach (born 1891). Two further sons were born – Marvin, on 19 March 1918, and Walter, on 28 November 1921.

Harold at Warners

Harold Mirisch left school aged fourteen, in 1921, the year Walter was born, and started work as an office boy at Warner Bros in New York.[1] The Warners, like the Mirisches, were a Polish Jewish family. Indeed, Warner Bros was Hollywood's only

---

[1] Mirisch, 2008: 8.

family-owned and operated studio, just as, almost forty years later, the Mirisch Company, was the only major independent production company, owned and run by one family. In 1961, the Mirisch Company returned the favour by hiring Doris Vidor, Harry Warner's daughter; Harold had probably known her since the 1920s.[2] In 1921, Warners produced only three films, but in 1923 the company reorganized as Warner Bros. Pictures, Inc. and began to expand, producing thirteen features that year and seventeen in 1924. In the early 1920s, Warner films were primarily distributed outside the big cities and to theatres unaffiliated with the majors. In 1924 Warner Bros bought their first theatre. The following year, when the company's baseball team beat Fox in a Motion Picture Baseball League match in Central Park, Harold, just eighteen, was one of the players, though apparently not one of the stars.[3] In the second half of the decade, Harold witnessed Warners' expansion, as the company duplicated the road show strategy of the then big three, Famous Players-Lasky (later Paramount), Loew's (later MGM) and First National (later acquired by Warners), making fewer, more expensive films, a strategy Harold would repeat thirty years later.

Harold learned from his years at Warner Bros the desirability of ensuring a clear division of labour between siblings: the Warner family comprised four brothers – Harry was chief operating and financial officer, Abe ran distribution, Sam was head of technical and exhibition activities and Jack was head of production. A similar division was subsequently instituted at the Mirisch Company, where Harold Mirisch became president, Marvin was vice president and secretary-treasurer, while Walter was executive in charge of production. (The oldest brother, Irving, despite his years in exhibition, never joined the company, though he received equal shares.) Harry Warner's office was in New York, at 321 W 44th Street, the headquarters of the legal and financial operation of the company, which was presumably Harold Mirisch's base.

In 1925, Warners' assets were valued at just over $5 million; by 1930 they were worth $230 million. Warners acquired a chain of theatres, from First National, in October 1928 (as well as its studios in Burbank) followed by the acquisition of Skouras Brothers Theaters in St Louis. (Harold subsequently dipped his toes into theatrical holdings too.) In January 1930, Harold was transferred from Warner's New York 'home' office to its Metropolitan distribution division where it was reported, 'Mirisch will work on booking for Warner houses'.[4] By 1930, New York was only one major city in which Warner Bros films were being screened in its own – as well as other companies' – theatres. However, following the Wall Street Crash, on 29 October 1929, Warners reduced the number of its first-run theatres in New York from five, in April 1930, to one by the end of 1934.

Advised by a Warner executive (probably his boss, Edward Alperson, then assistant head of Warner Theaters) to learn the theatre-management side of the business,

---

[2] 'Doris Vidor to a Top Post with the Mirisch Company', *Boxoffice*, 2.10.61: 16.
[3] 'Baseball', *Moving Picture World*, 11.7.25: 199.
[4] 'Along the Rialto', *Film Daily*, 2.1.30: 4.

Harold decided to move into exhibition. His brief first posting was to St Louis.[5] In November 1928, Warners had bought the city's best cinemas from the Skouras Brothers, appointing Spyros Skouras as general manager of what were now Warner Theaters.[6] By the summer of 1930, Harold had been, 'sent to Memphis . . . to manage the Warner theater there' which had reopened that spring.[7] Memphis's Pantages Theater had been acquired by Warners in 1929 and re-modelled for sound, becoming the Warner Theater. Soon after Harold arrived, the trade press reported that 'Warner Bros have announced a $50,000 remodelling plan for their house here. H.J. Mirisch recently succeeded George Overend as manager of the theater'.[8] By the end of the year, Harold had transformed its fortunes. 'Following a thorough renovation, which converted it into the most attractive house in town, the Warner is now playing to big business. Success of the house, since it reopened two weeks ago, has proved a surprise here.'[9] Under Mirisch's management Memphis Warner had seen 'A 100 per cent increase in business' and up to 300 per cent improved box office during the evening hours.[10] As manager of the 2300-seater theatre, Harold hired his elder brother, Irving (whose farm had gone bankrupt during the Depression), as assistant manager.[11] In December 1930, Harold's Memphis Warner Theatre was one of four picture houses to run free screenings for the unemployed.[12] That month Mirisch attended the Motion Picture Theater Operators convention in Memphis.[13]

Exhibition was itself hit hard by the Depression. Annual moviegoing attendance fell from 110 million weekly in 1930 to 70 million in 1931 and less than 60 million by 1933. Ticket prices were cut and a four-day emergency national bank holiday in 1933 left theatres accepting IOUs or groceries, in lieu of cash. In 1930 there had been some 23,000 picture houses operating in the United States; by 1932, 8000 had closed their doors. Warners lost nearly $8 million in 1931, $14 million in 1932 and a further $6 million in 1933. By the end of the Depression, the company had closed or sold more than half its theatres. To survive, exhibitors had to innovate. Warners developed a so-called 'day-and-date' strategy, linking Broadway openings with regional releases and a one city, multiple theatre strategy, maximizing the returns from national publicity for premieres.[14] Warner Theaters began offering monthly 'day and date' bookings across the country, simultaneous with Broadway openings, including, in August 1930, an adaptation of Herman Melville's *Moby Dick*, *The Sea Beast* (Webb, 1926)[15] which the

---

[5] 'Harold Mirisch Who Has Been with the Warner Here Left Last Night for St Louis', 'Along the Rialto', *Film Daily*, 13.2.30: 4.
[6] Douglas Gomery, *The Coming of Sound*, Routledge, 2005, 118.
[7] 'Harold Mirisch Rejoins Warners Booking Staff', *Film Daily*, 17.7.31: 2.
[8] 'May Remodel Warner Memphis', *Film Daily*, 28.9.30: 3.
[9] 'Warner-Memphis Turned into a Winner', *Film Daily*, 3.12.30: 1.
[10] 'Memphis Take Double Under Warner Wing', *Motion Picture Daily*, 22.12.30: 4.
[11] Mirisch, 2008: 9–10.
[12] 'Memphis Gathers in 3000 Shekels to Aid Jobless', *Motion Picture News*, 20.12.30: 15.
[13] 'Keep Government Out of Business, Convention Told', *Motion Picture News*, 6.12.30: 16.
[14] Brian Hannan, *In Theaters Everywhere: A History of the Hollywood Wide Release 1913–2017*, McFarland and Co, 2018, 24.
[15] Ibid, 24: note 187.

Mirisches were to remake, twenty-five years later, as a Moulin Production, released, appropriately, through Warners. Among other Warner Bros films that Harold would have booked were *Public Enemy* (Wellman, 1931) and *Little Caesar* (LeRoy, 1931), two of the gangster films pastiched in *Some Like It Hot*. James Cagney's role in the former was based loosely on Capone, as was Edward G. Robinson in the latter, and Mirisch even attempted to get Robinson to play Little Bonaparte in *Some Like It Hot*.[16]

By the summer of 1931, Harold was back at work for what was now 'the Warners-First National' circuit.[17] That November, with his friend Alperson newly appointed as Warners' general sales manager, a wave of promotions saw Harold confirmed in charge of bookings.[18] He must have proved himself swiftly for, in spring 1932, Harold was transferred again, this time to work in the 'Chicago zone'.[19] and he was already being described in the trade press as 'a well-known exhibitor', far beyond Warner Bros circles.[20] In 1933, Harold moved once more, to Milwaukee, where he subsequently became general manager of Warner's entire Wisconsin theatre circuit.[21] Wisconsin was one of the states overseen by the Chicago zone office.[22] The so-called geographic area or zone system maximized profits by maintaining a clear distinction between the first-run and subsequent-run theatres and ensuring an adequate clearance period passed between these consecutive exhibition 'windows'. As one Wisconsin exhibitor put it, 'Hollywood may be a long way from "main street" of your town or my town but talking pictures bridge the gap.'[23]

Small-town and rural theatres made up a significant proportion of the Warner circuit and Harold learned the hard way that mid-Western tastes were not necessarily in synch with the East and West Coasts. Indeed, his own company's subsequent predilection for Westerns, the epitome of the rural story, may owe something to his hard-won experience in what such audiences preferred to see, at least before the war. The operator of one small-town Wisconsin cinema, the Garrick Theater, Fond du Lac, stressed that a cinema is 'a necessity in every community. It is the center of social and business life of the community'.[24] Perhaps it was partly Harold's experience of exhibition, reinforced by the brothers' years at Monogram/Allied Artists with their own often rural and small-town outlets, which explains the Mirisch brothers' enthusiasm for an early project like *Man in the Net* (Curtiz, 1959), with its depiction of a couple who leave the New York rat race for the countryside. Similarly, Mirisch's final film for United Artists, *Mr Majestyk* (Fleischer, 1974) dramatizes the conflict between a melon farmer and a mobster, between the countryside and the big city.

---

[16] Mirisch, 2008: 101.
[17] 'Waugh at Warner Memphis House', *Film Daily*, 1.7.31: 12; *Film Daily*, 17.7.31: 2.
[18] 'Moe Silver Named Assistant Manager of Warners Circuit', *Motion Picture Herald*, 14.11.31: 18.
[19] 'Coming & Going', *Film Daily*, 26.4.32: 8.
[20] 'Exhibs at RKO Convention', *Film Daily*, 20.5.32: 7.
[21] 'Harold Mirisch Takes Over as Milwaukee Booking Manager', *MPH*, 10.1.33: 7.
[22] *MPH*, 24.11.34: 2.
[23] Ken W. Thompson, Wisconsin Exhibitor, quoted in *Hollywood in the Neighborhood: Historical Case Studies of Local Moviegoing*, Kathryn H Fuller-Seeley (ed), University of California Press, 2008, 177–8.
[24] Ibid, 179.

By 1933, a release pattern taking 'a year or more penetrating the hinterland' had been replaced by 'blanket simultaneous coverage of the whole market'.[25] Indeed, Warners broke studio records when over 400 theatres simultaneously released *Footlight Parade* later that same year.[26] It is unclear what role, if any, Harold Mirisch played in such a strategy, but as conventional film history associates such wide releases with blockbusters like *Jaws* in the 1970s, it is striking that such saturation release was deployed decades earlier and was a strategy that Harold himself dusted off at Monogram. Harold proved both a keen observer of – and participant in – such movie marketing strategies and, thirty years later, the Mirisch Company was to re-popularize several of them with some of its early UA releases. Indeed, this period was to prove formative for the brothers' subsequent exhibition strategy.

According to Schatz, 'Harry Warner saw himself in the early 1930s as the Henry Ford of the movie industry, and the studio as a factory that produced consistent, reasonably priced products for a homogenous mass of consumers'.[27] Schatz describes how Warners' filmmakers, even their best-paid directors, Roy Del Ruth and Michael Curtiz, were accustomed to 'a factory-based assembly-line production system'.[28] Harold Mirisch cannot have been unaware of their prestige – Del Ruth became the first director signed by the Mirisches to a multiple film contract at Allied Artists, while Curtiz subsequently directed one of the Mirisch Company's earliest productions, *Man in the Net*. One of the latter's biggest 1930s hits, *Captain Blood (Curtiz, 1935)*, starred Errol Flynn, and in 1954 the Mirisches hired Flynn to star in another swashbuckler, *The Black Prince*/aka *The Warrior* (Levin, 1955). The other two top Warners' stars of the 1930s, while Harold worked for the company, were James Cagney and Bette Davis. Cagney was later pastiched in *Some Like It Hot* and starred in *One, Two, Three* (Wilder, 1961) while Mirisch remade the Davis vehicle, *Dark Victory* (Goulding, 1939), as *Stolen Hours*. But Warner was not merely a film factory. According to a profile in *Fortune* magazine in 1937, Harry Warner and the company that bore his family name had two major interests, 'business and morals'. Or as the company motto put it, 'Combining Good Picture-Making with Good Citizenship.'[29] Warners' celebrated anti-fascist films provided a model for the depictions of intolerance and its ugly effects painted in Mirisch movies as different as *The Children's Hour* and *In the Heat of the Night*.

By the mid-1930s, in the wake of the Depression, Warners had reduced its theatre holdings from 700 to 400 and staff, budgets and wages were cut back.[30] Perhaps because of such economies, Harold briefly left Warner Bros in 1935, to join the Standard Theatre Company in Wisconsin, but he was soon back at his old position with Warner-Saxe Theaters in Milwaukee.[31] By May 1936, he was working as 'Warners District Publicity Manager', arranging visits by stars like Gertrude Niesen before being appointed as

---

[25] *MPH*, cited in Hannan, 2018: 27.
[26] Hannan, 2018: 28.
[27] Schatz, 1988: 136.
[28] Ibid, 139, 141.
[29] Quoted in *We'll Always Have Casablanca* by Noah Isenberg, Faber and Faber, 2017: 94.
[30] Douglas Gomery, *The Hollywood Studio System: A History*, London: BFI, 2005, 132.
[31] *Motion Picture Herald*, 11.5.35: 66 and *MPH*, 18.6.35: 2.

Warners' booking manager for the whole state of Wisconsin.[32] Harold finally left Warners for good in June 1937.[33] One of the last films he booked, therefore, would have been *Kid Galahad* (Curtiz, 1937) released by Warners that May. The Mirisch Company remade the film, with director Phil Karlson and starring Elvis Presley, in 1962.

Exhibitors needed gimmicks to attract patrons back to their cinemas after the Depression. Pre-screening games and giveaways, like Bank Night, provided one way to tempt them.[34] By 1937, bank nights were giving away an estimated $1 million annually, while other prizes added a further $3 million.[35] But such attractions, from book nights to bank nights, ultimately paid off in ticket sales. Another innovation was the double bill, which had already been adopted by 40 per cent of theatres by 1932. In 1937, so-called bank nights and other 'prosperity games' were being played at over 6,000 of the country's 15,000 cinemas – though not without opposition.[36] Local Grievance boards even banned bank nights in Kenosha and Milwaukee, Wisconsin.[37] In August 1935 the Milwaukee district court declared bank nights illegal in a case against the city's Hollywood theatre.[38] But as soon as local legislators outlawed one gimmick, or cinemagoers tired of another, exhibitors came up with new variations.

Harold as independent exhibitor

Harold's next job, from August 1937, was managing two first-run, independent theatres in Milwaukee, owned by the Annenberg family, the Oriental (opened in 1927, and so ornate that Garbo apparently dubbed it 'the last word in motion picture theaters') and the Tower.[39] In the autumn of 1938, the company which owned the two theatres, the Oriental Theatre Corp, was sued for damages for failing to screen the film *Blockade* (Dieterle, 1938) for two days as advertised. The plaintiff, The American League for Peace and Democracy, claimed that 'certain individuals and groups, hostile to the program and purposes of the league, coerced and intimidated the theatre management into withdrawing the picture'. Mirisch replied that the film was withdrawn when it failed to do the anticipated business.[40] Pickets protesting the film's withdrawal were dispersed by the police.[41] The case was eventually settled out of court. *Blockade* was produced by Walter Wanger and this appears to have been how Wanger and Harold

---

[32] 'Niesen Personal Appearance Nets Newspaper Publicity', *Motion Picture Herald*, 1.5.36: 78 and 'Name Executives in Warner-Saxe Pool', *Motion Picture Daily*, 6.10.36: 4.
[33] 'Mirisch Gives Up Warner Film Buying', *Boxoffice*, 3.6.37: 71.
[34] Frank H Ricketson Jnr, *The Management of Motion Picture Theaters*, McGraw Hill, 1938, excerpted in Gregory A. Waller, *Moviegoing in America: A Sourcebook of Film Exhibition*, WB, 2001, 192.
[35] Douglas Gomery, *Shared Pleasures*, University of Wisconsin Press, 1992, 70.
[36] *Hollywood in the Neighborhood*, 209.
[37] 'Two Federal Courts Sustain Bank Night', *Motion Picture Herald*, 18.5.35: 18.
[38] 'First High Court Decision Awaited', *Motion Picture Herald*, 10.9.35: 59.
[39] *Boxoffice*, 26.10.40: 31.
[40] 'Public Group Sues Over Withdrawal of "Blockade"', *Boxoffice*, 24.9.38: 32-A.
[41] Ibid, 58.

Mirisch first met; if so, it seems not to have resulted in any resentment on either side. Harold brought Wanger to Allied Artists as a staff producer in 1951.

The year 1938 saw both of Harold's theatres equipped with new marquees.[42] That same year, the two theatres were 'host to some 1000 Sentinel-Post carrier boys . . . to see the current episode of The Lone Ranger'.[43] At Hallowe'en 1938, 'H.J. Mirisch's Tower and Oriental theaters offered stage contests, spooky films and Hallowe'en masks'.[44] The following Hallowe'en it was reported that 'Harold J. Mirisch featured an 18-unit Hallowe'en Jamboree at his Tower and Oriental theatres here. The program included eight stage contests, costume parades, five Walt Disney cartoons, Our Gang comedy, The Wizard of Oz, and free masks'.[45] The hugely popular *Our Gang* cycle (the original was made by Hal Roach in 1922) was acquired and resuscitated by Monogram as *The Little Rascals* in 1948, in a deal Harold negotiated.

Also in 1939, Harold inaugurated a book night each Monday and Tuesday, with tokens towards a fifteen-volume set of encyclopaedias as the attraction.[46] Consolidated Book Publishers, a branch of the Cuneo Press, originated the idea and introduced it at the Tower and Oriental theatres. Patrons obtained coupons with their tickets and one volume of the Standard American Encyclopaedia was exchanged for two coupons plus 10 cents – though a deluxe edition could be acquired for 25 cents. According to press reports, the Tower and Oriental, with 25- and 35-cent tickets, had given out over 8,000 copies of volumes 1 and 2 of the Encyclopaedia. 'Business at both houses was reportedly considerably boosted by the new stunt.'[47]

In March 1939, the Tower was one of several Milwaukee theatres accused of infringing bans on Bingo and similar games. A warrant was sought against the Tower for playing Ten-O-Win, though the District Attorney reportedly refused to issue arrest warrants.[48] That same month Mirisch was appointed to an industry committee to consider such premiums and prizes. At a meeting of exhibitors, representatives from sixty-three of Milwaukee county's seventy-three theatres discussed double features and 'early bird' admission discounts, as well as games, gimmicks and giveaways.[49] Mirisch's two theatres were singled out for a reminder that such Sunday discounts were frowned on. Later that same year, both the Oriental and the Tower were 'offering "Kwiz Kash" each Friday night with $75 or more in prizes'.[50] That Christmas, Mirisch's two theatres 'were hosts to the kids at a Saturday Matinee Christmas party'.[51] By 1940, probably to avoid falling foul of prosecution, the name of the game had changed to 'Movie Kwizzo'.[52] That same month, 'H.J. Mirisch's Tower and Oriental staged a fur fashion

---

[42] 'Milwaukee', *Boxoffice*, 10.12.38: 83.
[43] Ibid, 1.10.38: 52.
[44] 'Hallowe'en Parties for Milwaukee's Youngsters', *Boxoffice*, 5.11.38: 52.
[45] 'Hallowe'en Parties Staged for Kids', *Boxoffice*, 4.11.39: 38.
[46] 'Milwaukee', *Boxoffice*, 15.7.39: 40.
[47] '"Book Night" A New Stunt', *Motion Picture Herald*, 22.7.39: 18.
[48] 'Fine in Milwaukee for Bingo Party', *Boxoffice*, 4.3.39: 26.
[49] 'Milwaukee Country Showmen Hold Parley on Problems', *Boxoffice*, 11.3.39: 56.
[50] 'Milwaukee', *Boxoffice*, 4.11.39: 36.
[51] 'Wisconsin Showmen Play Santa Claus', *Boxoffice*, 30.12.39: 35.
[52] '10 Autos, $5000 in One Giveaway', *Motion Picture Herald*, 6.4.40: 23.

revue on their stage in cooperation with a local furrier'.[53] The synergies between film and fashion in particular and motion pictures and product placement in general, were to be explored again the following decade at Monogram, in the *Teenagers* series.

In January 1940, the two theatres boasted 'the 20-volume home library of the world's greatest literature as giveaways'.[54] Indeed, Mirisch's two theatres were credited with being the 'originators' of such book nights, in Wisconsin at least.[55] In April, Mirisch's theatres gave away '64-page comic magazines free to kids attending the Saturday matinee shows'.[56] This combination of Monday and Tuesday book nights, Friday night Kwiz Kash and Saturday and Sunday matinees saw Mirisch's theatres doing their utmost to keep box offices busy. The reliance on books as promotional pretexts for exhibition was to be reprised in the brothers' adoption of adaptation as a key production strategy at their own company, two decades later. That summer, 'members of the Cubs and Giants baseball teams appeared on the stage of H.J. Mirisch's Oriental and Tower' and cannot but recall Harold's teenage role in Warners own baseball team.[57]

Most such gimmicks were intended to attract the whole family to the box office. When gimmicks no longer worked, some theatres tried adjusting box office prices. In the run-up to Xmas 1940, the Tower and Oriental inflated their ticket prices from 36c to 40c admission, but to little effect, and abandoned the experiment after a week's trial.[58] Giveaways, on the other hand, still sometimes succeeded. Where female filmgoers could be targeted, Harold was a proponent of single features and, in 1939, personally promoted a single bill of *The Women* (Cukor, 1939), at both The Tower and The Oriental, 'in tribute to the season's finest photoplay'.[59] The theory was that if the women of the family were tempted to buy tickets, the whole family would go along.[60] At the Capitol Theater in Racine, Wisconsin, meanwhile, Dish Nights allowed female filmgoers to win an inexpensive set of crockery.[61] The same strategy could be used to tempt children too. At Xmas 1940, *Boxoffice* reported that 'Tower and Oriental theaters here have already conducted shows, admission to which was a game or a jig-saw puzzle. Toys collected at the theaters were turned over to the WPA toy lending project here'.[62] While toys targeted children, there were attractions for teenagers and twentysomethings too. Valentine parties were held by the Tower and Oriental theatres, alongside other Milwaukee venues, on 10 February and 11 February 1940, with five valentines given to every boy and girl buying a ticket.[63] That same month the Tower

[53] 'Milwaukee', *Boxoffice*, 23.12.39: 57.
[54] Ibid, 13.1.40: 44.
[55] Ibid, 12.8.39: 62.
[56] Ibid, 20.4.40: 40.
[57] Ibid, 22.6.40: 96.
[58] 'Price "Hikes" Flop in Milwaukee Houses', *Showmen's Trade Review*, 7.12.40: 6.
[59] 'Milwaukee', *Boxoffice*, 16.12.39: 47.
[60] Gomery, 1992: 71.
[61] *Motion Picture Herald*, 13.4.40: 32.
[62] 'Wisconsin Theaters Spread Yule Cheer', *Boxoffice*, 21.12.40: 47.
[63] 'Valentine Parties Held by Warner-Saxe Houses', *Boxoffice*, 17.2.40: 36.

and Oriental were also named among those independent Milwaukee theatres raising money for the Finnish Relief Fund.[64]

Second-run, independent theatres, like the Tower and Oriental, faced a new financial hurdle in 1940 – a Federal Defence Tax. Mirisch's two theatres, like other subsequent-run cinemas, dropped their admission prices so that, even with the tax added on, total ticket prices remained the same, absorbing the levy.[65] In September 1940, Milwaukee theatres agreed to revert to single feature programmes and drop double bills altogether. However, 'With all but one house of the county's 72 theatres sold on the proposed policy, Harold Mirisch . . . withdrew his pledge to the policy change'.[66] According to *Variety*, 'Mirisch's pronouncement was a body-blow to the exhibs as well as a startling surprise for . . . a couple of weeks previously he had been one of the most outspoken and enthusiastic promoters of the change back to solos.'[67] Mirisch explained his change of mind as based on the advice of his attorneys that the new strategy might be construed as restraint of trade.[68] As producers, two decades later, the Mirisches also remained, somewhat anachronistically, attached to double bills, continuing to make B movies long after most of their independent producer peers had abandoned them.

Variety reported in depth on this dispute, revealing details of the ownership of the two cinemas in question. 'While there is doubt generally as to the actual ownership of the Oriental and Tower, they were originally the property of A.I. Annenberg . . . who recently surrendered to authorities in Chicago to begin a three-year prison sentence for evasion of $1217,298 in Federal income taxes.'[69] Was Harold persuaded, having initially supported a reversion to so-called 'solos', back to the status quo of 'duals' or double bills, by Annenberg's concern to avoid the mortgages in all his properties becoming public knowledge – and hence taxable assets? One anonymous source suggested that since Annenberg

> had to strain his resources to the utmost to get together the huge sum he must pay the Government he simply could not risk the possibility of any litigation clouding title in these collateral mortgages to the Government. Such litigation would become a distinct possibility were the Oriental and Tower theatres to become part of a combination that might be construed as illegal.[70]

Annenberg's gratitude may have helped Mirisch buy the Hollywood theatre in Milwaukee two years later.

---

[64] 'Theaters Collecting Thousands for Finns', *Motion Picture Herald*, 24.2.40: 25.
[65] 'Both Tax Absorption and Price Hikes in Milwaukee', *Film Daily*, 3.7.40: 10.
[66] 'Milwaukee, After Announcing It, Abandons Singles Test', *Boxoffice*, 7.9.40: C.
[67] *Variety*, 28.8.40: 12.
[68] 'Drop Plan to End Milwaukee Duals: Mirisch Refuses to Cooperate on Advice of His Attorneys', *Showmen's Trade Review*, 7.9.40: 4.
[69] 'Last Minute Deflection from Plan, where 69 of M'kee's 72 Cinemas Were to Solo Pix, Snarls Entire Zone', *Variety*, 28.8.40: 12.
[70] Ibid.

Harold was obliged to become something of a showman as an exhibitor, and he later became the front man of the Mirisch Company, from its formation until his death in 1968, both as formal president and public face. He hosted Hollywood parties and was the best known of the brothers. In Milwaukee, Harold focused his energies on devising promotional stunts to retain audience attention.

> Wisconsin exhibitors helped take the sting out of returning to school for hundreds of youngsters by staging special parties for them with prizes ranging from pencils and erasers to bicycles and coaster wagons. Local houses conducting school parties included H.J. Mirisch's Oriental and Tower, where a 98-page, pencil tablet and ruler was given to each youngster.[71]

As an independent exhibitor, Mirisch was free to exhibit films from whichever majors would rent him prints, for instance, in 1941 one matinee double bill combined RKO's *Kitty Foyle* (Wood, 1940) with Paramount's *Victory* (Cromwell, 1940).[72] *Kitty Foyle* proved so popular as a day-and-date attraction at the Tower and Oriental that Mirisch sent the star, Ginger Rogers, a giant 5' by 7' lobby card signed by hundreds of fans.[73] The following year Mirisch became RKO's head booker.

Harold at RKO

In October 1940, Annenberg's Oriental and Tower Theater Corp sued Fox for 'Fraud, conspiracy and enrichment of themselves at the expense of the people for whom they were to operate theatres.'[74] Annenberg lost the case.[75] Within weeks of the verdict, it was reported that Harold was returning to Warner Bros on 1 September.[76] Warners, meanwhile, acquired the Oriental and the Tower.[77] Harold seems to have remained in Milwaukee until January 1942, when he took up a post in New York at RKO. 'Harold J. Mirisch, of the Warner booking office in Milwaukee, joined the RKO booking department of the home office.'[78] That August, *Variety* reported that Harold and Marvin had acquired 'The Hollywood, deluxe nabe', a neighbourhood, first-run theatre in Milwaukee, an acquisition presumably funded from the brothers' cinema confectionery business.[79] That same month, Harold was appointed head buyer and booker for the entire RKO circuit (Figure 2).[80]

---

[71] 'Help to Take Sting Out of Returning to Classes', *Boxoffice*, 14.9.40: 85.
[72] *Boxoffice*, 29.3.41: 93.
[73] 'Mirisch Sends Rogers Congratulatory Message', *Motion Picture Herald*, 29.3.41: 64.
[74] 'M.L. Annenberg's Tower and State, Milwaukee, in Trust Suit Vs Fox', *Variety*, 23.10.40: 16.
[75] 'Annenberg Loses VS Fox Milwaukee', *Variety*, 5.2.41: 6.
[76] 'Mirisch to WB', *Variety*, 27.8.41: 27.
[77] 'Warners Acquire Two', *Motion Picture Herald*, 13.9.41: 40.
[78] 'Sales Personnel Shift in Field, Home Offices', *Motion Picture Herald*, 16.5.42: 88.
[79] . 'Mirisches Takeover', *Variety*, 12.8.42: 16.
[80] 'RKO Met Theater In Three Divisions', *Film Daily*, 24.8.42: 1.

ACE DIRECTOR Alfred Hitchcock arrived in New York last fortnight and was snapped in a candid mood with RKO theatres' executive Harold Mirisch, just back from sales meetings. Hitchcock will test Broadway players for roles in his next thriller for RKO, "Notorious."

Figure 2 Alfred Hitchcock, Producer, and Harold Mirisch, RKO Theaters Executive, in New York where the producer is testing Broadway stars for his next RKO picture, *Notorious* (*Motion Picture Herald*, 8.9.45: 12).

The Theatres Candy Co

In 1939 Harold had set up a confectionery business in Milwaukee, The Theatres Candy Co. Incorporated, whose slogan was 'Serving the Midwest's Finest Theaters with Quality Confections'.[81] The purposes of the company were described in its state licence as 'to manufacture, deal in, buy and sell candies, popcorn, gum, confectionery, non-intoxicating beverages, toys, novelties and all kinds of personal property'.[82] The firm was registered on 16 January 1939. Harold was the president, and Irving officially became the vice president in 1940. That same year, under the headline '20 Million Nickels From Concessions', it was reported that 'Confection Sales ... Pay Rent in Some Small Houses' and that, 'Candy Profits Cut The "Nut" in Picture Theater Operation'.[83] *Film Daily* reported that the Theatres Candy Company 'will install venders of their own development in the theaters in the Illinois and Wisconsin territory'.[84]

By 1941, *Motion Picture Herald* was even running a regular supplement, 'The Vender Vane ... A Department Devoted To Candy and Popcorn Sales and Vending Of All Kinds For Extra Theatre Income' under the headline 'There's More Than One Way To Make Refreshments Pay'.[85] Two years earlier, it had reported that

---

[81] *Boxoffice*, 18.12.48: 102.
[82] 'Articles of Organization of Theatres Candy Co', 19.1.39, Wisconsin Historical Society, Series 365 Box 1500, 1–94.
[83] *Motion Picture Herald*, 24.2.40: 42 and *Boxoffice*, 7.12.40: 48, 49, 67.
[84] 'Candy Nets Chicago a Sweet "Take"', *Film Daily*, 23.1.41: 4.
[85] *Motion Picture Herald*, 28.6.41: 34.

Lobby vending machines in theatres in Milwaukee county grossed for exhibitors approximately $75,000 last year. Practically all theatres in Milwaukee have the machines, the majority of which merchandise box candy and bars exclusively . . . Milwaukee theatres are serviced by the manufacturers and receive up to 40 per cent on the gross sales of the machines as rental fees. Candy is purchased from the owner of the machine and the exhibitor is billed once a week for the merchandise.[86]

For Harold and Irving, who both managed theatres *and* owned their own confectionery company, this was a win-win. Initially, the company's annual reports described the nature of their business as 'operating candy vending machines' but in 1947 this changed subtly to 'Vending in Theatres', whereby sales were conducted not simply via vending machines but across the counter.

By the mid-1930s, annual sales of candy in American cinemas had already passed $10 million. 'Then came popcorn. For decades, vendors had sold this snack to movie patrons from the nearby convenience store or from wagons positioned outside theatres. During the late 1930s theatre owners simply moved the popcorn stand into the lobby.' The Movie Palaces purchased popcorn in bulk, easing cost savings so they 'could produce a fifteen-cent box for three cents and a nickel bag for about a penny'. The US popcorn harvest grew from 5 million pounds in 1934 to 100 million pounds in 1940 and over 400 million pounds by the time the United States entered the war.[87] While candy sales suffered a setback during the Second World War, because of sugar rationing, popcorn production got the go-ahead from the War Production Board because of its alleged health benefits and popularity. Popcorn flourished, solidifying its hold over the cinema concession business, not least for the new Mirisch family firm. In 1941, with Harold leaving for New York, the two older brothers exchanged roles at the Theatres Candy Co., with Harold now vice president, and Irving president and treasurer. Business was booming. 'Huge Jump in Theater Candy sales is Recorded' was one front page headline in 1943, with sales figures at an all-time high, double the previous year's.[88] In 1945 Marvin's name was added to the board of directors. The firm eventually grew to serve some 800 theatres in the midwest and was only finally dissolved in 1961.[89]

On a double-page spread taken out by Milwaukee businesses for Xmas 1948, The Theatres Candy Co offered 'Seasons Greetings', opposite a similar message from Monogram Midwest Film Company and Allied Artists Productions.[90] Harold was on equally familiar terms with most such production companies and their regional representatives. But by the late-1940s, theatre owners were grappling with another threat – television – that made it more important than ever to capitalize on confectionery. Between 1948 and 1956, despite a 50 per cent decrease in cinemagoing,

---

[86] *MPH*, 24.7.37: 1.
[87] Gomery, 1992: 80–1.
[88] *Film Daily*, 5.11.43, 1.
[89] Email from Susan Krueger, Reference Archivist, Wisconsin Historical Society, 26.8.19.
[90] *Boxoffice*, 18.12.48: 103.

concession sales increased fortyfold. In 1948 alone, theatre candy sales in the United States amounted to $600,000,000![91] Adding salt to popcorn, meanwhile, accelerated the sale of soft drinks and, with wartime sugar rationing ended, colas became equally ubiquitous in cinemas. By 1948 Theatres Candy Co Inc, while still based in Milwaukee, had branches in Omaha, Minneapolis, Portland, Los Angeles, Indianapolis and Cincinnati.[92] (Although only 1 per cent of retail outlets for candy were in theatres in 1948, they already accounted for 27 per cent of American confectionery sales!)[93] As late as 1956, the Theatres Candy Company was installing a new Formica counter, with a built-in Manley popcorn machine, Butter Mat dispenser and Supurdisplay ice cream freezer – to the Tower in Milwaukee, the very cinema once run by Harold himself.[94] Only the previous year, the brothers' candy company had opened a new warehouse for its confectionery in Milwaukee, doubling its storage space.[95]

Marvin and Walter

Marvin worked as a theatre usher during his high school years and while he was a student at City College New York, but, in 1938, Harold secured him a summer job as an assistant booker at Grand National Pictures.[96] Grand National was a B film production company, formed in 1936 by Edward Alperson, Harold's friend and ex-colleague from Warners. For his third and final year at CCNY, Marvin switched to evening classes, while continuing working during the day at Grand National.[97] 'Marvin continued with Grand National, rising to booker and then branch manager in the New York Exchange.'[98] In 1939, the year Marvin finally graduated from CCNY, Grand National was declared bankrupt and Marvin lost his job. Alperson resigned in February 1939 and the company itself was liquidated in 1940. The final Grand National film was released in December 1939.[99]

Marvin relocated to Wisconsin with the rest of the family, where Harold secured him another position, this time with the National Screen Service, which, at its height, had some 1200 depots nationwide, including one in Milwaukee.[100] The NSS supplied film trailers and other publicity material for theatres nationwide, up to three times

[91] *Motion Picture Herald*, 4.12.48: 51.
[92] *Boxoffice*, 18.12.48: 102.
[93] *MPH*, 4.12.48: 51.
[94] Ibid, 11.2.56: 52–3.
[95] Ibid, 24.12.55: 38.
[96] *Boxofffice*, 19.10.38: 30A carries a photo of Marvin, identified as from the 'New York branch', alongside his colleagues at Grand National.
[97] Mirisch, 2008, 11.
[98] 'Mirisch Careers in Horatio Alger Tradition', *Boxoffice*, 1.10.62: 9.
[99] *Grand National, Producers Releasing Corporation, and Screen Guild/Lippert*, McFarland: Ted Okuda, 1989, 2.
[100] 'Enthusiastic Meeting for Wisconsin TO', *Boxoffice*, 11.11.39: 74.

per week.[101] By the late 1930s, the NSS was serving 12,000 screens nationally and had twenty major exchanges across the country.[102] In the spring of 1940, the National Screen Service rented an office in Milwaukee, announcing it 'will open quarters here shortly'.[103] This was presumably where Marvin worked.

In 1942, Marvin acquired a theatre with Harold, the Hollywood in Milwaukee.[104] However, he was probably still working for the National Screen Service, as his name does not appear in the family confectionery firm's annual reports until 1945. In 1950, Harold also acquired the Penn and Victor theatres in downtown New Castle, PA, but he sold them again two years later.[105] Nevertheless, this may have been a symbolic acquisition for the family, since it was the very town where the Warner Brothers had famously opened their first theatres in 1907. As late as 1948, Marvin was still at the Theatres Candy Co. and only began work in Hollywood in 1953.[106]

Walter, meanwhile, graduated from high school in 1938 and, like Marvin, became a freshman at CCNY. That summer, Harold secured him a holiday job, working seven days a week as an usher at RKO's State Theater in Jersey City, some ninety minutes from the family home in the Bronx by subway. Once his studies started at CCNY, Walter continued working on Saturdays and Sundays and two weekday evenings as an usher at the Park Plaza Theater, part of the Skouras family chain. (This is the oft-cited 'background' as an 'executive' in exhibition the trade papers reported when Walter was hired and then rapidly promoted by Monogram in the mid-1940s.) When the rest of his family relocated to Milwaukee, Walter joined them there in May 1940. (Milwaukee was to provide the location for the brothers' film, *Gaily, Gaily*, almost three decades later.) That summer, he began working at the Oriental Theater, which Harold then still managed, but decided to continue his undergraduate studies at the University of Wisconsin, Madison. The Theatres Candy Co supplied confectionery to the Capitol Theater in Madison, and Walter subsequently secured a holiday job there, checking the stock, to keep his brothers' Milwaukee warehouse informed of sales, earning enough to pay his way through college.

At Madison, Walter majored in history. He later admitted, 'I've done a number of films with historical background, such as *Wichita*. I also produced a biography of Sam Houston called *The First Texan*, and an English historical picture about the Black Prince that was called *The Warriors*, and then later on I did the *Battle of Midway*, about the crucial World War II battle.'[107] Walter wrote his history dissertation on the wartime pact between Nazi Germany and fascist Italy. (A subsequent Mirisch film, *What Did You Do in the War, Daddy?* (Edwards, 1966) plays on Italy's role in the war.)

---

[101] 'From Advertisement to Entertainment: Early Hollywood Film Trailers', Keith J. Hamel, *Quarterly Review of Film and Video* vol 29, no 3, 2012: 268–78.
[102] 'Brass Tack Talk', *Motion Picture Daily*, 14.12.38: 12.
[103] 'Nat'l Screen Names Patz Milwaukee Branch Head', *Boxoffice*, 27.4.40: 100.
[104] 'Mirisch Takeover', *Variety*, 12.8.42: 16.
[105] 'Clips From Film Row', *Variety*, 15.3.50: 24 and 'Clips from Film Row', *Variety*, 24.12. 1952: 18.
[106] *Boxoffice*, 3.7.48: 78.
[107] 'A Conversation with Walter Mirisch', Department of History, University of Wisconsin-Madison, Fall 2008 https://history.wisc.edu/wp-content/uploads/sites/202/2017/05/history_newsletter2008.pdf

Walter formally graduated in June 1942, just as the Battle of Midway was being fought in the Pacific (from 4 June to 7 June). More than thirty years later, Mirisch's film about that battle, *Midway*, was one of several Mirisch productions for which historical events provided pretexts – from *The Gunfight at Dodge City* (Newman, 1959) to *The Great Escape*, from *Cast a Giant Shadow* (Shavelson, 1966) to *The Thousand Plane Raid* (Sagal, 1969). Indeed, the latter, historical raid had occurred in May 1942 and Harold was already recommending that RKO theatres book Pathe News' coverage of it that September.[108] Harold's other specific newsreel recommendations included *Battle of Midway* (10.9.42) and a seven-minute newsreel entitled *Salvage*, a theme which became central not only to *The Thousand Plane Raid* itself but also to *Hell Boats* (Wendkos, 1970).[109] Harold also ensured that 'a new program known as 52 War Information Shorts, released in conjunction with the War Activities Committee', were booked by RKO theatres on a weekly basis from June 1943.[110]

Walter at Harvard

In the spring of 1942, Walter was offered a postgraduate scholarship in History at Wisconsin but was told, in no uncertain terms, that there was no future for a Jew in academia. Casting about for alternative careers, he remembered a talk he had heard at Madison by recruiters from Harvard Business School. 'It seemed fascinating to me, these people who, among other things, computed the probabilities of hitting targets and the amount of tonnage required to fall on a given target to yield a statistical probability of destroying it.'[111] He immediately applied to Harvard Graduate School of Business Administration and began his studies there on Monday, 15 June 1942.[112] Walter enrolled in a twelve-month programme for the degree of Industrial Administrator, which was designed to train men for jobs of immediate usefulness in government service or in industries related to national defence. 'All the courses were skewed to preparing you for war service. My accounting instructor was Robert McNamara, who later became Secretary of Defence on John F. Kennedy's cabinet.'[113] McNamara was an associate professor at Harvard at the time.[114]

According to Harvard Business School's Baker Library records,

> Walter Mirisch took the following courses for the Industrial Administrator (IA) degree. Accounting for War Industries I, II, and III. Financing War Industries,

---

[108] Telegram to George French, 10.9.42, Harold J. Mirisch Film Bookings 1942–43, Iowa Digital Library.
[109] Letter to George French, 25.9.42, Harold J. Mirisch Film Bookings 1942–43, Iowa Digital Library.
[110] Letter to Dave Lewis, RKO Albee Theatre, 15.6.43, Harold J. Mirisch Film Bookings 1942–43, Iowa Digital library.
[111] Mirisch, 2008, 18.
[112] Ibid, 19 and https://iiif.lib.harvard.edu/manifests/view/drs:423141930$9i
[113] Mirisch, 2008, 19.
[114] 'The Contribution of the Harvard Business School to Management Control, 1908–1980', *Journal of Management Accounting Research* vol 2, 2008: 182.

Industrial Management Engineering, Management Statistics, Management Reports, Procurement and Distribution, Industrial Mobilization and War Policies I, Production Organization and Engineering, Management Controls, and Human Problems of Administration. The IA program was one year long and had three terms. Mirisch entered in June 1942 and received his degree in May 1943.[115]

Harvard on Hollywood

Perhaps surprisingly, Harvard's curriculum had included Hollywood since at least 1927. Wall Street financier and sometime movie mogul, Joseph P. Kennedy, himself a Harvard alumnus, had arranged a series of talks at the business school in March and April 1927 by leaders of the American film industry, including Will H. Hays, Jesse L. Lasky, Adolph Zukor, William Fox, Marcus Loew, Samuel Katz, Cecil B. De Mille and Harry M. Warner. Kennedy subsequently compiled the transcripts of these talks into an anthology on the industry, which was published as *The Story of the Films* (1927). Given Walter Mirisch's passionate interest in Hollywood, he undoubtedly read this book, just as Harvard insisted that he read the case studies of other American businesses, around which the curriculum was structured. The movies were, after all, the industry in which, by 1942, all three of his older brothers were employed.

The thrust of these talks – and of the book that anthologized them – was that film production was both standardized and differentiated, a lesson whose ambivalence Walter seems never quite to have shaken off.

> There is no such thing as standardization of product. Every successful picture must be different from any that has gone before. It is as if an automobile manufacturer had to turn out an entirely new model every week. . . . Fortunately for the automobile manufacturer, there is no demand for such variety in his product. In the world of the motion pictures there is. Entertainment must be varied. There is standardization only in that the popularity of certain stars is rather well known and that the ability of directors, camera men, and scenario writers can be measured fairly well. Of course, the news reel is wheat in the bin, a standard commodity. Among the feature pictures, too, 'westerns' follow well defined rules – a good story surrounded by riding, thrills and fine outdoor scenery.[116]

Jesse L. Lasky described another kind of Hollywood standardization, claiming 'there are three fundamental types of picture', the programme picture 'the very backbone

---

[115] Email to the author, from Clarissa Yingling, Harvard Baker Library Special Collections, 26.7.19. Curriculum for Harvard Business School's 'Twelve Month's Course Leading to the Degree of Industrial Administrator', 15 June 1942 to 12 June 1943 https://iiif.lib.harvard.edu/manifests/view/drs:423141930$1i

[116] Will H Hays, 'Supervision from Within', in Joseph P. Kennedy (ed) *The Story of the Films: As Told by Leaders of the Industry*, A. W. Shaw, 1927, republished 2018, 36.

of the industry', the special and the road show picture.[117] (This balance between the programmer and the special was to characterize Mirisch's output and lead to a consequent equivocation between maximizing reputational capital and potential profitability in a project and minimizing risky outlay.) Lasky went on to discuss the crucial search for familiar screen material and the reliance on best sellers and 'timely topics' as well as historical subjects – those 'the public know best'.[118] He also noted the over-supply of war films but the comparative rarity of aviation films. These observations may also have lodged in Walter's memory. The disproportionate number of Westerns, adaptations and aviation pictures in the Mirisch filmography is certainly striking, as is the retention of programme pictures, well after their deletion from the production portfolios of many of the company's competitors.

While at Harvard, Walter may also have increased his knowledge of filmmaking by reading some of the Hollywood screenplays recently donated to the University.[119] The number of writers of those twenty-five films who were later associated with Mirisch is certainly striking. Ben Hecht, who wrote or co-wrote three of them – *Wuthering Heights* (Wyler, 1939), *A Star Is Born* (Wellman, 1937) and *The Prisoner of Zenda* (Cromwell, 1937) – was subsequently both the source and fictionalized subject, of the Mirisch's bawdy 'biopic', *Gaily, Gaily*; *Naughty Marietta* (Leonard, 1935) was co-written by John Lee Mahin, who later wrote *Horse Soldiers* for the Mirisch Company. *Winterset* (Santell, 1936) was written and *Stage Door* (La Cava, 1937) co-written by Anthony Veiller, who subsequently scripted *Moulin Rouge* for the Mirisches. Both *Dead End* (Wyler, 1937) and *These Three* (Wyler, 1936) were written by Lillian Hellman, whose plays provided the basis for two Mirisch productions, *The Children's Hour* and *Toys in the Attic* (Roy Hill, 1963*)*. It thus seems more than likely that Walter's Harvard reading included at least some of these scripts, alongside his strictly curricular case studies. As with directors, the Mirisches were subsequently to prove reluctant to employ untested screenwriters, and to rely on previously published works more than their competitors.

Among the twenty-five films whose screenplays were in the Harvard Library, one, *The Informer* (1935*)*, was directed by John Ford, who later directed *Horse Soldiers* for the Mirisch Company. Three more (*These Three, Dead End, Wuthering Heights*) were directed by William Wyler, who subsequently directed *Friendly Persuasion* (1956) for Allied Artists and *The Children's Hour* for the Mirisch Company). Another, *Broadway Melody of 1936*, was directed by Roy Del Ruth, who went on to direct three films for Allied Artists. A sixth, *The Prisoner of Zenda*, was remade by Walter Mirisch two decades later.[120] Of course, such coincidences may also be explained by a consensus over conceptions of 'quality' shared between Hollywood and Mirisch, since the list, described as of 'outstanding films', included prestigious adaptations from the page – *David Copperfield* (Cukor, 1935), *Pride and Prejudice* (Leonard, 1940), *Wuthering Heights*, and the stage – *Pygmalion* (Asquith/Howard, 1938), *A Midsummer Night's*

---

[117] Jesse Lasky, 'Production Problems', in *The Story of the Films*, 101–2.
[118] Ibid, 106–7.
[119] 'Harvard University's Theatre Receives 25 Film Scripts', *Motion Picture Herald*, 24.5.41: 31.
[120] 'Harvard Receives 25 Film Scripts', *Motion Picture Herald*, 30.8.41: 31.

Dream (Dieterle/Reinhardt, 1935) as well as from 'real life', with biopics like *The Barretts of Wimpole Street* (Franklin, 1934) and *The Story of Louis* Pasteur (Dieterle, 1936). Nevertheless, all three kinds of adaptation, or 'pretexts' for production, in which, arguably, the R&D had already been done, were to become default strategies for the Mirisch Company.

The Harvard Curriculum

The Industrial Management Engineering (subsequently retitled Industrial Administrator) curriculum, stipulated that 'Throughout the course, such management devices as time study, standardization, wage incentives, production planning and control, inspection, safety campaigns to reduce accidents, and industrial cost analysis are studied as aids in clarifying and solving management problems'.[121] This focus on time and motion study, scientific management and standardization was to continue to influence Mirisch's corporate strategy into the 1960s and 1970s, in the company's commitment to remakes, sequels, cycles, spin-offs and overall efficiency. The curriculum also included a 'Control of Plant and Equipment' case study of the Thaler Candy Company, which may well have informed the management of Walter's brothers' own, still new, confectionery enterprise.[122]

In the 1940s, Harvard Business degrees followed the tenets of so-called scientific management, espoused by sometime Harvard lecturer, Frederick Taylor. Taylor lectured at Harvard annually from 1908 until his death in 1915 and was one of the pioneers of management studies. As evidence of his legacy, one of the courses Mirisch took, Industrial Management Engineering, stressed such 'management devices as time study, standardization, wage incentives, production planning and control inspection' while another, Production Organization and Engineering included 'a wide range of specialized functional activities such as planning, method development, motion and time study, inspection, worker selection, worker training, inventory control, maintenance and plant traffic'.[123]

While at Harvard, Walter also learned some of the latest marketing techniques. The summer he completed his studies saw the launch of a research project into broadcasting as a marketing tool for retailers. 'The Harvard Business School is starting a study of radio advertising by retailers, service operators, wholesalers and manufacturers with limited territorial distribution.'[124] The resulting report, *Radio Advertising for Retailers*, was published in January 1945, by Harvard University Press – the year Mirisch finally

---

[121] *Harvard Curriculum*, 52.
[122] Industrial Management Engineering V2, vi, Harvard Curriculum, IndustrialManagementEngineering.pdf
[123] *Harvard Curriculum*, 52, 59.
[124] 'Harvard Studies Air Use by Retailers: Report Will Be of Aid to Buyer, Seller of Radio Time', *Broadcasting*, 3.5.43: 18.

entered the film industry.¹²⁵ Coincidentally or not, Monogram first deployed radio advertising the following year, in its tie-ins with Koret Fashions. In 1959, 'United Artists and the Mirisch Company . . . pulled off one of the outstanding showmanship coups of recent years by acquiring the radio broadcast rights to the Floyd Patterson-Ingermar Johannsen title bout . . . The $100,000 deal, made on behalf of "The Horse Soldiers", marked the first motion picture sponsorship of a prize fight'.¹²⁶ A radio audience of 20 million listeners was predicted.

Walter at Lockheed

After Harvard, Walter moved to Los Angeles, where his first job was not in Hollywood, but in the aircraft manufacturing industry. Turned down by the Navy as physically unfit because of a heart defect, Walter contacted Harvard for advice and was put in touch with Lockheed, the very company which the University's recruiters had eulogized in the talk which brought him to Harvard in the first place. At Lockheed, he was initially 'assigned to a project involving the simplification of assembly-line procedures'.¹²⁷ His first position was as 'Engineering Assistant, Vega Aircraft Corp, Burbank, Calif'.¹²⁸ In June 1943, Lockheed's P38 Lightning assembly line at Burbank, California, was mechanized, more than doubling the rate of production. The transition to the new system was accomplished in only eight days, but production never stopped and even continued, under camouflage, outdoors.¹²⁹ Mirisch's arrival at Lockheed also coincided almost exactly with the creation of the so-called Skunk Works (recently republicized in the UK by Dominic Cummings, the former chief adviser to former prime minister Boris Johnson). The Skunk Works was created and run by the young engineer Clarence L. 'Kelly' Johnson, and his team, to deliver a fighter jet for the US Air Force. The formal contract for the XP-80 did not arrive at Lockheed until 16 October 1943; some four months after work had already begun and by which time Mirisch was himself either an assistant engineer or a managing engineer.

This is not to suggest that Walter played any part in the Skunk Works, nor that he necessarily witnessed its operation first-hand. Nevertheless, while the celebrated production of the P38 undoubtedly reinforced his Harvard-ingrained belief in assembly line, continuous production, the existence of the Skunk Works, an innovation-driven team (its official designation was the Advanced Development Program), given a high degree of autonomy and unhampered by bureaucracy, with the task of working on advanced projects, may also have had an impact on his thinking. At least once in his subsequent career Walter supported just such an initiative, the proposed Roth-

---

¹²⁵ *Broadcasting*, 16.1.45: 59.
¹²⁶ 'Promotion Pioneering: UA To Plus "Horse Soldiers" via Heavy Title Bout', *Film Bulletin*, 8.6.59: 16.
¹²⁷ Mirisch, 2008, 21.
¹²⁸ 'Keeping Up to Date with the Alumni', *Harvard Business School Bulletin*, Autumn 1943: 155.
¹²⁹ https://enacademic.com/pictures/enwiki/77/Mechanized_P-38_conveyor_lines.jpg

Kershner production unit dedicated to the making of 'arty' and 'offbeat' films for young cinephiles, rather than the mass audience.[130]

Walter as management theorist

By the autumn of 1944, Walter was a managing engineer at Lockheed Aircraft Corporation, which had absorbed Vega in a merger.[131] Walter was subsequently to take Lockheed's ideas of setting and hitting targets, rationalizing assembly-line processes and minimizing staff numbers, into the film industry. In August 1944, *Factory Management and Maintenance* journal, of which Walter Mirisch was already a reader and to which he was soon to be a contributor, published an article which was not only about Lockheed but also about the work simplification programme on which Mirisch had by then worked for a year. That article was entitled 'To Get Ready For Lower Unit Costs Take Advantage of Work Simplification Methods: Case of Lockheed Aircraft Corporation' and began by announcing 'Proposals for improvement made by employees at Lockheed Aircraft Corporation, Burbank Calif., are saving enough man hours annually to build 1000 big bombers'.[132] These two ideas – of 1,000 American bombers and of work simplification through scientific management – were to stay with Mirisch for over twenty years, feeding into the plot, title and mode of production of *The Thousand Plane Raid*, the one US production among the six, otherwise 'British', films in a cycle of 'standardized' Second World War-set Mirisch movies.[133]

The following month's issue of *Factory* included an article entitled 'Scientific Management in a Post-War Plan'.[134] This article outlines the use of a Gantt chart for project management in a confectionery company and was thus intrinsically of interest to Walter, both for its methodology and its focus.

> Basically the manufacturing problem consists of obtaining approximately a 50% increase in production . . . and to accomplish this with as small an increase in productive personnel as possible. The only way in which this can be done is to abandon the standard batch method of manufacture and to devise continuous methods of production. . . . There is but one objective . . . a continuous manufacturing cycle which will initiate an unexcelled product under constant scientific control.[135]

[130] Roth-Kershner Proposal, March 1962, United Artists Collection, Box 5, 3.
[131] 'Measuring Drafting Output', *Factory Management and Maintenance* vol 102 no 11, November 1944: 101.
[132] Ibid, August 1944: 129.
[133] Lockheed was a frequent subject and source of articles in both *Factory Management* and *Personnel Journal* in the 1940s, including other reports on 'Chronic Attendee *and* Good Attendant', *Factory Management*, December 1944: 23; 'Lockheed's Full Testing Program', *Personnel Journal*, September 1942: 21; 'Why Workers Quit', *Personnel Journal*, September 1944: 23; 'Industrial Relations Research', *Personnel Journal*, July 1944: 22: 7.
[134] 'Scientific Management in a Post-War Plan', *Factory Management and Maintenance* vol 102 no 9, September 1944: 96–101.
[135] Ibid, 101.

The shift from the 'standard batch method' to the 'continuous manufacturing cycle', through the provisions of scientific management, maximizing production while minimizing personnel, combines characteristics of the package-unit system, of which independents like the Mirisch Company were pioneers, with aspects of the 'continuous manufacturing cycle' associated with assembly-line production – of the kind practised at Lockheed and, of course, studio-era Hollywood. Strikingly, this shift reverses the trajectory of industrial change undergone by the film industry in the 1940s, when, as Staiger demonstrates, the continuous production model of the firm was being replaced by the one-off production of individual films.[136] This differentiated the Mirisch Company from its independent peers in the 1950s and 1960s and begins to explain the company's productivity.

Both these pieces were almost certainly read by Walter Mirisch. The first, anonymous, article (it is more than conceivable he wrote it himself) was about his current employer and the specific system he was charged with overseeing. The second described scientific management in operation – a management system he had been taught at Harvard and was responsible for implementing at Lockheed, and the example, a confectionery company, proved equally close to home, as his brothers ran just such a company.

Mirisch later recalled,

> I thought I could make available to other companies some of the methods and practices that we had developed at Lockheed. I began to write articles . . . for various industrial magazines. I wrote a number of them for Factory, one of which, called 'Drafting Controls', was quite detailed. It was an intricate system that we had devised and put in place at Lockheed.[137]

This article seems to be 'Measuring Drafting Output' and was his first signed piece, co-written with Kenneth R. Cole. The authors noted that 'progressive managers have been applying the principles of scientific management to manufacturing operations and have achieved wide betterment'.[138] These 'principles' were designed 'properly to weight final ratings both for speed and preciseness, separate ratings are determined for quality and for quantity, and these twin ratings are then combined into a final rating'.[139] The quality rating was calculated according to a percentage of incorrect work; the quantity rating was derived from the work rate per hour of each employee. Mirisch and Cole were convinced that 'Quality control supplies a scientific, impartial measurement of performance eminently to be preferred to personal estimation', thus 'eliminating supervisory personal prejudice from the ratings'.[140]

---

[136] Bordwell, Staiger, Thompson, 1985: 330.
[137] Mirisch, 2008: 23.
[138] 'Measuring Drafting Output', 1944: 101.
[139] Ibid.
[140] Ibid, 103.

Significantly, the authors acknowledged that 'One of the plan's great advantages is at the same time a marked disadvantage. Since the device is an empirical mechanism, it leaves out of the rating personal, intangible factors such as knowledge, dependability and cooperation'. Of course, in a knowledge-based field like film production, where, as Walter subsequently discovered, collaborative skills and creativity are crucial attributes, such a disadvantage could prove decisive. Nevertheless, the authors argue that there is no need for their proposal to be met with 'the dismal reception' which greeted 'time study' (or 'time and motion' study) and other aspects of Taylorism.[141] Subsequently, both *The 1000 Plane Raid* and *Submarine X-1* (Graham, 1969) were to dramatize and enthusiastically endorse such scientific measurement. Indeed, as we shall see, time and motion studies were to have a significant impact on Mirisch productions, not only behind the camera but also in front of it. Mirisch and his co-author note that, 'The plan can serve as an invaluable guide to judgment but not as an inflexible measure to be arbitrarily applied'.[142] The Mirisch Second World War cycle itself demonstrates this flexibility on-screen by allowing the commanders and their subordinates to change their minds and their plans when necessary. But there was comparatively little room for manoeuvre on-screen as far as the tropes and types these films deployed, and even less off-screen, in the schedules and budgets negotiated for their production.

Walter's second signed article critiques the lack of training many managers and industrial administrators had – and their consequent resistance to innovation. He notes that 'Cost control has received but little heed from men acting on the theory that the more you spend the more you produce. Line administration, with little intrinsic appreciation of the industrial cost concept, has often seemed ignorant of the fact that efficiency is often consonant with cost'.[143] Such 'efficiency' was subsequently to prove a watchword at the Mirisch Company, not only off-screen but also on-screen. (See, for instance, the emphasis on precision in planning the robbery in *The Thomas Crown Affair* in which a series of meticulously timed phone calls give the go-ahead for the heist. ('At the tone the time will be 3.17 exactly.') The heist is preceded by a montage of Crown and his anonymous subordinates all checking their watches. Or, as the hero is told by his commanding officer in *633 Squadron*. 'Since you took over, the squadron has attained a high degree of efficiency'. Mirisch himself, of course, could thank Harvard for his education in management.

Walter's training in Taylorist principles valorized the imposition of constraints on costs and staffing and a simultaneous increase in productivity.

> Most managers cannot see the waste of man power. They feel they need all the people they can possibly secure under them. For the more people the manager places under him, the wider the petty bureaucracy reporting to him, the better is his own position fortified. The more impressive is his prestige standing in the plant

---

[141] Ibid, 105.
[142] Ibid, 104.
[143] 'Emergency Administration', *Personnel Journal: The Magazine of Labor Relations and Personnel Practices* vol 14 no 1, May 1945: 37–40.

community. He seeks to make himself so important a part of the line or staff that he will be irreplaceable when the day of reckoning comes. And well he might be if he succeeds in constructing a maze of red tape, winding octopus-like through his department, branch, or company with himself at the core.[144]

This paragraph could stand as a blueprint for the bloated, bureaucratic corporations caricatured in *The Apartment* or *How to Succeed in Business Without Really Trying* (Swift, 1967). The Mirisch Company, by contrast, was subsequently celebrated, not least by the Mirisches themselves, as '... a small, effective organization'.[145]

Indeed, in the Mirisch Company's very first release, *Fort Massacre* (Newman, 1958) a character bemoans the ubiquity of bureaucracy along precisely these lines. Private McGurney conducts a one-sided conversation with a silent, fatally wounded lieutenant, slumped over his horse, as they ride. The private throws his empty water bottle away, before remarking,

> I shouldn't have done that now. Should have more respect for government property. Even when a thing is useless, you pin a medal on it and toot a horn and bury it in a deep hole. Of course, you've got to have the proper orders. Yes, orders. The date, the regimental seal. Signed by three colonels, two generals, maybe even the Pope himself. Isn't that right, Sir? Ah, can't even spit without that. You can't even retreat when the whole sweet platoon is being killed like mayflies. Not without orders.

I am not suggesting here that Walter, as producer, necessarily had a hand in writing that speech. But it is certainly more than possible that the anti-bureaucratic corporate culture at the Mirisch Company contributed to – and even welcomed – it.

Mirisch's 'Work Simplification' programme at Lockheed was 'directed toward correcting ... inefficiencies and abuses' and he was to take such ideas with him to Monogram and subsequently to the Mirisch Company.[146] The article ends with the warning that 'Those companies that do not purge themselves and redesign their organizations on the sole basis of ability and enterprise will find themselves at the mercy of those who do'.[147] In a subsequent article, Mirisch proposed ensuring such efficiencies by dividing up the stages of each production line, with every stage having its own cost centre.[148] Walter continued to work at Lockheed until the war ended with the dropping of atomic bombs in August 1945. 'At that point I decided I could now pursue the real ambition of my life, and I started to look around for a position in the movie business.'[149]

---

[144] Ibid, 39.
[145] *Boxoffice*, 1.10.62: 8–9.
[146] 'Emergency Administration', 1945, 39.
[147] Ibid, 40.
[148] 'Efficient Production and Cost Control', *Factory Management and Maintenance* vol 103 no 12, December 1945: 109–13.
[149] Mirisch, 2008: 23.

Walter Goes to Hollywood

Since Walter continued to contribute to *Factory Management* at the end of 1945, it seems likely that he was also still reading other articles endorsing Taylor's time and motion studies.[150] The following year, by which time Walter was already working in Hollywood, another article even espoused something of the 'small is beautiful' philosophy. It reported that at Johnson and Johnson, 'the size of each new unit is geared to what one man can fully comprehend and where all the workers can know each other by name, not by number like license plates'.[151] The article described how, at Stillwater Worsted Mills, the policy was that 'No industrial unit should ever grow beyond the point where the person at the top can know not only the individual workers, but also their families'.[152] This was to chime with the family business approach at the Mirisch Company, where the number of permanent staff employees, at least initially, was small and everyone was on familiar terms.

While the leap from Lockheed to Hollywood may sound surprising, in fact the crossover between war factories and film factories was a familiar one in wartime. In 1944, for instance, *Variety* listed a range of entertainers including Harry Jolson (Al's brother) and his wife, Alvino Rey and his entire orchestra, the comic, Joe Whitehead, Max Lerner and his instrumental trio, the skaters, the Glorias (Gloria Nord had appeared that same year with Betty Grable in *Pin Up Girl* (Humberstone, 1944)), George Mann (of Barto and Mann) Ed Gardner, comedians Gracie Deagon, Harry Fox and Emily Darrell and lion tamer Mabel Stark, all working on the assembly lines at Lockheed.[153] But if some were taking shift work on the assembly lines, whether to raise morale or to compensate for ever-increasing gaps between freelance contracts, Walter was keen to move in the opposite direction, and in the late summer or early autumn of 1945, he secured his first job in Hollywood.

---

[150] See, for example, 'Rating a Plant's Efficiency', Ralph Irving, *Factory Management and Maintenance* vol. 103 no. 6, June 1945: 115–118 and 'Motion-Time Standards: A Modern Technique', J. M. Quick, W. J. Shea, R. E. Koehler, *Factory Management and Maintenance* vol. 103 no. 5, May 1945: 87–108.
[151] 'Decentralization in Doing Things for these Industrial Concerns', *Factory Management and Maintenance* vol. 104, 12 December 1946: 144.
[152] Ibid, 145.
[153] 'Lefty Writes a Letter', *Variety*, 16.8.44: 13.

2

Prequel

The first time: The Mirisches at Monogram, Allied Artists and Moulin Productions

Walter at Monogram

The year 1945 must have seemed like an optimum moment to enter the film industry. Ticket sales peaked at an astonishing 100 million a week the following year, equivalent to some two-thirds of the entire American population! However, by 1948 that figure had fallen to 85 million a week and it continued falling to 40 million a week by 1957. Germany had surrendered on 8 May 1945, and VJ Day was celebrated on 2 September, so it seems likely Walter Mirisch had left Lockheed by autumn at the latest. Harold recommended Walter contact Samuel 'Steve' Broidy, who had been a salesman for Warner Bros in the early 1930s, when Harold was based in WB's New York booking office, but was now general manager and vice president of Monogram Pictures Corporation.[1] Broidy offered Walter a job as his assistant, initially to check figures, but he was soon answering questions like 'How do we make this place work better? Do we have too many guards at the gate? Can we operate the editorial department differently? Should we move it off the lot?'[2] Mirisch's role, based on the combination of his Harvard education and his Lockheed experience, was to ensure that the company was 'operating in the most cost-effective way possible'.[3] Harvard's curriculum, after all, had been designed to 'make it possible for men to go immediately into such departments as planning, scheduling, dispatch, routing, time study and inspection, where they may serve as assistants to departmental heads and supervisors'.[4] This chapter discusses the Mirisches period at Monogram not just as an apprenticeship in production, but also as a formative experience providing customs and practices which retained an influence

---

[1] 'Who's Who in Hollywood', *Film Daily*, 7.8.45: 7.
[2] Mirisch, 2008: 25.
[3] Ibid.
[4] 'The Graduate School of Business Administration', *Harvard Business School Course Catalog*, June 1942: 30 https://iiif.lib.harvard.edu/manifests/view/drs:423141930$37i

on the brothers for the rest of their careers, either through adoption or conscious reaction to and differentiation from prior strategies and standards.

Monogram in the mid-forties was a Poverty Row, B movie factory. It released 402 films between 1940 and 1949, an average of forty a year. The lowest annual amount was twenty-nine in 1945 and again in 1947. Monogram's stock-in-trade was series films, producing eleven distinct series in the 1940s, including *Charlie Chan*, *Bowery Boys*, *Mr Wong*, *Cisco Kid* and *Bomba the Jungle Boy*. (Its low-budget competitor, Republic, was known for its serials.)[5] In the mid-1940s, some 75 per cent of the majors' releases were adaptations, a key distinction between A films and Bs.[6] Indeed, Steve Broidy, then president of the studio, admits that adaptations were largely beyond Monogram. 'We had to use ninety-five percent original material, unless it was something in the public domain. . . . We very rarely bought a book. We made *Treasure Island* (1934), *Kidnapped* (1948).'[7] Of course, both those novels were then out of copyright, as was *Ivanhoe*, which the young Walter Mirisch hoped to produce, and *Hiawatha*, which he eventually did. Another Monogram characteristic was a predisposition towards 'the rural' or outdoor film, as a broad generic category, as distinct from more urban, urbane genres.[8] Warner's product, by contrast, was by then characterized by city-based storylines – and audiences – and while Walter's formative years at Monogram may have inclined him towards more rural and often period subjects and settings, Harold's experience in Milwaukee exhibition perhaps predisposed him more to cityscapes and contemporaneity.

By the mid-1940s, Monogram, having only just relocated from New York, owned a small studio on Sunset Drive, with one New York street set. It also ran the Monogram Ranch in Newhall, California, for its Westerns, subsequently bought by Gene Autry and renamed Melody Ranch – which recently provided the location for the Spahn Ranch in *Once Upon a Time . . . in Hollywood* (Tarantino, 2019). There was no sound department or camera department – sound was provided by Sound Services, while all cameras were rented – but there were several cutting rooms and scoring and dubbing was done on site. Films were mostly shot in eight days or less, one at a time, as there were only three sound stages. The budgets of series pictures – the bread and butter of Monogram – were between $80,00 and $100,000.

On 14 November 1945 Broidy became president of the company.[9] Walter recalls Broidy's promotion in his autobiography, so he must have joined the company by November. Like Harold Mirisch, Broidy's background was in distribution – after his spell at Warner Bros he had run Boston's Monogram Exchange, before becoming national

---

[5] For Monogram's *Charlie Chan* series see Kyle Dawson Edwards, '"Monogram Means Business": B Film Marketing and Series Filmmaking at Monogram', *Film History* vol 23 no 4, 2011: 391–6, and Yannis Tzioumakis, *American Independent Cinema*, Rutgers University Press, 2006, 77–82.

[6] Bordwell, 2017: 22.

[7] Broidy, quoted in *Kings of the B's: Working Within the Hollywood System*, Charles Flynn and Todd McCarthy (eds), New York: E. P. Dutton, 1975, 274–5.

[8] Tim Onosko, 'Monogram: Its Rise and Fall in the Forties', *The Velvet Light Trap* vol 5, Summer 1972: 5–9.

[9] 'Monogram Elects Broidy President', *Motion Picture Daily*, 15.11.45: 1.

sales director in 1940. Perhaps predictably, therefore, under Broidy Monogram stepped up its reliance on series production. Broidy's strategy was to focus on 'Monogram's core competencies in the current B-film market and increased attention to exhibitors'.[10] In 1945, Broidy even asked his bosses at Monogram to halt studio production. 'The first thing I said when I got to (Monogram headquarters) was, "Stop making pictures . . . Your product, which you've made for the past year and a half or two, is practically new in every situation in the country. Why not concentrate on trying to sell those pictures and get as much as we can out of that."'[11] Sweating the assets, ensuring that every film was efficiently and exhaustively marketed, was to become ingrained with the Mirisches. Meanwhile, Walter was tasked with taking inventory of those assets and identifying opportunities for saving money.

Walter as producer

That Broidy was impressed with his young assistant is obvious. Early in 1946, he gave Walter, not yet twenty-five and after barely six months in the industry, the opportunity to produce his first film. In May, the trade press reported 'Walter Mirisch has incorporated Pembroke Productions to produce that million dollar production of Sir Walter Scott's Ivanhoe for release next season'[12] noting that 'Producer Walter Mirisch is making big plans for Ivanhoe, a costume romance'.[13] However, *Ivanhoe*, despite being out of copyright, came to nothing. Nevertheless, its attraction for Walter Mirisch is worth considering. It had been an MGM project in the late 1930s and briefly developed by Paramount after the war, before returning, via RKO, to MGM. In the interim, Monogram's interest emerged in May 1946 when Aeneas Mackenzie wrote several drafts for Paramount. Perhaps Mackenzie showed Mirisch a draft, or perhaps trade reports alerted Mirisch to its potential. Certainly, John Rosenberg was hired to adapt, and the Jewish themes Mackenzie was developing might have been an additional inducement.[14] As the trade press reported in 1946, 'Scott wrote in Ivanhoe: ". . . there was no race existing on the earth, in the air, or the universe, who were the objects of such an unintermitting, general, and relentless persecution as the Jews of this period"'.[15] Mackenzie subsequently scripted an unmade adaptation of Kipling's *The Man Who Would Be King* for Mirisch a decade later, so Walter certainly knew him.[16]

In the event, however, the only film credited as a Pembroke production, was *Bomba the Jungle Boy* (Beebe, 1949), but the other entries in this series were listed simply

---

[10] Edwards, 2011: 388.
[11] Broidy quoted in Edwards, 2011: 389.
[12] 'Along the Rialto', *The Film Daily*, 6.5.46: 3.
[13] 'Monogram in Fast Pace', *Showmen's Trade Review*, 11.5.46: 42.
[14] 'Hollywood's Middle Ages: The Script Development of Knights of the Round Table and Ivanhoe, 1935–53', Jonathan Stubbs, *Exemplaria* vol 21 no 4, Winter 2009: 398–417. Mackenzie's co-scripted *Ivanhoe* (Thorpe) was released in 1952.
[15] Ibid.
[16] Mirisch, 2008: 82–3.

as Walter Mirisch productions, evidence that Walter swiftly dropped his status as an independent, with the seven subsequent *Bombas* all in-house, Monogram productions. In June 1946, Mirisch was among the eight producers, including the three King Brothers, attending Monogram's annual convention at the Drake Hotel in Chicago, alongside the company's top executives.[17] Like the majors, Monogram worked with both in-house, staff producers and independents, under what Staiger refers to as the Producer-Unit system.[18] There was a group of 'loosely associated producers' including the King Brothers, Lindsley Persons, Paul Malvern, Scott Dunlop, Philip N. Krasne and James S. Burkett. Edwards argues that Monogram sold 'the prospect of product quality via the company's association with a pool of experienced, relatively autonomous producers. At the same time, Monogram's corporate backing . . . ensures the stability and smooth operation of the supply chain that would lead those films to the theater'.[19] (This system of devolved relative autonomy was also to be replicated at the Mirisch Company.)

Walter and Woolrich

Still not quite twenty-five, Walter acquired the rights to a Cornell Woolrich short story, *Cocaine* (also known as *C-Jag*) originally published in *Black Mask Magazine* in October 1940. The film went into production in winter 1946, exploiting an amendment to the Production Code, making such subject matter viable for the first time.[20] The story even made the front page of *Motion Picture Daily*, under the headline, 'Code Change Starts Dope Film Cycle', reporting that

> Evidence of appearances in the near future of a cycle of dope films followed immediately upon the announcement by the Motion Picture Association last week that the Production Code provision barring narcotics as a motion picture theme had been amended to permit use of the subject in productions. . . . Monogram has purchased Cornell Woolrich original story 'Cocaine', assigned Walter Mirisch to produce.[21]

This implies that Mirisch's role was a passive one, but Walter selected the story and acquired it himself. The controversial subject matter and its marketing potential therefore owe a great deal to him.

Subsequently, pushing the envelope, as far as censorship was concerned, became an occasional Mirisch reflex – and one with marketing value. Nor was *Cocaine* Mirisch's only acquisition. *Motion Picture Daily* reported a group of forthcoming 'A' pictures,

---

[17] 'Monogram Heads Off to Convention', *Motion Picture Daily*, 25.6.46: 13.
[18] Bordwell, Staiger, Thompson, 1985: 320–9.
[19] Edwards, 2011: 391.
[20] 'Cocaine to Monogram: Mirisch to Produce Cocaine', *Showmen's Trade Review*, 21.9.46: 36.
[21] *MPD*, 17.9.46: 1, 9.

including *In the Fog*, to be written by Richard Harding Davis and produced by Walter Mirisch, and *One Way Street* by Cornell Woolrich, also to be produced by Mirisch.[22] Woolrich was clearly a preferred source, but Walter's affection for the noir novelist seems more than fashionable. Subsequent Monogram/Allied Artists hires included Philip Yordan – who had scripted an adaptation of Woolrich's *The Chase* (Ripley, 1946), Jacques Tourneur – who had directed an adaptation of Woolrich's *Leopard Man* (1943), William Cameron Menzies – who had co-directed an adaptation of Woolrich's *Deadline at Dawn* (Clurman, 1946) albeit uncredited) and William Castle, who had directed an adaptation of Woolrich's *The Marked Man* as *Mark of the Whistler* (1944). Walter Mirisch also worked with other noir novelists including W. R. Burnett, on *The Great Escape*, Steve Fisher on *I Wouldn't Be in Your Shoes* (Nigh, 1948) and *Flat Top* (Selander, 1952), Daniel Mainwaring, on *The Phenix City Story* (Karlson, 1955), *An Annapolis Story* (Siegel, 1955) and *Invasion of the Body Snatchers* (Siegel,1956), and Elmore Leonard, on *Mr. Majestyk* (Fleischer, 1974) and *Desperado* (NBC, 1987).

Other 'A's announced included *The Hunted*, to cost over 1 million dollars and be produced by the King Brothers with Barry Sullivan and Belita, and Phil Karlson's *Black Gold* (Karlson, 1947). The King Brothers signed a deal to make four films for the company in 1945.[23] This was presumably the first multi-picture contract Walter was aware of and may well have reinforced his determination to form a comparable company with its own output deal. One of those four proposed King projects was yet another Woolrich adaptation, *I Wouldn't Be In Your Shoes*, which Walter ultimately produced himself. The other three were *Suspense* (described as an adaptation of *Crime and Punishment*), *Absent Without Love* and *The Honest Gambler* to be written by Philip Yordan, who subsequently scripted the King Bros' *The Big Combo* (Lewis, 1955) for Allied Artists, by which time Walter was head of production.

Finally, a screenplay for *Cocaine* was complete – and Mirisch was ready to produce his first film. 'Walt Mirisch is one of the newest additions to the ranks of Monogram producers.'[24] The trades mistakenly described the new producer as a 'former theatre executive', when in fact his only real exhibition experience had been as an usher.[25] *Cocaine* began shooting on 11 November 1946.[26] The very week it went into production, Monogram also announced its acquisition of the narrative poem, *The Highwayman*, probably further evidence of Walter's influence at the studio. (He subsequently produced a loose adaptation of another narrative poem, *Hiawatha*, for Monogram and acquired a third as the source for an abortive project for the Mirisch Company.) *Cocaine*, retitled *Fall Guy*, was shot in eight days, cost $83,000, and was released in March 1947, very visibly limited by its budget and schedule.[27] Three subway entrances appear in the film, all too conspicuously shot on the same, minimally redressed, set – with only the respective subway signs, a candy bar poster on the wall, a garbage can in

---

[22] Ibid, 28.6.46: 7.
[23] 'King Brothers to Make Four Pix for Monogram', *Film Daily*, 1.6.45: 2.
[24] 'Hollywood Indie List Growing', *Film Daily*, 18.11.46: 24.
[25] 'New Producers of 1947', *Showmen's Trade Review*, October–December 1947: 122.
[26] 'One Starts at Monogram', *Showmen's Trade Review*, 9.11.46: 40.
[27] *Film Daily*, 7.3.47: 7.

the foreground, and a weighing machine, to differentiate them as 18th Street, 28th Street and 50th Street sets.

Trouvailles and talking points

In another scene (Figure 3), the hero, Tom, arranges to meet his girlfriend, Lois, and friend, Mac, at the Bijou cinema, where a lobby poster advertises *Don't Gamble with Strangers* (Beaudine, 1946), while the cinema marquee boasts '*Decoy* Plus 2nd Feature'. By the box office is another poster, for *Wife Wanted* (Karlson, 1946). This appears to be an in-joke, since Mac was played by Robert Armstrong, who co-starred in *Decoy* (Bernhard, 1946), and Lois by Teala Loring, who co-starred in *Wife Wanted*, while all three films were low-budget noirs made by Monogram. (Armstrong's claim to fame was his appearance in *King Kong* (Cooper/Schoedsack, 1933), an unmade remake of which was one of the first films announced by the Mirisch Company.)[28] Of course, this selection of titles might simply be a function of the film's low budget, using those posters available at no cost. Bordwell, however, calls such things 'trouvailles', in which, for instance, billboards for one film appear in another by the same filmmaker, attributing their inclusion to auteur directors like Preston Sturges and Orson Welles, for whom 'cinematic narrative creates a parallel world in which the author can link

Figure 3 The Bijou cinema in *Fall Guy*.

[28] 'RKO vs. Mirisch "Kong"', *Variety*, 11.9.57: 7.

different stories in ways that only a devotee will notice'.²⁹ But this is to disparage ordinary cinemagoers, since it is perfectly possible that audiences for Monogram movies recognized that all three titles were from the same stable, and that the same actors appeared in both the present film and its predecessors. Bordwell perhaps unintentionally implies that while auteur directors are capable of such touches, producers or, indeed, production companies, let alone less than prestigious ones, like Monogram, are not.

It is worth noting, furthermore, that the candy advertised in the subway was an 'Oh Henry!' chocolate bar. Whether or not Monogram had 'devotees', it certainly had regular customers, some of whom might well have known that the celebrated writer, O. Henry, was the creator of the Cisco Kid character, protagonist of one of Monogram's most successful series. Oh Henry! was a real chocolate bar, and one already associated with mysteries as the sponsor of *True Detective Mysteries*, a CBS radio series based on *True Detective Magazine*. Such touches – with their passing references to candy and movie theatres – might even be a hidden homage to Walter's brothers' business interests in exhibition and confectionery. Walter even ensured the film received a special screening in Milwaukee, the family home and HQ of the Theatres Candy Co.³⁰

The film did receive some press attention, not least because of its controversial subject matter.

> Based on the Cornell Woolrich story, Cocaine, this is the first to be produced in sequel to the revision of the Production Code, in such a way as to permit the presentation of drug addiction on the screen, and it presumably rates special consideration in the trade . . . it does deal with the use of drugs (referred to in dialogue both as 'drugs' and as 'narcotics') and therefor does offer the exhibitor disposed to exploit it on this ground an opportunity to do so, but does not offer his audiences the type of thing that sort of exploitation would suggest. In point of fact, nothing has been done with the 'dope' element which could not have been done with drunkenness, amnesia or even an accidental bump on the head.³¹

Mirisch's good taste or sensitivity may have prevented him pressing the exploitation button – a reticence which would subsequently characterize the brothers' own company's productions, not always to their benefit. Nevertheless, the free publicity caused by a provocative, code-challenging theme was not forgotten and subsequent Mirisch films including *The Children's Hour*, *Town Without Pity*, *Irma La Douce*, and *Kiss Me, Stupid* (Wilder, 1964), were all subject to considerable press attention because of their controversial content.

---

[29] Bordwell, 2017: 436.
[30] 'Walter Mirisch, former Milwaukeean, now a Monogram producer, will give localites a look at his first Monogram production, Fall Guy, at the Warner in July'. 'Milwaukee', *Boxoffice*, 31.6.47: 68.
[31] *Motion Picture Daily*, 3.3.47: 5.

Monogram and narrative forms

According to Bordwell, a handful of narrative options dominated the 1940s, the flashback narrative, the multiple protagonist film, the social comment film, the new realist film, the self-consciously stylized film, the film reliant on subjective imagery and voice-over, and the psychological thriller.[32] Three of Mirisch's own early productions fit into the first category – *Fall Guy*, *I Wouldn't Be In Your Shoes* and *Flat Top* (aka *Eagles of the Fleet*). The first and second were both Woolrich adaptations, the second and third both scripted by Black Mask alumnus, Steve Fisher. *Fall Guy* also relies on subjective imagery and voice-over and is one of some seventy 1940s films deploying amnesia as a plot device.[33] In this case, the hero cannot remember what happened on the night of a murder, because he had been drugged. *Fall Guy* is also one of some twenty-five films a year, between 1942 and 1950, which deployed flashbacks.[34] *Flat Top* is another. As in Allied Artists' *The Gangster* (Wiles, 1947), these flashbacks are cued by the protagonist's voice-over narration. *Flat Top* is also a multiple protagonist film; *Riot in Cell Block 11* (Siegel, 1954) and *Crime in the Streets* (Siegel, 1956) meet the criteria of the social comment film; *The Phenix City Story* and *Crime in the Streets* both qualify as new realist films; *The Big Combo* and *The Maze* (Cameron Menzies, 1953) are self-consciously stylized films, the former expressionist noir, the latter 3D gothic. Several of these narrative devices were to be redeployed in Mirisch productions once the brothers had their own company. Indeed, small-scale social realism and multi-protagonist, ensemble quests were to remain characteristic of many of the Mirisch Company's own productions. So too was a reliance on voice-over narration (both in the first and third person). Perhaps Tevye's direct address to the audience, in *Fiddler on the Roof*, felt less radical to Mirisch because of such early experiments with narration.

After overseeing another Woolrich adaptation, *The Guilty* (Reinhardt, 1947), based on the story, *He Looked Like Murder*, Walter produced his second film, based on yet another Woolrich story, *I Wouldn't Be in Your Shoes*. *Film Daily*'s review notes it as a collaboration between 'Veteran director William Nigh and young producer Walter Mirisch'.[35] The film features two dancers, hoping to make it in California with 'jobs in the studios'. Again, it is tempting to see this as appealingly parallel to Walter's own professional ambition. As Walter would learn, if he had not already, the producer was the industry's fall guy, blamed if things went wrong, but rarely praised if they went well. And like the title of his second film, the role of producer was far from a default aspiration for Hollywood wannabes. More than two decades later, a Mirisch screenwriter wrote to his producer, 'I tip my toby to you – I wouldn't be a producer, not no-how I wouldn't.'[36] Characteristically, *Shoes* starts on death row and then flashes

---

[32] Bordwell, 2017: 15.
[33] Ibid, 6.
[34] Ibid, 69.
[35] 'Film Daily Reviews of New Features', *Film Daily*, 5.5.48: 8.
[36] Letter from Donald Sanford to John C. Champion, Walter Mirisch Collection, Wisconsin, File 2, Box 42.

back to how the protagonist got there. Strikingly, neither amnesia nor flashbacks were devices deployed by Mirisch once the brothers had their own company. (There is one fleeting flashback, and even an imagined flash-forward, in *The Spikes Gang*.) Whether this is a consequence of changing cinematic fashions over the decades, or because such tropes felt like residues of Poverty Row productions and genres, which the brothers hoped to have left behind, is unclear. Nevertheless, *The Landlord*, their most formally inventive film, certainly plays with linear time.

The press release announcing the start of filming on *Shoes*, also revealed that 'Monogram has acquired the rights to "Isle of Hate", murder mystery, which Walter Mirisch will produce' so Mirisch's first projects were all apparently adaptations, necessitating acquiring copyright.[37] Mirisch was already proving prolific, convinced that acquiring literary pretexts for productions made economic sense. In August 1947, in a week in which acquisitions from publishers were at a new low, he ensured Monogram was buying. Under the headline, 'Only Four New Stories Sold During the Week', *Boxoffice* reported that 'there was a noticeable trend on the part of the studios toward holding off on the acquisition of new properties, with the result that only a meager quartette [*sic*] of stories found their way into producers' hands. Of these, Monogram accounted for a pair'. They were *Tijuana*, to be produced by the King Brothers and *Advice of Counsel,* to be produced by Walter Mirisch.[38] Neither was made, but a nascent film industrial strategy was being sketched.

The search for a series

Mirisch's producer fee for each film was $2500, but his first taste of independence, and the freelance insecurities that went with one-off productions, proved worrying. 'I soon realized that I could quickly starve to death while waiting for subsequent films to be approved. Now I understood the value of the series pictures to their producers.'[39] Recognizing the unpredictability of one-off productions, Mirisch 'started to look for a subject that could become a series and that would provide a minimum income for me while I was searching for better films to do'.[40] In December 1947, *MPH* reported that, 'Monogram purchased the screen rights to the famous adventure stories of Roy Rockford's "Bomba the Jungle Boy" including 20 published books . . . Walter Mirisch will handle the production chores on all of the "Bomba" series which will be filmed in color. More than a million copies of the books have been sold to date.'[41] Broidy agreed they should produce two films in the series each year, the first being shot for $85,000 in eight days.[42] The films were based on bestsellers and deployed considerable

---

[37] 'Production Holds Level With 39 Shooting as Three are Started', *Motion Picture Herald*, 15.11.47: 34.
[38] *Boxoffice*, 30.8.47: 30.
[39] Mirisch, 2008, 27.
[40] Ibid, 28.
[41] 'Hollywood Causes Drop at Studios', *MPH*, 6.12.47: 33.
[42] Mirisch, 2008, 34.

stock footage, two strategies the Mirisch Company would deploy repeatedly later.[43] Walter once again received a flat fee of $2500 for producing the film, plus 50 per cent participation in profits, once overheads and other Monogram expenses had been deducted. A full-page advertisement in *Showmen's Trade Review* revealed some of the exploitation strategies for the film, including 'Monkey face bally man with giant Bomba book', 'Monkeys in Lobby: Livewire showmen promote crowd-drawing simians!', 'Nationwide Book Tie-up! Thousands of dealers get free poster selling film!' and 'Newsboys Ballyhoo! Kids in Bomba T-shirts make tip-top walking ads!'[44] ('Bally', short for ballyhoo, echoes Harold's own marketing activities, and describes any appropriately costumed, walking and talking promotion for a film.) The poster for *Bomba* also ensured Walter's name as producer was considerably larger than Ford Beebe's as director.

The *Bomba* series starred Johnny Sheffield, famous for appearing as 'Boy' in *Tarzan* films – a role he had been playing since 1939. The *Tarzan* series had been made by MGM for some time, but in 1942 the independent producer, Sol Lesser, took *Tarzan* with him to RKO. That same January, coincidentally, Harold Mirisch started working there, initially supervising all non-New York bookings, but by the end of the year he was head buyer and booker for their entire circuit. Lesser's *Tarzan* films would thus have been among his first bookings.[45]

Such series were predicated on the promise of further films, thus satisfying Monogram's marketing claims about the company's long-term viability as a supplier.[46] Broidy also revived the *Cisco Kid* series, developed a new one around comic strip character, *The Shadow*, adopted *Joe Palooka* from radio, adapted *Jiggs and Maggie* from the *Bringing Up Father* comic strip and launched *Freddie Turnbull*, the screen persona of bandleader Freddie Stewart. Monogram also transformed *The East Side Kids* into *The Bowery Boys*.[47]

Whether or not Walter influenced the decision to double down on series production, it certainly influenced him, while B movies remained a component of the Mirisch Company's own dual strategy and series proved a reliable way of sweating the company's assets. In June 1949, *Variety* announced that Monogram's ten current film series constituted an industry record. Broidy was adamant that 'This policy has proven immensely popular with exhibitors and the theatre-going public through the years and we intend to continue along the line which has proven so successful'.[48] Edwards explains this policy by quoting Broidy's infamous remark that 'Not everybody likes to eat cake. Some people like bread and even a certain number of people like stale bread

[43] Ibid, 35.
[44] *Showmen's Trade Review*, 2.7.49: 13.
[45] Derral Cheatwood, 'The Tarzan Films: An Analysis of Determinants of Maintenance and Change in Conventions', in Janet Staiger (ed), *The Studio System*, Rutgers University Press, 1995, 176. See also a Telegram from Harold J. Mirisch to Dave Lewis, RKO Albee Theater, Providence, confirming a booking for *Tarzan's Triumph*, 12.4.43, Harold J. Mirisch Film Bookings 1942–43, Iowa Digital Library.
[46] Edwards, 2011: 392.
[47] Ibid, 394.
[48] 'Mono Sets Record: Ten Different Pix Series at Work', *Variety*, 28.6.49: 5.

rather than fresh bread. . . . Quality of product . . . was not necessarily the yardstick by which we could gauge our potential success or failure.'[49] The Mirisches, however, remained convinced that quality product – where possible based on a quality pretext – was its own guarantee at the box office.

Product placement

In early 1946, just as Walter became a producer, a California clothing company, Koret, which manufactured female sportswear, made a deal with Monogram. The contract guaranteed that 'Every link in a merchandising chain reaction has been carefully forged to show returns to the store, theatre and advertising in the town booked for a showing of a specially produced film highlighting Koret garments'. Merchandizing was certainly one of the aspects of business which Mirisch had studied at Harvard and it seems possible that he was involved in the deal. This was apparently the first time a major manufacturer not only provided the costumes for a film but also mass-produced the same item for sale to the cinemagoing – and non-cinemagoing – public.[50] The films in question, *High School Hero* (Dreifuss, 1946), *Vacation Days* (Dreifuss, 1947) and *Smart Politics* (Jason, 1948) all brought 'screen fashions to the American woman at prices within her reach'.

Variety's review of *High School Hero* began by identifying just how much product placement there was in the film.

> Monogram might well go into the advertising business on the strength of this picture. Cross-plugs come so fast that it's hard to keep up with them, going from Capitol Records to Koret Fashions to Royal Crown Cola ad infinitum, all of which makes the exhibs' exploitation job somewhat simpler, but doesn't add a great deal to the pic's b.o. value.[51]

Walter may have learned from Harold how to maximize customer interest, as exhibitors were put in touch with both the film's stars and the sportswear company, attracting teenagers to the box office with the chance to win free outfits, at reduced ticket prices.[52] His Harvard education may also have contributed to the campaign, which involved co-star June Preisser appearing on Koret's sponsored radio show, *Show Stoppers,* as well as in full-page ads in *Photoplay* and *Seventeen*.[53]

The success of *High School Hero* convinced Koret to repeat the experiment. 'Cooperative effort on High School Hero was so effective that Koret bounced back

---

[49] Edwards, 2011: 388.
[50] Kerry Segrave, *Product Placement in Hollywood Films: A History*, McFarland and Co, 2004, 93.
[51] 'Film Reviews', *Variety*, 22.10.46: 10.
[52] 'Adolescent Appeal Tops "School Hero" Campaign', *Showmen's Trade Review*, 7.12.46: 16.
[53] 'Monogram Sets National Tie-Ups on "School Hero"', *Showmen's Trade Review*, 7.9.46: 18.

with even bigger magazine campaigns for Vacation Days.'[54] *Vacation Days* was part financed by Koret, in return for a confident campaign. Clothing stores were told that '1. Your merchandise shares the limelight with the glamour of Hollywood and a famous designer; 2. Your customer is presold at the theatre. She will be in a buying mood when she enters your shop. For these reasons Vacation Days is a natural for lively promotion and sparkling publicity.'[55] Walter Mirisch's Harvard-imbibed understanding of merchandizing may well have played a part in securing or at the very least endorsing this deal. Certainly, the concept of 'pre-selling the customer' was one with which Walter was already extremely familiar.

These pictures were part of an eight-film series featuring 'The Teen Agers', and starring Freddie Stewart and June Preisser. The relationship between Koret and Monogram continued with the next film in the series, *Sarge Goes to College* (Jason, 1947).[56] Stephanie Koret was once again credited for the girl's costumes in the penultimate film in the series, *Smart Politics*. Certainly, Walter must have been aware of The Teen Agers series; indeed, he was looking for a series of his own. That September 1947, two further Monogram films, *Maggie and Jiggs in Court* (Beaudine, 1948) and *Shep Comes Home* (Beebe, 1948) contained product placements for beers made by the National Brewing Company.[57] The Mirisch Company later deployed its own spin on product placement with *One, Two, Three*, which starred James Cagney as European head of Coca Cola, in an echo of Monogram's earlier product placement deal with a rival Cola company. (*Time*'s review of the former film even coined the term 'Coca-colonisation' to describe the soft power the film depicted.) Writer-director Billy Wilder had created a character who worked for Pepsi Cola, in *Love in the Afternoon* (Wilder, 1957), and felt this was simply cinematic balance.

Hollywood and assembly lines

Series like The Teen Agers were not only Broidy's 'bread', however, they were also Monogram's bread and butter. And Walter Mirisch was not unique in thinking that assembly lines had something to offer their production. One prominent industry observer in 1946, Hortense Powdermaker, agreed. In her anthropological study of Hollywood, *Hollywood The Dream Factory: An Anthropologist Looks at the Moviemakers*, for which she did the field work between July 1946 and August 1947, she wrote, 'In this age of technology and the assembly line, many people wish to escape from their anxieties into movies. Collective day-dreams themselves manufactured on the assembly line.'[58] She goes on to qualify this statement by suggesting:,

---

[54] 'Koret, Princess Pat in Monogram Film Tie-Ups', *Showmen's Trade Review*, 7.12.46: 14.
[55] Quoted in Segrave, 2004, 94.
[56] 'Monogram-Koret Tie Up', *Showmen's Trade Review*, 12.4.47: 10.
[57] Segrave, 2004, 96.
[58] Hortense Powdermaker, *Hollywood the Dream Factory: An Anthropologist Looks at the Movie-Makers*, Martino Fine Books, 2013, reprint of 1950 edition, 12.

Although the production of movies . . . is unbusinesslike in many ways, at the same time it has some of the characteristics of the assembly line. Producer, writer, director, actor, cameraman, cutter, musician, make-up man, set designer and many others all have a set place and timing in that production. A unit manager endeavors to keep all efficiently geared to a schedule and a budget. The filming of sequences in a different order from that in which they finally appear contributes to the assembly-line analogy. So also does the breaking up of the script into many separate and seemingly disconnected elements.... The emphasis given to technical details such as lighting and the great concern with appearances – costuming, sets and make-up – as compared to the meaning of the picture as a whole or its emotional validity are other characteristics similar to those of the assembly-line factory.[59]

Nor was Powdermaker alone is deploying the assembly-line analogy. That same year, *Box Office Digest* reviewed a 'formulaic' film, *Strange Journey* (Tinling, 1946), under the headline 'Assembly Line Meller Job', commenting, 'The Wurtzel organization had produced its meller [*sic*] in efficient, assembly-line fashion'.[60] The previous year, just as Walter was entering the industry, *The Screenwriter* (September 1945) noted that 'writing does not lend itself to belt-line production. The story which is passed from writer to producer, to another writer, to director, to writer and so on back and forth across the assembly line – is bound to emerge with standardized parts and no individuality'.[61] In 1946, producer Robert Riskin suggested that sustaining mass consumption of movies depended on an end to such mass production. 'Going to the movies is a habit' Riskin points out 'which can only be established and maintained by producing good movies . . . In my opinion it's the B product which will go by the board. The superior picture, made with care and craftsmanship will continue to justify at the box office its high budget . . . ' Riskin concluded that 'you can't make quality films on an assembly line basis'[62] In fact, Poverty Row companies were among the last to abandon these techniques. The *Motion Picture Daily* review of Monogram's *Rainbow Over the Rockies* (Drake, 1947) began 'Latest of the Jimmy Wakely series comes right off the assembly line with little effort to distinguish it'.[63] The Mirisch Company was to retain aspects of assembly-line production for its programme pictures, while abandoning such economies for its A films and top-line filmmakers.

The antidote to such endemic standardization was that the proposed 'elimination of double-features, with resultant letdown in the tempo of Hollywood's assembly line production methods, would permit greater emphasis on individual creative effort'.[64] B movies and double bills were seen, at least by some, as the last bastion of assembly-line production practices. *The Exhibitor* agreed that 'A large percentage of Hollywood's

---

[59] Ibid, 30–1.
[60] *Box Office Digest*, 28.9.46: 5.
[61] *The Screenwriter*, September 1945: 54.
[62] 'Good Picture Benefits the Entire Industry, Riskin Believes', *Motion Picture Herald*, 7.12.46: 35.
[63] *MPH*, 19.3.47: 8.
[64] *Screenwriter*, 1945: 54.

product arrives stamped with the "Made in Hollywood" trademark, an indication of assembly line production methods'.[65] But this trademark was apparently of decreasing value. 'American producers have found out that meritorious pictures cannot be produced on an assembly line basis. It doesn't work.'[66] Meanwhile, proponents of specialist film crafts, like cinematography, increasingly objected to the idea of assembly-line procedures. 'Cinematography is an art and a science. It cannot be regimented nor placed on an assembly line basis.'[67] Nor were B movies as profitable as A's. Exhibitors paid studios a percentage of the box office for A movies, while Bs simply received a flat fee. Phil Karlson, one of the directors who worked at Monogram and Allied Artists under Broidy, described the former as resembling an assembly line in a factory 'I was like a mechanic that worked on a line' and that only changed 'with Steve Broidy, after Trem Carr had left, and we started getting the Mirisches in there, then I started making these pictures that really said something'.[68]

Harold at RKO

At the beginning of 1942, Edward Alperson became the general manager of the RKO Theater Circuit and offered Harold, with his background in distribution and exhibition, a job back in New York. Alperson and Mirisch knew each other from Warners, and both had been board members of the Milwaukee branch of the Variety Club, Alperson having previously worked in the midwest, as assistant head of Fox Wisconsin Theatres.[69] Alperson had joined RKO in June 1941 and tempted Harold with a position supervising all non-New York RKO bookings.[70] The role involved regular trips to the coast to see new product and plan promotional campaigns. In August, Mirisch was promoted to take charge of film buying and booking for the entire RKO circuit.[71] That same month, Marvin and Harold Mirisch acquired the Hollywood Theater in Milwaukee.[72] If standardization was one strategy Harold imbibed at RKO, another was differentiation. As he put it in a letter to George French at RKO Albee Theater, Providence, 'I think it would be a good idea when listing the opposition bookings on the back of the booking sheet, that you also list all other types of oppositions, such as ice shows, circuses etc . . ., so that we may be guided accordingly.'[73]

By 1942, RKO owned some hundred cinemas across the United States, almost all of which were first-run, except those in New York, where it operated a chain of

---

[65] 'Exhibitors Must Help Hollywood', *The Exhibitor*, 9.6.48, SS2.
[66] *Harrison's Reports*, 21.8.48: 136.
[67] 'The Case for the Cameramen', *American Cinematographer*, February 1949: 66.
[68] Karlson, in *Kings of the Bs*, 334–5.
[69] 'Gran Named Head of Milwaukee Club', *Motion Picture Daily*, 17.12.40: 2.
[70] 'Mirisch Joins RKO', *MPH*, 19.1.42: 4.
[71] 'Realign RKO Circuit: Mirisch Head Buyer', *Motion Picture Daily*, 24.8.42: 1.
[72] *Variety*, 12.8.42: 16.
[73] Letter to George French, 1.3.42; Harold J. Mirisch Film Bookings 1942–3, Iowa Digital Library. http://aspace.lib.uiowa.edu/repositories/2/archival_objects/398

neighbourhood, second-run, screens. The president of RKO, George Schaefer, resigned in June 1942, having failed to control allegedly profligate filmmakers like Orson Welles. (Harold himself recommended booking Welles' *Magnificent Ambersons*, in a telegram to exhibitors.) Charles Koerner, whose own background was in theatre operations (he had been appointed head of all RKO theatres in 1941), became the new head of production.[74] Koerner cancelled a pair of allegedly over-budget Welles and Pare Lorentz productions and installed 'Showmanship in Place of Genius' as his production policy.[75] The implicitly non-genius directors working for and/or releasing through RKO in this period included Jacques Tourneur, John Ford, William Wyler and Robert Wise – all of whom went on to work for the Mirisch brothers. In 1943, Harold was among the RKO executives attending a meeting at Samuel Goldwyn Studio in Hollywood to discuss distribution plans for *The North Star* (Milestone, 1943).[76] The Goldwyn Studio later became the Mirisch Company's own base for almost eighteen years.

In 1943–4, as in the previous year, Harold oversaw RKO's distribution of Warners, 20th Century Fox and half of Universal's films, as well as the studio's own output.[77] The Koerner period proved a successful one financially. RKO showed a $7.6 million profit in 1943, ten times that of the previous year and RKO stockholders approved a pension plan for 2000 of its employees on 14 March 1944. In May, however, Alperson abruptly resigned and Harold's own career prospects, though he remained chief booker and film buyer for RKO, stalled. Nevertheless, he was an increasingly public figure in the business, quoted in trade advertising for RKO films, with hyperbole like 'A box office whopper . . . Will set record grosses' on ads for the studio's *Incendiary Blonde* (Marshall, 1945) and to promote *The Song of Bernadette* (King, 1943); 'It set a new all-time record . . . and did smash business . . . '[78] Mirisch was also instrumental in opening *Song of Bernadette* 'in the heart of Harlem, with a view to testing it among the coloured trade. The business in both houses turned out very big'[79] Whether this was simply a business decision on a high-ticket film, or early evidence of Mirisch anti-racism, or a blend of both, is unclear. In the summer of 1945, Harold was one of the speakers at RKO's annual convention, 'to discuss film product for the various cities in which RKO houses are located'.[80] And his position ensured he was having increasing contact with major filmmakers, including the likes of William Wyler and Alfred Hitchcock.

Koerner entered into an agreement with the independent producer, David O. Selznick, to co-produce with the latter's Vanguard Films and signed deals to co-finance and distribute for Liberty Films, the director-led independent production company comprising Frank Capra, William Wyler and George Stevens, and with Argosy, John

---

[74] Richard Jewell, *Slow Fade to Black: The Decline of RKO Radio Pictures*, University of California Press, 2016, 3.
[75] Ibid, 8.
[76] 'RKO Executives Meeting at Studio', *The Exhibitor*, 22.9.43: 20.
[77] 'RKO, Loew in Same Deals in 1943–44', *Motion Picture Daily*, 11.8.43: 1&6.
[78] *Motion Picture Herald*, 25.8.45: 38 and *The Exhibitor*, 9.8.44: 11.
[79] 'Record $285,000 Gross Struck on Limited 3-Day Runs in 37 RKO Houses', *Variety*, 12.7.44: 8.
[80] 'Kingsberg Tees Off RKO Conv.', *Variety*, 27.6.45: 25.

Ford's company, to include *The Fugitive* (Ford, 1947) to be shot in Mexico.[81] Indeed, Koerner made RKO something of an oasis for independent producers, a strategy Harold can hardly have been unaware of. Among a series of trips in 1945, Koerner visited Churubusco Studios in Mexico City, which RKO was then building to take advantage of lower labour costs south of the border.[82] Fifteen years later, the Mirisches shot additional scenes for *The Magnificent Seven* there. However, Koerner died suddenly in February 1946 and was replaced by Dore Schary and RKO's new owner, Floyd Odlum, decided to get out of the movie business altogether. It was in this brief period that RKO produced a number of social problem pictures including *Crossfire* (Dmytryk, 1947), *The Farmer's Daughter* (Potter, 1947) and *So Well Remembered* (Dmytryk, 1947), a strategy which cannot have escaped Harold's attention and subsequently informed that of his own company. Also in 1947, RKO's distribution department dismissed twenty-seven members of staff as part of a general cost-cutting exercise. 'Even the theatre company, then the healthiest division in the RKO organization, was not immune. Its mandate was to reduce costs by hundreds of thousands of dollars.'[83]

Harold himself was one of the casualties, after a row with the new management.[84] According to the trade press, he resigned as a buyer for RKO in February 1947 and acquired the Keith Theatre in Indianapolis, once again planning a move into exhibition.[85] With a partner, Arthur Steel, Harold bought the lease for $250,000, as the initial acquisition in a projected circuit of cinemas in major cities.

> A national circuit of independent first-run theatres in cities of 250,000 population or more will be headed by Harold Mirisch, formerly chief booker and film buyer of RKO Theaters, in partnership with Arthur Steel, independent theatre owner.... The first link, the Keith, in Indianapolis, will be inaugurated on April 30th opening with Samuel Goldwyn's The Best Years of Our Lives, Mirisch said.[86]

Mirisch also announced, somewhat hyperbolically, that he was 'to add two new offices in the West to those now maintained in Minneapolis, Milwaukee, Indianapolis, Cincinnati, Omaha, Los Angeles and in Brooklyn'.[87] Irving Mirisch was described as managing the LA branch of this notional national chain, while Marvin purportedly headed the Milwaukee HQ 'as well as over-all operations of the company'.[88] There were certainly industry plans for an expansion of exhibition in 1947, with the trade press reporting that 'an assembly line in Los Angeles can start rolling out such theaters as fast as the orders arrive'. [89]

---

[81] '$85,000,000 Will Be Spent on Indie Production on West Coast During Year', *Film Daily*, 26.12.45: 10.
[82] Jewell, 2016: 31–2.
[83] Ibid, 71.
[84] Mirisch, 2008: 36.
[85] *Motion Picture Daily*, 20.2.47: 2.
[86] 'Nat'l Circuit for Mirisch', *MPH*, 1.4.47: 1.
[87] Ibid, 1.4.47: 5.
[88] *Motion Picture Daily*, 17.4.47: 1.
[89] 'New Pre-designed Theater is Ready', *MPH*, 18.1.47: 32.

By early 1947, however, the trades were reporting Harold's plans to launch a new production company of his own, 'Harold J. Mirisch plans to head an important new producing group, fast taking shape on the coast . . . now holding conferences with industry execs'.[90]

> Mirisch leaves New York Friday (7) on his way to the coast with a stopover in Milwaukee. Headquartered there is the popcorn and candy biz which has made him independently wealthy in the past five or six years. The outfit will continue, incidentally, to service RKO theaters, despite Mirisch's exit from the chain. Production deal on which Mirisch is going to the coast may be in association with Edward L. Alperson, indie producer for 20th-Fox.[91]

By the spring, *Variety* was also reporting that 'A long term deal is being negotiated by Harold Mirisch . . . with the King Bros, by which he'll become partner with them in their indie production unit. They have been releasing through Monogram, but with Mirisch joining the unit, it will begin releasing via Mono's higher budget subsid, Allied Artists'.[92] On the same page, *Variety* reported that the King Bros had signed a deal with AA for four new films, including *Gun Crazy* (Lewis, 1950).

Harold joins Monogram

In fact, Harold was also already talking to Steve Broidy about a possible role at Monogram instead and he soon sold off his share of the Keith lease.[93] Broidy and Mirisch already knew each other well – in 1943, for instance, they had been pictured together at a lunch to launch Monogram's *Women in Bondage* (Sekely, 1943).[94] In late May, the Hollywood trade press announced, 'Mirisch to AA as Vice-Prexy'.[95] By June, the King Bros deal had 'chilled'.[96] *Gun Crazy* was instead released by United Artists, but a relationship with the King Brothers subsequently saw another Joseph H. Lewis film noir, *The Big Combo,* released by Allied Artists. (Lewis had previously directed *That Gang of Mine, Boys of the City* and *Pride of the Bowery* for Monogram in 1940 and *Invisible Ghost* in 1941.)

As the traditional double bill began to decline in the late 1940s, Broidy revised Monogram's corporate strategy, creating a production arm for 'A' movies, Allied Artists, while steadily reducing the number of films produced under the old

---

[90] 'Along the Rialto', *Film Daily*, 25.3.1947: 4.
[91] 'Mirisch Eyes 25 St Loo Theaters. Also Plans Prod', *Variety*, 5.3.47: 3 & 18.
[92] 'Mirisch Kings Expansion Set', *Variety*, 7.5.47: 9.
[93] *Variety*, 9.4.47: 6.
[94] 'This Week: The Camera Reports', *Motion Picture Herald*, 27.11.43: 11.
[95] *The Film Daily*, 28.5.47: 1.
[96] 'Mirisch-King Bros Deal Cold', *Variety*, 4.6.47: 24.

Monogram label.⁹⁷ This was partly a consequence of the 1948 Paramount Decree, which opened the first-run market beyond the big five and little three studios. But already, by 1947, Allied Artists had initiated its 'nervous A' strategy, with films like *It Happened on Fifth Avenue* (Del Ruth, 1947), *Black Gold* and *The Gangster*. These were necessarily distinct from Monogram's B and series pictures – indeed the Del Ruth film was budgeted at $1,700,000, an unprecedented sum for the company. Walter convinced his boss that 'a separate sales chief would help differentiate the Allied Artists pictures from the Monogram product' and persuaded Broidy – to whom Harold had himself recommended Walter, only two years earlier – to hire Harold to run distribution for Allied Artists.⁹⁸ Harold was duly appointed as vice president at $400 a week, in 1947. *The Gangster* was directed by Gordon Wiles, who had been Walter's art director on *Bomba, the Jungle Boy*. It is initially narrated by the protagonist, who is killed in the course of the action, rendering his narration posthumous. (Wilder's 1950 film, *Sunset Boulevard*, did something similar, in a much more sustained and celebrated way, three years later.) While the Mirisches were never to experiment in such a way themselves, they did subsequently deploy voice-over in several of their films, with first-person narration in *The Apartment*, *Fort Massacre* and *Town Without Pity* and third-person narration in *Irma La Douce*, *Hawaii* and *The Hallelujah Trail*.

Harold's first task was to devise a distinctive distribution strategy for *It Happened on Fifth Avenue*, *The Babe Ruth Story* (Del Ruth, 1947) and *Red Light* (Del Ruth, 1949). Reporting Mirisch's appointment, *Showmen's Trade Review* noted that Broidy and his new vice president 'discussed plans for merchandising Roy Del Ruth's It Happened on Fifth Avenue, AA's first release, which opens at the Rivoli in New York on June 10'.⁹⁹ This strategy was not unconnected with the trade press's perception that the time for assembly line, B productions was over.¹⁰⁰ Nevertheless, Harold's distribution contacts led to a deal with Josef Auerbach to reissue the *Our Gang* series through Monogram, under a new series title, *The Little Rascals*.¹⁰¹ Before the end of the decade, Harold was vice president of both Allied Artists and Monogram itself.¹⁰² As such, his role involved frequent trips to the exhibitor exchanges to see how the companies' films were being marketed and to plan future campaigns. In January 1948, for instance, he 'was on an extensive tour of the company's Southern exchanges to set release plans for Allied product'.¹⁰³

Three months later he was setting off on an 'extensive tour of the company's Western branches'.¹⁰⁴ This gave him a familiarity with audiences, albeit not necessarily those for first-run theatres, and with what worked – or did not – at the box office. It

---

[97] *Kings of the Bs: Working Withing the Hollywood System*, Todd McCarthy and Charles Flynn (eds), EP Dutton, 1975, 38.
[98] Mirisch, 2008: 37.
[99] 'Regional Newsreel', *STR*, 7.6.47: 32.
[100] 'Assembly Line Filming Doomed, Warns Small', *Boxoffice*, 11.12.48: 15.
[101] Mirisch, 2008: 38–9.
[102] *Showmen's Trade Review*, 2.6.47: 9 and *Motion Picture Herald*, 20.11.48: 22.
[103] 'Coming and Going', *Film Daily*, 20.1.48: 2.
[104] Ibid, 19.4.48:2.

also may have reinforced his recognition of the importance of so-called 'programmers'. *Panhandle* (1948) and *Stampede* (1949), both directed by Lesley Selander and starring Rod Cameron, for instance, were B Westerns produced and scripted by Blake Edwards and John Champion. Edwards even played the villain in *Panhandle* and appeared, uncredited, as a bank teller in *Stampede*. Edwards and Champion put up $40,000, Monogram provided the other $140,000.[105] Both Champion and Edwards subsequently worked for the Mirisch Company, the former on a Second World War cycle, the latter on a succession of comedies.

Harold's responsibilities at Allied seem to have combined attracting top production personnel to work for the company with marketing their subsequent productions. He was appointed as 'a vice president', serving as 'a producer-contact for the sales department for the company'.[106] This involved intimate contact with filmmakers as well as promotional work.

> Allied Artists is having encouraging results from its special exploitation for 'Black Gold' now in release, and the company also plans a similar campaign for the King Bros' 'The Gangster' scheduled for November distribution. Firm veepee Harold Mirisch, who conceived the Black Gold promotion, arrived from the coast this week to set up ideas for The Gangster. For Black Gold's ballyhoo Allied Artists have been using . . . two troupes of Cheyenne Indians which have covered more than 100 towns on behalf of the film. In their nationwide tour, made in station wagons and trailer truck, the Indians set up tepee villages in the average small town.[107]

In 1948 the Justice Department won its anti-monopoly case, with the so-called Paramount Decree, and the big five slowly began to divest themselves of their theatrical holdings. This, in turn, reinforced the single-bill strategy, since from now on each movie had to be marketed on its own merits, 'A's were increasingly prioritised and there was an end to block booking. Launching its 1948–9 schedule, the company announced fifty-one Monogram releases and ten Allied Artists films.[108] This cautious move upmarket seems to have paid off. After initial losses in 1948 ($497,696) 1949 ($1,108,433) and 1950 ($603,342) Monogram turned a record profit in 1951 ($1,061,648). In 1950, Harold Mirisch announced that, following a test of three Cinecolor features released that year, Monogram planned six colour features for its 1950–1 schedule and had 'more films in work now than at any time in the past two years'.[109] Indeed, the following year, the trade press reported the company's increased output.

---

[105] 'Round the Hollywood Studios: United Artists Buys RKO Pictures to Bolster Program – A Bit of Horatio Alger in Wonderland – Libel Suit – Other Items', *New York Times*, 5.10.47: X5.
[106] *Showmen's Trade Review*, 31.5.47: 12.
[107] 'AA's Big Indian Chief Bally on Gold Pays Off', *Variety*, 10.9.47: 6.
[108] Edwards, 2011: 395.
[109] *Variety*, 11.10.50: 22.

Production activities of Monogram and Allied Artists in the 1951-52 fiscal year are expected to be considerably expanded because of the new ownership control brought about by the purchase of 82,500 shares acquired by Harold Mirisch and G. Ralph Branton. Mirisch, the vice president of the two companies, is known to be making a careful survey of story properties and personnel, with an eye toward increasing the new slate.[110]

This placed Mirisch, Broidy and Branton in complete control of Monogram-Allied Artists for the first time. 'Kenilworth Investment Co, controlled by Harold J Mirisch, reported acquiring 41,250 shares of common, the company's entire holding. Mr Mirisch personally holds 1200 shares.'[111] 1920 Kenilworth Place, Milwaukee, was the Home Office base and HQ of Theatres Candy Co.

The move upmarket was balanced by negotiations to sell the company's back catalogue to television and the launch of a TV subsidiary to produce small screen series, under Walter's management.[112] Indeed, Allied quietly retained its commitment to 'extracting maximum value from its assets' and leased fifty-two of its films for broadcast, while continuing to produce its *Bowery Boys* films until 1956.[113] In August 1950, Walter Mirisch announced a series of thirty-minute episodes of *Simbar, The Jungle Queen* for screening in 1951, if a sponsor could be found. The pilot episode was budgeted at $12,500, but the series was never made.[114] In October 1951, *Variety* reported 'Mono Joins Vidpix trek of H'wood Film Studios: Branton, Mirisch Heads'[115] Walter Mirisch and Branton headed a new 'vidfilm unit', or TV production arm, for Monogram. One of the few projects attributed to Monogram's TV subsidiary, Interstate Television Corp (mooted *Buffalo Bill* and *Raffles* series, the latter to star George Raft, never materialized), was an, as yet untitled, anthology programme, scheduled to be 'femceed' by actress Joan Bennett – in a package her agent, Jennings Lang, of MCA, had put together.[116]

Walter Wanger and the Mirisches

Meanwhile, Allied Artists was loudly promoting its increased budgets and film quality, announcing a three-year, nine-picture deal with Bennett's husband, producer Walter Wanger, and promising to increase the use of Technicolour in its productions.[117] The contract with Bennett might, indeed, have been a sweetener for – or even part of the deal with – Wanger. On 13 December 1951, however, Wanger shot Lang in the groin

---

[110] 'Studio Size-Ups', *Film Bulletin*, 19.12.51: 18.
[111] 'SEC Report', *Motion Picture Herald*, 13.10.195: 16.
[112] *Film Bulletin*, 2.2.52: 12.
[113] Edwards, 2011: 396.
[114] 'Jungle Telepic Series', *Variety*, 9.8.50: 31.
[115] *Variety*, 17.10.51: 13. See also *Film Bulletin*, 19.12.51: 27.
[116] *Variety*, 19.12.51: 2.
[117] 'Wanger Enters 3-Year Deal', *Variety*, 21.6.51: 8.

because of the latter's alleged affair with Bennett – an affair which was reportedly consummated at the apartment of another, more junior, MCA agent. Production on the proposed Bennett series was postponed on the 18th – the same day Wanger was released on bail – and the show was eventually cancelled.

Subsequently, this affair, conducted in a subordinate's apartment, seems to have provided one of the inspirations for Wilder's *The Apartment*, though Wilder himself claimed the idea came from a scene in *Brief Encounter* (Lean, 1945) perhaps to deflect attention from Hollywood's homegrown, real-life scandal. Furthermore, the Mirisches were close friends with Wanger. It was Harold Mirisch who went to the police station to post Wanger's $5000 bail. The day after the latter's arrest, but before he was incarcerated, Wanger turned up to work at Monogram as usual and, that evening, Walter Mirisch invited him home for dinner. While Wanger was in prison, Walter oversaw two films for him, giving him producer credit and ensuring he still received his salary. Returning the favour, among the films Wanger went on to produce for Walter Mirisch at Allied Artists, following his release from prison, were two classics – Don Siegel's *Riot in Cell Block 11* and *Invasion of the Body Snatchers*. Harold Mirisch ensured the former was well-marketed by securing the services of General Teleradio Corp 'to handle a special television-radio campaign'.[118] *Invasion of the Body Snatchers* was shot in twenty-three days and cost $382,000. Wanger having already brought Don Siegel to the Mirisches' attention, Siegel, in turn, brought Sam Peckinpah into the company and he worked as a dialogue director on *Crime in the Streets* and *World Without End* (Bernds, 1956) among others.[119] Neither, perhaps predictably, given their generic track records and kinetic style, ever worked for the Mirisch Company. Peckinpah appeared as a bank teller in the robbery sequence in the 1955 AA production, *Wichita*, which Walter produced, as well as appearing as a pilot in Walter's production of *An Annapolis Story*, as Charlie in *Invasion of the Body Snatchers*, and uncredited in *Dial Red O* (Ullman, 1955) – all for Allied Artists.

'Accent on Quality Pictures'

By the early 1950s, Walter and his brothers 'wanted to upgrade the types of films' they were making and produce more 'presold' films in colour.[120] The trade press reported this as an 'Accent on Quality Pictures'.[121] By 'presold', Mirisch meant properties with name-recognition – either through stars, source material (books, plays, biopics, film remakes) or subject matter. Examples of the latter included such Cinecolor productions as *County Fair* (William Beaudine, 1950), followed by *Rodeo* (Beaudine, 1952), *The Rose Bowl Story* (Beaudine, 1952) and *Roar of the Crowd* (Beaudine, 1953) – all of which included authentic and festive location footage as colourful background to

---

[118] 'Plan Radio-TV Drive for AA "Cell Block"', *Motion Picture Daily*, 24.8.53: 3.
[119] Mirisch, 2008: 49.
[120] Ibid, 40.
[121] *Film Bulletin*, 3.12.51: 12.

their dramas. Mirisch also produced Westerns, starting with *Cavalry Scout* (Selander, 1951) and war films, the first of which was *Flat Top*.

In the summer of 1951, Walter was made the executive producer and head of production for Monogram and Allied Artists, at a weekly salary of $1000.[122] *Variety*, reporting Walter's promotion, noted that his comparative youth was characteristic of recent appointments. 'In mostly all cases the studio toppers are showing marked preference for youth when they hand over the reins on production and direction to newcomers.'[123] One of his first actions in his new role was to initiate 'a thorough inventory of the companies [*sic*] properties and production personnel prior to setting the 1951–52 schedule'.[124] He was also 'seeking new producing, directing and acting talent'. The company swiftly announced that there would be four productions a month.[125] Inventory and efficiency were, of course, among the business skills he had learned at Harvard. *Film Bulletin* was impressed.

> One of the first moves made by Walter Mirisch . . . was to start hyping budgets on a larger portion of the company's forthcoming product. At the same time, he started agitating for an increase in the quantity of production in order that the company might rank equally as a production and distribution organization. . . . Feeling, generally around Hollywood, is that Mirisch's appointment is one of the best things that has happened to the sister companies in a long time. Only 29 years old, Mirisch is aggressive, enthusiastic, and possesses a freshness that is sorely needed around the industry.[126]

Such productions sometimes benefitted from the sort of saturation release Harold had witnessed two decades earlier at Warners. The trade press reported that 'A five-day advance of dates for national "Monogram Drive-In Week" May 24th–30th will coincide with a planned national saturation booking of the Walter Mirisch Cinecolor production, Wild Stallion, which stars Ben Johnson'.[127] There was even a science fiction film, *Flight to Mars* (Selander, 1951) and a 3D spectacle, *The Maze*, though Walter's heart does not appear to have been in either. Nevertheless, *Flight to Mars* did deploy Mirisch's default strategy of recycling, in this case the spaceship interior was from *Rocketship XM* (Neumann, 1950), while the Martian costumes came from *Destination Moon* (Pichel, 1950).

Flat Top was one of the first of Walter Mirisch's personal productions following his promotion. It is therefore tempting to read one speech by the film's hero, played by Sterling Hayden, as something of a declaration of intent.

Squadron Leader Collier:

[122] Mirisch, 2008: 43; *Motion Picture Herald*, 19.7.51: 1.
[123] 'Films' New Blood', *Variety*, 1.8.51: 20.
[124] 'Mirisch To Expand Allied Production', *Motion Picture Daily*, 7.8.51: 1.
[125] 'Monogram, Allied List 45 Features for the New Season', *Motion Picture Daily*, 7.9.51: 1.
[126] 'New Studio Chief Spurs More Bigger Mono-AA Films', *Film Bulletin*, 13.8.51: 12. See also 'Mirisch Ups 52 Program: Accent on Quality Pictures', *Film Bulletin*, 3.12.51: 12.
[127] 'News in Brief', *Motion Picture Daily*, 12.3.52: 7.

All you've got to remember is that we're a team, something like a football team, it's just that our stakes are a little bit higher. I'll be calling the signals. But we're not going to have any stars on this team, and certainly no aerial acrobats . . . one thing we're not going to have in this squadron – an individualist is dangerous to the group and to himself. In fiction he is invariably the hero who breaks formation to fly out and shoot down some zero he spotted. In reality, nine times out of ten, he is killed for his efforts and has left his squadron one plane and one pilot short. . . . This squadron must and will fly as a unit.

This emphasis on the unit over and above individuals is striking and pre-echoes the corporate, or more accurately, family firm culture of the subsequent Mirisch Company itself as a business. But it might also explain what amounts to a virtual antipathy to virtuosity in Mirisch movies. It is also an articulation of the ensemble movie ethos, in contrast to the single-star vehicle, an ethos which *Flat Top* itself epitomized and which the Mirisch Company went on to popularize with films like The *Magnificent Seven* and *The Great Escape*. The premiere of *Flat Top* was on 'Armistice Day aboard the USS Princeton, off San Diego, Calif' and was arranged with 'top Navy cooperation for promotion and the premiere' including the attendance of 'political, naval and military dignitaries'.[128] This 'special relationship' with the military was also to characterize the Mirisch Company's own films from *633 Squadron* to *Midway*.

The Korean-War cycle

The outbreak of the Korean War (1950–3) saw a number of topical movies produced in Hollywood, and Walter Mirisch's productions in this cycle alongside *Flat Top*, the story of a Naval Commander during the conflict and his memories of having led a squadron of pilots during Second World War, include *An Annapolis Story* (1955), AA's first widescreen film, a love triangle about two midshipmen – and the object of their affections – set at the Naval Academy at Annapolis and the Naval Flight School at Pensacola, prior to their deployment in Korea. Other films which Walter supervised in this cycle, include *Battle Zone* (Selander, 1952), *Dragonfly Squadron* (Selander, 1954) and *Hold Back the Night* (Dwan, 1956). The latter, also told in flashback, was about a Marine platoon leader and his men, fighting on despite being surrounded by Chinese soldiers. It was produced by Hayes Goetz, one of AA's in-house producers, under Walter's supervision, and directed by Allan Dwan. Like *Flat Top*, it involves a serving officer in the Korean War 'remembering' the Second World War, in this case when he was given a bottle of Scotch as a present. But this time the Korean War present-day story dominates, with flashbacks to the original gift of the bottle, a flirtation with a married Australian woman in Melbourne, the hero's eventual return from the Second World War, and several occasions in Korea when he takes the bottle out, but then

---

[128] 'Increase in Gross Seen by Branton', *Motion Picture Herald*, 4.10.52: 12.

changes his mind about opening it. The film, therefore, deploys what Bordwell refers to as a 'recurring object' – the bottle – to structure its multiple flashback narrative.[129] Thus, at least two of the Korean-War films which Walter was responsible for were built around flashbacks, as well as both Woolrich adaptations.

Moulin Rouge and *Moby Dick*

Soon after Walter's promotion, the agent, Alvin Manuel, pitched him a biopic of the artist, Toulouse-Lautrec, to be directed by John Huston and star Jose Ferrer. Manuel had persuaded the Woolf brothers in the UK, through their company Romulus Films, to pay the below-the-line costs, but needed an American company to stump up the above-the-line fees for Huston, Ferrer and the rights to the book on which the script was based. The author, Pierre La Mure, was one of Manuel's clients. Harold and Walter Mirisch and Steve Broidy were receptive to the idea, but Ferrer refused to contemplate making a film for what was still perceived as a B movie outfit. Harold's New York contacts were able to raise enough money to bankroll the above-the-line budget independently and, together with Broidy and all four Mirisch brothers, they became joint stockholders of a new company, Moulin Productions.[130] (This seems to have been the only production in which all four brothers were involved.) Harold and Walter then brought the project to Arthur Krim and Robert Benjamin, who had recently taken control of United Artists. UA assumed the bank loan, which had been arranged in New York, leaving Moulin with 20 per cent of the profits, without any outlay of its own. *Moulin Rouge* began shooting in Paris in the summer of 1951 and turned out to be a critical and commercial success. According to the *New York Times*, the film pioneered 'a new way to finance the movies . . . with three kinds of money – a foreign partner, a domestic partner and Wall Street venture capital'.[131] This was early evidence of the brothers' ultimate aim of launching their own independent. Indeed, in the *Production Encyclopaedia* for 1952 (covering the period from 1947 to 1951), in a list of members of the Independent Motion Picture Producers Association, after Monogram Productions comes Mirisch Productions.[132]

Between them, *Moulin Rouge* and *Moby Dick* (Huston, 1956) provided early examples of the 'quality' cinema which the Mirisches aspired to. The former was a biopic of an artist, the latter an adaptation of a literary classic. Moulin Productions also gave the brothers their first experience of running their own independent. In *Moulin Rouge* there is a scene in which Lautrec arrives at a bistro to meet some of his artist friends, including Seurat. There is an exchange in which Seurat says,

---

[129] Bordwell, 2017: 176–81.
[130] Mirisch, 2008: 50–1.
[131] Lucian K. Truscott IV, 'Hollywood's Wall Street Connection', *NYT Encyclopedia of Film*, 26.2.78A. See also United Artists Collection, Wisconsin Historical Society, Box 4, Folder 14.
[132] *Production Encyclopedia*, 1952: 556 https://lantern.mediahist.org/catalog/productionencycl1952holl_0616

> Seurat: We missed you at the meeting last night.
> Toulouse-Lautrec: Meeting, what meeting?
> Seurat: The Society of Independents.
> Toulouse-Lautrec: I have better things to do. Independents? Bah! Pariahs rather. Outcasts. It is not ideals which bind us together but failure.

The Society being referred to, of course, was the Society of Independent Artists or Salon of Independents founded in Paris in the 1880s. As it happens, the Society of Independent Motion Picture Producers had been active since 1941 and Mirisch producer, Walter Wanger, had been a founder member. In 1951 Walter Mirisch had received a call from Arthur Hornblow Jr, one of the producers setting up a new Screen Producers Guild.[133] It too represented independent producers. Walter joined and, in 1960, became its president and editor of its *Journal*. But in 1951, the very year *Moulin Rouge* began pre-production, Walter had himself joined the Guild.

The *Moulin Rouge* bistro scene quoted above continues with a conversation about the artistic value of the *Mona Lisa* in the Louvre, which Toulouse-Lautrec calls a graveyard, a painting which they describe as 'truly the greatest painting in the world'. Again, Toulouse-Lautrec provokes them:

> Toulouse-Lautrec: And how do you know it is the greatest painting in the world? And how do you know that it was painted by Leonardo? . . .
> Seurat: . . . Only Leonardo could have painted that smile. She smiles with her eyes.
> Toulouse-Lautrec: I don't care if she smiles with her navel, that still doesn't say that Da Vinci painted it.
> Seurat: The techniques, the brushstrokes. Each one bears his signature.
> Toulouse-Lautrec: Rubbish. There is only way you know that the Mona Lisa is by Leonardo. By the little brass plate with his name on it. That is what you bow down to. A name printed on brass.

The importance of having their name on their work was dramatically brought home to the Mirisches by the fact that the film fails to credit Moulin Productions at all and is exclusively credited to Romulus. Later in the film, at a gallery exhibition of his work, a customer complains,

'For me, I do not see the signature. I buy nothing that is not signed.'

Toulouse-Lautrec's dealer replies, 'The signature is on the back, Monsieur. But if you want one on the front of the painting, I am sure Monsieur Lautrec will be glad . . . '

Strikingly, the signing of contracts and the ownership of intellectual and other property were later to become a recurrent motif of Mirisch productions. Similarly, there is a conversation about the value of works created and the payments for those who work on them.

> Marie: Toulouse, how much is a painting worth?
> Toulouse-Lautrec: All depends on who painted it.

[133] Mirisch, 2008: 61.

> Marie: One of yours I mean?
> Toulouse-Lautrec: It's too soon to say . . .
> Marie: How much do you pay your models?
> Toulouse-Lautrec: Oh, the usual rate is 3 francs for the morning and 5 francs for the whole day.
> Marie: Then you should pay me.

And we discover that just as the artists all have their dealers, taking a percentage, so too Marie has her pimp.

When Huston approached the Mirisches to back another of his projects, an adaptation of Melville's novel *Moby Dick*, he was reluctant to be associated with a B studio like Allied Artists.[134] Instead, he told them,

> You know, I'm ready to do this deal, but I don't want to do it alone. I've talked to some friends about it and suggested to them the advantages of working in a company where we would have independence, where there isn't going to be a great deal of overhead charged to our pictures, and where we can have a more meaningful participation in profits.[135]

Those friends were William Wyler and Billy Wilder, two of the first filmmakers to be signed by the Mirisch Company.

Allied Artists

In 1952, Walter Mirisch and Steve Broidy negotiated a deal to co-produce two films with Associated British Pictures Corp in the UK.[136] Monogram/AA had signed a multi-picture deal with ABPC in 1947 but only one film had resulted by 1952, *Affair in Monte Carlo* (Saville, 1952) based on Stefan Zweig's story, so Broidy, Harold and Walter Mirisch had sailed to the UK to agree further co-productions and watch the shooting of *Moulin Rouge* in Paris. Walter stayed behind, agreeing that one of a promised pair of productions would be *Yellow Knife*, based on a *Saturday Evening Post* serial.[137] Mirisch's knowledge of production conditions and subsidies in the UK subsequently fed into 'British' films he oversaw in the 1960s, and the Mirisch Company's exploitation of the Eady Levy.

That summer Walter Mirisch launched a new AA corporate policy ensuring 'important box office personalities in every upper bracket picture turned out by the studio' and asserting that 'players, agents and other studios are now cognizant of the fact that strong properties, colour and added production values we are giving our films

---

[134] Ibid, 73.
[135] Ibid.
[136] 'Broidy Sets Plans for Two in England', *Motion Picture Daily*, 9.7.52: 1.
[137] 'Mono-AA Execs Hypo Filming with England's ABPC', *Variety*, 9.7.52: 5.

today are worthy of the best talent available'.[138] In September Walter announced to a convention of 200 Allied Artists salesmen that 'retooling' the studio facilities for stronger product was the biggest hurdle the company faced.

> We are crossing our barriers in Hollywood, and by doing so we are helping to place you in a position to overcome any sales resistance. There is no production problem, whether it concerns cost, story acquisition, technical obstacles or casting that we won't tackle during 1953 if it results in bringing to the screen the best in entertainment value. Allied Artists quality has passed the proving grounds stage. It has won strong exhibitor acceptance.

Edward Morey, New York vice president, acknowledged, 'This in part may be attributed to a better quality of picture produced under the guidance of Walter Mirisch.'[139]

That same year, Walter produced another 'presold' 'better quality' title, in Cinecolor, *Hiawatha* (Neumann, 1952), based on Longfellow's poem. That October, Broidy revealed that the company had the second-best year in its history, convincing him to confirm the move upmarket. Walter, as head of production, announced an increasing commitment to colour, widescreen and even four further 3D films following *The Maze*.

> We feel people will be flocking back to theaters to see the new processes and systems, and we want our pictures to be the ones they will be flocking back to see. Our diversified program will include high, medium and small budget pictures. We will film in CinemaScope, in color by Technicolor, in 3-D and wide-screen as well as two-dimension and black-and-white.[140]

Allied's run of Technicolor CinemaScope films, released through 20th Century Fox included *The Black Prince/The Dark Avenger* and *The Adventures of Haji Baba* (Weis, 1954). In 1954 Walter Mirisch even succeeded in persuading Technicolor to process – and put their name on – an Allied Artists film that he had personally produced – *The Annapolis Story*. That same year, the last of the 'Bomba' films, *Lord of the Jungle* (Beebe, 1955) was released, and Mirisch followed up with a 'fact-based' Western, *Wichita*, which became the highest-grossing picture he had produced up to that time.[141]

Finally, on 11 November 1953, Monogram officially became Allied Artists and aimed at bigger budgets, longer running times and an increasing proportion of widescreen, colour productions. As a business, one strategy for securing such a move upmarket was doing package deals with talent, since almost no on- or off-screen talent remained contracted to the majors.[142] As Broidy announced it at the autumn 1953 Allied Exchange Owners convention, a series of such package deals would lead to

---

[138] 'Says Monogram Star Policy is "Just the Beginning"', *Motion Picture Herald*, 28.6.52:14.
[139] '"Re-Tool" AA Studio for New Product', *Motion Picture Daily*, 26.9.52: 1&4.
[140] *MPH*, 25.7.53: 35.
[141] Mirisch, 2008: 70.
[142] 'Monogram Studio Changes Its Name Stockholders Approve Shift to Allied Artists Pictures, Hear Reports of Earnings Rise', *New York Times*, 13.11.53, Thom M. Pryor.

Allied joining 'the leading major companies'.[143] By the spring of 1954 Allied was finally able to announce such deals with John Huston, Billy Wilder and William Wyler, all of whom were also subsequently to work for the Mirisch Company; indeed, it was the Mirisch brothers who secured their commitment to Allied.[144] Package-unit production was officially the new corporate strategy. Later that year, Broidy himself contributed an article to *Variety* entitled 'A Packager's Place in the Sun'.[145] The currency of the package in the mid-fifties was thus as prevalent on Poverty Row as it was in Beverly Hills.

In 1954, while waiting for the first films made by their major director signings, Allied experienced a brief shortfall in product.[146] The following year, with production levels back to normal, the trades reported that AA was 'interested in acquiring for distribution the best in independent and foreign pictures' as well as co-productions.[147] Allied was, in fact, already negotiating with independents. Indeed, one such deal was with both Theodora Productions and Security Pictures to co-produce *The Big Combo*. The former was co-star, Cornel Wilde's, company; the latter belonged to the film's producer, Sidney Harmon, and screenwriter, Philip Yordan. The agreement was that AA would co-produce the film with these two companies under Walter's supervision.[148] Such joint productions were to become the Mirisch Company's modus operandi.

Like Monogram, Allied Artists worked with both in-house producers and independents (like the King Brothers, Katzman and Corman). It hired established filmmakers, but also gave opportunities to first-time directors. 'They had worked as assistant directors, or some of them had just been promoters . . . Don't forget, working for us provided hard, fast, tried proof. If you could make pictures for Monogram, you could make pictures for anybody.'[149] Broidy referred to such opportunities as 'screen tests' and cited Edward Dmytryk, William Friedkin, Mark Rydell and Jerry Thorpe as directors whose debuts were at Monogram and AA.[150] This proved to be one, perhaps crucial, corporate initiative which the Mirisch brothers subsequently failed to follow at their own company. Broidy gave several young talents a break, including, after all, the then twenty-four-year-old Walter, but the Mirisches themselves subsequently proved reluctant to offer comparable opportunities to untried behind-the-camera talent at their own company. Nor did those B filmmakers they subsequently rehired include such distinctive directors as Don Siegel or Joseph H Lewis, perhaps because of the generic and budgetary associations they brought with them. Mirisch equated certain genres with low budgets and had correspondingly low aesthetic expectations of them.

According to *Variety*,

---

[143] 'Broidy in Speech to Owners Bullish on Films' Future', *Variety*, 17.10.53: 9.
[144] 'Allied Enters a Name Class', *Variety*, 26.5.1954: 1, 29.
[145] *Variety*, 4.11.54: 156.
[146] 'AA at Low Ebb; Exhibitors Would Welcome Programmers', *Film Bulletin*, 13.12.54: 37.
[147] 'Allied Artists Ready with Big Program', *Motion Picture Herald*, 9.7.55: 25,
[148] 'Theodora, Security, AA to Make "Combo"', *Motion Picture Daily*, 24.7.54: 1.
[149] Broidy, quoted in McCarthy and Flynn (eds), 1975: 281.
[150] Flynn and McCarthy, 279–81.

Huston's tie with Moulin served to set the stage for his stock option deal with Allied Artists as a producer-director-writer. AA vp Harold J. Mirisch and G. Ralph Branton, also an Allied vp, are associated with Moulin Productions and were also involved in the financing and Western Hemisphere distribution of Huston's Moulin Rouge and their association with Huston on this project and on Moby Dick eventually led to the signing of this pact with Allied Artists.[151]

However, Huston remained reluctant to be the only top director to break ranks with the majors, and he told Harold and Walter that he had discussed leaving the majors with Billy Wilder and William Wyler, both of whom, he implied, were ready to work with the company. Wilder and Wyler, however, were both represented by MCA, which proved harder to convince.[152] The deal Harold eventually proposed was that established directors would not only receive the same salary as at the majors, but also stock options. Wilder proved agreeable, still furious with Paramount over changes it had imposed on *Stalag 17* (Wilder, 1953) to ensure the film's acceptability in post-war West Germany. Wyler, meanwhile, had previously been a partner in Liberty Films, an early incarnation of a talent-led independent, and was eager to join another ambitious, director-centred, company.

The trade press was impressed with Allied's announcement of its move into the big time.

> The announcement of the Wyler-Huston-Wilder Allied story was reminiscent of the big deal that was to have brought Frank Capra, William Wyler and George Stevens . . . to Paramount . . . under the heading of Liberty Pictures. . . . It pushes Allied up to major rank and gives the creators participation AND ownership arrangement that's something new in this business because the trio will not only get stock in the parent company, but will have an option to buy more plus their participation in the profits of their individual pictures. . . . Harold Mirisch spent weeks and months on this deal that is now beginning to be fulfilled. It will add up to quite an accomplishment and may be the forerunner of other such deals that Mirisch now has in negotiation.[153]

Mirisch's ambitions were explicitly upmarket.

> Allied Artists move into the 'big time' . . . has now become fact. Last week negotiations were completed with John Huston, Academy Award-winning director-writer for a minimum of three features. In conjunction with his announcement of the Huston deal, AA President Steve Broidy revealed that deals are almost consummated with two more Academy winners, producer-director-writer Billy Wilder and director William Wyler. . . . Broidy credits Harold J. Mirisch and G. Ralph Branton with

---

[151] *Variety*, 2.6.54: 4.
[152] Mirisch, 2008: 73–4.
[153] 'Hollywood Reporter Tradeviews', *Motion Picture Daily*, 14.9.55: 3.

swinging the Huston deal.[154] Certainly, Harold was well rewarded for his efforts – his remuneration for 1953-54 was $53,183.00. Despite this endorsement, Harold Mirisch sold 18,125 shares of common stock in AA in May 1954.[155]

Meanwhile, the company also had to contend with a dearth of on-screen talent, and Walter announced 'A long-range move in the direction of alleviating the talent shortage, caused by production curtailment and losses to television '.[156] Mirisch's plan was to 'establish a dramatic school and start interviewing young performers shortly after the first of the year, with the view to building up a stock company of promising actors and actresses.'[157] The trade press reported that 'Mirisch will supervise the school personally, his aim being to select from eight to fifteen people each year. Screen tests will be given the most likely prospects and they will be awarded contracts for varying periods'.[158] This ambition, essentially to wind back the clock to pre-Paramount Decree days of studio contract staff, seems never to have been implemented.[159] Nevertheless, the announcement evidences a commitment to continuous rather than batch production, an attempt to reverse, or at least mitigate, the wider industry's impetus towards one-off production. It is equally possible, however, that it was as much self-promotion as a practical proposal. It kept Mirisch himself – and Allied Artists – in the headlines, without involving any outlay.

Nevertheless, Allied Artists was spending like never before. 'Walter Mirisch cast a flicker of sunshine on the product outlook for exhibitors with the announcement that Allied Artists will release approximately 15 features within the last half of the year, five of them "big ones". Two are in Cinemascope.'[160] Monogram had been listed on the American Stock Exchange and when W. Ray Johnston and Trem Carr stood down, Broidy, the two Mirisch brothers and Ralph Branton (who had invested in an AA subsidiary, Trans-Western Pictures, to produce Westerns) bought their stock. By the mid-1950s, Walter and Harold had proved pivotal in attracting a range of experienced independent producers to the company, the King Brothers and Walter Wanger among them.

By now, however, 'The theater concession business in Milwaukee was running into serious difficulties, as the larger theaters, and the theatre chains, moved to own their own candy and popcorn operations . . . Harold and Irving now began to consider the possibility of selling their concession business'.[161] In 1953, Marvin, who had remained in Milwaukee with Irving at the Theatres Candy Co., finally joined them in Hollywood. Marvin's first position was at AA's Trans-Western Pictures, before becoming assistant to George Burrows, the vice president and treasurer of Monogram, just as it became

[154] 'Huston Deal Closed, Wilder Wyler to Follow', *Film Bulletin*, 31.5.54: 10.
[155] *Motion Picture Daily*, 13.10.54: 2 and 'Mirisch Cuts Holdings', *Motion Picture Daily*, 22.6.54: 2.
[156] *Independent Exhibitors Film Bulletin*, 13.12.54: 17.
[157] *Motion Picture Herald*, 24.7.52: 14.
[158] *Film Bulletin*, 13.12.54: 17.
[159] 'Allied Artists Recruits 8 Actors as Core of its First Stock Company', *Variety*, 15.12.54: 3.
[160] 'They Made the News', *Film Bulletin*, 11.7.55: 19.
[161] Mirisch, 2008: 60.

Allied Artists. Marvin received what seems to have been his first credit, as associate producer, on *Arrow in the Dust* (Selander, 1954).[162] He was also credited as associate producer on *The Human Jungle* (Newman, 1954), produced by Hayes Goetz, that same year. In 1955 he became 'assistant secretary' of Allied.[163]

Moulin, meanwhile, helped arrange finance for *Beach Head* (Heisler, 1954) which starred Tony Curtis, was shot in Hawaii and distributed by United Artists. Like the connection with Wilder and Wyler, this project laid the foundations for future relationships – in this case with the star, the state and the distributor – all of which were to pay off for their own company in due course. Moulin also acquired nine films which had been produced by International Pictures as a package to resell to television. That package included *Tomorrow Is Forever* (Pichel, 1946), *The Stranger* (Welles, 1946), *Along Came Jones* (Heisler, 1945), *Casanova Brown* (Wood, 1944), *The Dark Mirror* (Siodmak, 1944), *The Woman in the Window* (Lang, 1944), *Belle of the Yukon* (Seiter, 1944), *It's A Pleasure* (Seiter, 1945) and *Temptation* (Pichel, 1946). Moulin also agreed to present another independent production, *Duel in the Jungle* (Marshall, 1954). However, *Moby Dick* went so far over budget that Moulin Productions was forced to sell all its assets – the International Pictures negatives, the rights to *Beach Head* and *Duel in the Jungle*, and its shares in both *Moulin Rouge* and *Moby Dick* itself.

Nevertheless, *Moby Dick* had provided the Mirisches with an opportunity to oversee the marketing of a film during production. Because of its status as a Romulus film for Warner Bros, they were forced to depend on Warner's in-house publicity and advertising division and on the outsourced work of PR firm Rogers & Cowan, which in turn hired Ernest Anderson, a London-based unit publicist with a wide array of contacts with the European and US press. Anderson published personalized press releases full of anecdotes about the gruelling logistical trials that the crew faced on location, transforming the unfolding drama of the shoot into a parallel narrative with the film's plot and material that publications both in the United States and abroad turned into news stories.[164]

Quality and adaptations

In January 1956 it became apparent that Allied Artists' move upmarket included a new emphasis on adaptations, announcing six new films based on published novels.[165] While the company was buying up books, it was also contracting directors to film them. Wyler came on board first, and *Friendly Persuasion* (Wyler, 1956), based on a novel by Jessamyn West, went into production starring Gary Cooper and Dorothy

---

[162] *Motion Picture Daily*, 19.4.54: 5.
[163] 'Marvin Mirisch Secretary of A.A.', *Motion Picture Daily*, 10.6.55: 2.
[164] '"Paris. . . As You've Never Seen It Before!!!": The Promotion of Hollywood Foreign Productions in the Postwar Era', Daniel Steinhart – In *Media. The French Journal of Media Studies*, 2013 - journals.openedition.org
[165] 'AA to Produce Six Films from Novels', *Motion Picture Daily*, 25.1.56: 5.

McQuire. *Film Bulletin* reported that it represented 'the giant step in Allied Artists transition from bread and butter to strawberry shortcake'.[166] It cost $3 million (Mirisch says $4 million), making it easily AA's most expensive production to date. It tells the story of a Quaker family against the background of the American Civil War, a conflict the Mirisch Company returned to with *The Horse Soldiers* in 1959. For various reasons, *Friendly Persuasion* never broke even, despite an Oscar nomination for Best Film and winning the Palme D'Or in Cannes in spring 1957. Indeed, AA was compelled to sell off its foreign distribution rights (and those of *Love in the Afternoon*) to finance the overspend.

Wilder, meanwhile, was ready to start shooting *Love in the Afternoon* a remake of *Ariane* (Czinner, 1931) a German film, itself based on a French novel. Wilder's adaptation, co-written by I. A. L. Diamond (who was to be his writing partner throughout Wilder's contract with Mirisch) starred Gary Cooper again, this time opposite Audrey Hepburn. Wilder originally wanted Cary Grant for the lead, but the star declined, which may have encouraged the pastiche of Grant in his next film, *Some Like It Hot*. Wilder's second choice was Yul Brynner, who would also star in one of the Mirisch Company's first productions, but when he too proved unavailable the director opted for Cooper. Like *Friendly Persuasion*, *Love in the Afternoon* went over budget, and was not a success on the domestic market, though it did much better abroad.

As Audrey Hepburn's Parisienne music student says of Americans in *Love in the Afternoon*, they have become 'immunized, mechanized, air conditioned and hydromatic' – or automated and mass-produced. Implicitly, the film accuses mainstream America – and American cinema – of the same impersonality. Only by escaping the assembly lines of both life and work was a real character, real art, to be found. Ironically, such 'personality' could only be secured by acquiring it from pre-existing works, rather than creating it from scratch. Seen today, however, both films reveal a dangerous disconnect with the tastes and demographics of contemporary cinemagoers, which perhaps parallels the latter film's May–September romantic pairing. Nevertheless, Harold Mirisch had negotiated a deal with United Artists' Arnold Picker to distribute the film, as well as Huston's promised project.[167] Huston had finally decided on his next film and AA had secured the rights to Kipling's short story, *The Man Who Would Be King*, though the director then changed his mind, opting for another Melville novel, *Typee*, instead – which proved prohibitively expensive. The brothers reluctantly acknowledged that Allied Artists was simply too under-financed for a sustained attempt to challenge the majors.

Allied Artists' ambitious strategy was deemed to have failed at the box office, with both *Friendly Persuasion* and *Love in the Afternoon* losing money, and Huston still prevaricating.[168] Furthermore, with *Friendly Persuasion*, Allied Artists suffered the humiliation of becoming 'the first studio to exercise the credit escape clause', by eliminating the name of blacklisted screenwriter, Michael Wilson, from the credits,

---

[166] 'The Allied Artists Story', *Film Bulletin*, 5.3.56: 17.
[167] 'Headliners', *Film Bulletin*, 11.6.56: 16.
[168] Balio, United Artists, 1987: 164–5; Mirisch, 2008: 78–83.

noting only that the script was 'from the novel by Jessamyn West'.[169] Mirisch's production of *Hiawatha* in 1952 had also been hit by accusations of pro-communism in the script, and the naming of its screenwriter, Arthur Strawn, in *Red Channels* and its production had been delayed. (Strawn had also scripted *Flight to Mars*.)[170] Filming had been postponed from summer 1951 to summer '52, because 'its theme might be construed as Communistic' according to Monogram bosses.[171] To make matters worse, the *New York Times* noted that in terms of the numbers of films released, 'Allied Artists is eight behind last year, with ten completed'; and, at AA, fewer did not necessarily mean better.[172]

The quality strategy fails

The Mirisch-backed decision to move upmarket was reversed, and Allied Artists retrenched into what it knew best: B movies. Indeed, Walter's final producer credit for Allied was for the B Western *The Tall Stranger* (Carr, 1957), starring Joel McCrea and Virginia Mayo, though it was not actually released until October 1958. Furthermore, Broidy's return to 'B' movies involved a shift towards such previously neglected genres as horror and science fiction. Walter Mirisch had only personally produced one sci-fi film, *Flight to Mars*, both Monogram and AA having previously tended to leave such subject matter to AIP. But increasingly, in the wake of the success of *Invasion of the Body Snatchers* in 1956, Allied produced and/or distributed movies like *Timeslip* (aka *The Atomic Bomb* in the United States) (Hughes, 1955) *World Without End*, *Indestructible Man* (Pollexfen, 1956), *Attack of the Crab Monsters* (Corman, 1957), *Not of This Earth* (Corman, 1957), *The Cyclops* (Gordon, 1957), *From Hell It Came* (Milner, 1957), *The Disembodied* (Grauman, 1957). *The Bride and the Beast* (Weiss, 1958), *Queen of Outer Space* (Bernds, 1958), *War of the Satellites* (Corman, 1958) and *Attack of the Fifty Foot Woman* (Juran, 1958). Allied Artists was also belatedly learning from Corman and Arkoff to deploy exploitable titles like *Teenage Doll* (Corman, 1957) and *Naked in the Sun* (Hugh, 1957). This, too, may have helped convince the Mirisches that they had a better chance to fulfil their cinematic aspirations for 'quality' by forming their own independent production company. Nor were they alone in their reluctance to abandon the family audience for the teenage market. In 1958 Sam Goldwyn was adamant that 'I believe in making pictures a man can take his whole family to see'.[173]

It was in the context of the critical disappointment and commercial failure of the 'quality strategy', alongside Allied Artists' subsequent decision to retrench and reorient, that the Mirisch brothers opted to leave and launch their own company. They even invited Broidy to join them, but he remained at Allied until departing to create

---

[169] 'Film Studio Bars Credit to Writer', *New York Times*, 21.9.56.
[170] Mars, of course, was the 'red' planet. Of such coincidences are conspiracy theories made.
[171] 'Studio Size-Ups', *Film Bulletin*, 15.1.51: 14.
[172] 'Film Production Below Forecast', *New York Times*, 8.7.57.
[173] 'Avoid Gats and Gams', *Variety*, 4.6.58: 1.

an independent company himself, in 1965.[174] Commenting on their decision, the Mirisches said, 'Naturally it is with a deep sense of regret that we leave Allied Artists after many years of pleasant and rewarding associations. These have not only been productive years but we honestly count them among the happiest of our professional and personal lives.'[175] In fact, Walter had only announced the next raft of Allied Artists Productions that same week.[176]

The new Mirisch Company was first announced, appropriately enough, in Milwaukee, with a paragraph in *Motion Picture Daily* reporting the creation of Mirisch Brothers Production Co. to produce and deal in motion pictures, stage plays and television.[177] Meanwhile, in November 1957, *Variety* announced that Allied Artists might cease in-house production altogether, relying exclusively on independent production. 'Allied Artists is moving towards a policy patterned after the United Artists type of operation – that is, tying up with independent producers. AA is to provide the necessary bank guarantee and take distribution rights. Expectation is that AA will cease production itself and in the future will look to the indies as the sole source of product.'[178] But if this marked 1957 as the end of old Hollywood, that same month saw the celebration of Hollywood's fifty-year anniversary with a 'Golden Jubilee Month' – the industry's 'organized institutional PR endeavour' to resuscitate the studio system and its cinema.

Yet that the days of studio-based, assembly-line production were over, at least for the majors, had been reported by the press as early as 1953.[179] That same year, *Hollywood Reporter* noting the decline of studio contracts, stated that 'Paramount is down to three in the star division – Crosby, Hope and Holden – but has another 12 others with young players . . . Twentieth-Century Fox has only Henry King and Clifton Webb holding what might be termed "long term" deals with the company . . . RKO has only 5 term-contracts operating.'[180] Meanwhile the number of independent producers with studio deals in Hollywood had more than quadrupled from 40 in 1947 to 165 by 1957.[181] The industry had reached a tipping point: 'a new upsurge in independent or semi-independent production . . . is expected to bring about a wider diversity of expression on the screen . . . The dominating influence exercised by a few studio heads over subject matter and styles in cinematic expression is dwindling accordingly.'[182] By the summer of 1957, while studio production was dropping, independent productions were rising dramatically, compared with the previous year's figures.[183]

---

[174] Mirisch, 2008: 89.
[175] 'Harold, Walter Mirisch to Leave AA August 31', *Motion Picture Daily*, 1.8.57: 2.
[176] 'They Made the News', *Film Bulletin*, 5.8.57: 23.
[177] *Motion Picture Daily*, 11.7.57: 6.
[178] 'Allied Artists May Rely 100% on Indie Units', *Variety*, 18.11.57: 3.
[179] 'Studios Indicate Assembly Line End: Selectivity of Public is Factor in Concentration on Fewer Films of Better Quality', Thomas M. Pryor, *New York Times*, 29.8. 1953A.
[180] 'Long-Term Deals on Way Out', *Hollywood Reporter*, 20.1.53: 1.
[181] Mann, 2008: 32.
[182] *New York Times*, 29.8.53A.
[183] 'Film Production Below Forecast: 10% Gain Over '56 Period Attributed to Independents – Big Studios Decline', Thomas M. Pryor, *New York Times*, 8.7.57.

By the time the brothers set up their own independent, only a few weeks later, the demise of both Fordist mass production of movies and American mass cinemagoing was even clearer. As the editor of the *Motion Picture Herald* put it in 1957, 'In the "good old days" of dimming memory, no one in the industry – be he producer, distributor or exhibitor – took any interest in the question *Who Goes to the Movies?* The answer was plain to Everyone...'[184] The implied answer was 'everybody'. The previous year the same paper had reported a national opinion poll finding that 'The need for pictures appealing to the 15 to 25 age group was listed as most important by all classes of exhibition and by production as well, but distribution placed it fifth.'[185] And Quigley was clear, 'it would be futile to adopt an ostrich-head-in-the-sand attitude and pay no heed to the fact that in relation to their numbers those in the 15 to 25 age-group are the motion pictures' best customers'.[186] *Variety*'s conclusion was similar, 'the demand for teenage pictures ... is coming from all quarters – from small theatres as well as large circuits, from rural towns as well as big cities'.[187]

Sam Katzman was one of the pioneers of the teen picture – indeed he began doing this at Monogram with *Junior Prom* (Dreifuss, 1946) and *High School Hero*, so the Mirisch brothers must have been all too aware of the strategy and consciously decided against it. Indeed, one exhibitor reported of the latter film that 'This is the second of the Teen Agers and they get me more business than any Western I have ever played.'[188] A decade later Katzman's *Rock Around the Clock* (Sears, 1956) changed everything. Walter and Harold had not entirely ignored this market. Apart from Monogram's *Teen Agers* and *East Side Kids* cycles in the 1940s, there was *Crime in the Streets*, about teenage gangs and juvenile delinquency, whose cast included John Cassavetes, in only his second featured film role and Sal Mineo in the wake of *Rebel Without a Cause* (Ray, 1955) and which could be seen as a blueprint for *West Side Story*. It was scripted by Reginald Rose and directed by Don Siegel, the dialogue coach was Sam Peckinpah, and it was based on a TV drama directed by Sidney Lumet with much the same cast. *Crime in the Streets* may have been filmed on Allied Artists' city streets sets, the antithesis of Cassavetes' authentic location aesthetic, but the Rydell character was given a jazz motif, and since Cassavetes' directorial debut, *Shadows* (1959) followed only a few months later, this conceivably influenced his own celebrated improvisational style and soundtrack.

Meanwhile, as Walter Mirisch put it in 1960, 'Picture making has become less and less a production line operation of skilled mechanics and more and more a custom design of highly artistic creators ... Today, the major companies are largely financiers and distributors and, as a result, the ties that formerly reached from the producer to the theatre operator have been severed.'[189] The three Mirisch brothers' backgrounds

---

[184] 'Who Goes to the Movies ... and Who Doesn't', *MPH*, 10.8.57: 21.
[185] 'Youth Must Be Served', *MPH*, 23.6.56: 7.
[186] 'For the Young Audience', *MPH*, 15.9.56: 7.
[187] 'Lost Audience: Crass vs Class', *Variety*, 5.12.56: 1, 86.
[188] 'What the Picture Did for Me', *Motion Picture Herald*, 31.5.47: 45.
[189] Walter Mirisch, 'Make Way for Tomorrow?' *The Journal of the Producers Guild of America* vol 6 no 7, December 1960: 21–2.

embodied just such ties, however, Walter with production and management, Harold with exhibition and distribution and Marvin with marketing, retail and finance. Indeed, the combination of industry experience the three Mirisch brothers brought to their own independent company was already exceptional. Harold's background as a theatre manager and in bookings for RKO and Warners and subsequently as sales head for Allied Artists, Marvin's in advertising at the National Screen Service, serving the appetites of cinemagoers at the Theatres Candy Co, and balancing budgets, as assistant to the treasurer of Monogram, and Walter's in film production and industrial administration were to prove a remarkable grounding for launching their own production company.

On the other hand, the specificity of those backgrounds may have contributed to an understanding of the film business, of American cinema and of the audience for it, which eventually became out of sync with reality. The cinemas that Harold ran and programmed were not first-run, major metropolitan venues. The films which Walter initially greenlit and the first few he personally produced were programmers and when his instincts at the Mirisch Company didn't tend to belt-tightening, the antithesis to B movies was assumed to be the expensive acquisition of rights to the kinds of books, plays, musicals and real lives that would have been beyond the dreams of Monogram and Allied Artists, although as it turned out, occasionally and perhaps increasingly, also beyond the dreams of the American moviegoing public. But for now, at least, their ambition to set up their own independent was unstoppable. In one of their final films for Allied Artists, *The First Texan* (Haskin, 1956) Sam Houston declines an offer to join a discussion about the future of Texas. Jim Bowie replies, 'You don't understand. This is big. We're talking about making Texas independent of Mexico.' To which Houston responds, 'Well, that is pretty good-sized talks.' Ultimately Houston joins those fighting for Texan independence, just as the Mirisches opted for independence themselves.

Their experience at Monogram had taught the Mirisches a number of things about Hollywood. Some of these structures and strategies they deployed throughout the rest of their time as producers – the economies of series and cycle production, the reputational and promotional benefits of a strategy of adaptation, the risk sharing of co-productions and the subsidies and frozen funds to be tapped for runaway productions, the autonomy of independence and the passing on of that relative creative autonomy to top talent. There was also the realization that release strategies and promotional techniques could be crucial to the success of a film. But there were other Monogram lessons that the Mirisches rejected – the failure of the quality strategy, the anachronism of the assembly-line approach – or refused to learn, like the changing demographics of the box office, the shifting generic appetites of the new audience and the emergence of a new generation of film school educated talent. These attitudes and aptitudes were to determine the successes and failures of the new company the brothers left Monogram to establish.

3

How to succeed in business without really trying

Towards a corporate history of the Mirisch companies

In the summer of 1957 United Artists signed a contract with the Mirisch brothers agreeing to finance a minimum of four films annually for three years beginning on 1 September. UA paid a weekly producer fee and overheads for their rental of office space and a skeleton staff at Goldwyn Studios. The Mirisches duly incorporated under the name Mirisch Company Inc. Two years into the contract UA extended the deal from twelve films to twenty. Mirisch's autonomy was relative – UA had approval over the story, stars, director and budget but these strictures were somewhat relaxed as the company proved itself. The Mirisches signed a second deal on 1 December 1963, for a further twenty films but once again this was renegotiated, resulting in a commitment effective from 1 September 1964 for another forty-eight films by 1974.

Managing creativity

In *The Classical Hollywood Cinema*, Janet Staiger notes that 'Pertinent . . . to a study of Hollywood's mode of production is an analysis of who managed the firms – an analysis which considers the stylistic paradigms and economic practices operating as received norms for these managers.'[1] In 1957, barely two months before the Mirisch brothers launched their company, the editor of *The Hollywood Reporter*, William 'Billy' Wilkerson, noted that 'Making pictures to entertain the people of the world is a big job, and requires top management and control, much of which the studios have passed to the big agents.'[2] But Mirisch was neither an agency nor a studio. Nevertheless, as owners of their company, the brothers prided themselves on their managerial skills.

In this chapter, I consider whether understanding how the seven Mirisch film companies (The Mirisch Company, The Mirisch Corporation, Mirisch Pictures, Mirisch Films, The Mirisch Production Company, Oakmont Films and Ashton Productions) operated, how they were managed, can help explain why so many memorable films

---

[1] Bordwell, Staiger and Thompson, 1985: 316–17.
[2] *Hollywood Reporter*, 13.6.57: 1, quoted in Denise Mann, 2008: 246.

of the period were Mirisch productions. Would expanding our knowledge of their competitive strategy and corporate working practices enable us to understand the characteristics such films have in common – and why – and distinguish them from other contemporaneous Hollywood productions and production companies?

First published in 1980, Michael E. Porter's hugely influential study, *Competitive Strategy: Techniques for Analysing Industries and Competitors*, on whose approach Tino Balio relies in his second volume on United Artists, helps illuminate the Mirisch business strategy.[3] Indeed, applying Porter's analysis beyond UA to Mirisch seems particularly appropriate, as, like Porter himself, Walter Mirisch attended Harvard Business School before entering the film business, making him (one of) the first Hollywood producer(s) to have studied there.[4] Of course, Mirisch was at Harvard long before Porter, in a course which included the techniques of so-called scientific management: cost accounting, control systems, management information, business statistics and decision science. Porter's 1980 Preface usefully includes a synopsis of what he calls the 'Classical Approach to the Formulation of Strategy',[5] covering the curriculum both Mirisch and Porter studied at Harvard, which was discussed in more detail in Chapter 1. Balio acknowledges Porter's influence on the first page of his introduction, noting that the latter's analysis is 'well suited to making sense out of a period of film industry history that underwent radical transformation as a result of changing audience tastes, federal anti-trust action, competition from television, and conglomerate takeovers'.[6] And if it helps explain the actions of UA under Krim and Benjamin, it is presumably equally pertinent to their most successful supplier, Mirisch.

Porter is, of course, far from being the only management theorist to have influenced thinking about business strategy in Hollywood. Two recent books on corporate Hollywood, by Jerome Christensen and Jeff Menne,[7] rely heavily on Peter Drucker's work.[8] But despite John Beckett's (chairman of the Board of Transamerica) pamphlet, *Principles of Management*, sent to Arthur Krim and his senior team at UA, along with copies of Drucker's latest book, *The Age of Discontinuity*, Krim and his colleagues did not welcome the management guru's statistics-based business strategy.[9] Indeed, Krim wrote a detailed rebuttal of Transamerica's (and, by implication, Drucker's) advice recommending separation between Transamerica and UA, referring to the latter as 'a volatile subsidiary' and arguing 'the vagaries of the business do not and will never fit

---

[3] Michael E. Porter, *Competitive Strategy: Techniques for Analysing Industries and Competitors*, Free Press, 1980, reprinted 2004; and Balio, 1987.
[4] Coincidentally, Porter's undergraduate degree was in Aeronautical Engineering – which was the very field in which Mirisch began his career.
[5] Porter, 2004: xxiv.
[6] Balio, 1987: 4.
[7] Jerome Christensen, *America's Corporate Art: The Studio Authorship of Hollywood Motion Pictures*, Stanford University Press, 2012, and Jeff Menne, *Post-Fordist Cinema: Hollywood Auteurs and the Corporate Counterculture*, Columbia University Press, 2019.
[8] Peter Drucker, *The Future of Industrial Man*, 1942 and *The Concept of the Corporation*, 1946.
[9] John R. Beckett, *Principles of Management*, remarks resented to the 1969 Management Conference of Transamerica Corporation, 11.3.69, Transamerica published these remarks as a pamphlet, n.d. See also Peter Drucker, *The Age of Discontinuity*, 1969.

into the TA emphasis on prognostication, per annum growth, patterns of return on equity or other guidelines applicable to other operations of TA'.[10] Krim insisted that the failures of 1968 and 1969 (when he and Benjamin had stepped back from managing the company) were not due to 'new management techniques' and that it would be foolish to assume that the successes of the previous few years were 'typical or automatically redoable merely by application of formulas or artificial prognostications'.[11]

Nevertheless, Drucker's work was among the foundations of Management Studies. *The Concept of the Corporation*, about General Motors, endorsed the practice of 'establishing high-level goals while devolving authority for executing them to self-governing units'[12] which closely coincided with United Artists' outsourcing strategy and Mirisch's similarly slimmed-down operation, with the latter's reliance on renting facilities and equipment rather than owning them and on hiring employees on short term contracts rather than as permanent staff and on 'runaway' projects rather than in-house filming and facilities.

Creating the customer

However, it is Drucker's contention that 'profitability is not the purpose of business enterprise' which is perhaps both the most counterintuitive and yet most consistent with Mirisch. For Drucker, the purpose of business is, instead, 'to create a customer' and this may help explain the presence of a six-film cycle and seven sequels among Mirisch's sixty-eight films for UA.[13] It also provides another rationalization for the prevalence of so-called runaway productions in the Mirisch canon, otherwise known as off-shoring – the taking of above-the-line Hollywood talent abroad to work with (cheaper) below-the-line international casts, crews, locations and studios, with the resulting films offering not only a tourist's eye view of a foreign city to American filmgoers but also the opportunity for cinemagoers in the host country to see their own land- and cityscapes as the backdrop for Hollywood stars and storylines, directed by Hollywood filmmakers. On the other hand, the adaptation of bestsellers and Broadway hits, another Mirisch strategy, was precisely predicated on recruiting pre-existing customers. Similarly, sequels, spin-offs and cycles functioned by re-attracting customers of previous products.

Given the centrality of creating customers for Drucker, it is striking that Mirisch was one of the first, if not the first, independent(s) to invest in 'promotional featurettes', short documentaries publicizing forthcoming films with 'making of' footage. Such films gave

> audiences behind-the-scenes insights into the filmmaking process. This soft-sell style was especially useful with the strengthening power of the 'pre-sell,' a strategy

---

[10] Arthur Krim, 'United Artists 1970–1973 Background Report', December 1973, United Artists Collection Addition, 1950–1980.
[11] United Artists, 1970–1973: 6.
[12] Menne, 2019: 14.
[13] Peter Drucker, *The Practice of Management*, Harper Business, 1954, 37.

to bring notice to a film before its release so that studios could increase the chances of recouping their costs on the theatrical first-run of a big-budget picture . . . preselling a movie was critical to helping each film appear distinct to the public.[14]

The Mirisch brothers had previously experimented with the form at Allied Artists when *The Phenix City Story* was publicized by a twenty-five-minute promotional documentary.[15] Of the *Phenix City* documentary, the trade press reported that 'The short is designed to hype interest in the feature, which Mirisch described as one of the company's important projects to date.'[16] Mirisch referred to the documentary as 'an advance selling agent'.[17] According to Steinhart, by the late 1950s, all the major studios 'had an exclusive deal with National Screen Services to create trailers.'[18] Marvin Mirisch, given his background in promotion, would have been aware of this marketing strategy. But the Mirisches, appropriately enough, preferred to outsource such featurettes to boutique agencies. The earliest featurette Steinhart identifies is UA's *How a Great Film Is Made* (1957), promoting *The Pride and the Passion* (Krämer, 1957) but Mirisch's AA was there two years earlier with their short promoting *The Phenix City Story*. Indeed, the brothers deployed similarly promotional documentary 'making-of' featurettes, not only to publicize individual Mirisch productions but also and simultaneously to foreground the Mirisch Company itself, notably with *The Declaration of Independents* in 1963, an ABC-TV *Hollywood Special*.[19]

The trade press reported on this development in detail, underlining its undoubted newsworthiness. 'Globe Photos has produced for the Mirisch Co and United Artists a 15-minute documentary film about independent motion picture production, with alternate versions for domestic and European viewing.' The short was originally narrated by Jack Lemmon and scheduled on ABC Sunday, 30 December 1963, but late in post-production, Arthur Knight, author of the popular film history book, *The Liveliest Art* (published in 1957), who had written the narration, recorded his own words. The Knight version was transmitted as scheduled, while the Lemmon version was apparently screened on TV or in cinemas overseas. 'Titled "*The Declaration of Independents*" the short subject traces the evolution of the motion picture industry which began as an independent filmmaking movement, progressed to a mass production major studio era, only to evolve back in recent years into an independent oriented outlook.' The documentary combined on-set footage, interviews and extracts from a number of upcoming Mirisch-UA pictures, including *Two for the Seesaw*, *Irma*

---

[14] 'Featurettes', *Cinema Journal* vol 57 no 4, Summer 2018: 100.
[15] *Motion Picture Daily*, 5.7.55: 3.
[16] *The Independent Film Journal*, 5.7.55.
[17] *Motion Picture Herald*, 9.7.55: 27 See also 'The Making of Hollywood Production: Televising and Visualizing Global Filmmaking in 1960s Promotional Featurettes', Daniel Steinhart, *Cinema Journal* vol 57 no 4, Summer 2018: 96–119.
[18] 'The Making of Hollywood Production', Steinhart, 101.
[19] I have been unable to locate a copy of this featurette. However, its role in authorizing (in both senses of the word) the new company echoes Jacques Derrida's remarks in his article, 'Declarations of Independence' (1986) in *New Political Science*, 7: 1, 7–15, about the process whereby new institutions constitute themselves.

La Douce, *The Great Escape*, *The Pink Panther* and *Toys in the Attic*.[20] The original title for this edition of ABC-TV's *Hollywood Special* was *Hollywood Goes Independent*. Subsequent Mirisch-promoting 'featurettes' include *One, Two, Three's A Company* (on the making of *The Thomas Crown Affair*, which had originally been titled *The Thomas Crown Comp*any) and *Who Is Beau Bridges?* – a short screened on ABC-TV to promote *Gaily Gaily* – by which time the star was already at work on his second Mirisch movie, *The Landlord*.

According to Steinhart, the networks began broadcasting these featurettes after feature films in strands such as *NBC Saturday Night at the Movies* (1961–78) and *The ABC Sunday Night Movie* (1964–98). The slot length for these weekly feature films allowed any unused screen-time to be filled with a 'making-of' featurette. Both the broadcaster and the production company benefitted from this arrangement, 'the network received programming that could occupy broadcast time, and the studio earned unpaid publicity for its films during prime-time hours. In addition, studios could target a TV audience who, research proved, were more likely to attend the movie theatre – a reflection of film promotion's evolution from focusing on mass appeal to more specialized audience segments'. Indeed, promotional featurettes performed a crucial role for the industry by accelerating and intensifying the convergence of film and television, as the latter became a primary site for advertising the former, as well as providing what was often its final resting place.[21]

Steinhart suggests that one of the key characteristics of such featurettes is the way in which the film's story becomes a metaphor for the film's production. *Declaration of Independents* is a perfect example of this, in which Mirisch as an independent producer is identified with the 'independence', the charismatic individuality, of the protagonists of *Two for the Seesaw*, *Irma La Douce*, *The Great Escape*, *The Pink Panther* and *Toys in the Attic* as well as of their difference from more mainstream films (by virtue of settings, styles, stars, scale and subject matter). Similarly, five years later, *One, Two, Three's a Company* played on the equivalence between the stylish corporate heist depicted in *The Thomas Crown Affair* and the implicitly stylish independent producer behind it, while also combining two Mirisch titles in one.

Mirisch management and management theory

Mirisch's relevance to management theory is also evident in that two of the exemplary films cited in Emma Bell's *Reading Management and Organization in Film*[22] are Mirisch productions – *The Apartment* and *How to Succeed in Business Without Really Trying*. That a book on management, published by an academic in the School of Management, should identify two, very different, Mirisch productions (a realist comedy-drama and

---

[20] 'Independent Filmmaking Shown Over ABC-TV', *Boxoffice*, 7.1.63: 11.
[21] 'The Making of Hollywood Production', Steinhart, 99, 107.
[22] Emma Bell, *Reading Management and Organization in Film, in the Management, Work and Organizations Series of Textbooks*, Palgrave, 2008, 99–109.

a heavily stylized musical) as emblematic of ideas about management reveals those films' role in representing the then contemporary consensus about corporations and corporate culture and careers, in both cases somewhat satirically, but each distinctly differentiated from their makers' own smaller, more personal production culture.

Balio, following Porter's maxims, notes that Mirisch saw its independent rivals as 'at a disadvantage from the start by not diversifying . . . (and) . . . devised a special brand of independent production'.[23] Porter identifies three key generic strategies for a new company in any industry – cost leadership (essentially low if not lowest-cost production), product differentiation (competitive advantage through a distinctive commodity) and focus (targeting one or a small number of markets for that selected strategy).[24] In what follows, I deploy Porter's concepts to identify how Mirisch attempted to differentiate itself and its products from its rivals, with 'quality', distinctive product as well as low-cost, less distinctive works – and to determine more precisely what distinguished its 'special brand of independent production'. Using Porter's model, Mirisch's corporate career and competitive strategy as a UA supplier fall into three periods – entry, maturity and decline – which closely correspond with the three contractual periods of the relationship between Mirisch and United Artists. As most of the key elements that come to define a company are introduced during the Entry period and continue to exist in the other two periods this chapter will discuss the entry period in more detail than maturity and decline.

The first United Artists contract

In the first years of its operation (1957–63) Mirisch prioritized a small number of strategies which not only helped to define the brand of the company – literally to make a name for itself – but also ensured its entry into the industry and critical and commercial success, its very visibility and viability, extremely swiftly. These characteristics are effective organization, dual strategy, family business, quality and adaptation – and this section discusses them in that order. By 1957, when the Mirisch Company signed its first multi-picture deal with United Artists which agreed to finance a minimum of four pictures a year for three years beginning 1 September 1957, 71 per cent of major studio releases were independent productions.[25] These films for UA were to be cross-collateralized with profits split 50/50 between the two companies. UA paid the overhead for the brothers' small offices at Goldwyn Studios and a weekly producer fee, divided equally between the brothers. Exactly two years later UA extended that contract from twelve films to twenty.[26]

Of the 'barriers to entry' for any new company Porter suggests of economies of scale that 'The benefits of sharing are particularly potent if there are joint costs. . . .

---

[23] Balio, 1987: 160.
[24] Porter, 1980 and 2004: 11–15.
[25] '3 Mirisch Bros. Set Up Indie Co. For 12 UA Films', *Variety*, 11.9.57: 7. Mann, 2008: 67.
[26] Balio, 1987: 15.

A common situation of joint costs occurs when business units can share intangible assets such as brand names and know-how. The cost of creating an intangible asset need only be borne once'.[27] The seven film production companies Mirisch ran were all based at the same address and staffed by essentially the same core personnel. Some were cycle-specific, some region-specific, others period-specific, functioning for the duration of a particular contract with UA. Mirisch was explicit about its desire to develop co-production arrangements with other smaller independents and writer-director hyphenates.[28] As *Variety* noted in 1958, Harold

> Mirisch reported that with unlimited financing and distribution to offer – through UA – his company is concentrating on joint production ventures and already has lined up with five outside units, four headed by stars and one by Billy Wilder. In each case, separate companies will be formed, such as Ashton Productions, set up by the Mirisches and Gary Cooper for the Cooper starrer, 'Man of the West'[29]

Ashton took its name from Cooper's old school – he had been educated in Dunstable in England – whose philanthropist founder was a Mrs Frances Ashton. But the name Ashton was also associated with Las Vegas dance director, Barry Ashton's sometimes bare-breasted showgirls, so the Mirisch brothers quickly used their own family name for their new firm. In 1958 the Mirisch Company produced *Cast a Long Shadow* (Carr, 1959) in which Audie Murphy plays the illegitimate heir to a ranch, Matt Brown. At one point, Matt says, 'You know what it's like not having a name? Like being the extra joker in a deck of cards. A nothing. You don't belong in the game. I haven't the most ordinary thing in the world. A last name.' The film's title and theme thus echo the necessity of establishing a name and a reputation.

Economies of scale are virtually absent in industries which are 'intrinsically hard to mechanize or routinize'.[30] This is particularly true of the film industry, where every product is also a prototype. Mirisch attempted to minimize the one-off-ness implicit in the package-unit system pioneered by independent film production companies with the efficiency, economy and rationalization that sequels, cycles, remakes and runaway productions afforded, while maximizing the 'difference' of the company's properties and the talent associated with them. Thus, the scientific management techniques that Walter Mirisch absorbed at Harvard and applied at Mirisch to their 'programme' pictures, were balanced by the creative freedom the company offered to 'name' directors for more ambitious, if often pre-tested, projects. This binary at the base of Mirisch's business strategy is echoed in the title of this book, both Hollywood and Independent simultaneously. Matthew Bernstein refers to 'independents' producing films for major studios, often on their back lots, as, at best, semi-independents.[31]

---

[27] Porter, 2004: 8–9.
[28] Brynner's Alciona, Sturges' Alpha and Jewison's Simkoe all subsequently reaped tax benefits from their status as co-producers with Mirisch.
[29] 'Mirisch Freres', *Variety*, 12.3.58: 3.
[30] Porter, 2004:196.
[31] Matthew Bernstein, 'Hollywood's Semi-Independent Production', *Cinema Journal* vol 32 no 3, 1993.

Porter suggests that 'Large size may be inconsistent with an image of exclusivity' and that often 'an artist ... wants to deal with a smaller, more personalized organization with a particular image or reputation'.[32] Several of Mirisch's independent peers developed out of talent agencies and Mirisch shared many of their characteristics but while some were co-founded by stars (Burt Lancaster's Hecht-Lancaster and Kirk Douglas's Bryna are among the best known of the period), Mirisch was built on its relationships with directors and its acquisition of IP. This was partly how it differentiated itself from its rivals. Rather than foregrounding their own stars or making stars of themselves as owners, the Mirisches prioritized directors and literary properties. According to Menne, 'The auteur theory functioned as a kind of management theory for a cohort of filmmakers who were made cine-literate through University education'. And while only Walter had such an education, all three brothers had an extensive background in the film business. 'Both auteur theory and business management theory ... had the same object in their sights: the large corporation, which was made sclerotic by a combination of its hypertrophy and its centralised command structure. In its place would emerge a smaller-scale, more flexible system of labor.'[33] The Mirisch Company was just such a small, flexible company and in *The Apartment* and *How to Succeed*... the sclerotic, large corporation was very much in its sights (Figure 4).

Figure 4 Tribute to Harold Mirisch, Motion Picture Pioneer of the Year, 1964. Source: Tribute To Harold Mirisch 'Published November 23, 1964 TRIBUTE TO HAROLD MIRISCH, MOTION PICTURE PIONEER OF THE YEAR, 1964'.

[32] Porter, 2004: 199–203.
[33] Menne, 2019: 6.

The package-unit system

Janet Staiger has identified several strategies deployed by independent production companies using the package-unit system – differentiation on the bases of its innovations, story, stars and director; targeting specific demographics; runaway production; profit-sharing; and the rise of the hyphenate.[34] She is at pains to avoid an exclusively economic explanation of the film industry's – or indeed any individual company's – business structure and strategies. Producers rarely aim to produce simply the cheapest film; they want to make films that encourage audiences to return repeatedly to theatres. Staiger identified the polarity between 'standardization versus product differentiation' to explain the balance between generic conventions and innovations.

Staiger stressed 'the transitory nature of the combination' in package production, and the fact that employment was based 'on a film not a firm'.[35] One distinctive characteristic of Mirisch was the impetus to mitigate this transitory, film-by-film, mode by the development of sequels (seven spun off from three originals), and a cycle (six spun off from one original) as well as multi-picture contracts with both directors (Sturges, Edwards, Jewison and Hill and an eight-film run with Wilder) and stars (McQueen, MacLaine, Lemmon, Bronson, Coburn and Garner among others). Balio added a big picture strategy and blockbusters; and differentiation from TV both formally, through Cinemascope and Panavision, as well as editorially, through the inclusion of sex and violence and 'adult' themes, particularly in response to a shift in audience tastes beginning in 1967 which resulted, at Mirisch, in a belated and somewhat half-hearted attempt to target the youth market.[36]

Mirisch prided itself on being a small family business and was initially owned 96 per cent by the brothers and 4 per cent by key employees. Harold Mirisch was the president, Marvin was the vice president and secretary-treasurer, and Walter was the executive in charge of production. The rest of the staff initially comprised only a production manager, a lawyer, the head of the television production unit, an in-house editor, a publicist and two secretaries.[37] Such a family business was already something of an anachronism in American industry, which had witnessed a transition to managerial capitalism in which any successful organization's structure followed its business strategies. But while the Mirisches prided themselves on their managerial skills, they were adamant about remaining a small family business. They thus occupied a corporate middle ground. Which, in turn, prioritized family films.

> An article in *Boxoffice* describes Mirisch's aims as to find the best filmmakers and provide them with the very best story material and most talented associates – enable the filmmaker to do the thing he most wants to do – concentrate completely

---

[34] Bordwell, Staiger, Thompson, 1985: 332–4.
[35] Ibid, 330.
[36] Balio, 1987: 161–96.
[37] Mirisch, 2008: 89.

on the films, on what appears on the screen and let a small, effective organization handle all the other complex matters that are part of making a movie, ranging from negotiating contracts and financing, to persuading actors to work under the Mirisch banner, to arranging pre-production logistics, and perhaps most important, taking the completed film and supervising its merchandising on a coordinated world-wide basis.[38]

The trade papers were quick to detect differences between this new, slimmed-down operation – a combination of what today we might describe as downsizing, outsourcing and casualization – and the old, vertically integrated studios. As *Variety* reported, 'the company will concentrate on low overhead while maintaining as high quality as possible ... Approximately 98% of all costs of a picture will be on the screen, rather than keeping expensive personnel, bricks and mortar, while not in operation'.[39] *Business Week* added: 'They rent office space by the week and sound stages by the day. The overheads stay low.'[40] As we shall see, that outsourcing encompassed everything from story material to studios and locations, from subsidiaries to co-production arrangements with directors who had their own businesses.

Mirisch negotiated deals with established, studio-era filmmakers like John Ford, Robert Wise, Michael Curtiz, Anthony Mann, Billy Wilder and William Wyler but also hired proven, somewhat younger directors like John Sturges, Norman Jewison, Blake Edwards and George Roy Hill. The contracts were generally for profit-sharing 'joint production ventures'. Wilder's first contract with the company, for instance, called for two features for which he was to be paid a director's fee of $200,000 per film plus 17.5 per cent of the gross after each film broke even (a figure which was set at about twice the negative cost). If a film grossed $1 million above that, Wilder's share rose to 20 per cent.[41] Those first two films turned out to be *Some Like It Hot* and *The Apartment*. As Wilder put it, 'All the Mirisch Company asks me is the name of the picture, a vague outline of the story and who's going to be in it. The rest is up to me. You can't get any more freedom than that.'[42] He reprised the tribute in another interview.

> I have complete freedom of choice of subject – they do not control me during shooting, or in cutting. Sometimes they have an opinion and I listen to it, of course. I do none of the bookkeeping, and have no taste for business arrangements – how can you spend your time with your lawyers and business managers and bookkeepers while you are trying to knock out a story? ... Unless what I choose is impractical, or censorable, I have complete authority to make what I choose.[43]

---

[38] *Boxoffice*, 1.10.62: 8–9.
[39] 'Casting Their Own UA Horoscope', *Variety*, 10.12.58: 4.
[40] 'Fade Out for Blockbuster Films', *Business Week*, 20.10.62: 178.
[41] Balio, 1987: 167–8.
[42] Billy Wilder, quoted in Tom Wood, *The Bright Side of Billy Wilder, Primarily*, Doubleday, 1970: 179.
[43] 'The Old Dependables', *Film Quarterly*, 5: 6.

John Ford told the same writer that 'all that happened to Horse Soldiers after he left it was that some of the humor was cut'.[44] In fact, as I hope to demonstrate, rather than merely freeing the filmmaker from business chores, companies like Mirisch played a crucial role in shaping, 'packaging' and (despite Wilder's 'Producer' credit) producing or co-producing, the films that carried their logo. Creative freedom was not only what Mirisch offered Wilder, but also what UA offered Mirisch. That this was dependent independence, a relative autonomy, does not diminish its significance (Figure 5).

A family business

Porter stresses the importance of consensus in any new business, asking 'How much unanimity is there among management?' noting that family businesses can be inherently cohesive.[45] As a family business, the intimacy of Mirisch was always a key factor. Unlike the siblings who founded Warner Bros., which swiftly became a major corporation, Mirisch was a comparatively small-scale operation, where everyone knew virtually everyone else and the brothers could be involved in every film they made, as there were rarely more than a handful of productions being made at any one time. Walter Mirisch remembers their offices being 'small enough to be intimate and for people to know most of the people on the lot' even as the company expanded and that he, Wilder and co-writer I. A. L. Diamond 'lunched nearly every day together, we dropped in on each other, we talked about all the decisions that needed to be made'. The creative freedom Mirisch offered filmmakers was based on 'the personal relationships that we had with the particular directors that we worked with . . . freedom is also based on trust and on mutual respect'.[46]

Alongside the core staff and those stars and directors who made multiple films for the company, many others worked repeatedly for them. Jack Lemmon made five films for the company, James Coburn made four, Charles Bronson, Steve McQueen, James Garner and Shirley MacLaine each made three. (Multiple picture deals thus replicated studio staff contracts by other means.) Lynn Stalmaster cast twenty-five Mirisch features and three TV series for them; Allen K. Wood was the production manager on thirty-nine successive Mirisch films and associate producer on another; Robert Boyle was the art director on seven; Emile LaVigne did the make-up and Sam Gordon was the props master on fourteen each; Robert Relyea was the associate producer on seven and worked on two more; Lewis Rachmil produced nine Mirisch films; Richard Heermance edited five Mirisch films and ran their TV arm, working as associate producer on one TV series, *Wichita Town* (NBC 1959–60), and as an editor on another, *Peter Loves Mary* (NBC 1960–1); Ferris Webster edited eight Mirisch

[44] Ibid, 9.
[45] Porter, 2004: 52.
[46] Interview with the author, for *Nobody's Perfect*, BBC2 2001.

films and the TV series, *Rat Patrol* (ABC 1966–8); Ralph E. Winters edited twelve Mirisch films; and Hal Ashby was editor or assistant editor on five, an associate producer on one more and, finally, director on another. So many familiar faces, in such a comparatively small company, contributed to the sense that this was indeed a family business.

At one point in *How to Succeed in Business Without Really Trying*, the hero's girlfriend, Rosemary, says 'Every company has a couple of relations floating around' And of course she's right. In Hollywood the old joke that 'the son-in-law also rises' was all too true. And yet it is striking, to say the least, that the Mirisch Company was not just a family business, it was also a business a disproportionate amount of whose output was 'about' families. A third of the Mirisch Company's productions focused on families or had family relationships central to them – the outlaw Tobin family in *Man of the West*, the Masterson brothers in *Gunfight at Dodge City*, the illegitimate son and heir in *Cast a Long Shadow*, Maria's 'Sharks' family in *West Side Story*, Elvis Presley's *Kwimper* family in *Follow That Dream* (Douglas, 1962) the dysfunctional Bernier family in *Toys in the Attic*, the homicidal Wulf/Pilgrin family in *Return from the Ashes* (Lee Thompson, 1965) the Norwegian Bergman siblings in *633 Squadron*, the flyers Scotty Scott and his adopted brother Quint Munroe in *Mosquito Squadron*, the Hale and Keoki families in *Hawaii*, the litigious brothers-in-law in *The Fortune Cookie* (Wilder, 1966) the rival Earp and Clanton brothers in *Hour of the Gun* (Sturges, 1967), the Enders family in *The Landlord*, the Hoxworth and Tsin families in *The Hawaiians* (Gries, 1970) Tevye's family in *Fiddler on the Roof* and even Wendell Armbruster Jr and Pamela Piggott, who reprise their respective parents' illicit affair, in *Avanti* (Wilder, 1972).

Efficiency, artistry and a social conscience

As a family business, Mirisch was determined to be business-like. In an article for the *Journal of the Screen Producers Guild*, Mirisch made the company's two-pronged strategy explicit. He diagnosed an industry in which 'there is still great inefficiency in production' but observed: 'Picture making has become less and less a production line operation of skilled mechanics, and more and more a custom design of highly artistic creators.'[47] This tension between balancing assembly line 'efficiencies' with individual 'artistry' came to characterize the dual strands of the Mirisch strategy – which proved a strength in their first decade but was becoming an anachronism by the late 1960s. It was by applying the simplified assembly lines of so-called 'scientific management' to the company's programme pictures, while relaxing creative controls on its more ambitious productions, that Mirisch's dual strategy operated. And such assembly lines implied not only how individual programme pictures were produced, but also continuity of production – how one film followed another, as in the days of the vertically integrated studios, before the Paramount Decree.

[47] Mirisch, 1960.

In the same article, Walter Mirisch admitted: 'We are all faced by the prospect of renewed television competition as the flood of post '48 films finds its way to the TV screens of the world. As producers, all we can do to meet this competition is to dedicate ourselves to continually higher standards of quality and showmanship.' He suggested that this might involve what he called 'new forms', but also new content: 'Many of our pictures today attempt to reflect reality in life – serious pictures, if you will. Pictures which provide a depth and treatment in character and direction which may not be possible on television.'[48] Differentiating its output from the small screen while approximating it more closely with lived reality was one of Mirisch strategies at the turn of the decade.

Almost twenty-five years later, in an article written for *Variety*, Walter Mirisch remained adamant about the social and aesthetic responsibilities of the producer.

> Greater autonomy for picture creators, whether they are working under the umbrella of a major studio or completely independently, also brings a responsibility to themselves, to the filmgoing public and to society itself, not to make films solely in pursuit of profits without any creative concept or vision, cynically corrupting their audiences by glorifying violence or distorting sex or exploiting rank sensationalism. The golden goose can be killed.[49]

In one of only a handful of references to the film industry, Porter salutes the role of two Paramount executives in the 1970s, who brought TV initiatives into cinema, including 'pre-selling of films, releasing films simultaneously in large numbers of theaters, and so on'.[50] More than a decade earlier, the Mirisches brought their background at Monogram and Allied Artists – and Harold Mirisch's exhibition expertise – to bear on their own marketing, and – while not distributors themselves – were centrally involved in the decision to give *The Magnificent Seven* a saturation release – a decade and a half before either *Jaws* at Universal, or, Porter's example, Paramount – were applauded for allegedly pioneering precisely the same strategy. Similarly, Porter notes that 'movie companies have boosted demand by advertising movies on television' – another strategy deployed by Mirisch in the previous decade.[51] *The Magnificent Seven* was the beneficiary of a major TV spot advertising campaign. As the trade press reported, 'This is the first time that saturation technique had been used for a picture of the scope of "Magnificent Seven". Mass bookings in key theatres surrounding each of the selected exchange cities will be backed by heavy television and radio campaign and hefty general ballyhoo on local level.'[52]

In a subsequent book, Porter developed the value chain concept which has since been applied to Hollywood studio films and, more recently, American

---

[48] Ibid, 21–4.
[49] 'Today's Producer Must Be More Daring and Creative Than Ever Before', *Variety*, 11.6.84, 19.
[50] Porter, 2004: 60.
[51] Ibid, 178.
[52] 'UA's $2,700,000 *Seven* is Given Saturation Booking in Switch', *Variety*, 30.8.60: 4.

independent cinema. Porter's concept has been used to 'disaggregate a firm into its strategically relevant activities'.[53] The concept was first applied to studio films, divided into production, distribution and exhibition. Subsequently, Peter Bloore applied it to recent British independent productions and James Lyons to recent American independent productions. Bloore produced a diagram to represent what he called the Independent Film Project Value Chain, comprising not three but seven specific stages – Development, Financing and Pre-sales, Production (shoot and Post), International Sales and Licensing, International Distribution, Exhibition and Exploitation, Consumption.[54] As Lyons notes, despite 'the extent to which scholarship and cinephilia maintain a strongly auteurist perspective on independent film, the diagram limits the director's input to three of the seven categories'.[55] An independent producer, on the other hand, is involved in four or even five of these categories or phases of activity.

The Mirisch Company could confidently claim to have had its corporate fingerprints on six of these stages at different points in its career. As Walter put it in 1960,

> The producer's interest in his films extends far beyond the time when the last preview has been held. He [sic] is interested in the merchandising and exploitation of his film and he is anxious to play an active part in these functions. The independent producer, particularly, feels that his job has been completed only after he has done everything within is power to assure the quality and success of his product. He has a greater financial stake in the success of his films than ever before.[56]

Of course, Marvin's background in trailers and promotion and Harold's decades of experience as an executive in both distribution and exhibition also proved invaluable, long after the last preview.

Prestige versus programmers

Mirisch seems to have continually operated on (at least) two fronts, aiming about two-thirds of its output at the top of the market (through a calculated combination of major stars and established directors with bestsellers, Broadway shows and occasional remakes) and the remainder at low-budget, formulaic films, often produced in series or cycles, whose earnings depended on double bills and early sale to television. United Artists' Annual Report for 1959 states, 'We are particularly pleased that among these

---

[53] Michael Porter, *Competitive Advantage: Creating and Sustaining Superior Performance*, Free Press, 1998: 33.
[54] 'Re-defining the Independent Film Value Chain', Peter Bloore, UK Film Council, 2009.
[55] James Lyons, 'The American Independent Producer and the Film Value Chain', in Andrew Spicer, Anthony McKenna and Christopher Meir (eds), *Beyond the Bottom Line: The Producer in Film and Television Studies*, Bloomsbury Academic, 2014, 200.
[56] Mirisch, 1960: 23.

projects are four of the most important number one best sellers of the last two years, namely, BY LOVE POSSESSED, EXODUS, ADVICE AND CONSENT and HAWAII. as well as four extraordinary Broadway successes of the same period, TWO FOR THE SEEESAW, WEST SIDE STORY, THE MIRACLE WORKER AND TOYS IN THE ATTIC.'[57] Two of these bestsellers and three of the Broadway hits were adapted by the Mirisch Company.

This strategy continued throughout Mirisch's association with UA, with at least twenty 'programmers' produced over that seventeen-year period, many of them so-called 'runaway productions', designed to exploit Britain's Eady Levy or other foreign subsidies and to recoup much of their costs at the international box office. And while cost leadership found its form in those programmers and under $1 million productions, product differentiation was managed through the employment of major filmmakers, often working with name-recognition IP.

Thus, among the company's first nine films, *Fort Massacre*, *Cast a Long Shadow*, *Man in the Net* and *Gunfight at Dodge City* are all 'programmers'. *Gunfight at Dodge City* was described as 'a competent Western of the kind the Mirisches used to turn out for Allied Artists and are now releasing via United Artists. . . . It's frankly a programme picture and it fits the bill'.[58] By contrast, during that same three-year period, Mirisch also produced *Man of the West*, *The Horse Soldiers*, *Some Like It Hot*, *The Apartment* and *The Magnificent Seven*. Three 'auteurs' and, arguably, four or even five canonical classics – though, surprisingly, perhaps, both *Some Like it Hot* and *The Magnificent Seven* were remakes. This combination of differentiated A films with minimally distinct Bs, or programmers, proved characteristic of Mirisch, 'quality' countered by 'quantity'. The former created the company's reputation, won awards and were occasionally big box office hits, but the latter were undoubtedly underrated contributors both to their return on investment (including sales to TV) and the satisfaction of their contractual obligations to UA.

According to Porter, 'Companies develop perceptions of themselves or images of themselves and their relative capabilities ("we are the quality leader") which are reflected in the implicit assumptions that form the basis of their strategies.'[59] As Walter Mirisch put it, 'Our company's aim is to become preeminent as *the* quality independent film-maker.'[60] This 'quality strategy' paid off in the short term, but eventually left them adrift as audience appetites – and tastes – shifted dramatically during the late 1960s and conceptions of quality were radically transformed. One symptom of this is that exactly half of Mirisch's UA output, thirty-four of their sixty-eight films, were set in the past. Another is the resolute eschewal of genres associated with exploitation cinema.

As Walter Mirisch put it in his autobiography, they wanted 'to produce a program of films of consequence'.[61] Their first few films were Westerns, but 'Due to the oversaturation

---

[57] 'United Artists' Annual Report for 1959', United Artists Collection Addition, Box 1, 4.
[58] 'Gunfight at Dodge City', *Variety*, 13.5.59: 3.
[59] Porter, 2004: 247.
[60] 'Mirisch Brothers: Oscar Monopolists – A Studio Without Walls', *Film Bulletin*, 17.9.62: 10.
[61] Mirisch, 2008: 85.

of television Westerns in the 1950s and 1960s, I felt strongly that we had to do more adult subjects for the genre'.[62] Mirisch avoided genres like horror and science fiction, with their B movie and exploitation cinema associations (while a rival independent enterprise like AIP specialized in such films) and instead attempted to position itself as a prestige producer. In this respect, Mirisch's output remained in such traditional, middlebrow, mainstream and masculine-leaning genres as Westerns, war movies and epics and family (and female-skewed) melodramas, musicals and comedies. Indeed, of their sixty-eight films for UA, thirty-eight were war movies, Westerns or comedies.

Nevertheless, Mirisch continued to produce what were widely perceived as comparatively unambitious, standardized, 'B' movies, albeit under other corporate names. This risked Porter's diagnosis of being 'stuck in the middle' between cost leadership and differentiation, by pursuing a dual strategy[63] – producing two types of films, some aiming to be the best, others to be among the cheapest on the market. Porter notes how 'an effective strategy for achieving above average results can be to specialize on a tightly constrained group of products (which can) allow the enhancement of product differentiation with the customer as a result of the specialist's perceived expertise and image in the particular product area'.[64] Indeed, differentiation necessitates 'creating something that is perceived industry-wide as being unique' and 'provides insulation against competitive rivalry because of brand loyalty'.[65] The brand here is simultaneously Mirisch itself, as a guarantor to UA, the banks and the independent exhibitors, but often perhaps more importantly, the property being adapted, which was also a recognizable 'brand' in its own right. The adapted IP thus facilitated the company – and the brothers – literally making a name for themselves. Furthermore, special prices could be charged for tickets for roadshow releases of prestige adaptations like *West Side Story*, *Hawaii* and *Fiddler on the Roof*.[66]

Adapt and survive

Mirisch's reliance on adaptation as a quality strategy distinguished its 'constrained group of products', a distinction which was achieved by relating those adaptations to another group of already pre-tested texts (novels, plays, musicals and other films). Indeed, of their sixty-eight films for UA, nineteen were adaptations of novels, five were based on works of non-fiction, twelve adapted stage plays or musicals, ten were series films (*The Magnificent Seven*, *The Pink Panther* and *In the Heat of the Night* between them spawned another seven Mirisch sequels, not to mention spin-off TV series and award-winning animation) and four more were remakes of other films. Some two-thirds of its output for UA, then, were adaptations and of those a significant number

---

[62] Ibid, 91.
[63] Porter, 2004: 41.
[64] Ibid, 208.
[65] Ibid, 37–8.
[66] Balio, 1987: 208–10.

piggy-backed on the original's prestige and reputation as well as its market-proven risk aversion. The adaptation of bestsellers and Broadway hits was thus predicated on recruiting pre-existing customers, albeit those of other media firms. In the early years, Mirisch married such risk aversion with risqué content, particularly with Wilder, but later this aspect of their work began to disappear as more middlebrow, mainstream projects were alternated with directorially indulgent projects like *The Party* and *Gaily Gaily*, which failed to garner audiences or awards, but nevertheless evidenced their increasing delegation of creative autonomy to their filmmakers. Indeed, it is striking that three of the first four of Wilder's films for Mirisch (the exception was *One, Two, Three*), two of the first three Sturges films, the first two Edwards films and the first three of Jewison's were major critical and/or commercial successes but subsequent projects, despite or perhaps because of increasing autonomy, proved far less consistent. If a moral can be taken from this, it is that when the company closely oversaw its key projects and personnel they performed better. But when talent outgrew such corporate oversight, it often over-reached itself catastrophically.

For Porter, another barrier to entry can be 'proprietary product technology'.[67] On *The Party*, the associate producer, Ken Wales, operated a Video Assist camera so that there was a video monitor on which to watch what was being filmed. Because all equipment was outsourced by Mirisch there was no attempt to exploit (or perhaps even awareness of) this by the production company and the system was subsequently developed by Video West Panavision and later adopted by Coppola on *Apocalypse Now* (Coppola, 1979). The Cinerama process had been introduced in the early 1950s and a decade later would-be spectacular films included *How the West Was Won* (Ford/Hathaway/Marshall/Thorpe, 1962), *It's a Mad Mad Mad Mad World* (Krämer, 1963), *Battle of the Bulge* (Annakin, 1965) and *The Greatest Story Ever Told* (Stevens, 1965). Mirisch's *The Hallelujah Trail* was a comparatively late entrant and as such had no rights in the process. Nor was the celebrated split screen technique (rather than any specific technology) deployed in *The Thomas Crown Affair* IP as such. Similarly, Nelson Tyler '... got the idea of trying to isolate [the] vibration while viewing the aerial credits on West Side Story. They were shaky and he knew that there had to be a way to create smooth footage from helicopters ... Nelson presented his Major Mount to the industry about six months later.' Within a year Tyler had put his new prototype mount to use on *The Satan Bug* in what may be that film's only memorable sequence, overhead shots of bacteria-stricken motorists. Tyler also worked on aerial photography on the company's TV series, *Rat Patrol*.[68]

But while proprietary technology is not necessarily pertinent to an independent producer, for whom such equipment is almost invariably rented, Mirisch did exhibit a proprietary approach, through its reliance on pre-tested talent and texts. Key to this strategy is the concept of 'reputational capital' – the acquisition of reputable literary properties from page and stage and the contracting of reputable, established,

---

[67] Porter, 2004: 16.
[68] 'A History of Aerial Cinematography', Stan McClain (*The Operating Cameraman: The Magazine of the Society of Camera Operators*, 1996) http://www.cinematographers.nl/DoPh4a.html

filmmakers to make them into films. The latter signings helped launch the company, with such auteurs as Ford, Mann, Wilder and Wyler loudly announced, but only one of the subsequent hirings proved comparably viable or visible, critically or commercially, Norman Jewison. Meanwhile, the brothers continued to snap up stage and book rights. Porter warns: 'Differentiation creates a barrier to entry by forcing entrants to spend heavily to overcome existing customer loyalties.'[69] But Mirisch spent heavily precisely to co-opt existing customer loyalties – acquiring proprietary properties from other narrative forms, including bestsellers, Broadway plays and even earlier films. This first contract period saw Mirisch acquiring more high-profile properties than subsequently, though *Hawaii* was only finally made in the second period. One of the most familiar of these is the 'proprietary character' identified by Altman (1999: 115).[70]

The social problem film

Adaptation was not the only avenue to quality for Mirisch. The company made several forays into the post-war prestige cycle, one aspect of which was the social problem film. Cagle argues that independents could use social relevance or realism as a passport to prestige and box office. For Cagle, 'social problem films were a central catalyst in the industry's shift in approach to "serious" filmmaking'.[71] To achieve that shift, on *The Apartment*, *The Children's Hour*, *Town Without Pity* and *Two for the Seesaw* – all 'medium budget art films' in social realist, 'artistic' black and white – Mirisch worked with directors like Wyler, Wilder, Petrie and Sturges and writers like Hellman, Schnee and Wilder again, all with a pedigree in social problem prestige pictures.[72] (However, such liberalism on-screen was based on neoliberal outsourcing off-screen.) Mirisch even ensured its adaptations of middlebrow bestsellers included 'issues' such as adultery, impotence and alcoholism in *By Love Possessed* (Sturges, 1961), and nymphomania in *A Rage to Live* (Grauman, 1965).

The second United Artists contract

By the early 1960s, Mirisch had clearly arrived. *The Apartment* won five Oscars including Best Picture, Best Director and Best Original Screenplay. The following year, *West Side Story* won ten Oscars, including Best Picture and Best Director, becoming the second biggest US box office attraction of the year. By 1963, three of UA's top four box office hits ever were Mirisch productions.[73] The Mirisches signed another deal

---

[69] Porter, 2004: 9.
[70] Altman, Rick (1999) *Film/Genre* London: British Film Institute.
[71] Cagle, C., *Sociology on Film: Postwar Hollywood's Prestige Commodity*, Rutgers University Press, 2016, 16.
[72] Mann, 2008: 121, 124.
[73] '"West Side" – The Lead "Story"' 'All-Time Top Film Grosses', *Variety*, 9.1.63, 18.

for twenty films on 1 December 1963.⁷⁴ The Mirisch Company and its first twenty films were acquired by UA, while a new firm, the Mirisch Corporation, was set up to replace it. After briefly flirting with Paramount, the Mirisches signed an extension on their UA deal on 1 September 1964, contracting them to produce a total of forty-eight films, in three groups – one of twenty, the other two of fourteen each (those final twenty-eight films were produced from 1968 on). In this period of its business (1963–8), the equivalent to what Porter refers to as maturity, Mirisch introduced two additional strategies to maintain its position in the industry. These two strategies he calls substitution and globalization.

Television and differentiation

Porter defines 'substitutes' as 'products that can perform the same function as the product of the industry'.⁷⁵ For American cinema in the 1960s, the primary substitute was television. The Mirisches were well aware of the threat/opportunity posed by the networks – they made series for them and sold movies to them, but at the same time ensured that their major productions were as unlike TV as possible. The Mirisch attitude to television as a medium in which the assembly lines of studio-era B movie filmmaking could still operate, differentiated the company's small screen output from all but its programmers for big screen double bills, which were often the first to be sold to the networks, having the shortest cinematic shelf life. Other potential entertainment 'substitutes' for cinema – the theatre, publishing, music – became the raw material for such differentiation themselves, via adaptation.

Most Mirisch films of this period were in Panavision or similar widescreen processes and several contained 'adult' themes – adultery, prostitution, racism, the Cold War and the Holocaust. *Kiss Me, Stupid* was condemned by the Catholic Legion of Decency. Meanwhile *Hawaii*, the Mirisch's first 'blockbuster' at 189 minutes, contained shots of bare-breasted islanders. The 'difference' from the mid-sixties small screen fare could not have been clearer. (Nevertheless, Mirisch sequels are evidence of the application of the company's TV logic to its film productions.)

Mirisch's strategy of sweating its cinematic assets, and monetizing its narrative arcs and characters, saw it initiating a series of sequels to *The Pink Panther* (the first of which was released in 1964), *The Magnificent Seven* (the first of three sequels appeared in 1966), two separate adaptations of different sections of James Michener's bestseller – *Hawaii* was followed by *The Hawaiians*, *In the Heat of the Night* spawned two sequels, while animated film and TV series were spun off from *The Pink Panther*. *The Pink Phink* (Freleng and Pratt, 1964) even won an Oscar for Best Animated Short. *Hawaii* was the number one box office attraction of the year in 1966.⁷⁶ In 1968 *In the Heat of*

---

⁷⁴ Balio, 1987: 180.
⁷⁵ Porter, 2004: 23.
⁷⁶ David Bordwell, *The Way Hollywood Tells It: Story and Style in Modern Movies*, University of California Press, 2006: 200.

the Night won five Oscars, including both Best Picture and Best Adapted Screenplay. Mirisch also proved a reliable earner for UA until the late 1960s. *West Side Story* was UA's fourth biggest box office hit of the decade, *Hawaii* eighth, *Irma La Douce* ninth, *In the Heat of the Night* eleventh and *The Russians Are Coming, The Russians Are Coming* (Jewison, 1966) twelfth.[77]

Runaway production

Porter notes that 'mobility of production' could be a significant contributor to a company's success in its maturity, as 'the firm moves its crew from country to country to build projects' and that mobile production can also facilitate a company's competitive strategy on the global market.[78] Three fundamental factors led Hollywood independents, like Mirisch, to consider shooting movies abroad. First, it was often considerably cheaper than filming in Hollywood. Second, it allowed American filmmakers to take advantage of generous foreign subsidies and legal loopholes surrounding 'co-production' deals. Third, it gave producers potential access to so-called 'frozen funds', foreign revenues earned in local currency by US distributors that often could not be withdrawn because of restrictive regulations. While such funds could not be removed, film rushes could. American distributors, like United Artists, could thus finance independent producers to make films using their own blocked currency and then exhibit them worldwide. It is thus ironically appropriate that the first literary property Mirisch acquired seems to have been the novel *The Border Jumpers* (Brown, 1955) which was the basis for *Man of the West*, as the company subsequently became controversial for its enthusiastic embrace of so-called runaway production.

Aware of the inflation of film production costs in the United States and the increasing impact of international box office takings on the profitability of American productions, Mirisch began producing more of its films abroad. Having identified 'inefficiency in production' in Hollywood and the appeal of foreign subsidies like the Eady Levy, Walter Mirisch concluded: 'American films must continue to fill the screens of the world . . . America must continue to be the center of the world's film making industry.'[79] Meanwhile Harold Mirisch argued: 'There are pictures which should be made overseas. The standard by which these pictures can be identified is simply this: If it is not made overseas, is it therefore impossible to make this picture?'[80]

The first of Mirisch's second group of twenty films was *633 Squadron* which subsequently spawned a cycle of six 'British' Second World War films, all also subsidized with support from Britain's Eady Levy.[81] In fact, eleven of these twenty films were shot outside the United States. Of the sixty-eight films Mirisch produced for UA,

---

[77] Bordwell, 2006: 191–204.
[78] Porter, 2004: 281.
[79] Mirisch, 'Make Way for Tomorrow?' 1960: 21–4.
[80] 'Pros and Cons re Runaway' (1960) *Variety*, 7.12.60, 11.
[81] Mirisch, 2008: 204.

thirty-one were produced entirely or largely outside the United States, as was the first season of its most successful live-action TV series, *Rat Patrol* (made in Spain). Mirisch produced three films in Mexico, four in Spain, four in Germany, nine in the UK, two in Italy, one in Ireland, one in Switzerland, one in Yugoslavia, one in France, one in Canada and another in Israel, as well as several in multiple international locations. This strategy caused conflict with the unions but the push factor of wage inflation at home, combined with the pull factor of lower salaries, national subsidies, and allowances abroad, proved irresistible.

The final United Artists contract

The final period of Mirisch's exclusive relationship with UA (1968–74) saw *Fiddler on the Roof* winning three Oscars and becoming the 'most profitable UA release up to that time'.[82] However, *The Thomas Crown Affair* and *Fiddler* and, to a lesser extent, *Mr Majestyk*, were Mirisch's last successes for UA, critically or commercially. Porter defines this period of any business as decline, often characterized by an inability to decide between cost leadership and differentiation. Mirisch continued attempting to balance low-cost production (for its 'programme pictures', the final entries in *The Magnificent Seven* franchise, a pair of unsuccessful *In the Heat of the Night* spin-offs and the Second World War cycle) with bigger budgeted 'quality films' which were decreasing as a proportion of output, with only a few prestige adaptations (*Fiddler*, *The Hawaiians* and *Gaily Gaily*, the latter pair even more unsuccessful than the first was successful) – indeed fewer adaptations of any kind.

Porter describes a strategy he terms 'harvesting' for companies in decline and outlines the threats and opportunities posed by demographics – both of management and consumers – by market shifts, and by the disadvantages of family businesses at a time of rapid change.[83] In the face of an industry-wide recession, Mirisch deployed Porter's 'harvest strategy' by 'taking advantage of whatever residual strengths the business has in order to raise prices or reap benefits of past goodwill'.[84] *Fiddler on the Roof* was its final roadshow film, with limited engagements, pre-booking and high-ticket prices. Otherwise, this period saw their final five sequels – *Inspector Clouseau* (Yorkin, 1968), *Guns of the Magnificent Seven*, *They Call Me MISTER Tibbs* (Douglas, 1970), *The Organization* (Medford, 1971) and *The Magnificent Seven Ride* (McCowan, 1972). But Mirisch, through its contract with UA, lost the IP of *The Pink Panther* franchise after the first three films, while for the same reason an *In the Heat of the Night* TV series was produced by a rival company.

In 1968 United Artists acquired the Mirisch Corporation's back catalogue[85] while the Mirisches formed the Mirisch Production Company, credited with fourteen

---

[82] Balio, 1987: 143.
[83] Porter, 2004: 269–70.
[84] Ibid, 269.
[85] Balio, 1987: 191.

films, as well as Mirisch Films and Oakmont, which between them oversaw several 'British' films, including the Second World War cycle. That cycle of six films based on *633 Squadron*'s blueprint was specifically designed so that they 'would all comply with the Eady Plan requirements, would all be made in the $1 million cost bracket, and would all have a military theme . . . each of the films had a recognizable American personality in the lead . . . and they all had American directors'.[86]

This was unequivocally a return to low-budget filmmaking, Porter's cost leadership strategy. *Variety*'s reviewers relegated *Submarine X-1* to the 'supporting half of a double bill';[87] *Mosquito Squadron* was 'For double bills';[88] and *The Last Escape* (Grauman, 1970) was 'Slated for double-bill programs'.[89] *Mosquito Squadron* was even promoted as a sequel to *633 Squadron*. These films recycled footage – the former even reused the air raid from the latter – as well as character tropes and narrative arcs and all were sold swiftly to television. Perhaps the most flagrant example of such 'harvesting', however, was *Massacre Harbor* which simply assembled three episodes of *Rat Patrol* (which had themselves recycled footage from Mirisch's *The Great Escape*) as a stand-alone feature, eliminating opening and closing episode credits and pre-title recaps while eschewing any additional sequences.

When Harold Mirisch died in 1968 the company still had twenty-eight films to deliver on its contract with UA. Harold is often credited as the most talented of the brothers, without whom, it is alleged, Walter and Marvin struggled. But the late sixties also proved problematic for Mirisch and its peers for less personal reasons. In 1967 UA was bought by Transamerica while Krim and Benjamin, with whom the Mirisches had nurtured longstanding relationships, decided to retire from day-to-day management. In 1968 a new rating system replaced the Production Code Administration and Mirisch entered an era of screen permissiveness around sex, violence and drugs with which they never seemed comfortable. Furthermore, the entire film industry was in recession in 1969–71. Porter notes that 'product innovation can improve an industry's circumstances' but Mirisch signally failed to innovate in this period, with the exceptions of *The Landlord*, *Gaily Gaily* and *The Party* – none of which worked at the box office and only the first of which, to this viewer, rewards critical re-evaluation.[90] However, *The Party* certainly has its admirers and is notable for its reliance on improvisation.

Porter remarks that 'there seems to be a tendency for firms in difficulty to flip back and forth over time among the generic strategies . . . such an approach is almost always doomed to failure'.[91] He identifies three contributory factors for corporate failure: 'Technological Substitution', discussed earlier; 'Demographics': 'shrinkage in the size of customer group that purchases the product' (which could be potentially offset by

---

[86] Mirisch, 2008: 20. The Eady Plan was intended to support the production of 'British' films via subsidy but attracted American subsidiaries and American top-line talent working with the required quota of British casts, crews, locations and facilities.
[87] 'Submarine X-1', *Variety*, 27.8.69: 3.
[88] 'Mosquito Squadron', *Variety*, 6.7.70: 3.
[89] 'The Last Escape', *Variety*, 29.5.70: 3.
[90] Porter, 2004: 169.
[91] Ibid, 42.

changes in the ages of the talent group making and/or the customer group purchasing the product); and 'Shifts in Needs' (which he defines as sociological or other factors resulting in changing tastes).⁹²

Discussing demographic change, Porter notes: 'products catering to the 25–35-year-old age group are currently enjoying the effects of a post-World War II baby boom'.⁹³ This change in the demographics of the market seems to have been virtually ignored by Mirisch until it was too late, and anyway, the brothers seem to have been out of sync – and sympathy – with the times. In 1970, *Daily Variety* reported that Walter Mirisch was sceptical about what he referred to as

> the new rules of picture making. We're not supposed to use any stars. Make only cheap pictures. Don't talk to anyone over 20 and get rid of all the studios. There's certainly much truth in them, but a lot of the present problems have developed from a terrible amount of mismanagement. We've tried to make the films of general satisfaction that did the job and covered the table. Those films tended to bleach out. Audiences have become more and more fragmented, and, of course, the young audience is the easiest to reach. But I'm still interested in the stay-at-homes. For Mr. Nixon, they are the silent majority. For us, they are the stay-at-home majority. We think 'Fiddler' has that immense worldwide appeal to reach them.⁹⁴

John R. Beckett's *Principles of Management*. which was sent to attendees among its subsidiaries at Transamerica's annual management conference in 1969, along with Drucker's latest book, *The Age of Discontinuity*, quotes Drucker on declining businesses. (Mirisch was not itself a subsidiary of Transamerica, though it was wholly dependent on its deal with one such subsidiary, United Artists.) 'Under such circumstances a major industry will rarely put its best brains to work on basic changes. It will rather tend to fritter away its energies on desperate efforts to keep yesterday going a little longer.'⁹⁵ Drucker's recommendation for reversing such decline was radical.

> When change is needed – when the return on equity capital begins to go into a declining trend line – we must look to our young men [*sic*], or men young in outlook, for leadership. . . . I would like to see us reduce the age of retirement of our top leaders, our board chairmen and our presidents. I would like to see our corporation move toward compulsory retirement of the top executive of the corporation and each of its subsidiaries by age 60.⁹⁶

---

⁹² Porter, 2004, 258–9.
⁹³ Ibid, 165.
⁹⁴ Walter Mirisch quoted in 'Just for Variety', *Daily Variety*, 23.2.70, 11.
⁹⁵ Drucker, quoted in John Beckett, *Principles of Management*, 5.
⁹⁶ 'Principles of Management', 7.

Fiddler was, indeed, a major hit, but such successes were both vanishingly rare and yet increasingly vital to the economic logic of the system – the days of relying on a range of, more or less profitable, productions were almost over and the era of the blockbuster was arriving. While Mirisch had made 'big pictures' in the past – notably *West Side Story* and *Hawaii* – they were never really central to its strategy, particularly once UA reined in Mirisch's budgets and productivity. There was another potential strategy, a renewed focus on more 'adult' material, challenging film censors and exceeding the permissible standards, verbal and visual, of the small screen. But Walter Mirisch was adamant: 'The public is fed up with X and R films. The business has been built up by moviegoers who don't go to theatres to hear four-letter words.'[97] For the time being, however, that business seemed to have run its course, bar one or two 'must-see' blockbuster family films every year.

Demographics and youth

The year 1968 was, in many senses, the end of the family audience (though Mirisch was slow to notice the youth audience – and distinctly unsuccessful at addressing it – *The Landlord* aside. *Halls of Anger* (Bogart, 1970), and worse *The First Time* (Neilson, 1969), *Some Kind of a Nut* (Kanin, 1969) featuring Dick Van Dyke as a rebellious banker (!) and *The Spikes Gang*, with its calculated reunion of *American Graffiti's* (Lucas, 1973) stars, all failed at the box office. Mirisch meanwhile continued to target those who were no longer regular cinemagoers, with films in familiar male and/or older audience genres which no longer tempted those who were.

In 1970, while the likes of Robert Evans (then forty) and Peter Bart (then thirty-eight) were running Paramount, the Mirisch brothers were a decade or two older – aged forty-nine (Walter), and fifty-two (Marvin). (Harold, had he lived, would have been sixty-three.) Porter asks: 'Are there patterns in the places from which outsiders are hired into the company as an indication of the direction the company might be taking?'[98] At Mirisch, none of the producer-director hyphenates they hired – like Wilder, Sturges, Jewison, Edwards and Hill – were among the 'younger' demographic in the industry hierarchy. Indeed, while the movie brat/film school directors were in their late twenties and thirties, Mirisch directors were all in their forties, fifties and sixties. None of Mirisch's directors were film school graduates; most were war veterans, and all had served long apprenticeships in the film and television industries. The only 'Movie Brat' director to work for the Mirisches, indeed their only first-time director, Hal Ashby, was not only the oldest of that entire group but had worked in the industry for almost two decades before getting his break. As well as hiring the 'wrong' directors, they worked in the 'wrong' genres for the movie brats, eschewing 'disreputable' and sensational forms like horror, science fiction and youth exploitation pictures for their

---

[97] *Daily Variety*, 30.10.70: 2.
[98] Porter, 2004: 52.

B movie associations. The Mirisch 'corporate culture' was no longer in sync with the culture of the cinema going audience, nor indeed with much of the cinema that appealed to it.

Having begun as a small family business with a handful of full-time staff, by 1969 the company had three vice presidents (including for Business Affairs and Advertising and Publicity), assistant VPs, assistant treasurers and assistant secretaries. With the death of Harold Mirisch, Marvin became CEO, while Walter became president and executive head of production. In fact, the end of the decade proved traumatic for the family. Walter, Marvin and Harold's father died in 1968. Harold himself died in December that same year. The mother of the two surviving brothers died in 1969. Their half-brother, Irving, died in 1971. As Walter recalled, 'It was devastating.'[99] But this seems to have only reinforced the two brothers' relationship. However, if the family business had been a force for cohesiveness a decade earlier, it was now arguably an obstacle to change. As Porter suggests, 'the old informality and personal friendships may be hard to maintain' noting that this may be particularly true of family businesses.[100] Hollywood business was changing – and so were the films themselves – old alliances and assumptions were being challenged.

The transformation of Hollywood in the decade and a half from the late fifties to the mid-seventies is echoed in the transformation of an independent production company from what had been a small family business into a corporation. UA itself was now owned by Transamerica, an insurance company of the kind satirized in *The Apartment*. It is ironic, to say the least, that a company that was satirizing corporations (including film corporations, with a pointed reference to 'the big five' in the opening narration of *The Apartment*) at the beginning of the decade, had become one itself by the end of it. The Mirisch brothers may not have been WASPs, but they were decidedly as unhip as the protagonist of *The Landlord*, if considerably more entrepreneurial.

Transamerica's acquisition of UA led to cutbacks and Mirisch was forced to reduce staff, cut overheads and cancel contracts with name talent. But Mirisch had demonstrated to UA that directors were key to critical and commercial success, while its own indulgence of some 'auteurs' pales in comparison with the *Heaven's Gate* (Cimino, 1980) fiasco which destroyed UA. The Mirisch back catalogue dramatically enhanced the value of UA's film library when the latter was finally sold to MGM. Both at the box office and industry awards ceremonies and among critics Mirisch films performed proportionally better than their peers, cementing UA's reputation as a distributor.

However, like UA, Mirisch failed to attract any film school directors. Nevertheless, Mirisch re-popularized sequels a decade before they became known as franchises, was an early adopter of remakes, particularly of international films, repopularized cinematic cycles, routinized runaway production and was an innovator in saturation release and spot advertising. But as a *family* business it proved, perhaps understandably, unresponsive to the decline of the *family* audience and unable or unwilling to cater to teenagers. The brothers eschewed what they saw as the exploitation genres which

---

[99] Mirisch, 2008, 272.
[100] Porter, 2004: 252–3.

they hoped to have left behind, but which were to fuel the success of *Jaws* and *Star Wars* and the movie brats who made them. However, Mirisch's dual strategy remains something of a missing link, both in business terms and cinematically, between the end of the studio system and the blockbuster franchise films and idiosyncratic Indiewood movies which characterize two aspects of Hollywood today. But in the age of *Easy Rider* (Hopper, 1969), those dual competitive strategies simply ran out of road.

4

The organization

Corporate culture and the Mirisch Company as 'author'

Calvera: What I don't understand is, why a man like you took the job in the first place? Why?

Chris: I wonder myself.

Calvera: Oh come on, come on, tell me why.

Vin: Like a fellow I once knew in El Paso. One day he just took all his clothes off and jumped in a mess of cactus. So I asked him the same question, why?

Calvera: And?

Vin: He said it seemed to be a good idea at the time.

(*The Magnificent Seven*, 1960)

House style

Vin's (Steve McQueen) response to Calvera in *The Magnificent Seven* prompts another question, why particular projects seem like 'good ideas' at specific times in Hollywood history. Too often the answers have revolved around either directorial genius or a more general context, either auteurism or the zeitgeist. Another, film industrially specific answer, the idea of studio 'house style' and the role it played in the era of the vertically integrated companies, when the majors had actors, writers, directors, designers, cameramen, editors and composers on contract, has been discussed elsewhere. In an essay on the director Raoul Walsh and his 1940s films for Warner Brothers, for instance, Edward Buscombe noted that 'What seems to be lacking is any conception of the relations between the economic structure of a studio, its particular organization and the kind of films it produced'.[1] Buscombe suggested that 'working for a studio

---

[1] Edward Buscombe, 'Walsh and Warner Bros', in Phil Hardy (ed), *Raoul Walsh*, Edinburgh Film Festival, 1974, 54.

with as distinctive a policy and style as Warners imposed a number of constraints on any director. Yet these constraints should not be thought of as merely negative in their operation. Working for the studio meant simply that the possibilities for good work lay in certain directions rather than in others'.[2] House style contests the auteur theory with what might be called an atelier theory, in which the studio rather than the director is ultimate author. But Mirisch was neither a studio, nor ever owned its own studio facilities.

'House style' is not a new idea. Leo Rosten, in his book, *The Movie Colony*, published in 1940, proposed that 'Each studio has a personality ... in the final analysis, the sum total of a studio's personality ... may be traced to its producers'.[3] Similarly, Mae D. Huettig's *Control of the Motion Picture Industry*, published in 1944, argued that 'the structure of the major companies is important because there is a real and direct connection between the way in which they are set up, the kind of people who run them, and the kind of films produced'.[4] This, it seems to me, is a far more inclusive approach to the production of Hollywood films, than one which attributes them either to the fingerprints of one particular figure, the director (auteur theory) or that sees in them only a reflection of a general American ethos (zeitgeist theory). Of course, Mirisch adapted properties which were currently Broadway hits or on Bestseller lists and addressed topical issues while tapping into box office trends and availing themselves of any industrial opportunities. More importantly, however, this approach includes both the moment and the conditions of production in its analysis of Hollywood (or any other) films. It reunites texts with their respective production contexts, insisting that the specific culture of (a) production (in this case a corporate culture) impacts on, and is imprinted in, its production of culture. As Denise Mann puts it, it reveals 'the intrinsic symmetries between the cultures of production and the production of culture'.[5]

The case for corporate authorship

Among several recent contributors to this field, Jerome Christensen's *Corporate Art: The Studio Authorship of Hollywood Motion Pictures*, focuses on the vertically integrated major studios and principally discusses the studio era. Christensen insists on a distinction between 'house style' and what he calls 'corporate art'. For while the former is intended to establish 'a brand identity in the eyes of the audience'.[6] Indeed, for Christensen,

> Corporate art always counts as a tool of corporate strategy – that is, as one of a set of actions taken to attain competitive advantage which are coordinated and

---

[2] Ibid.
[3] Leo Rosten, quoted in Schatz, 1988: 7–8.
[4] Mae D. Huettig, quoted in Christensen, 2012: 14.
[5] Mann, 2008: 24.
[6] Christensen, 2012: 2.

implemented by executives, who can successfully claim the authority to interpret the intent of the corporation and project a policy that will advance its particular interests, whether financial, social, cultural, or political.

And he suggests that 'A studio . . . may find certain dramatic situations . . . convenient vehicles for allegorizing its corporate strategy.'[7] Corporate art is thus, for Christensen, aimed not only at the cinema audience, but also at competitor companies and among potential employees in the film industry itself.

Christensen's insight that the Hollywood studios' output was thus always, at one level, about Hollywood itself, is also neither a new nor even an exclusively academic one. Films reflect, or refract, not 'the zeitgeist', nor, indeed, only the specific and carefully constructed world in front of the camera, but also the particular conditions of production behind it. JD Connor begins his book, *The Studios After the Studios: Post-Classical Hollywood 1970–2010*, by quoting Peter Biskind's remark about *Greystoke* (Hudson, 1984), 'Like every Hollywood movie, on some level, it was about the business.'[8] Of course, if all films are 'about the business' then the question is what distinguishes them? What specifically do they have to say about the business, and at which moments in a company's history do they say it most audibly? In this chapter, I attempt to identify particular moments when rebranding a production company or stressing a specific characteristic of the way it does business might have amounted to a conscious corporate strategy or, at the very least, an unconscious concern for the Mirisch Company.

Connor's book is just one of several recent studies of Hollywood which have attempted to flesh out Huettig's 'connection' more precisely, arguing the case not only for corporate authorship but also for the contention that Hollywood films have often, if not always, allegorized the corporate strategy of their producing organizations. Christensen's *Corporate Art* devotes five of its seven chapters to the period up to 1968. Connor brings this approach up to date, by focusing on the period from 1970 to 2010. Jeff Menne's recent *Post-Fordist Cinema: Hollywood Auteurs and Corporate Counterculture* fills in the gap between those two volumes by discussing the so-called American Renaissance, specifically the years 1962–75. Between them, then, these three studies describe the industrial terrain from the founding of the Mirisch Company in 1957 to the two surviving brothers' move from UA to Universal in 1974, the year *Jaws* was greenlit (a film which both Connor and Menne discuss at some length). None of them, perhaps predictably, mentions Mirisch.

Christensen explains that 'With the phrase *corporate studio*, I include those Hollywood production companies that were actually incorporated (such as Samuel Goldwyn Inc) . . . and production companies that shared the structure, practices, and objectives of the major studios (Universal Pictures, Selznick International, and United Artists after 1950).'[9] In fact, of course, UA was *not* then a production

---

[7] Ibid, 2, 7.
[8] Connor, 2015: 1.
[9] Christensen, 2012: 13.

company at all – instead it financed and distributed the films made by independent production companies – and the Mirisch Company was one such company, with a distinctive corporate culture of its own. As such, a corporation like Mirisch was indeed constituted, among other things, of a hierarchy of 'actual persons', comprised at its top by the three Mirisches, Harold, Marvin and Walter. The Mirisch brothers were, crucially, both the owners of the company and its managers. In Schein's seminal study *Organizational Culture and Leadership* and specifically his article on media culture from an organizational culture perspective, he defines organizational culture as 'a pattern of shared assumptions that was learned by a group as it solved the problems of external adaptation and internal integration'.[10] To deconstruct that culture, Schein suggests the analysis of artefacts, espoused beliefs and underlying assumptions – and I analyse all three in what follows. For Schein, 'artefacts' refers to logos, promotional materials and artistic creations; 'espoused beliefs' to officially expressed strategies in interviews, industry reports and PR pronouncements; and 'underlying assumptions' to taken-for-granted beliefs and feelings.[11]

The Mirisches as social commentators

The three brothers did, apparently, have pronounced socio-political views. Walter explained the company's selection of projects to film critic Elvis Mitchell, in 2008, in a radio interview to publicize his autobiography, 'When they were serious subjects, they reflected my own or my brothers' viewpoints on society . . . We try basically to make films that are gonna please ourselves and then we hope that audiences will agree with us. They don't always'.[12] This was certainly the case for films which replicated the Mirisch's own liberal social attitudes, including such hymns to tolerance and against bigotry as *West Side Story, The Children's Hour, In the Heat of the Night* and *Fiddler on the Roof*, all of which shared a literal reliance on pretexts.

According to Schein, an organization's underlying assumptions are often revealed through the ways in which resources are allocated and the rewards and status conferred on its members.[13] In the case of the Mirisch Company, the tradition of allocating large budgets to adaptations of middlebrow hits of stage and page and of being parsimonious at best with more traditional genre productions (including Westerns, thrillers and war movies) led them to reinforce the cultural class system between prestige and 'programme' subjects and styles, a system which was to be

---

[10] Edgar H. Schein, *Organizational Culture and Leadership*, 2004, San Francisco Jossey-Bass, 2004; and Schein, 'The Culture of Media Viewed from an Organizational Culture Perspective', *The International Journal on Media Management* vol 5 no iii, 2003: 17.
[11] Schein, 2003: 171.
[12] *The Treatment*, KRCW, 18.6.08 https://www.kcrw.com/culture/shows/the-treatment/walter-mirisch
[13] Schein, 2004: 257–9.

turned on its head by the genre exercises which established the Movie Brats in the 1970s, with what were essentially inflated science fiction, gangster and monster movies – or, as has often been said, the equivalents of B films on A budgets. The Mirisch Company made no such science fiction or gangster films. Indeed, having overseen some successful and stylish 'B' film noirs at Allied Artists, the Mirisches turned their back on such fare and aimed, increasingly, at 'A' subjects and styles. Their one independent horror film, *Dracula* (Badham, 1979) had to wait until their arrival at Universal, the ancestral studio home of the genre, and it too was a stage adaptation.

The culture at the Mirisch Company was socially liberal but also literal, Jewish, entrepreneurial, Democrat-leaning, anti-racist, social realist, middlebrow and family-friendly. Their films touched on topical 'issues', not only because of these views but also because controversy brought publicity and publicity brought cinemagoers to the box office. Nevertheless, their liberal leanings are evidenced by some of the people they hired. Leo Penn, the star of Walter Mirisch's first film for Monogram as producer, *Fall Guy*, was making his screen debut as a leading man, after an uncredited appearance in *The Best Years of Our Lives* (Wyler, 1946). Penn was a leftist, subsequently blacklisted for refusing to name names by HUAC. At Allied Artists and Moulin Productions the Mirisches worked with Jose Ferrer (star of *Moulin Rouge*), Orson Welles (co-star of *Moby Dick*), John Huston (director of both), screenwriters Michael Wilson (who was uncredited for *Friendly Persuasion*) and Richard Collins (who scripted both *Riot in Cell Block 11* and *Invasion of the Body Snatchers*), all of whose names were included on the infamous 1950 *Red Channels* list of 151 alleged 'un-Americans' in broadcasting, accused of having communist affiliations.[14]

The Mirisch Company itself also employed ex-blacklistees and friendly witnesses alike. Dalton Trumbo, screenwriter of *Hawaii* and, uncredited, of *Town Without Pity*, actors Lee J. Cobb, who had been a friendly witness in front of HUAC – as had the film's star, Gary Cooper – in *Man of the West*, and the blacklisted actress, Lee Grant, who appeared in both *In the Heat of the Night and The Landlord*, being cast in the former after an enforced twelve-year absence from the screen. Such well-known liberals as composer Leonard Bernstein, Walter Bernstein, the uncredited, but primary, screenwriter of *The Magnificent Seven* and Elmer Bernstein, who composed the latter's celebrated score, all worked for Mirisch. Martin Ritt, briefly in line to direct *The Magnificent Seven*, Garson Kanin, who wrote and directed *Some Kind of a Nut*, Howard Koch, who scripted *633 Squadron*, Isobel Lennart, a friendly witness who regretted testifying for the rest of her life, and adapted *Two for the Seesaw, By Love Possessed* and *Fitzwilly (Mann, 1967)* also worked for the company. Mirisch also produced adaptations of two plays by the once blacklisted Lillian Hellman – *The Children's Hour* and *Toys in the Attic*. All of the above were also named in *Red Channels*' eponymous list. (*The Children's Hour* itself, of course, filmed in the immediate aftermath of HUAC,

---

[14] *Red Channels: The Report of Communist Influence in Radio and Television*, 1950, American Business Consultants, publishers of Counterattack, 'the newsletter of facts to combat Communism'.

functions as a commentary on the destructiveness of gossip, bigotry and indeed mass hysteria, as does *Town Without Pity*.) That amounts to 15 of the 151 *Red Channels* names, 10 per cent of the total, who were employed, sometimes repeatedly, by the Mirisches, individually or corporately, over their career. This seems to me a significant percentage, but one might argue that, by 1957, and certainly after 1960, such signings were considerably less controversial. Nevertheless, such an employment policy can be taken as, at the very least, an indication of a lack of antipathy towards leftists. (It is also the case, however, that ex-blacklistees may have been cheaper to hire than their industry peers.)

Trumbo and Koch had both been named as early as 1946. Huston had been one of the organizers of the Committee of the First Amendment in 1947, which Billy Wilder was involved in, too. Richard Collins was called to testify before the first HUAC hearings in 1947 and was only subsequently hired by Allied Artists to write *Riot* and *Body Snatchers*, having renounced his previous membership of the Communist Party. *Invasion of the Body Snatchers*, of course, has been the subject of intense debate regarding its alleged allegory of a communist invasion or, conversely, the perils of McCarthyism. In 1949, the Americanism Division of the American Legion published its own blacklist and Lillian Hellman was on it. In 1951 HUAC launched its second investigation of Hollywood and communism and Elmer Bernstein was an Unfriendly Witness. It is often claimed that it was Kirk Douglas publicly hiring Dalton Trumbo to write *Spartacus* (Kubrick, 1960), which finally broke the blacklist, but it is worth noting that both Trumbo and Douglas also worked for Mirisch about the same time. Daniel Taradash, the original screenwriter on *Hawaii*, left the project, to be replaced by Trumbo in October 1961, but Trumbo must have been employed by Mirisch at least a year earlier himself, since *Town Without Pity*, on which he did rewrites, was released in Germany and Austria in March that same year and was already shooting in October 1960.

Mirisch as a Jewish company

It is often argued that HUAC anti-communism was, among other things, a convenient cover for antisemitism, and it is indeed striking how many of those named were Jewish, just as it is unmissable how many Mirisch employees were Jewish. But without research beyond the capacity of this volume, it is impossible to say whether the Mirisch Company hired a disproportionate number of people with Jewish heritage compared with other Hollywood companies. Certainly, antisemitism figured on-screen in several of its films (the post-Holocaust premise of *Return from the Ashes*, the struggle for an independent Jewish homeland in *Cast a Giant Shadow* and the pogroms of *Fiddler on the Roof*) and anti-racism more generally is pivotal in several more, from the scene in which Chris and Vin first meet in *The Magnificent Seven*, over a town's refusal to bury a dead Indian, to the colonialism depicted in *Hawaii* and *The Hawaiians*, to the racially reverberating slap in *In the Heat of the Night*, school bussing in *Halls of Anger* and accusations of miscegenation in *The Landlord*. Similarly, if *West Side Story*'s

Polish emigree youths pre-existed the Mirisch film, in the original Broadway musical, *Some Like It Hot's* half-Polish Sugar Kane Kowalczyk did not. Mirisch also considered buying the rights to black playwright, Lorraine Hansberry's stage hit, *Raisin in the Sun*. After the Broadway premiere, UA, Paramount, Fox, Mirisch and Harry Belafonte all expressed interest, but in March 1959 the film rights went to David Susskind.

Racial difference motivates the antagonism between the Puerto Rican and white (Polish) gangs in *West Side Story* and is explicit in the song "America". Counter-intuitively, the Broadway production had bowdlerized Stephen Sondheim's original lyrics so that, on stage, the song 'cites almost exclusively the material advantages of the American experience... The movie version of "America" emphasizes quite sharply the social disadvantages, the ethnic and racial prejudice, and even the violence to which the immigrant is exposed'.[15]

> **Girls**: Life is all right in America
> **Boys**: If you're all white in America
> **Girls**: Here you are free and you have pride
> **Boys**: 'Long as you stay on your own side
> **Girls**: Free to be anything you choose
> **Boys**: Free to wait tables and shine shoes.[16]

According to Acevedo-Munoz, the impetus for these changes came from screenwriter, Ernest Lehman (163), but Misha Berson notes that 'Sondheim, obliged to tweak some "objectionable" lyrics at the request of the producers, was pleased about certain changes – the substitution of the original version of "America"'.[17] These 'producers', of course, included the uncredited Producer Robert Wise and Executive Producer Walter Mirisch. The Mirisches would have specifically felt the sting – and the familiarity – of the Polish Jets being described as 'immigrant scum'.

More significantly, perhaps, the brothers' Jewishness, their father having fled to New York from pogroms in Poland, the family then having to relocate themselves again to Wisconsin, when his small tailoring business went bankrupt, and Walter's own experience of antisemitism in academia, all contributed to an inevitable feeling of otherness for the family. This sense of illegitimacy created an instinctive empathy for projects focusing on protagonists exhibiting precisely such homelessness ('bezdomność' in Polish). This may explain a disproportionate deployment of the 'fish out of water' formula in their films, from *In the Heat of the Night*, included in the BFI's top ten fish-out-of-water films list, to *Some Like It Hot* (also mentioned in that list).[18] Indeed, a predilection for or predisposition towards stories which presented such situations sympathetically seems to

---

[15] Ernesto Acevedo-Munoz, *West Side Story as Cinema: The Making of an American Masterpiece*, University Press of Kansas, 2013, 162–3.
[16] Lyrics from 'America' in the 1960 film, but not the original Broadway show, quoted in Acevedo-Munoz, 164.
[17] Misha Berson, *Something's Coming, Something Good: West Side Story and the American Imagination*, 2011, Applause Theatre and Cinema Books, 157.
[18] https://www2.bfi.org.uk/news-opinion/news-bfi/lists/10-great-fish-out-water-films

have been characteristic of Mirisch, providing some of the parameters and perimeters, the premises – and lack of premises (in both senses of the word) – for many of their productions and protagonists. Ironically, perhaps their best-known previous production, *Moby Dick*, was a literal attempt to get a 'fish' (or marine mammal) out of water, but one which almost sank them. Of course, director-centred criticism traditionally sees such themes as auteurist fingerprints.[19] But, as I hope is demonstrated in what follows, the theme of homelessness, the fish-out-of-water formula, recurs regularly throughout the Mirisch filmography, far beyond the films Wilder made for them.

A quick scan of Mirisch's sixty-eight titles for UA reveals *Fort Massacre* (cavalry troop lost in Indian territory), *Man of the West* (ageing outlaw going 'straight'), *Some Like It Hot* (two male musicians on the run passing as members of an all-girl band), *Man in the Net* (New York couple escaping the big city for life in the countryside), *Cast a Long Shadow* (illegitimate son claiming his inheritance), *The Apartment* (office worker increasingly uneasy living the life of the corporate conformist), *The Magnificent Seven* (Americans in Mexico), *Town Without Pity* (American military in post-war Germany), *West Side Story* (Puerto Ricans and Poles in racist America), *One, Two, Three* (Americans in West Berlin), *Follow That Dream* (an Elvis vehicle, based on the novel *Pioneer, Go Home*, about a poor family forced to move their temporary home), *Two for the Seesaw* (small-town lawyer living as – and with – a big city beatnik), *Irma La Douce* (cop as pimp), *The Great Escape* (allied POWs in – and escaping from – Germany), *The Pink Panther* (idiot as detective), *Kiss Me, Stupid* (wife as hooker, hooker as wife, Dino as dinner guest), *Return from the Ashes* (Holocaust survivor in disguise returns to post-war Paris only to be asked to impersonate herself), *Cast a Giant Shadow* (American as Jewish freedom fighter), *What Did You Do in the War, Daddy?* (Americans in Italy), *Hawaii* (American missionaries as colonizers in Hawaii), *How to Succeed in Business Without Really Trying* (window cleaner as an executive), *In the Heat of the Night* (northern black cop in the deep south), *Fitzwilly* (butler as criminal mastermind), *The Party* (blacklisted actor at Hollywood party), *The Thomas Crown Affair* (businessman as bank-robber), *Some Kind of a Nut* (bank clerk becomes beatnik), *Gaily Gaily* (country boy in the big bad city), *The Landlord* (white millionaire moves into Brooklyn brownstone tenement, 'Everyone wants a home of his own, you know'), *Fiddler on the Roof* (Jewish villagers in – and ultimately forced out of – antisemitic Russia) and *Avanti* (brash American businessman and free-spirited British shopgirl-meet cute in Italy).

Mirisch films and anti-racism

Fort Massacre, Mirisch's first production and first release, set a precedent and laid down a marker for the company. It follows a cavalry troop, led by an Indian-hating sergeant,

---

[19] See, for instance, 'Home/Sick Locating Billy Wilder's Cinematic Austria in The Apartment, The Private Life of Sherlock Holmes and Fedora' by Robert Dassanowsky', *Journal of Austrian Studies* vol 46, no 3, Fall 2013: 1–25.

played by Joel McCrea. As the Paiute Indian says of him, 'The only good Indian is a dead Indian. That's what he thinks.' In the end, the last survivor, Travis, shoots the sergeant, to prevent him from killing the peaceful Paiute in cold blood. There are Black characters in *The Horse Soldiers* (featuring the first African-American tennis Grand Slam winner, Althea Gibson), *The Man in the Net*, *Irma La Douce* and, more centrally, in *The Fortune Cookie*, not to mention the later, more self-consciously 'black' projects. *Variety*'s otherwise extremely critical review of *They Call Me MISTER Tibbs*, concluded with the following aside:

> More than any film in memory, principals, supporting players, and extras are integrated, so that the police department, criminal elements, political campaign workers and street crowds of San Francisco become an unself-conscious, casual blending of blacks and whites. Unlike 'In the Heat of the Night,' race is never an issue. In fact, it is not even mentioned, let alone exploited. It is one of the very good things about 'Tibbs'.[20]

Such integrated casting could hardly have happened without the Mirisches' tacit approval, at the very least.

Social issues, like race, were implicit in the 'adult' movie strategy the company pursued, and its association with a notion of quality which was both aesthetic and ethical but also always economic. As Walter Mirisch himself put it, 'We try to make movies that have mass appeal, yet are first-rate artistically and state a meaningful theme,' explaining his idea of first-rate quality in terms of good taste. 'To me, good taste means good taste in terms of writing, directing, acting, scoring, editing, and all the other phases of the picture business,'[21] (This tautological notion of 'quality' cinema related, among other things, to the seriousness of the subjects they dealt with, the reputations of those involved and the provenance of the projects, including Broadway hits and best sellers, prize-winning authors, award-winning 'veteran' filmmakers and, indeed, previous films).

Liberalism and/as 'quality'

I have already discussed the Mirisch 'quality' strategy and will detail the corporate reliance on adaptations in a later chapter, but here it is worth briefly indicating other aspects of prestige and gestures towards an adult or art cinema mode in the company's output. Denise Mann notes that 'the number of social problem films dropped from 21 percent of all Hollywood films in 1947 to 9.5 percent by 1955'[22] But for Mirisch, a black and white, social realist aesthetic was characteristic of many of its 'serious' issue

---

[20] They Call Me Mr Tibbs, 'Review', *Variety*, 4.7.70.
[21] Mirisch quoted in Jeanine Basinger, Film Reference http://www.filmreference.com/Writers-and-Production-Artists-Me-Ni/Mirisch-Walter.html
[22] Mann, 2008: 148.

films of the early 1960s including *The Apartment, Town Without Pity, The Children's Hour, Two for the Seesaw* and even the shocking opening scene of *Return from the Ashes*. And the 'problems' depicted both centrally and peripherally in Mirisch productions, particularly in its early years, are striking. According to a 1959 survey, audiences could be lured back to the cinema by 'a realistic treatment of a social problem'[23] Meanwhile, controversy, including problems with the censors over the depiction of just such social problems, could also function as a marketing device. Ambitious attempts to deal sympathetically with hitherto taboo topics like rape – *Town Without Pity*, lesbianism – *The Children's Hour* and adultery – *Kiss Me, Stupid*, and all three ran into trouble with the censors.[24] The latter was even accused of 'moral brinkmanship' by the Legion of Decency[25] and was distributed by UA subsidiary, Lopert Films, to distance it from United Artists. If this was a strategy, it was one decidedly discontinued in the final years of the UA contract.

Despite such liberal good intentions, unconscious racism was occasionally detectable too – examples include Sellers' brownface in *The Party*, and the treatment of Arabs in *Cast a Giant Shadow* and *Rat Patrol/Massacre Harbor*. Mirisch movies may indeed have sympathetically depicted lesbianism (albeit tragically, in *The Children's Hour*), transvestism (albeit comically, in *Some Like It Hot*), rape (*Town Without Pity* and *A Rage to Live*) suicide (*Town Without Pity, The Children's Hour, By Love Possessed*) and attempted suicide (*The Apartment*). However, those committing or attempting suicide in such films are all women (Lemmon's Bud had attempted suicide off-screen), and all too often in Mirisch films, female characters are prostitutes. Thus, Polly the Pistol in *Kiss Me, Stupid*, the eponymous *Irma La Douce* and every other female character in that film, virtually every female role in *Gaily Gaily* and the murder victim in *They Call Me MISTER Tibbs* are all prostitutes. Such stereotypes perhaps reveal something of the sexism at Mirisch – as well as more widely in Hollywood at the time. (Significantly, the criticism embedded in the lyrics of *America* in *West Side Story* is delegated to the boys, the girls only see the sunny side of the United States.) Although the period of the company's third and final contract with UA coincided with women's liberation, this seems not to have impacted significantly on Mirisch productions, though civil rights and Black power visibly did. The liberalism of Mirisch movies was amply evidenced by the themes they tackled, and the language they used, but rarely by explicit images of sex or glamorized violence. These were post-studio-era productions, made largely within studio-era cinematic paradigms.

Indeed, if the period of prestige Mirisch productions up to the mid-sixties was often marked by a restrained social realism, the era from the mid-sixties on was dramatically different – and this cannot be entirely explained by wider industry shifts. The retreat from liberal social attitudes was mirrored by a withdrawal from tightly plotted narratives. Where the emphasis had previously been on understatement, now the tone

---

[23] 'Art Films and Eggheads', *Studies in Public Communication* no 2, Summer 1959: 10.
[24] See 'New Film Denied Seal of Approval', *New York Times*, 9.5.61: 45; 'Films Challenge Censorship Code', *New York Times*, 11.8.61: 18 and Mirisch, 2008: 209–11, respectively.
[25] 'Film Resume 1964', *Variety*, 6.1.65: 56.

was wilfully excessive, with the on-screen results including the would-be hilarious *The Hallelujah Trail, What Did You Do in the War, Daddy?, How to Succeed in Business Without Really Trying, The Party, Some Kind of a Nut*, as well as sections of *Sinful Davey* (Huston, 1969), *The Private Life of Sherlock Holmes* (Wilder, 1970) and *Gaily Gaily*. In *The Hallelujah Trail, The Party, Sinful Davey, The Private Life of Sherlock Holmes* and *Gaily Gaily* Mirisch paid the price for indulging its top talent, those filmmakers with multiple film contracts with the company – though Huston's second film for Mirisch never materialized and his relationship with Walter Mirisch never recovered. The comparative creative autonomy the company delegated to directors ultimately proved both critically and commercially catastrophic and subsequently the autonomy allocated to the company itself by UA was radically reduced, both financially and aesthetically. That a corporate culture can change and develop and that, in the case of a media company, the culture it produces can change too is central to Schein's argument. He writes that as companies grow, they mutate, and that 'deciding which elements become changed or preserved then becomes one of the tougher strategic decisions that leaders face'.[26] The shift from restrained social realism to a comedy of excess was just such a decision and one which eventually expensively backfired.

The films as evidence

The meanings of a company's films, Christensen proposes, 'cannot be deduced from a flow chart or a biography of an executive, or a table of revenues, or a theoretical model of the development of finance capitalism or a policy statement . . . but must be discovered by close examination of the particular motion pictures that are each corporation's individualized speech'.[27] To demonstrate this, Christensen selects a handful of films which he claims speak for the studio in question ('ventriloquizing corporations', as he puts it), implicitly omitting a far larger number of titles which conceivably do not.[28] This is necessarily less persuasive than an analysis of a larger selection of films combined with a consideration of the records of the company and the remarks of its employers and employees – as Schein suggests. In this volume, I discuss all sixty-eight films Mirisch produced for United Artists (as well as the subsequent five for Universal and a final film for UA) and its corporate strategy and explicit policy decisions. I draw on both biographical, financial and promotional data as well as on the films – and filmmakers – themselves.

Assuming Christensen, Biskind and Connor are correct, then every Mirisch film is also, in some sense, about the movie business, if not about the specific company itself. There is, indeed, a striking degree of reflexivity about many Mirisch films – *Some Like It Hot,* with its entertainment industry setting, *The Party,* which starts out in *medias*

---

[26] Schein, 2004: 317.
[27] Christensen, 2012: 13–14.
[28] Ibid, vii.

res on a film set with an actor on a movie being made by General Federal Studios, being sacked and indeed blacklisted by the industry, the opening shot of *The Landlord* and the final frame of *Gaily Gaily*, which both break the fourth wall of cinema. Steven Cohan's book on the 'backstudio picture' phenomenon contextualizes the several cycles of this 'genre' to 'significant crises in and transformations of the political economy of US film production' one of which he identifies as the mergers and takeovers of the majors in the late 1960s.[29] Certainly the merger with/acquisition of United Artists by Transamerica in April 1967 immediately precedes the production of *The Party* (which was filming from May to July that same year) and coincides with the pre-production of both *Gaily Gaily* and *The Landlord*. Curiously, Cohan does not discuss *The Party* or indeed mention Mirisch or any of its films. (For a discussion of the reflexivity of the Mirisch cycle of British war movies, which also coincides with this acquisition, see Chapter 8.)

There are even in-jokes about sequels in *Fitzwilly* and (the screenplay of) *The Pink Panther*. Furthermore, the Mirisch Company's entrepreneurial journey from being a small producer, itself the tenant of a studio (*The Apartment*, courtesy of Samuel Goldwyn Studio) to becoming a major independent player and dealmaker (*The Landlord*, made once the Mirisches were themselves shareholders in Transamerica/UA) is a paradigm-shifting one. Nevertheless, perhaps the small scale of the company meant that it was simply impossible to insulate the creatives from the business; nor indeed, does there seem to have been any desire for such a separation.

According to Connor, in the cinema's neoclassical era, 'Movies are movie movies.'[30] For Connor, '1970 serves as a rough beginning to a neoclassical era that had largely consolidated by 1975 '[31] This roughly coincides, perhaps significantly, with Mirisch's final deal with UA (1968–74). But neoclassical knowingness was visible in Mirisch movies well before 1970. *The Party* begins with a sequence set in India, in which it is revealed that the Peter Sellers character is in fact a ham actor in an Indian epic, which is being filmed on location. *The Landlord* opens with a brief glimpse of the director, Hal Ashby's, on-set wedding, with the film's producer, Norman Jewison, a visible guest. *Gaily Gaily* ends with a shot revealing that the brothel setting of the story was actually a film set.

Mirisch and the majors as 'authors'

For Connor, the history of film texts is also a history of the film industry in the studio era. As he explains,

> The Jazz Singer is the story of the assimilation of European Jews and the story of the Warner brothers becoming Warner Bros. On the Waterfront is the story of

---

[29] Steven Cohan, *Hollywood by Hollywood: The Backstudio Picture and the Mystique of Making Movies*, Oxford University Press, 2009, 11.
[30] Connor, 2015: 44.
[31] Ibid, 17.

organized crime on the waterfront and the story of naming names before HUAC. Red River is the story of the civilization of the West and the story of independent production and the perils of contract.[32]

Even if we accept the premise that the major studios' films ventriloquized their corporate masters' voices, however, can the same be said for independent production companies, which often entirely depended on those majors for finance and distribution, as Mirisch depended for seventeen years and sixty-eight films on United Artists? Menne's answer is definitive.

> The filmmaking, then, was farmed out to small production companies – sometimes housed in bungalows on the studio lot, sometimes located off-site – and in them, the auteur theory was like a management doctrine that helped to structure the small firm, insulate its labor from the executive layer, and generally lend its workplace the look of a maverick redoubt despite its dependency on the larger conglomerate enfolding it.[33]

The Mirisch Company was based very close to United Artists' Los Angeles HQ, renting a small suite of offices at Samuel Goldwyn Studio. According to Harold Mirisch, 'We do not own the bricks and mortar of studio buildings but utilize such facilities only when we need them. Nevertheless, we feel that we are a "major" studio in our thinking and our ability to translate this thinking into motion picture entertainment.'[34] This studio without walls was thus an ad hoc production base, just as the fortress in *Fort Massacre* was not a real fort, but simply a cliff dwelling, given its name by an embittered soldier tasked to defend and transform it into a makeshift fortress.

Menne, whose periodizing of New Hollywood (from 1962) is informed by the work of Denise Mann, identifies the self-incorporation of talent in independent production companies, which worked closely with the talent agencies, as decisive.

> I posit the small firm – the small production company in particular – as the unit of analysis for New Hollywood . . . Because these small firms were often started by actors or directors, individually or severally, it was more straightforward for them to project their personhood (i.e. star power) onto the firms' corporate agencies, and in turn for the firms' personhood to reflect on the stars.[35]

Mirisch, however, was founded and run not by actors or directors but by producers. Menne discusses two examples of such 'small firms', Kirk Douglas's Bryna Productions and Robert Altman's Lion's Gate.[36] Douglas himself starred in two films for Mirisch –

---

[32] Ibid, 42.
[33] Menne, 2019: 15.
[34] *Boxoffice*, 1.10.62: 8.
[35] Menne, 2019: 21.
[36] Ibid, 22.

Town Without Pity and *Cast a Giant Shadow*, the latter a co-production with his own Bryna Productions. Altman, meanwhile, only founded Lion's Gate, having twice lost out on an opportunity to direct *The Bells of Hell Go Ding a Ling a Ling* (the title has also been recorded as . . . *Ting a Ling a Ling* and . . . *A-Ling-A-Ling* as well as being known as *Death, Where is Thy Sting* and *The Chicken and the Hawk*) for the Mirisch Company.

In the mid-1960s Altman had developed a black comedy about First World War flyers and, with Cary Grant's agreement to participate, took it to Mirisch, who, despite a self-funded flying stunt which Altman shot, remained unconvinced he was experienced enough to direct. In February 1970, after an aborted five-week shoot with director David Miller and star Gregory Peck in Switzerland, the film was quietly abandoned. However, Altman seems to have been briefly re-involved as putative producer/director on the film in 1970, barely a month after the hugely successful release of *MASH* (Altman, 1970). But once again the project came to nothing.[37] Altman founded his own independent, Lion's Gate, later that same year.

Menne discusses Bryna Productions as analogous to the Cuban revolution era 'guerrilla warrior'.[38]

> A sign of how equivocal a figure it was appears in the rather unmotivated scene from . . . *The Apartment* . . . in which the company man C.C. Baxter is asked by a fellow carouser on New Year's Eve what he thinks of Fidel Castro. In this scene it would have been a year since the fidelistas had seized Havana, and the throwaway question suggests the unsettling fascination with their revolution. The fidelistas exerted fascination, I believe, not for ideological reasons per se but because they were an object lesson in organizational theory.[39]

If this seems something of a stretch, it is not least because the carouser in question is married to one of the Bay of Pigs mercenaries and wants her husband out of Castro's prison. Indeed, it is the mercenary, not the guerrilla, who is the subject of her concern. Menne's 'argument is predicated on Bryna's oblique representation of guerrilla war even though . . . *Lonely are the Brave* does not address guerrilla war but simply resembles it'.[40] But Douglas's film for Mirisch, *Cast a Giant Shadow*, which Menne does not mention, was explicitly about guerrilla warfare and the struggle for an independent state. (It is worth remembering that Mirisch produced a film about precisely the same imperative, *The First Texan*, while at Allied Artists.)

Menne's book

> assesses the industrial shakeup that led to the New Hollywood by disclosing the crucial part that a radicalized management theory played in both its formation and stabilization. The auteur theory functioned as a kind of management theory for a

---

[37] 'Mirisch In Prod'n Lull', *Daily Variety*, 23.2.70: 1.
[38] Menne, 2019: 48.
[39] Ibid, 53.
[40] Ibid, 58.

cohort of filmmakers who were made cine-literate through university education ... in the same moment that management theory was gaining a foothold in the university by way of proliferating MBA programs. Both auteur theory and business management theory, I argue, had the same object in their sights, the large corporation, which was made sclerotic by a combination of its hypertrophy and its centralized command structure. In its place would emerge a smaller-scale, more flexible system of labor.[41]

Is it a coincidence, then, that just such large corporations, made sclerotic by hypertrophy and a centralized command structure, provide the settings but also function as the antagonists in both *The Apartment* and *How to Succeed in Business Without Really Trying*? Both, of course, were produced by just such a smaller-scale, more flexible company. One song in the latter, "The Company Way", both undermines corporate identity but also underlines it for the anti-corporate Mirisch Company family firm.

Discussing *Ocean's Eleven* (Soderbergh, 2001) Connor concludes that 'the film testifies to the producers' powers of assembly'. *Ocean's Eleven* was a remake of a 1960 film, directed by Lewis Milestone, and produced by the independent production company, Dorchester Productions Inc. Indeed, the assembling of a team provides much of the first act in several early 1960s independent productions, notably Mirisch films, particularly in precisely this period (*The Magnificent Seven* and *The Great Escape* among them). According to Connor, 'Operating under the modern "package-unit" system of production – where each film is mounted by a new and one-off collection of talent rather than assembled from studio labor already under contract – studios face a great deal more uncertainty about their continuity as creative enterprises.'[42] But such studios were no longer the companies assembling such labour, that role having been largely assumed by independent production companies, like Mirisch, though their films were still financed and distributed by those same majors. As an exchange between two characters in *Hawaii* has it, 'From now on we don't own. We just handle.' – 'Well, I'll be damned. You don't put up a dollar of your own money. And yet you handle anything that passes in and out of the port.' To which the response is, 'For a fee!'

Connor discusses film packaging, the process of assembling on and off-screen 'talent' and identifies its narrative equivalent, noting that 'collective aesthetic endeavor is almost everywhere in Hollywood movies: in a criminal band, a movie crew, a TV crew, a submarine crew, in a newsroom, a bachelor penthouse, a garage.'[43] This list of 'collective endeavours', or more precisely the process of assembling such collectives for the purpose of, but prior to, their embarking on a specific endeavour, corresponds closely with early scenes from *The Magnificent Seven*, *The Great Escape*, *The Thomas Crown Affair* and the British Second World War cycle. Moreover, the openings of, respectively, *Some Like It Hot* (the Chicago mob), *The Party* (the movie crew) and *The Fortune Cookie* (the sports TV crew) and the key submarine location of *The Russians Are Coming, The Russians Are Coming* and *Gray Lady Down* (Greene, 1976), the

[41] Ibid, 6.
[42] Connor, 2015: 12.
[43] Ibid, 322.

eponymous *Apartment* and *The Landlord* and the setting of TV sitcom, *Hey Landlord* (NBC 1966-7) (bachelor pad) plus 'grease monkey' Walter Gulik's garage in Presley's *Kid Galahad* correspond precisely to the locations Connor enumerates.

Mirisch films and allegory

The Mirisch Company was set up in 1957 with a deal to produce films for United Artists and several of its first contractual productions – *Some Like It Hot*, *The Magnificent Seven* and *The Great Escape* function, in part at least, as allegories of contemporary Hollywood filmmaking – including freelancing, and the temporary assembly of teams of professionals, just as *The Apartment* operates as an acidic depiction of its opposite, an impersonal, bureaucratic corporate culture. The pair of producer/directors responsible for those four films were John Sturges and Billy Wilder, two filmmakers who could hardly have been more different, so that searching for an auteurist explanation for this shared theme seems futile. That initial UA deal was renewed in 1963-4 and several early results of the second contract period prove equally revealing (including films as fundamentally distinct as *633 Squadron* and *Kiss Me, Stupid*). A third and final contract was signed with UA in 1968 (UA having been acquired by The Transamerica Corporation in 1967) and once again several films, notably *The Thomas Crown Affair* and *Mr Majestyk*, dramatically foreground brands and contracts in their opening sequences, and are, in Connor's terms, 'allegorically autobiographical'. As Schein notes, mergers or acquisitions or changes of ownership are key moments at which companies regularly reassess and reassert their core beliefs.[44]

Discussing *Jaws*, Connor notes that 'the midpoint . . . involves the signing of a contract, Act 1 concludes with Quint's offer to kill the shark for ten thousand dollars. That is, the plot of the terrestrial first half of the film pivots around the poles of New Hollywood labor, independence and contracting'.[45] But Mirisch films had already been doing this for some time in *Man of the West* (Link is on his way to hire a schoolteacher when his train is attacked), or *Some Like It Hot* (with agents securing contracts for performances), or *The Magnificent Seven* (with the hiring of the seven), or *The Thomas Crown Affair* (which opens with the hiring of a 'getaway' driver and whose second scene includes a close-up of the signing of a contract), while *Mr Majestyk* begins with the hero hiring fruit pickers for his watermelon crop.

Some Like It Hot

Denise Mann's study of agency-dominated Hollywood, barely mentions *Some Like It Hot*, referring to it only three times – as the work of a writer-director, as a characteristic

---

[44] Schein, 2004: 315-16.
[45] Connor, 2015: 60.

shop window of talent assembled by MCA, and as an example of cinematic self-referentiality, in the sending up of Cary Grant (by Curtis) and George Raft (through an exchange between Edward G. Robinson Jnr and Raft himself). Grant and Raft were both, of course, studio-era stars. According to Mann, 'self-referential themes and self-reflexive strategies' were characteristic of independent films in post-war Hollywood in transition, a distinct cinematic style illustrating an aesthetic shift from the classical to post-classical.[46] One such scene occurs early in the film, though Mann doesn't mention it. Tony Curtis and Jack Lemmon are in a hallway entering a series of different talent agencies looking for work. As the door of one office closes, with no job offers forthcoming, the viewer can see the nameplate, which reads: Jules Stein, Music Corporation of America.

INT. CORRIDOR OF MUSIC BUILDING – DAY

Joe moves down the corridor, Jerry tagging along grimly beside him. Other job-seeking musicians mill around, and a melange of musical sounds and singing voices issues from the various offices, studios and rehearsal halls.

Joe and Jerry come up to a door marked: KEYNOTE MUSICAL AGENCY – BANDS, SOLOISTS, SINGERS.

Joe opens the door, revealing a crummy office, with a secretary behind a desk.

    JOE
Anything today?

    FIRST SECRETARY
Nothing.

    JOE
Thank you.

Joe shuts the door, and they shuffle along to the next agency, which is marked:

JULES STEIN – MUSIC CORPORATION OF AMERICA.

Joe opens the door. This is like the other office – except a little crummier. There is a secretary behind the desk.

    JOE
Anything today?

---

[46] Mann, 2008: 117.

SECOND SECRETARY (drinking from a bottle)
Nothing.

JOE
Thank you. (See Figure 6)

This, right down to the illicit swig of prohibition liquor, is, of course, an in-joke, a bit of 'self-referentiality', of the kind Mann refers to. But it is also much more than that. It is a denial of corporate agency and an implicit avowal of human agency. I trust that what follows will make this distinction clear.

The film begins in 1929 in Chicago and tells the story of two unemployed musicians in prohibition America who witness the St Valentine's Day Massacre. This period and location also saw the beginnings of MCA. Mann's chapter about MCA begins in the 1940s, so she omits to mention that The Music Corporation of America was founded in Chicago by Jules Stein in 1924 – specifically as a band-booking agency. MCA helped pioneer the business of booking touring jazz bands and musicians for clubs, concert halls and speakeasies, many of them run by the Capone mob. It was in 1920s Chicago that Stein's MCA first deployed the arts of packaging and block booking talent. Block booking works essentially on the same principle as packaging – leveraging unwanted acts or products on a customer as obligatory parts of a deal involving one or two specifically required performers/films.

The connection between a story about two freelance musicians who need work, and the history of the agency, MCA, that arranged the signing of the actors who played those roles is far from accidental. This is both the story of the pre-war origins of MCA itself and, by analogy, the story of all talent in the post-anti-trust era. In the late 1950s, Hollywood was, for the first time ever, dominated by independent

Figure 5 Joe and Jerry visit MCA's Chicago office in *Some Like It Hot*.

producers and the package-unit system, with employment on a single film (like the musicians hired for specific dates and locations) rather than by a particular firm (with employees sometimes spending years, if not decades, on staff at a specific studio). Indeed, Hollywood's own musicians were negotiating new contracts with the studios in 1958, just as the film was in pre-production, and subsequently film work for all studio musicians would be freelance. *Some Like It Hot* was shot between 4 August 1958 and 6 November 1958. The studio musicians had gone on strike in February 1958 and the dispute was only finally settled on 11 July. The Screen Actors Guild followed the dispute closely and began its own negotiations with the studios in late 1959. Thus, this film about freelance musicians was made precisely as Hollywood's own musicians were being forcibly casualized by an industry in which they had previously enjoyed staff contracts and was acted by performers whose own job security had already been hit in the same way.

Of course, this brief agency-visiting scene could be explained autobiographically – as a quintessentially auteurist fingerprint, a trace of Wilder's reflexive writer-directorial DNA. But in the late 1950s, for the first time in his Hollywood career, Wilder, as a freelance talent for hire, was in the same position as his film's protagonists. That the premise of *Hot* reflected the economics and employment practices of Hollywood, not at the time the film was set but precisely at the moment of its production, is intriguing. But it is also the case that much of the film's key talent – the human aspect of the 'package' – Wilder himself, of course, but also Curtis and Monroe, the biggest box office names above the title, not to mention Persoff and O'Brien, were all MCA clients. Indeed, Wilder, Curtis and Monroe all enjoyed MCA negotiated profit-sharing percentages on the film, from each of which the agency took its share. And Wilder, the consummate hyphenate, with his three credited roles, was a particularly valuable MCA client. Wilder's first casting choices for the film meanwhile – Frank Sinatra, Danny Kaye and Mitzi Gaynor – all of whom, incidentally, were William Morris clients – were all rejected. Even the title, *Some Like It Hot*, previously the name of a Bob Hope comedy, was IP owned by MCA through its recent acquisition of Paramount's pre-48 back catalogue (for $50 million) and could thus be re-charged to Mirisch/UA. The original title, *Fanfares of Love* – a literal translation of the German original, *Fanfaren der Liebe* (Hoffmann, 1951) – was changed during production to *Not Tonight Josephine*, before that too was jettisoned; neither would have led to profits for MCA.

As Christensen puts it, 'Certain Hollywood films allegorically reflect on the motives and methods of the studio and its agents.'[47] Christensen uses the phrase 'studio allegory' to describe such films, arguing that 'It is an allegorical characteristic of a certain privileged class of motion pictures that their extra-diegetic aims, such as an aspiration for Oscars, must be "invisible" to the studio and to the trade – not just in the promotion of the picture but in the picture itself.'[48] It is my contention here that, consciously or not, the Mirisches entrusted Wilder with an allegory of – or subliminal

---

[47] Christensen, 'Studio Authorship, Warner Bros, and The Fountainhead', *The Velvet Light Trap* vol 57, Spring 2006: 19.
[48] Ibid.

marketing campaign for – their new company and its package-unit system. It was, after all, a critical moment in Hollywood, and for the new company specifically. A moment which facilitated, if not actively necessitating, an exercise in corporate legitimation and branding.

Some Like It Hot was crewed and cast by hiring freelance on-camera and behind-the-camera workers, on short term, daily or weekly contracts, for the duration of its production (or less). As Monroe's Sugar Kane puts it, 'So you pull yourself together, you go on to the next job, the next saxophone player; it's the same thing all over again.' This is very much the life of the freelance artist, going from film to film, gig to gig, rather than the staff contract player on salary at a studio. But the role of the successful independent producer was to ensure that each production was precisely not, or *not precisely*, 'the same thing all over again'. And casualization played a crucial role in this differentiation, ensuring that each new collaboration never quite told the same story or reassembled the same team as before. The film thus functions as an allegory for the business strategy deployed by the Mirisch Company and a showcase for the adaptability, mobility and flexibility of independent producers like themselves and the package-unit system they adopted. In doing so it foregrounds the skills of freelance performers (whose roles involve 'acting', singing etc), a fluency with costumes, genres and generic hybridity. Thus, we see Curtis as Joe, Josephine *and* as a Shell heir Cary Grant, George Raft both as a gangster and as a pastiche of his own gangster roles, and Edward G. Robinson Jnr in a pastiche of Raft's coin-tossing character from *Scarface* (Hawks/Rosson, 1932) and an implicit reference to his own father's iconic roles in the gangster genre. (Robinson Snr was another 'unavailable' William Morris client.) Indeed precarity is a theme that Mirisch films repeatedly reference, from *Some Like It Hot* to *The Magnificent Seven*, from *The Thomas Crown Affair* to *Mr Majestyk*. But the increasing insecurity of their freelance protagonists on-screen and freelance employees off-screen was in inverse proportion to the built-in risk aversion of a cinematic sequel and cyclical production.

Christensen discusses 1930s gangster films, the very period of the genre so precisely pastiched in the opening sequence of *Some Like It Hot*. He also refers to *Bonnie and Clyde*'s (Penn, 1967) homage to old Warner Bros gangster movies, as 'mothballed irony' of which *Some Like It Hot* is surely another example.[49] But the gangster setting and characters in the latter are not there simply to provide opportunities for genre pastiche. The gangster board meeting also functions as a pastiche of a meeting of a big American corporation – like the vertically integrated studios themselves (with delegates from across the country). The same applies to Jnr's (Curtis in his Cary Grant persona) assumed role in his fictional family business, the Shell Corporation. In Wilder and the Mirisch's next collaboration, *The Apartment*, the office set was specifically designed as a pastiche of the anonymous workspaces of contemporary corporate bureaucracy – and, implicitly, one of the 'big five' (to quote Lemmon's opening voice-over) vertically integrated majors that companies like Mirisch were challenging.

[49] Christensen, 2012: 251.

Writing of the allegorical function performed by *Mrs Miniver* (Wyler, 1942) for MGM, Christensen concluded that '*Mrs Miniver* was the chosen vehicle for Mayer to vindicate MGM's commitment to quality, both in the eyes of its public audience, whom the film endeavours to confirm in its choice, and in the hearts and minds of the Hollywood faithful, for whom the film attempts to devise its future and perform quality.'[50] This chapter has argued that the independent, package-unit production of *Some Like It Hot* was a vehicle for the Mirisches to vindicate their own and United Artists' commitment to quality, both in the eyes of the new young adult audience and in the hearts and minds of the industry, for whom the film attempts to lay out a blueprint for its future business and aesthetic strategy. *Some Like It Hot* is thus both textual evidence of the company's on-screen differentiation from mainstream studio product (a one-off in every sense) and, at the same time, an allegory about the company's ability to reliably – and repeatedly – undertake just such a differentiation.

For Christensen, *Vertigo* (Hitchcock, 1958) is 'an allegory of the director's own struggle for independence in the 1950s'.[51] He suggests that 'Vertigo is a film about agency – about how things get done and undone – specifically, an allegory of the transformation of motion picture authorship into a new type of agency with a potent social character of unprecedented independence, an agency called "Alfred Hitchcock".'[52] *Some Like It Hot* is also a film about agency, including, in passing, an agency called MCA, but its playful project precisely denies the agency of such agencies, by celebrating the unique performative charisma or agency of its on-screen and off-screen talent. Indeed, the film dramatizes the uselessness of talent 'agencies' – including the one which represented the film's own stars, MCA – and instead celebrates the flexibility and adaptability of those stars – and by implication of the company that hired them.

Vertigo, of course, is an auteur classic. *Man in the Net* is neither a classic nor made by an auteur. (The director was an end-of-career, Michael Curtiz, of *Casablanca* (1942) fame. Mirisch subsequently hired *Casablanca* screenwriter, Howard Koch, to (re-)write *633 Squadron,* but the result was equally far from the classic he had co-scripted twenty years earlier). And yet, *Man in the Net* is about a painter who opts to escape corporate life, preferring the independent existence of a freelance artist to being 'Head of the Art Department' at a Madison Avenue advertising agency. He receives a letter announcing that 'An important opening has developed in our organization' but tells his wife, 'If I go back to that agency, I'll be working 24 hours a day. We both decided to give up the rat race in New York.' An opposition is being constructed not only between business and art but also between the rat race of a corporate career and the freedom of freelancing. Similarly, in *Man of the West* we hear Dock Tobin ask Link, 'Why did you leave me?' To which Link replies, 'I wanted to strike out on my own.'

---

[50] Christensen, 'Studio Identity and Studio Art: MGM, Mrs Miniver and Planning the Postwar Era', *English Literary History* vol 67, Spring 2000: 271.
[51] Christensen, 2012: 23.
[52] Ibid, 222.

Indeed, the success of Mirisch films was seen as a direct consequence of the company's 'independence'. Thus the *New York Times* report 'Oscar Triumphs of "West Side Story" seen as Victory for Independents' noted that

> ... last Monday night at the Santa Monica Civic Auditorium was a happy one for all moviemakers who believe that the future of films – commercially as well as artistically – is in the hands of the independent, that the only way in which a major studio can hope to compete any longer is to hire talented men and women and to allow them artistic freedom. That has been the secret of the success of United Artists and of the Mirisch Company.

The victory 'greatly gratified the Mirisch Company, which assembled "the package" for the production'.[53] The success of *West Side Story* may have meant more to the Mirisches precisely because of their own roots in Polish neighbourhoods in Harlem and the Bronx.

The Magnificent Seven

The Magnificent Seven deployed all seven of the strategies Staiger identifies as characteristic of 'package-unit' production.[54] It was shot on location in Mexico (as a so-called 'runaway production') by a freelance, casualized cast and crew, with only the director, star and executive producer on contracts beyond that single film. It assembled an ensemble package of co-star talent to surround its one legitimate movie star lead (Yul Brynner) and that assembly is mirrored in the film's own fictional narrative. The film's origin in a recent art cinema and festival hit provided it with both a narrative model and a pre-marketed storyline and functioned as something of a risk aversion strategy (characteristic of many Mirisch productions). As a one-off, the film distinguished itself from the then epidemic of multi-episode TV Westerns while the deaths of so many of its leads differentiated it from the recurring and apparently 'unkillable' casts of such series.

The producer/director John Sturges had a profit-sharing deal and indeed Sturges made several million dollars from the project. The ensemble package of on-screen, comparatively new, young talents assembled to complement – and contrast – with the presence of big screen (familiar, older) star, Brynner, clearly functioned both to attract, but also to mirror, the new majority youth audience – and the casting of Steve McQueen (Vin), Robert Vaughan (Lee), James Coburn (Britt), Charles Bronson (Bernardo) and Horst Bucholtz (Chico) was evidence of this. Indeed, the eventual script and cast contrast dramatically with the older stars originally approached by Brynner and Alciona, when they tried to develop the project, and the characters outlined in Bernstein's original screenplay draft.

---

[53] 'Hollywood Sweeps', *NYT Encyclopaedia of Film*, 15.4.62.
[54] Bordwell, Staiger, Thompson, 1985: 330–5.

Chris's reputation with a gun attracts the six other gunmen to work with him in much the same way that the film's director attracted male action stars to the project. As Walter Mirisch noted, 'with Sturges we have a definite asset in attracting top male stars'.[55] Similarly, Sturges admitted to modelling the role of Calvera on his old studio bosses at Columbia and MGM: 'I didn't want a big tough guy because the style of that part was not that of a big tough guy. Like Cohn and Mayer, he's a conman, a negotiator ... this hypocritical guy who sanctifies what he's doing by turning things around.'[56] This is not to recruit Sturges into the auteur pantheon through some anecdotal back door. But it is to insist that those who worked in Hollywood worked there in specific contexts and under precise corporate contractual conditions, at particular moments in film industrial history and under particular pressures. Such pressures and contexts partially determined not only the ways they were employed but also the kinds of projects they were employed to work on and even the nature of their contributions to those projects.

Much is made in the film's dialogue of the fact that the seven are doing a 'job as hired guns', that they 'took a contract' and are to be paid '$20 for six weeks work'. Vin joins up because he is broke, and the alternative – clerking in a store – 'good, steady work', one of the Mexicans informs him – is anathema. Meeting Calvera for the first time, Vin says 'We deal in lead, friend.' Calvera replies, 'So do I, we are in the same business.' And later, asked about what happens to the villagers, Calvera replies 'Can men of our profession worry about that?' The language is of business, of doing a job, of being hired professionals. As Vin explains to Chris,

> 'You know, the first time I took a job as a hired gun, a fella told me, "Vin, you can't afford to care."' Or as Chris explains earlier in the film, 'Men in this line of work are not all alike. Some care about nothing but money. Others, for reasons of their own, enjoy only the danger. And the competition.'

O'Reilly tells the children, 'This is my work.' And later one of the Mexican villagers says, 'That is not what you were hired for.' As Harry says on his first meeting with Chris 'I heard you got a contract open'. When Vin proposes abandoning the village, Chris is adamant. 'You forget one thing. We took a contract.' The Mirisch Company supported Newman's shooting script (and Roberts' minimal on-set revisions) and defended it against UA's suggested cuts when the film was in post-production. It is particularly pertinent that the early scenes, in which the seven are 'hired' and individuated, remained intact. Thus, the relative autonomy which Mirisch granted producer-directors like Sturges replicated the relative autonomy the company had from United Artists.

The case I am arguing here is that, rather than reflecting the wider cultural zeitgeist, whether that be America's foreign policy or domestic corporate economics, *The Magnificent Seven*'s narrative embodies, in homologous structural form, its own

---

[55] Walter Mirisch quoted in Balio, 1987: 173.
[56] John Sturges quoted in Glenn Lovell, *Escape Artist: The Life and Films of John Sturges*, The University of Wisconsin Press, 2008: 196.

mode of production – the package-unit system deployed by independents at the end of the 1950s.[57] I suggest that this explains why the project seemed like a good idea at the time to the Mirisch Company. Raymond Williams deployed the term homology in discussing the relationship between base and superstructure in Marxist cultural theory. 'There is the notion of "homologous structures", where there may be no direct or easily apparent similarity . . . between the superstructural process and the reality of the base, but in which there is an essential homology or correspondence of structures, which can be discovered by analysis.'[58]

In Williams' sense, *The Magnificent Seven* is a homology for the replacement of the old, vertically integrated, Hollywood studios with their salaried staffs, by new package-unit independents, with a small team put together to do a particular one-off job. The cast and crew are 'hired guns' in just the same way that the seven gunfighters are, paid a fee for their services for fulfilling a specific contract.

The Magnificent Seven was not necessarily a consciously 'autobiographical' project for the filmmakers. (That such 'messages' were intended, implied by the term allegory, explains my preference for the phrase structural homology, since such homologies are potentially unconscious.) Nevertheless, such stories relating to individual professionals being brought together to work on specific projects, were, at that precise moment in Hollywood, in that specific sector of the industry, in the very air that those filmmakers breathed. It is therefore significant that when UA wanted 15 minutes cut from *The Magnificent Seven* specifically from the early sequences involving the hiring of the seven, Mirisch resisted their efforts and won the resulting argument.[59]

Perhaps *The Magnificent Seven* felt like a good idea in 1958 – and an exceedingly appropriate one in 1960 – not because it mythologized a stage in American corporate capitalism, the development of which was far from synchronous across all the nation's industries, and the experience of which was not necessarily particularly positive at such a transformative moment in the film industry. Nor, perhaps, because it was a story in synch with its times because of an allegedly allegorical relationship with a war not yet begun, by a president not yet elected. Perhaps its story rang bells with a community of filmmakers whose own experience of employment, whose own sense of themselves as professionals, but also, virtually overnight, as freelancers, rather than staff, was deeply de-stabilized. And perhaps the way that the story squared the circle between their increasingly insecure professional status and the positive spin they could put on that insecurity as creative, autonomous, vocational, elective and even ethical – helped them to live that contradiction. That may, in part, explain why the film seems to have meant more to its makers than it did, at least on its initial release, to its American audience.

---

[57] See my essay, '"It Seemed Like a Good Idea at the Time"', 2020.
[58] Raymond Williams, 'Base and Superstructure in Marxist Cultural Theory', in *Problems in Materialism and Culture*, Verso, 1980: 33.
[59] TELEX to Harold Mirisch 15.9.60, United Artists Collection Addition, Wisconsin Historical Society, Box 5, Folder 12.

The Great Escape

Three years later, in *The Great Escape*, there are similar scenes dramatizing the assembly of the escape team. As Big X identifies the skillsets of the tunnellers and escapees:

We'll get Cavendish to do a survey . . . Dennis is surveyor. Willie, you and Danny will be tunnel kings. Danny, you'll be in charge of traps and I'll work out the exact location with you tomorrow. Sedgwick – manufacturer, Griff, as I said tailor, Maynard Haynes diversions, Mac, of course, will take care of intelligence, Hendley, we haven't met, scrounger?

> Henry: Right.
> Big X: Dennis – maps and surveys. Colin (Blythe), you'll take your usual job?
>   Eric, (Ashley-Pitt, Dispersal) have you thought how you'll get rid of this dirt?
> Eric Ashley-Pitt: Yes, I have, usual places, I hadn't anticipated three tunnels, but we'll manage.
> Roger: Who's going to handle security for this outfit?
> Big X: You are. . . .
> Hendley: What do you do here?
> Blythe: Here, oh, I'm the forger.

The Great Escape was based on the book by Paul Brickhill, who had also written *The Dam Busters*, which inspired not just the film of that name but was also an unacknowledged source of *633 Squadron*. Brickhill's subsequent book about escapee Johnny Dodge was also optioned by Mirisch for Sturges but went unmade until it belatedly provided the source for the two-part teleplay, *The Great Escape; The Untold Story* (NBC, 1988) co-directed by (one-time Mirisch regular) Paul Wendkos and Jud Taylor (who had played Goff in *The Great Escape*) and starring Christopher Reeve as Johnny. Dana Polan's recent book about the latter film notes the assembly of talents for a collective endeavour and concludes, 'It's important to the caper film that each team member has an irreducible personal talent: this is not about anonymous labor, or worker interchangeability, or loss of identity.'[60] Significantly, therefore, while the if not interchangeable then at least multiple screenwriters who worked on the film include William Roberts (who had been credited, unfairly, with the screenplay for *The Magnificent Seven* which was largely Newman's) provided an initial sixty-four page treatment, Walter Newman (whose name had been taken off *The Magnificent Seven*), produced the first full-length script, W.R. Burnett (who had worked on Sturges' previous picture, *Sergeants 3* (Sturges, 1962) and written the multiple protagonist heist novel *The Asphalt Jungle*) James Clavell (who had just published his own fictionalized POW experiences in the novel *King Rat* and subsequently scripted *633 Squadron* and *The Satan Bug* for Mirisch), and Ivan Moffat (who worked up McQueen's part, on location). Thus, none saw the project through from start to finish, while the Mirisches

---

[60] Dana Polan, *Dreams of Flight: The Great Escape in American Film and Culture*, University of California Press, 2021, 168.

remained committed to it from acquiring the rights to the book in 1957 to the film's release in 1963.

Polan goes on to compare *The Great Escape* with the heist film, *The Thomas Crown Affair*, without acknowledging that both were Mirisch productions. That the Mirisches were intimately involved in *The Great Escape* is revealed by the letters Polan cites from Walter re acquiring the book in August 1957, *before* their company had even been set up, and from Marvin, re the brothers' concern that,

> [R]egardless of where we have the laboratory work done, it is imperative that we here [i.e., in Los Angeles] see the dailies so that we may stay on top of John Sturges, who has a penchant for over-shooting. We feel certain that whatever reasonable cost is engendered by our seeing the dailies will be saved many times over by the pressure that we will be able to put on Sturges to cut down his coverage and over-shooting. Sturges, by the way, also is most anxious that we see the dailies as he goes along so that we may give him our advice and opinions.[61]

The Apartment

Before *The Great Escape*, Mirisch had, of course, produced *The Apartment*, a film which famously depicted the downsides of corporate America. '*The Apartment* (1960) foregrounded and harshly critiqued the corporatization and commodification of the advertising and broadcasting industries – and by extension, the New Hollywood film industry . . .'. According to Mann, 'the rise of the "independents" and the rise of the "organization man" are integrally related, given that independent filmmakers ended up having to take on the mantle of the businessman once they had set up their own companies.'[62] But *The Apartment* is an independent film which critiques 'the organization man', an idea which was very much in the air at the time. Indeed, David Riesman's *The Lonely Crowd* (1950), C. Wright Mill's *White Collar* (1951), William Whyte's *The Organization Man* (1956) and Vance Packard's *The Status Seekers* (1959) all confirmed the extent to which post-war America had become a corporate culture. Indeed, as Mann notes, 'The quasi-satirical literature includes Shepherd Mead's How to Succeed in Business Without Really Trying (1952)' though she fails to note that Mirisch acquired the rights to the musical based on that book and produced an adaptation of this comparatively toothless 'satire' too.[63]

For Mann, 'the self-referential aspect of the insurance company milieu of *The Apartment* is self-consciously metaphorical: one of Wilder's inspirations for writing the screenplay was a behind-the-scenes scandal involving MCA.'[64] The auteurist assumption here is that, of the two screenwriters, Wilder, and not co-writer I. A. L. Diamond, came up with the idea, and that the story of Walter Wanger shooting MCA

---

[61] See Ibid, 93, 148.
[62] Mann, 2008: 63, 65.
[63] Ibid, 76.
[64] Ibid, 88.

agent, Jennings Lang, for having an affair with his wife, an affair which took place in fellow agent, Jay Kanter's, apartment, was Wilder's 'inspiration' for the film. But it was the Mirisches, not Wilder, who were close friends of Wanger. Harold Mirisch had known him for thirteen years before the scandal and over two decades by the time of *The Apartment*. Walter had hired him at Allied Artists several years before the shooting and continued to employ him after he came out of prison, even taking him home to dinner the day he was arrested. Wanger's wife, Joan Bennett, had been hired to host an Allied Artists TV show, in a deal negotiated by Mirisch with Lang, so perhaps the brothers felt some responsibility for the events. Walter even gave Wanger a producer credit on two films which were made while the latter was in prison.

As Denise Mann puts it, 'Wilder took this juicy morsel of an idea and simply moved the setting of his film, The Apartment, from a talent agency to a less reflexively conspicuous insurance firm.'[65] However, this version of events completely ignores the fact that talent agencies in general and MCA, in particular, had already featured conspicuously in *Some Like It Hot* and the 'juicy morsel' may well have been nurtured not only by Wilder and Diamond but also by the Mirisch brothers themselves. Walter, after all, had lunch with Wilder and Diamond virtually daily. And if evidence is required for their closeness, apart from the seventeen years and eight films in which Wilder worked with Mirisch exclusively, then there is also this. Mr Sheldrake, in *The Apartment*, is head of Personnel – a profession about which Mirisch himself had written several articles in a journal of that name. Mr Kirkeby in *The Apartment*, is characterized by a verbal tic, 'Premium-wise and billing-wise, we are eighteen percent of last year, October-wise.' One of Mirisch's own admonitions to Hollywood ended 'All segments of the American industry must unite to take whatever steps may become necessary, public relations-wise, tax-wise or legislate-wise.'[66] Whether Wilder was channelling Walter or Walter was echoing Wilder, this is, at the very least, affirms their intimacy.

Diamond himself remembers the genesis of the script as follows.

> The project had originated the previous January (1959), right after we had finished 'Some Like it Hot'. Before the picture was even previewed, we were already searching for another vehicle for Jack Lemmon . . . 'The Apartment' is the story of a young bachelor working for an insurance company, who ensures his advancement by lending the key to his apartment to his married superiors. . . . It is a film that tries to say a few pertinent things about the society we live in, in this Year of Payola, 1960. No writer would sit down and deliberately try to whip up a plot about The Organization Man or The Lonely Crowd or The Status Seekers. But every writer is attuned to his times and dealing with the subject as we were, it was almost impossible to avoid some comment on the mores of the American business community.[67]

---

[65] Ibid, 109.
[66] Mirisch, 1960: 24; This article was based on a speech Walter gave earlier that year.
[67] 'Apartment' With View', by I. A. L. Diamond, *New York Times Encyclopedia of Film*, 12.6.60A.

The specific business community about which Diamond and Wilder had inside knowledge, of course, was the film industry. It is thus notable that *The Apartment* begins with a voice-over which characterizes the insurance company in which Bud works as 'one of the big five' – echoing the 'big five' integrated Hollywood majors which had been specifically named in the Paramount Decree and obliged to divorce production (their studios) from their exhibition arms. Ben Rogerson's essay on *The Apartment* begins by stating that 'There could be no starker critique of the Mid-Century white-collar workplace than The Apartment' and argues that the firm in which the story takes place, Consolidated Life, does just that, 'depicting work and leisure as increasingly indistinct' since Fordism depends on both mass production and mass consumption and the vertically integrated corporation.[68] Rogerson argues that 'The Apartment . . . levels a polemic that accuses Paramount, as well as the other "big five" Old Hollywood Studios, of resembling Consolidated Life, an inhuman, bureaucratic workplace that is "one of the top five companies in the country"'.[69] Arguably, Consolidated Life is an image both of the major studios and of the large talent agencies, like MCA, which did so much to replace them. Indeed, Rogerson argues that the film 'closely follows the contours of the film industry in the aftermath of the Supreme Court's 1948 Paramount decision'.[70]

The films' depiction of Fordism begins with the workplace, which is a skyscraper, where, at 'desk number 861' on the nineteenth floor, the protagonist C.C. Baxter sits in an immense open-plan office inhabited by hundreds of other clerks at identical desks with identical equipment, all dominated by an office clock. The very first scene inside Consolidated Life includes a close-up of this clock at precisely 5.19 pm, so that, moments later, when the clock shows 5.20 pm, a bell signals that the shift for this floor is over – there are so many floors that working hours are staggered, enabling each floor's employees to exit without the elevators overflowing.

And while work is repetitive, regimented and routine, so too is private life, with sex 'run on schedule like a Greyhound bus'. Fran recognizes that such affairs are simply part of an executive's annual schedule – 'Happens all the time. The wife and kids go away to the country and the boss has a fling with the secretary or the manicurist, or the elevator girl. Come September, the picnic's over.' Fran's affair is limited to the time between the end of the working day and the 7.14 train to White Plains. In much the same way, one of Fran's predecessors, Miss Olsen, informs her of a virtual assembly line of previous affairs: 'And before me there was Miss Rossi in Auditing, and after me there was Miss Koch in Disability, and just before you there was Miss What's-Her-Name on the twenty-seventh floor.' Similarly, Baxter's free time is either spent in the office, as executives make use of his apartment for their assignations or eating TV dinners while

---

[68] Ben Rogerson, 'Wilder's Mensch: United Artists and the Critique of Fordism', *Arizona Quarterly* vol 70 no 1, Spring 2014: 53.
[69] Ibid, 55.
[70] Ibid, 72; The foreword to Isobel Lennart's final draft screenplay of *Garden of Cucumbers* (*Fitzwilly*) in the Walter Mirisch Collection, starts with the words 'Any statements made herein about the rich, the poor, department stores, insurance companies, honesty etc are the opinions of the characters who voice them – and are not shared by the director, the actors, the writer, or anyone they know.' Center for Film and Theatre Research, Box 1, Folder 9.

Figure 6 The anonymous corporate office in *The Apartment*, antithesis of the small family business that was the Mirisch Company.

flicking desultorily through a range of all but identical TV shows. When Baxter regains something of his humanity at the end, rejecting the corporate life, returning the keys to the executive bathroom and dispensing with his bowler hat, the film ends without a kiss between Fran and Baxter or even a shot of them gazing into a shared future, in a pre-echo of the uncertainties of *The Graduate*'s (Nichols, 1967) final frames.[71]

Ian Brookes' essay on *The Apartment* also discusses it as a critique of Fordism with its iconic echoes of 'scientific management', derived from Henry Ford's mass production assembly lines and mass consumption society and Frederick Taylor's 'The Principle of Scientific Management'.[72] Brookes quotes David Noble's remark that 'the most important extension of the concept of standardisation was into the area of "personnel", management's scientific term for standardized labor'.[73] Brookes notes the importance for the film's critique that the villain, Sheldrake, is the director of personnel at Consolidated Life. Of course, Walter Mirisch was himself a past contributor to *Personnel Journal* in which he criticized over-manning in industry and its incipient inefficiencies, abuses and petty bureaucracy.[74] And if the film's focus on personnel and promotion recalls Mirisch's own contribution to the journal of that name, then its framing of regimented and routinized work echoes his articles on efficiency and the quantification and quality control of the individual output. Whether, therefore, the project appealed to Mirisch because it dealt with a world he recognized, or indeed depicted his own ambivalence about that world, is impossible to know. But it remains striking that *The Apartment*, like so many Mirisch productions, was not only a corporate production but was also *about* corporate life. That Sturges and Wilder both made a pair of films for Mirisch which explored such themes suggests at the very least that the company as well as the individual filmmakers was interested in them.

---

[71] Rogerson, 2014: 74.
[72] Ian Brookes, 'The Eye of Power: Postwar Fordism and the Panoptic Corporation in The Apartment', *Journal of Popular Film and Television* vol 37 no 4, 2009: 151–3.
[73] Noble quoted in Ibid, 154.
[74] See, for instance, Walter's article 'Emergency Administration', 1945: 37–40.

Other Mirisch films set in – or against – the world of business, or whose protagonists are businessmen include *Man in the Net*, in which the hero is attempting to escape the world of business, *The Thomas Crown Affair*, *The Organization*, *How to Succeed in Business Without Really Trying*, *One, Two, Three*, *The Fortune Cookie* and *Mr Majestyk*.

Crediting corporate authorship

To attribute such a recurrent business setting, or the narrative assembly of a team, simply to an individual screenwriter or director seems inadequate. Following Christensen, Connor and Menne, I propose that there is at least some corporate responsibility for such decisions and that corporate authorship requires and rewards recognition in film history. In fact, there have been several court cases revolving around precisely this question.[75] In both cases the corporation won and the individual's claim for joint authorship was refuted. As Christensen suggests,

> The credits at the beginning and end of a motion picture include the prescribed acknowledgment of artistic, technical, and financial contributions; the statement of copyright, which identifies the formal owner of the narrative representation imprinted on the reel of celluloid; and the formal opportunity for the display of the logo, which represents the corporate brand that subsumes all residual symbolic revenue that the motion picture generates.[76]

The literal meaning of the word 'credit' is made explicit in a letter written by Marvin Mirisch to Robert Benjamin of United Artists in 1966, which is worth quoting at length.

> we think it is vitally important, not only to the Mirisch Corporation, but also to United Artists, that the image of our corporation, particularly here in Hollywood and among the exhibitor fraternity, be made and kept sufficiently important so as to continue our image as the most progressive and most important independent producers in this country. I trust that you believe and understand that I personally have no desire to see my name in print, nor have we ever sought to take undue amounts of credit in the press. However, knowing the snob situation as it exists in Hollywood, you must be cognizant of the fact that there is no second best. In maintaining our position, we realize that the best way to do it is to present hit pictures, and we feel strongly that we have and will continue to deliver to United Artists pictures which will be important box office successes. This, of course, rebounds to the credit of both our companies. However, you cannot but agree

---

[75] See, for example, 'Controversy in Film Contract Construction – "That's Show Biz, Booby"', *San Fernando Valley Law Review* vol 1 no 37, 1967: 87–9; and 'Clouseau Would Have Been Confounded: Ninth Circuit Throws Out "The Pink Panther" Joint Authorship Claim', *Journal of Intellectual Property Law & Practice* vol 4 no 6, 2009: 402–3.
[76] Christensen, 2012: 277.

with me that, when we see ads in which our presentation credit is smaller and less prominent, not only than the credit of United Artists, but also the credits of Panavision and Deluxe Laboratories, I cannot but get the impression that not sufficient thought is being given to the importance of maintaining our reputation.[77]

A desire for accreditation can be explicit – as exemplified by Marvin's memo. But it can also be implicit. There are a striking number of occasions in Mirisch films when a logo, the 'image of the corporation' is framed in a key sequence. The opening shot of *Kiss Me, Stupid* is of a truck bearing the logo of The Las Vegas Sign Company. The opening shot of *Mr Majestyk* is of the protagonist's truck bearing the logo, Majestyk. Of course, this is an economic way of establishing a protagonist's profession and the story's setting. But it is also a curiously literal image, foregrounding a brand or logo to establish a professional identity, name and/or location. In *Cast a Long Shad*ow, when Matt discovers he is the heir to a ranch and is brought back home to inherit it, he initially decides to sell it but is told, 'Stay, Matt. This place is yours.' To which he replies, 'Words on a piece of paper don't make it mine. To hold a place like this together, people have to respect you, look up to you.'

In *The Thomas Crown Affair*, Crown sells one of his properties and the following conversation ensues:

Crown: Is the cheque certified?
Ty: Everything seems to be in order
Sandy: Tommy, just sign there at the top right, take your acknowledgements.

Figure 7 Thomas Crown (Steve McQueen) signs a contract in the opening scenes of *The Thomas Crown Affair*.

---

[77] Letter, 8 March 1966.

Once the signing is completed the buyer concludes:

> Ty: Well, I guess we bought ourselves a property. A Tommy Crown property.
> Crown: It's always been very good to me.
>> Ty: You know the first thing I'm gonna do? Juice up all the rent. Well, aren't you going to wish us luck, Mr Crown?
>
> Crown: You overpaid. (Crown's team leave the boardroom)
> Sandy: Mr Crown wishes you good luck.
> Crown turns to Sandy and says, 'Oh, Cancel the insurance. Take my name off that building.' (Figure 7)

As Menne puts it, 'It is a feature of the creative economy . . . to inscribe one's marketplace authority in the very product of one's labor'.[78] Conversely, it is also a feature of that economy to remove such inscriptions when that property (including Intellectual Property) changes hands.

Cultural legitimacy

In *Cast a Long Shadow* the hero is in pursuit of legitimacy. *Man of the West*'s protagonist is attempting to 'go straight', to become legitimate. This, of course, could also function as a synonym for the strategy of the newly formed Mirisch Company, after the brothers had been associated with B movies and Poverty Row for over a decade. They were themselves, finally, going straight, cinematically. *Man in the Net*, *The Apartment*, *How to Succeed in Business Without Really Trying* and *The Thomas Crown Affair* all depict characters expressing their individuality against the grey conformity of corporate life. The press release for *Some Kind of a Nut* describes the film as 'a timely spoof on conformity and the establishment'.[79] The initial periods of each contract with United Artists were marked by a renewed desire to brand themselves, to demonstrate their own strategic imperatives and priorities on the big screen, and to differentiate themselves from their competitors.

This is not to argue that a decision had been taken to ensure such reputation building was integral to each and every film project, at the script level. Nonetheless, projects which already had such characteristics, whether on the page, stage or screen, naturally appealed to the brothers as appropriate vehicles for steering their company towards legitimacy, quality, recognition and reputation. Strategies for accomplishing these ends included the acquisition of appropriate properties which already accommodated or could accommodate just such thematic exercises in brand and reputation building, via *adaptation* of middlebrow material and avoidance of exploitation genres, on the one hand, and the adoption of methods epitomizing efficiency and economy through outsourcing and off-shoring, and in the form of sequels, cycles and television series on the other. The former strategy is the subject of the next chapter; the latter are discussed in Chapters 6, 7 and 8.

[78] Menne, 2019: 216.
[79] Press Release, *Some Kind of a Nut*, Wisconsin, Box 24.

5

'This book is all that I need'

Adaptation as aesthetic and business strategy at the Mirisch Company

Pretexts and contexts

Neither prioritizing original screenplays nor indeed screenwriting itself, while largely relying on veteran directors and those younger filmmakers trained in television rather than at film school, and maintaining an aversion to directorial virtuosity, the Mirisch Company was able to safeguard its corporate authority and authorship and exercise its corporate taste. The result was the continuity of a classical studio-era style but tempered by the inclusion of contemporary issues and identity politics to an extent that their predecessors and peers could not or would not accommodate – issues that the next generation of filmmakers, the so-called movie brats, would exclude and ignore even as they addressed a hitherto underserved demographic.[1]

The importance of literary and indeed cultural and historical pretexts in film production was understood by Walter Mirisch well before he joined the film industry. At Harvard Business School in 1942 he could read the twenty-five Hollywood screenplays deposited there the previous year.[2] Ten of those screenplays were based on novels, including *David Copperfield*, *Pride and Prejudice* and *Wuthering Heights*, while another ten were adaptations of plays, including *Pygmalion* and *A Midsummer Night's Dream*. In Harvard's Baker Library, Walter could also peruse a case study of the film industry. After all, Walter's three brothers were already working in the business, which was his own career ambition too. Furthermore, such case studies were central to the Harvard Business School curriculum. That book, *The Story of the Films* (Kennedy, 1927), included Hollywood mogul, Jesse L. Lasky, explaining his determination 'to keep in close touch with the current fiction and magazines, with the current stage

---

[1] I discuss the selection of directors and specifically the Mirisch's failure to work with the Movie Brats in Chapter 9.
[2] 'Harvard University's Theatre Receives 25 Film Scripts', *Motion Picture Herald*, 24.5.41: 31.

successes'. Lasky also admitted that he 'read The Saturday Evening Post as if it were my Bible' and that 'our business is akin to book publishing. We try to make best sellers, only ours are on celluloid'.[3] One shortcut to securing such kinship was to acquire the rights to selected bestsellers, short stories and Broadway hits and adapt them for the screen.

Walter Mirisch's definition of his role as a producer prioritizes this relationship with the page and stage. Less than eighteen months after the brothers formed the Mirisch Company, he wrote,

> As a producer of pictures, my function is to choose literary properties which appear to me to have motion picture potential, and then to acquire the rights to produce films based upon those properties. For each story I choose a suitable writer and work with him in the development of the material into a screenplay. After this has been successfully accomplished, a director is chosen and cast selected. A production crew is hired and studio facilities are contracted for, and then the cameras are ready to roll.[4]

His article concludes that 'the most important role the producer plays is in choosing his material. Then, working with the writer in the development of the screenplay, he makes his real creative contribution, as he also does in his artful selection of both cast and directors ... In this way we hope to present our international audiences with the finest stories on film.'[5]

Prioritizing the choice of 'literary properties', as a part of the package, implies an attitude to cinema as an almost inherently adaptive medium and this shaped many Mirisch productions. More than a third of Hollywood's output, in the classical studio era (an era Anderson dates from 1930 to 1948) was based on novels, a proportion which would be considerably higher if plays and short stories were also included.[6] Before 1948 almost two-thirds of Hollywood films were based on original screenplays; 15–20 per cent were based on novels and 5–6 per cent were based on plays.[7] In 1957, the Writers Guild of America/West reported that between 1938 and 1952 nearly 65 per cent of hit movies were original stories, but from 1953 to 1956 this figure dropped dramatically to 28 per cent, while interest in Broadway shows, as well as bestsellers, 'intensified'.[8] The years 1957–62 saw the percentage of originals recover somewhat, with the balance split approximately 52 per cent adaptations and 48 per cent originals.[9] Nevertheless, an increasing reliance in Hollywood on pre-tested literary and theatrical

---

[3] In Kennedy, *The Story of the Films*, 1927, 106.
[4] 'Walter Mirisch', *Harvard Business School Association* vol 35, 1959: 17.
[5] Ibid, 17.
[6] Carolyn Anderson, 'Film and Literature', in Gary R. Edgerton (ed), *Film and the Arts in Symbiosis*, 1988, 97–132.
[7] Drew Casper, *Postwar Hollywood 1946–1962*, Blackwell Publishing, 44.
[8] Robert McLaughlin, *Broadway and Hollywood; A History of Economic Interaction*, Arno Press, 1974, 239.
[9] Casper, *Postwar Hollywood 1946–1962*, 44.

texts was the context in which the Mirisch Company was founded. Mirisch's first instinct, therefore, was, understandably, adaptation and it went on a rights raid, buying options and outright ownership of plays and novels as if there was literally no limit to its budget.

That the Mirisch Company privileged literary pretexts probably also owes something to the frustrations the brothers had felt at Monogram/Allied Artists, where such adaptation was often out of the question. 'We had to use ninety-five percent original material, unless it was something in the public domain . . . We very rarely bought a book. We made Treasure Island (1934), Kidnapped (1948).'[10] Copyright costs prohibited expensive acquisitions and only the occasional short story or out of copyright work was adapted (as period settings were also prohibitive). But this attitude to recent literary and theatrical work was not simply a function of financial constraints. Monogram's primary audience was in small towns and rural areas and there was a consensus among exhibitors that literary adaptations didn't necessarily play well there. The predisposition towards pre-existing storylines also allowed Mirisch to preselect the narratives their films would follow while enabling their directors and stars to design and populate those narratives within those pre-determined limits.

The Monogram approach was the antithesis of the adaptation strategy at Warner Brothers in the 1930s when Harold Mirisch worked there. Nearly half the studio's productions in this period were based on 'pretested' sources, about 20 per cent from recycled stories, while only 14 per cent were originals generated by Warner's paid screenwriters.[11] In the 1930s, Warner Bros' 'approach to film adaptation reflected a corporate strategy centred on efficient operations, a policy with the full exploitation of company resources as its goal.' Edwards relates this idea of resource management, of efficiently exploiting the inventory, to Frederick Taylor's ideas of scientific management.[12]

Edwards argues that 'Perhaps no other filmmaking corporation embodied the tenets of efficiency like Warner Bros., where the concept permeated nearly all areas of long-term planning and day-to-day business operations. Efficiency represented a corporate strategy that extended from production scheduling to employee management, to set design, to story development.'[13] If Harold absorbed that ethic of efficiency at Warners, Walter absorbed it at Harvard. As well as developing scripts based on published stories, Warners was renowned as the studio which found Hollywood plots in newspaper headlines. The former tendency is also apparent in the Mirisch Company's approach to developing source material, but rather than finding stories in contemporary headlines, Mirisch often found them in history. The title card of *Cast a Giant Shadow* states, 'The major events in this film actually happened. Some of them are still happening. The major characters actually lived. Many of them are still living. Although it was not easy.'

---

[10] Monogram President, Steve Broidy, quoted in *Kings of the B's*, 274–5.
[11] Kyle D. Edwards, *Corporate Fictions: Film Adaptation and Authorship in the Classical Hollywood Era*, Thesis, University of Texas at Austin, 2006, 6.
[12] Ibid, 270–4.
[13] Ibid, 289.

The title card of *The Great Escape* reads, 'This is a true story. Although the characters are composites of real men, and time and place have been compressed, every detail of the escape is the way it really happened.' And the card at the front of *Hour of the Gun* says, 'This Picture is Based on Fact. This is the Way it Happened.'

Edwards also discusses Selznick International Pictures, concluding 'this independent studio distinguished itself by purchasing the most expensive stories, producing them on a large scale, and attracting the largest audiences; to distributors and exhibitors an SIP picture was an unparalleled cinematic event that could bring patrons into theaters at a higher admission price than other studio releases'.[14] The Mirisch Company followed the same strategy, with the publicity for *West Side Story*, *Hawaii* and *Fiddler on the Roof* all promoting the high cost of rights acquisition, and all three films exhibited initially as high ticket, roadshow releases. It is important to mention here that Mirisch did not only adapt novels and non-fiction, or musicals and plays. They also 'remade' films, which were adaptations of a kind too. *The Magnificent Seven* and *Some Like It Hot*, the company's first two box office and critical successes, were both remakes of non-American films, while *The Children's Hour*, *Kid Galahad* and *Stolen Hours* were also remakes.[15] Meanwhile, *Massacre Harbor* was a composite film, not remaking but simply merging three consecutive TV episodes into a single narrative film.

Outsourcing development

For Mirisch, then, adaptation was essentially another form of outsourcing – dispensing with the development costs and associated overheads of originating material by acquiring market-proven IP and then amortizing the often eye-watering amounts involved in 'rights' as pre-production marketing, simultaneously recruiting new and alerting existing customers. Mirisch, like other successful independents, minimized fixed costs as a default strategy, but it took that strategy into entirely new territory. Outsourcing development to 'pretexts' functioned as a pre-production parallel to production off-shoring, a kind of 'off-shelfing' which was to remain a core characteristic throughout the company's existence. Such adaptation ensured that risk was outsourced to those publishers and theatres which had always already 'piloted' the raw material with their readers and audiences. Mirisch won the Oscar for Best Adapted Screenplay twice, for *West Side Story* and *In the Heat of the Night* but was nominated another four times – for *Friendly Persuasion*, *Some Like It Hot*, *The Russians Are Coming, The Russians Are Coming* and *Same Time, Next Year* (Mulligan, 1978). Mirisch films were only nominated twice for best original screenplay, winning with *The Apartment* and nominated for *The Fortune Cookie*. But such outsourcing of story development was counterbalanced by an implicit in-housing of story selection, whereby ready-made

---

[14] Ibid, 373–4.
[15] *Some Like It Hot*'s credits note that it was merely 'Suggested by a story by Robert Thoeren and Michael Logan' while *The Magnificent Seven*'s include an acknowledgement that 'This Picture is based on the Japanese film Seven Samurai'.

texts were acquired (including unsolicited screenplays like *The Thomas Crown Affair*) rather than the risk inherent in the company commissioning original screenplays.

Of the four musicals the company acquired, three were hits, starting with *West Side Story* and concluding with *Fiddler on the Roof* (the adaptation of *Irma La Douce* dropped the songs altogether) and only *How to Succeed in Business Without Really Trying* failed to repeat its theatrical success in cinemas. Of the bestsellers they adapted, *Hawaii* was a big hit, but *By Love Possessed* and *A Rage to Live* proved disappointments. Of the hit Broadway plays they produced for the screen, *Two for the Seesaw* and two Lillian Hellman dramas, *The Children's Hour* and *Toys in the Attic*, failed to catch fire at the box office while only the non-hit, *A Shot in the Dark*, transformed into a *Pink Panther* sequel, was a success. Curiously, their early film remakes *Some Like It Hot* and *The Magnificent Seven*, and non-adaptations like *The Apartment*, *The Pink Panther* and *The Thomas Crown Affair* were among their biggest successes (Figure 8).

Figure 8 *Hawaii* poster.

Like Selznick, the Mirisch Company deployed adaptation as part of its competitive strategy as well as its cinematic brand. Mirisch built its commercial and critical reputation on films based on bestsellers like James Michener's *Hawaii* and John Ball's *In the Heat of the Night*, Broadway musicals like *West Side Story* and *Fiddler on the Roof* and stage plays like *Two for the Seesaw* and *Same Time, Next Year*. The critical and commercial reputation of these works – and their authors – allowed those brands to be assumed, by association, by the production company adapting them.[16] As Edwards suggests of Selznick, independents 'needed to accumulate capital to sign talent, produce pictures and remain solvent; simultaneously, they sought to develop an identity – a brand that could help them cultivate relationships and maintain good will with prospective and current employees, industrial counterparts and cinema audiences'. Despite Mirisch's contract with United Artists, the brothers knew that adapting internationally known novels, plays and musicals would 'streamline the story development process, promise a built-in audience to distributors and exhibitors, and fulfil its goal of producing "prestige" pictures.'[17] Edwards explains that adaptations were thus both short and long-term investments, in the sense of both box office receipts and rentals and the construction of a corporate identity, a branding strategy differentiating both itself and its products.[18]

The Mirisches, corporately or individually, produced seventy-four feature films in the quarter century between 1957 and 1983. Twenty were adaptations of novels, eleven of stage plays and another four of musicals; of the remainder, three were based on non-fiction and two more were sequels to a previous adaptation. Even their so-called 'Originals' included *The Private Life of Sherlock Holmes*, whose eponymous protagonist was already a literary pretext in his own right, while a 'British' cycle of six formulaic Second World War films were all based on the blueprint of a previous Mirisch war movie, *633 Squadron*, which was itself an adaptation of a novel. One of the subsequent six was also based on an uncredited book. (This calculation does not even consider Mirisch's four remakes.) By this count, forty-nine films, or two-thirds of their output, were based directly or indirectly on literary properties. Adaptation was thus, for the Mirisch Company, a calculated corporate strategy as well as a cultural practice.

Adapting non-literary fiction

Most critical work on adaptations is based on 'literary' fiction and classic theatre (e.g. Shakespeare, Austen, Dickens in the UK, Henry James, Tennessee Williams, Scott Fitzgerald in the US). However, Mirisch not only eschewed 'disreputable' fictional genres but also their cultural opposite – prestigious literary fiction. Their projected Sherwood Anderson adaptation – *Winesburg Ohio* – was not made. Nor was an

---

[16] Edwards, 'Brand Name Literature: Film Adaptation and Selznick International Pictures' *Rebecca* (1940)', *Cinema Journal* vol 45, no 3, Spring 2006: 32–3.
[17] Ibid, 33–4.
[18] Ibid, 35.

announced reworking of Daniel Defoe's *Robinson Crusoe*.[19] Nor was a Peter Yates project, based on a poem. *The Judgment of Cory*.[20] Walter Mirisch had previously produced Monogram's *Hiawatha*, loosely based on Longfellow's poem.

Literary adaptation aside, adaptations of bestsellers of the kind Mirisch specialized in are less frequently analysed.[21] But Mirisch almost entirely ignored contemporary genre fiction – with the exception of *The Satan Bug* and the issue-led, *In the Heat of the Night*. One reason for the avoidance of more prestigious fare may well have been the disastrous commercial consequences of producing John Huston's adaptation of *Moby Dick*, which went so catastrophically over budget that Moulin had to sell its rights in both *Moulin Rouge* and *Moby Dick*. The Mirisches made nothing from the production. The downsides of fidelity to an ambitious literary work could not have been made more painfully apparent. Walter Mirisch himself suggests *Moby Dick*'s commercial (rather than critical) failure may have been because it was 'perceived as an "art" film'.[22] If so, this was an avenue the brothers would not pursue again until, perhaps, *The Landlord*, in 1970. Similarly, the artist biopic, *Moulin Rouge*, was a one-off. The closest they came to another biopic of an artist was the adaptation of Ben Hecht's disguised autobiography, *Gaily Gaily*, which was a complete failure, both critically and commercially.

As a risk-averse independent, Mirisch prized the pre-testing that buying existing literary and theatrical (presold) properties provided (and the simultaneous, ready-made marketing that the most successful titles in other media brought with them), and the kudos – and custom – that accompanied adaptations of bestsellers and Broadway hits. This reliance on page and stage initially served the company well critically and commercially, and Mirisch retained the strategy, even when its independent production company peers preferred 'originals' – until social and cultural shifts in the late 1960s meant that cinemagoers could no longer be assumed to belong to the same demographic as either bestseller readers or Broadway theatregoers.

All independent producers in post-Paramount Decree Hollywood needed a brand, a distinctiveness, a unique selling point and if 'Quality' was Mirisch's official slogan, one shortcut to it was adaptation, specifically, adaptation of works which had already acquired that label. And it was a shortcut, dramatically reducing the risk of, and requirement for, original screenplays. Mirisch thus minimized the need for R&D – and the development staffing which went with it. However, adaptation was always a fragile brand – since its very 'uniqueness' resided in the 'translation' of an existing story in one medium into another. The resulting films were always simultaneously unique and yet familiar, different but not too different. Furthermore, the success of any screen adaptation, not least because of the time it took for it to reach the screen, made the strategy vulnerable to the vagaries of box office trends and vacillating audience tastes. This chapter analyses the reasons for the success of this strategy at Mirisch – and why

---

[19] 'Musicalized "Robinson Crusoe" by Sammy Cahn and Jimmy Van Heusen is Now at the Mirisch Film Factory...', *Daily Variety*, 9.11.60: 2.
[20] *Variety*, 23.10.68: 5.
[21] Geraghty discusses 'middlebrow' bestsellers in her chapter on Ferber and Buck in *Now a Major Motion Picture*, Christine Geraghty, Rowman and Littlefield, 2007: 103–33.
[22] Mirisch, 2008: 77.

it eventually stopped working, as the company's films no longer found large audiences or won critical approval or awards as it once had done so successfully.

The Mirisch strategy was based, from its formation in 1957, on established stars, directors and literary properties and the 'reputational capital' all three brought with them. 'We felt we couldn't attract the stars without either outstanding material or directors with whom they were anxious to work. We obviously tried to develop material, but at the same time we continued to develop the relationships with directors.'[23] The 'outstanding material' the Mirisches 'tried to develop' was based primarily on adaptations. By implication screenwriters, or at least writers of original material, were relegated behind directors, actors and of course producers in the filmmaking hierarchy at Mirisch. (This relegation coexisted uneasily with the presence of writer-director Wilder at Mirisch for some seventeen years.) The first two years of the company's existence saw a large number of literary properties acquired by Mirisch – simultaneously creating a catalogue of content for adaptation and splashily announcing their arrival as major players. Thus, of Mirisch's first dozen productions, three were based on novels, two were based on films, one was based on a stage play and another on a musical. Published on 26 August 1957 (less than a week before the Mirisch Company was officially launched), *By Love Possessed* was one of three adaptations handed to Mirisch to produce by UA after the latter had a falling out with Seven Arts. The novel had been a surprise success, spending thirty-four weeks on *The New York Times* Best-Seller list, rating #1 on 22 September 1957, three weeks after its release, after holding the number-two position below *Peyton Place* and remained number one for several months, becoming the top-selling novel of 1957, before *Anatomy of a Murder* displaced it.

Over 500,000 copies of *By Love Possessed* were initially sold. The *Readers Digest* Condensed version sold another 3,000,000 copies. Mirisch first announced it in April 1959, for production later that year. In the event, it wasn't filmed until late 1960 and was released in 1961. 1959 also saw the acquisition of *A Rage to Live*. That same year saw a deal with Leon Uris (author of another adapted bestseller, *Exodus*) to write a novel, *The Ghetto*, which Mirisch would own and adapt as a movie. Although the deal dissolved, and Uris subsequently published the novel as *Mila 18*, the concept of commissioning a novel to be then adapted and filmed, all by the same company, was a pioneering one. (Uris had previously scripted Sturges' 1957 *Gunfight at the OK Corral*.) There was a contractual dispute over the rights to Sherwood Anderson's *Winesburg, Ohio*, while Marcia Davenport's bestseller *The Constant Image* was acquired in 1960 as was the stage play *Roar Like a Dove*, intended as a Doris Day vehicle, but none of the latter four were ultimately made by Mirisch.[24]

The best known of these 'adapted works' were thus well-publicized, popular and prestigious. For instance, James Michener had won the Pulitzer Prize in 1948 for *Tales of the South Pacific*, which was the basis of 1958's non-Mirisch musical, *South Pacific* (Logan, 1958); Mirisch bought the rights to *Hawaii* the following year. John

---

[23] Walter Mirisch, quoted in Balio, 1987: 167.
[24] *Variety*, 19.3.58: 3; *Daily Variety*, 3.8.59: 4; *Daily Variety*, 24.4.59: 12; *Variety*, 16.3.60: 17.

O'Hara, the author of the 1949 novel, *A Rage to Live*, won the National Book Award for a subsequent novel in 1956; the Mirisches acquired the rights to *Rage* in 1959. James Cozzens' *By Love Possessed*, adorned the coveted cover of *Time* magazine on 2 September 1957, and was number one on *The New York Times* Best-Seller list three weeks later. The film adaptation was released in 1961. All three books became number one bestsellers. John Ball's *In the Heat of the Night*, meanwhile, won the Edgar Award for Best First Novel and the Crime Writers' Association's Gold Dagger Award.

However, these were just the very visible tip of the iceberg. Most Mirisch 'properties', whether originally produced for the stage or the page, were less successful or celebrated works, like the novels *The Border Jumpers*, *The Man in the Net*, *Cast a Long Shadow*, *Pioneer Go Home* (filmed as *Follow That Dream*), *Return from the Ashes*, *The Russians Are Coming, The Russians Are Coming*, *633 Squadron*, *A Garden of Cucumbers* (filmed as *Fitzwilly*) and *The Hallelujah Trail*. Some had built niche critical reputations – like *The Landlord* and *In the Heat of the Night*, but while the rest didn't necessarily bring significant custom or kudos with them, they did provide blueprints for plot and character.

Instead of buying the rights to *A Rage to Live* for a flat fee of $500,000, the company took a five-year lease on the property, making a down payment of $100,000, with the author John O'Hara guaranteed 25 per cent of any profits.[25] *Rage*'s publication in 1949 perhaps explains the disjunction between it and the popular audience – a 1949 novel acquired in 1959 and finally ready for release in 1965 proved a cultural anachronism, the adaptation of a book from the immediate post-war era offered on-screen to an entirely different America in the mid-sixties.

The adaptation strategy and industry trends

An article in *Daily Variety* in 1960 announcing Mirisch's renewed contract with UA for an additional fourteen films noted this reliance on pretexts. *Variety* noted that

> Mirisch program is interesting in that, despite its two biggest successes – 'Some Like It Hot' and 'The Apartment' – being originals for the screen, all of the 14 projects will be based on bestsellers or hit stage plays. Reason, according to Walter Mirisch, is that there is a shortage of people who have the germ of a story. Said Harold: 'There is a tremendous amount of story material left on the shelves of studios. They can reactivate them and get creative filmmakers to get the best out of them.'[26]

What is most striking about this Mirisch strategy is that it ran increasingly counter to industry trends. In 1961 *Variety* reported, 'Despite current attention on big-money

---

[25] *New York Times*, 2.2.59 and 11.3.59.
[26] '"Presold Material", $3,500,000 Average for the Upcoming 14 Films, All Based on Bestsellers or Stage Hits', *Variety,* 17.8 .60: 7.

purchases of legit properties or bestsellers, film companies have reported a general surge towards material written directly for the screen. A total of 88 vehicles with no previous basis are in various stages of preparation, production/or awaiting release by major studios.'[27] But Mirisch remained undeterred. As *Variety* confirmed the following year, 'The Mirii record for adult transfer of the written word to the screen will remain intact in "Toys in The Attic," confirms Walter M. . . . Mirisch also stressed that about 98% of all literary properties bought had either been or were being made, which further hopped up company' s economy.'[28]

The adaptation strategy was based on several premises. That the existing readership or audience of a work could be attracted to a film based on that work and that the publicity for the book or stage show would function as marketing for the adaptation. That the 'original' worked as R&D for the adaptation, road-testing the plot with consumers. That the sometimes eye-watering expenditure on rights acquisition provided early promotion for the subsequent adaptations. That the kudos or reputation of the original was being acquired with the literary property itself. And that acquiring ready-made raw 'material' was more efficient than commissioning original screenplays. Nevertheless, of their originals, *The Apartment* remains one of Mirisch's most popular and prestigious films and *The Pink Panther* launched Mirisch's most productive and profitable franchise.

It is worth adding that Mirisch didn't always match the right property with the right filmmaker. The director and writer first hired for *Hawaii*, Fred Zinneman and Daniel Taradash, the pair behind *From Here to Eternity* (Zinneman, 1953) left the project when they couldn't agree with the producers about the budget or length of the epic they envisaged. The male action genre director John Sturges was employed to make the 'women's' melodrama *By Love Possessed*, largely to keep him occupied at Mirisch between *The Magnificent Seven* and *The Great Escape*. The film flopped. George Roy Hill was inappropriately tasked with directing the tortured family saga, *Toys in the Attic and* the tortuous epic, *Hawaii*, when his talent turned out to be better suited to buddy movies like *Butch Cassidy and the Sundance Kid* (1969) and *The Sting* (1973).

Promotion and adaptation

The trailers for Mirisch's major film adaptations made much of their literary roots (perhaps significantly, remakes concealed such roots). The trailer for *By Love Possessed* contains the caption 'Pulitzer Prize Winner James Gould Cozzens' Famous Novel' and the voice-over 'One of the most important and distinguished of all bestsellers. Time magazine called it the best book of the year . . . The bold bestseller that sent a fever through America now fires the screen.' Similarly, the opening credits of the trailer for *A*

---

[27] 'Return to Original Scripts – Presold Theory Less Compelling', *Variety*, 26.6.61: 5.
[28] *Variety*, 29.10.62: 2.

Rage to Live begin with the caption, 'The Mirisch Corporation Presents John O'Hara's A RAGE TO LIVE' while the voice-over promotes 'Famed novelist John O'Hara's startling bestseller, A Rage to Live.' The narrator of *Hawaii'* s trailer announces, 'Now James Michener's Monumental novel, his beautiful, fierce vision of paradise, comes to life, from the broad sweep of its epic drama to its most intimate emotions' (this, over shots of bare-breasted Hawaiians). The trailer for the sequel, *The Hawaiians*, states 'This is the continuation of James A. Michener's epic novel, Hawaii.'

Indeed, nothing demonstrates the promotional double duty of such acquisitions better than *Hawaii*, the rights for which were acquired for a record-breaking $600,000 in 1958.

> In order to bridge the two-year span between the publication of James R. Michener's novel, 'Hawaii,' by Random House on Nov. 10 and the release of the film version in late 1961, the publishers, United Artists and the Mirisch Co. are embarking on a joint promotional campaign to keep the book on the top of the bestseller lists. Plans to allocate $100,000 towards that end were outlined here today by Bennett Cerf, Random House prexy, Fred Goldberg, UA' s national ad-pub and exploitation director, and Leon Roth, veep of the Mirisch Co. The publishing house, which is printing an initial 100,000 copies of book, will handle the campaign until the end of the year. From there on, the joint effort takes effect. The Mirisch outfit acquired the Michener novel about the origins and history of Hawaii for $600,000 against 10% of the profits. . . . 'Hawaii' is already assured of a wide readership via two instalments in Reader's Digest Condensed Book Club, a piece in Reader's Digest magazine, and an illustration of the first section of the book in Life Magazine. It's also the choice of the Book-of-the-Month Club for December. The promotional push will include a heavy newspaper and mag campaign, window displays, radio and tv plugs, etc. First for the book alone and later tying in the picture. Cerf said that, unfortunately, the same thing was happening in the book world as has been happening in films, legit and tv. 'Big books by well-known authors are bigger than ever and you can't give away a first novel,' he said. 'Everyone goes for big things. It' s too bad for the culture of the country, but it' s great for someone like Michener. Everything that man touches seems to turn to gold.' Cerf figured the novelist would get about $1,000,000 out of Hawaii.[29]

The Mirisch Company was going for 'big things' too and while not quite everything it touched turned to gold, a combination of Oscar successes and box office records kept the company in business throughout the 1960s. The eventual film of *Hawaii* was based on the book's third chapter, *From the Farm of Bitterness*, which covered the settlement of the island kingdom by the first American missionaries. Zinnemann and Taradash, eventually left when their plan for a two-part epic was turned down and they were replaced by George Roy Hill and writer Dalton Trumbo. In the United Artists Files on

---

[29] 'UA, Random to Co-Plug Hawaii', *Daily Variety*, 16.9.59: 1, 4; 'Hawaii' Topping Lists' *Daily Variety*, 12.2.60: 2.

Hawaii there are letters from Fred Zinneman regarding the two parts plan of *Hawaii*, admitting that, 'We discussed at great length the question of breaking the film into two evenings' and the casting of Rock Hudson as Whip.[30] The Pressbook for *Hawaii*, *Hawaii: Story in Pictures*, notes that the book was 'one of the most popular novels of all time' and had probably been read by more people than any other work of fiction 'in the neighbourhood of 100,000,000'. Under the heading, 'GREAT BOOKS MAKE GREAT MOVIES; HAWAII IS LATEST EXAMPLE', it stresses that

> Aside from the undoubted draw of Julie Andrews and several others, the film version of James A. Michener's 'Hawaii' has something particularly potent going for it that no other current movie can claim. It is that title billing – James A. Michener's 'Hawaii' . . . This is the way it has been through the annals of the movies, that a large proportion of the finest, the most memorable and the most successful movies have stemmed from books that were successes in themselves. Their ingredients of storytelling were proven by success at the bookstalls. All that remained was successfully to adapt the stories of the books to screen, and what emerged was at least as successful . . . To the literary quality of Michener's undoubted great story telling has been added the great visual realism of the story re-told on the giant Color by Delux and Panavision screen[31]

Much the same strategy was deployed with the adaptation of *Toys in the Attic*.[32] In the event, William Wyler, for whom the play was acquired, departed the project and George Roy Hill directed it. Foregrounding the expenditure on rights in the publicity for its acquisitions seems to have been a conscious strategy for Mirisch. *Variety* reported, for instance, that the rights for *How to Succeed in Business Without Really Trying* and *Same Time, Next Year* cost a record-breaking $1,000,000 each; *Hawaii* cost $600,000, *A Rage to Live* cost $500,000 with a down payment of $100,000, *Toys in the Attic* cost $400,000 and *Two for the Seesaw* cost $350,000.[33] Such early outlay may have been high, but by making unprecedented payments for properties like these Mirisch ensured that their adaptations were in the news even before pre-production began. If the price of acquiring a literary property is generally seen as a pre-production or screenplay cost, for Mirisch it doubled as a marketing or publicity cost too, differentiating such high-profile adaptations from mainstream Hollywood productions and promising pictures of blockbuster proportions – which *West Side Story* and *Hawaii*, at least, delivered on.

Best sellers and the box office

Of course, not all Mirisch adaptations were successful. *By Love Possessed* may have been based on a 1957 bestseller, but by 1960, when Mirisch's adaptation finally went

---

[30] Zinnemann letter to Harold Mirisch 25.11.60, UA Collection Addition, Box 5, File 10.
[31] Walter Mirisch Collection, Center for Film and Theatre Research, Box 4 File 7.
[32] 'Hellman Play Buy: 400G', *Variety*, 23.3.60: 4.
[33] *New York Times*, 2.2.59 and 11.3.59; *Variety*, 23.3.60: 4.

into production, the project had lost its moment and the publicity its momentum. It had initially been acquired for production for UA by Seven Arts, alongside the stage play *Two for the Seesaw* and the musical *West Side Story*, but UA passed all three on to Mirisch when UA's relationship with Seven Arts soured. *Two for the Seesaw* and *By Love Possessed* both flopped at the box office, but *West Side Story* more than compensated for their failure, becoming the top box office attraction of 1962, placing it fifth on *Variety*'s 1963 list of all-time box office winners, behind *Gone with the Wind* (Fleming, 1939) *Ben-Hur* (Wyler, 1959) *The Ten Commandments* (DeMille, 1956) and *Around the World in 80 Days* (Anderson, 1956) all, perhaps significantly, epics and all also adaptations.[34] Such success, incidentally, could hardly have dampened Mirisch's enthusiasm for the adaptation of *Hawaii*.

Of the first twenty films Mirisch produced for United Artists, seven were adapted from novels, one was based on a non-fiction book, five were adapted from stage plays, two from Broadway musicals, four were remakes – one of which had itself been based on a stage play. Only four were original screenplays. Of the second twenty-film deal, nine were adapted from novels, one was based on a non-fiction work, two were adapted from stage plays, and one was from a Broadway musical. The final 28-film contract included four films adapted from novels, one based on a non-fiction book, one adapted from a musical, and one based on a stage play. This reduction in the number of adaptations is, no doubt, partially due to the reduction in UA's financial commitment to Mirisch in this period, resulting in a return to lower budget productions, of the kind with which the brothers had been associated at Monogram. Such restrictions ironically coincided with their penchant for increasingly indulging those major directors with whom Mirisch had multi-picture contracts, on bigger budget productions, in spite or perhaps because of their lack of pre-existing 'outstanding material'. Perhaps the best example of this is Blake Edwards' *The Party*, the original screenplay for which was barely half the length of an average script, allowing for improvisation for a considerable amount of the film's running time. The script of The *Thomas Crown Affair* was similarly brief. As Jewison remarked, 'It ended up as an 85–90-page screenplay because there wasn't much story there. It was an exercise in style. It was such a short script we were sort of making it up as went along.'[35]

Having paid out mouth-watering amounts of money for the rights to bestsellers and Broadway hits in its early years, Mirisch was reduced to acquiring the rights to little-known novels like *The Spikes Gang* and *The Landlord* in its final contract period with United Artists, while also adapting a second section of the already acquired *Hawaii* for *The Hawaiians* and borrowing Conan Doyle's out of copyright protagonist for *The Private Life of Sherlock Holmes*. The latter was commercially disastrous, mistakenly assuming that Wilder's take on the character was as interesting as Conan Doyle's. Norman Jewison's *Gaily, Gaily*, an adaptation of Ben Hecht's autobiographical novel, *A Child of the Century*, proved equally self-indulgent.

---

[34] '"West Side" – The Lead "Story": All-Time Top Film Grosses', *Variety*, 9.1.63: S18.
[35] Director's Commentary of the DVD release, *The Thomas Crown Affair* (DVD released, 2000).

In general, Mirisch spurned innovation in both source material (the properties they acquired were, mostly, resolutely mainstream and middlebrow – *The Landlord* is probably the exception) and in those they hired to adapt them (established filmmakers and TV veterans were their default directors, with Hal Ashby, appropriately enough, as *The Landlord*'s director, the company's sole directorial debut – and even in that case, the Mirisches only agreed on condition that the originally slated director, Norman Jewison, served as producer). *In the Heat of the Night* and *Fiddler on the Roof* were Mirisch's last two major adaptation successes for UA, though, strikingly, the company's best late film, a commercial failure, is probably *The Landlord*, also an adaptation, but of a book by a Black novelist, adapted by a Black screenwriter – a rare exception to the established white adaptors and adapted works usually relied on.

Fredric Jameson restates a familiar observation: 'A great film can be made from a mediocre novel; most great novels only yield second-rate movie versions.'[36] Mirisch avoided great novels (Huston's *Moby Dick* had been the exception that proved that rule for them), but by also ignoring much contemporary genre fiction they attached themselves too closely to respectable historical genres acceptable to middlebrow, middle-aged readers and theatregoers, at precisely the moment when this demographic was in drastic decline at the box office. Mirisch adaptations included high-profile Broadway productions and bestselling novels, but also Westerns and comic fiction, rather than the crime stories, horror and science fiction that provided the bases of many of the breakthrough films of the so-called movie brats. The success of a second preview, at a campus cinema, of *Some Like It Hot*, after a disastrous first screening at a mainstream picture house, should also have alerted them to this problem early in the company's history, but seems not to have done.

If they had taken their action thriller genre successes with *In the Heat of the Night* and belatedly, *Mr Majestyk*, more seriously, they might have found another literary lifebelt in the 1970s, but in the former it seems to be the anti-racist message, rather than the police procedural format, which attracted them (as evidenced by two, utterly lacklustre, but also curiously colour-blind sequels) while the latter is largely distinguished by Elmore Leonard's screenplay (which he subsequently novelized). Instead, Mirisch proved more comfortable adapting mainstream fiction, often melodramas, of the kind referred to as airport novels, which became so central to 1970s cinema, with bestseller-based genre blockbusters like *The Godfather*, *Jaws* and, of course, *Airport* itself (Seaton, 1970). (*Airport*'s author, Arthur Hailey's subsequent novel, *Wheels*, was optioned by Mirisch as their final UA production, but they never made it.) The Mirisch heyday preceded the airport novel era, but their reliance on books and plays for armchair travellers as well as would-be tourists – notably *Hawaii, Avanti, Fiddler on the Roof* – remains prescient (both in on-screen exhibition of local landscapes and off-screen exploitation of national subsidies). Appropriately, when, in 1961, TWA began showing in-flight movies on a regular

---

[36] Jameson, in *True to the Spirit: Film Adaptation and the Question of Fidelity*, McCabe, Murray, Warner (eds), Oxford University Press, 2011: 217.

basis, *By Love Possessed* kicked off the program and became the first-ever movie screened in-flight by an airline.

International adaptations

Mirisch's appetite for adaptations was international and, presumably, potential foreign box office receipts, as well as foreign filming benefits, were part of the calculation. *Town Without Pity* was based on a German novel *(Stadt ohne mitleid)* and was shot in Germany; *Return from the Ashes* was based on a French novel (Le Retour des cendres) but filmed in the UK; *A Shot in the Dark* was based on the Harry Kurnitz play, which in turn was an adaptation of Marcel Achard's play, *L'Idiote* and was shot in France and the UK. Four of Billy Wilder's Mirisch films were adapted from theatre – *Irma La Douce* (from Alexandre Breffort's play), with only scene-setting exteriors shot in Paris, *Kiss Me, Stupid* (from Anna Bonacci's play L'orra della fantasia), *Avanti* (from Samuel Taylor's play), filmed in Italy and *One, Two, Three* (from Ferenc Molnar's play, *Egy, kettő, három*) filmed in Germany. And of course, both *Some Like It Hot* and *The Magnificent Seven* were adaptations – or remakes – of foreign films.

The brothers' aversion to what they saw as exploitation cinema may be partly a residue of their previous career at Monogram, which specialized in such genres, and partly an attempt to retain the family audience rather than target the young. Indeed, as soon as they could comfortably afford to acquire the rights to the best work of a writer like Cornell Woolrich, they avoided it. The preference for war movies and Westerns, meanwhile, may in part be a consequence of Walter Mirisch's passion for history. But it was also a pursuit of the middle ground, the mature, male mainstream and respectability – and nothing is as respectable in Hollywood as middlebrow literary work. Mirisch's reliance on adaptation as a quality strategy distinguished its output, a distinction which was ironically achieved by basing those adaptations on already pre-tested texts (novels, plays, musicals and, indeed, other films). Adaptations could piggy-back on their originals' prestige and reputation as well as provide risk-averse insurance through their market-proven success in other media.

Of Mirisch's most successful films – *Some Like It Hot* and *The Magnificent Seven* were remakes, *The Apartment*, *The Pink Panther* and *The Thomas Crown Affair* were originals, *Hawaii*, *In the Heat of the Night* and *The Russians Are Coming, The Russians Are Coming* were based on novels, *West Side Story* and *Fiddler on the Roof* were adaptations of hit Broadway musicals, *The Great Escape* and *Midway* were based on non-fiction. Even *The Pink Panther* sequel, *A Shot in the Dark,* was based on a stage play. That divides 5/8 between 'originals' and 'adaptations' (from all media, including movie remakes). The Mirisch adaptation strategy may not have always been a reliable recipe for commercial and/or critical success, but it was always also an investment in IP – *Hawaii* and *Heat* both spawned sequels – though for Mirisch, IP didn't have the long tail it does now, as UA ultimately acquired its assets at the end of every contract period. It was also a marketing strategy (generating pre-publicity for the films, which every paperback edition and theatre ticket subsequently sold helped promote) and insurance against risk.

Books as props and plot points

This attitude to the strategic benefits of books is occasionally reflected in the adaptations themselves. The title sequence of *How to Succeed in Business Without Really Trying* sees the hero, J. Pierrepoint Finch, emerge from a New York Metro station on the way to work and buy at a newsstand a paperback copy of the (actually satirical) how-to book, *How to Succeed in Business Without Really Trying* (on which the musical itself was based). The first line of the film is voice-over as Finch reads the book in the street. 'Dear Reader, this little book is designed to explain everything you need to know about the science of getting ahead in business. Your first step is to memorize all the simple rules in the chapters which follow. If you have education, intelligence and ability so much the better, but remember that thousands have reached the top without any of these qualities. If you are anxious to rise quickly and easily to the top of the business world, the time is now. Strike while the iron is hot. Are you ready?' (To which the hero replies, 'I'm ready' – his first on-camera line in the film.) He carries the book with him in early scenes, and, by following its advice, makes his way from being a window cleaner to a corporate executive. The film's first song even contains the couplet – 'This book is all that I need, How to, How to Succeed.'

In *Fitzwilly*, the hero, played by Dick Van Dyke, tries to keep his bankrupt philanthropist employer afloat by criminal acts, but at the end of the film the apparently unpublishable dictionary the latter has been working on is sold for $500,000 to Hollywood and it is thus her book which bails them out. There are also writer protagonists in *The Russians Are Coming, The Russians Are Coming* (the playwright hero), *Town Without Pity* (the reporter), *Gaily Gaily* (the writer manqué hero), *Sinful Davey* (the latter pair being both based on loose autobiographies) and *Kiss Me, Stupid* (the songwriter protagonists).

The literary provenance of much of the company's output could prove critical in qualifying the package in UA's eyes, but it could also reinforce a literal, prosaic, proscenium cinema – in which the depth of field characteristic of Wyler and Toland's black and white filmmaking was replaced by the breadth of frame of widescreen colour. Books, for Mirisch, were thus both literary properties (off-screen sources) and props (on-screen objects). But such properties – and props – can ultimately prove disposable too. Many of Mirisch's acquisitions went unproduced. Others outlived their bankability. In an early scene in their utterly disposable *The First Time* we see the hero's father packing books into cardboard boxes with his secretary/lover, Pamela. 'Honey, remind me never to collect books again' Pamela: 'Right' She carries a cardboard box full of books, he picks up another armful, including two very visible copies of the oversized paperback bestseller, *Hawaii*.

In his anthology on literary adaptation, James Naremore wrote that 'We now live in a media-saturated environment dense with cross-references and filled with borrowings from movies, books and every other form of representation. Books can become movies, but movies themselves can also become novels, published screenplays, Broadway musicals, television shows, remakes and so on.'[37] Mirisch was doing most of these things three decades before Naremore's 'now'. *Mr Majestyk*, *Kings of the Sun* and *The Last Escape* were all novelized after production; the scripts of *The Apartment* and *The Fortune Cookie* were published by Studio Vista in 1971; *In the Heat of the Night* span off two sequels and a TV series. As such, Mirisch's adaptation strategy helped pioneer the industry's shift from vertical to horizontal integration in the late 1960s as multinational corporations, including media conglomerates, replaced the studio system and increasingly combined publishing and film production companies under the same corporate roof.

---

[37] James Naremore, *Film Adaptation*, New Brunswick: Rutgers University Press, 2000, 12–13.

6

Same time next year *or* the return of the seven

The Mirisch Company's sequels and series for cinema and television

Why series?

The Mirisches' experience at Monogram and Allied Artists – studios whose production processes approximated Fordist assembly lines as closely as Hollywood filmmaking could – reinforced the Fordist and Taylorist principles Walter had imbibed at Harvard and implemented at Lockheed, while minimizing costs and personnel. The brothers' subsequent career at their own small independent production company, packaging individual film projects with minimum permanent staff and almost exclusively freelance labour, epitomized post-Fordism. Mirisch was, then, a transitional company, a halfway house between the studio era's vertical integration and the – albeit relative – independence of its package-unit output deal with United Artists, and the company survived by combining residual Fordist with emergent post-Fordist strategies. Series production proved one profitable way of reconciling those two strategies, of squaring that cinematic circle.

The Mirisch Company is something of a forgotten episode in the history of Hollywood's cinematic series, not only an echo of studio era, often B movie series but also a precursor to the film franchise era which began in the 1970s. As producers of both film and TV series *and* as executives who worked in the industry before and after the Paramount Decree put an end to vertical integration, the Mirisches saw the financial benefit and risk avoidance inherent in a business strategy that included an impetus to continuity and repetition with minimal difference. That strategy facilitated the perpetuation, whenever possible, of continuous production, rather than on a film-by-film, or programme-by-programme basis.

That the company was intent on, and aware of, this strategy is evident not only in the industrially disproportionate number of cinematic sequels it produced in the period but also in the dialogue of a film which was not itself a sequel. Thus, in *Fitzwilly*, the titular hero, played by Dick Van Dyke, tries to keep his bankrupt philanthropist employer afloat by criminal acts, but eventually, the apparently unpublishable dictionary she has been working on is sold for $500,000 to Hollywood.

Miss Vicky: 'It was new money I earned from the Dictionary, so it makes it all right.'
Juliet: '$500,000! From Opal Pictures!'
First Man: 'And that's only for A-K. L-Z shall sell later, for more.'
Second Man: 'If the movie about Miss Vicky's father is the sensation Opal Pictures thinks it will be, they will undoubtedly make a sequel.'

Similarly, in the screenplay for *The Pink Panther*, Charles remarks 'We can call the sequel . . . Nephew of the Phantom'.[1]

Sequels, series and serials

As Stuart Henderson points out, 'the boundaries of any definition between the sequel, the series, the serial and the saga will always be highly porous'.[2] In a series each episode is, conventionally, a self-contained, complete narrative. In a serial, on the other hand, the narrative continues from one episode to the next. One crucial distinction between a sequel and a series film, meanwhile, seems to be that the latter, while featuring recurring characters, almost never acknowledges the events of previous films. Of course, the boundaries between these forms remain fluid, but the essential distinctions remain useful. Whatever form such films took, however, they mitigated against the one-film-at-a-time logic of the film-centred, rather than firm-centred approach of the average post-Paramount Decision independent.

Within the film industry, as trade press usage confirms, the terms series, serial and sequel are often equally blurred. For instance, in 1959, *Variety* reported that Mirisch was one of four production companies developing '60-minute film stanzas for the 1960-1961 tv season' for NBC.[3] A stanza, in *Variety*'s lexicon, is a series episode. Two years later, *Variety* reported that the Mirisch Company was developing another series, this time for the cinema. Under the headline, 'Shepherd's Mirisch Series' it noted that producer Richard Shepherd 'has set a deal with Mirisches for series of pix, first of which will be "Seven Men At Daybreak"'.[4] Industry use of the term 'series' often referred to a contracted number of otherwise unrelated projects, rather than a sequence of similar ones. This chapter, while relying heavily on trade press reports of Mirisch activities, retains academic rather than industry or trade paper terminology.

Nevertheless, the regularity with which the terms 'serial', 'series', 'sequel', 'spin-off' and 'franchise' are sometimes used virtually interchangeably makes it difficult to speak with precision. Here I use the words 'series' and 'serial' as earlier, while the term 'sequel' is deployed to refer to a further episode about a character or characters without

---

[1] *The Pink Panther* script, Walter Mirisch Papers, Center for Film and Theater Research, Wisconsin Historical Society, Box 7, Folder 1., 147A.
[2] Stuart Henderson, *The Hollywood Sequel: History and Form 1911-2010*, Bloomsbury, 2014, 5.
[3] *Variety*, 2.9.59: 33.
[4] *Variety*, 2.8.61: 3. The film was not made.

a continuing storyline (and indeed often without coherent causal or chronological continuities with its predecessor and progenitor). Following Henderson, I use the term 'spin-off' to refer strictly to films, TV programmes and other material featuring what were secondary characters from the initial episode. I acknowledge that these definitions are themselves relative but hope that they provide some fireproofing against confusion and conflation. Henderson suggests that

> the defining characteristic of the sequel is its acknowledgment of a chronological narrative relationship with a prior instalment. . . . The dividing line between the sequel and the series film is this: while both forms revisit characters from an earlier episode, the latter can be identified primarily by its general lack of commitment to maintaining narrative continuity from one instalment to the next.

He also distinguishes usefully between sequels which were 'preconceived' and those which were 'ad hoc'.[5] Recent scholarship on the history of Hollywood series, serials and sequels (e.g. by Henderson, Jess-Cooke, and Jess-Cooke and Verevis) reinforces the critical consensus that they were a commonplace of the early silent period, that in the sound era they were largely, though not exclusively, relegated to second feature status, and that they only re-emerged into respectability (even, occasionally, increasing rather than decreasing box office receipts for subsequent episodes) in the era of the Movie Brats with *Jaws*, *The Godfather* and *Star Wars* in the mid-1970s. It is the contention of this chapter, on the other hand, that sequels and series (and some aspects of seriality) were re-introduced into mainstream Hollywood cinema in the 1960s by the new independent production companies created in the wake of the Paramount Decree, one of which was the Mirisch Company. I also argue that the Mirisch Company contributed disproportionately to the production of such films. 'From 1964 to 1968, sequels and reissues combined accounted for just under five percent of all Hollywood releases. From 1974 to 1978, they comprised 17.5 percent.'[6] This is a striking statistic when one considers that, between 1964 and 1968, 14 per cent of Mirisch productions were sequels. But in 1974, Mirisch's final contract with UA came to an end, and neither the company nor the surviving brothers were ever again in the comfortable position of having both guaranteed finance from – and an output deal with – a distributor for which a similar sequel strategy might make sense (Figure 9).

In 1957, the year the Mirisch Company was founded, the majors released 268 movies, 58 per cent of which were produced by independent production companies. Among the films produced by the Mirisch Company and its corporate successors for UA between 1957 and the end of their corporate relationship in 1974, several spawned sequels or series. Mirisch titles with returning characters are *The Magnificent Seven* quartet – *The Magnificent Seven* (1960), *The Return of the Seven* (1966), *Guns of the Magnificent Seven* (1969) and *The Magnificent Seven Ride* (1972); *The Pink Panther*

---

[5] Henderson, 2014: 4.
[6] Thomas Schatz, 'The New Hollywood', in Jim Collins, Hilary Radner and Ava Preacher Collins (eds), *Film Theory Goes to the Movies: Cultural Analysis of Contemporary Film*, Routledge, 1993, 21.

Figure 9 *Return of the Seven* poster.

(1963) and two sequels, *A Shot in the Dark* (1964) and *Inspector Clouseau* (1968) and *In the Heat of the Night* (1967); and its two follow-up films *They Call Me MISTER Tibbs* (1970) and *The Organization* (1971). To these seven 'returns' on three 'originals' can arguably be added *Hawaii* (1966) and its semi-sequel *The Hawaiians* (1970) – both films were adapted from different sections of the same novel and continue the stories of the Hale, Hoxworth, Whipple and other families on the island. The *Pink Panther* franchise also included a series of *Panther* cinema shorts, as well as multiple TV series including *The Pink Panther Show* (NBC 1969–71) *The Pink Panther Meets the Ant and the Aardvark* (NBC 1971–6), *The Pink Panther Laugh and a Half Hour* (NBC 1976–8), *The All New Pink Panther Show* (NBC 1978–9), *The Pink Panther and Sons* (NBC 1984–5) and *The New Pink Panther Show* (Syndicated, 1993–4).

There were fewer than 130 Hollywood sequels and series films between 1955 and 1974.[7] The Mirisch Company and its successor corporations produced twelve of them (three 'originals', seven sequels, plus *Hawaii* and *The Hawaiians*) – almost 10 per cent of Hollywood's output in the categories over those years. Considering how many majors and independents were then producing features, the proportion made by Mirisch is striking. More specifically, Hollywood produced some seventy sequels and series films between 1965 and 1974. Mirisch companies between them were responsible for nine of these, so over 12.8 per cent of Hollywood's sequels and series films in that ten-year period were Mirisch productions. A total of sixty-two sequels and series films were among the hundreds of films made in Hollywood during the 1960s. Of those, six were produced by Mirisch companies. Given that the major studios and numerous independent production companies were then making hundreds of features annually, this too is impressive at almost 10 per cent of the total. Sequels were clearly a crucial part of the Mirisch production strategy throughout this period, initiated soon after the company came into existence and only abandoned shortly before the end of their output deal with UA in 1974.

The rationale for series production

What explanatory frameworks have been provided for the re-emergence of 'cinematic seriality' in post-studio era Hollywood? Three overlapping industrial imperatives – horizontal integration, television series production and the package-unit system – can be mentioned here and the Mirisch Company and its corporate successors were active participants, if not actual pioneers, in each of these spheres. First, in the form of media conglomeration and convergence; second, the advent of production not only for film but also for TV and, crucially, of TV as a destination for film (as well as other media spin-offs including soundtrack albums, novelizations and so on) and including industrial synergies across and between media; and third, the package-unit system of production, by which the film, rather than the firm, became the organizing principle of the movie business.[8] Perhaps paradoxically, it was thus the rejection of the assembly-line production model characteristic of the vertically integrated studios that, in the case of independents like Mirisch, propelled them towards series and sequels. Furthermore, these imperatives proved mutually reinforcing. After all, Mirisch had a distributor, UA, which was anticipating an average of four of the company's films to release every year, and the sequel provided one default strategy for fulfilling that contractual obligation. Indeed, the impetus towards sequels and series was clearly with the brothers before their company's formation.

At Warners in the 1920s and 1930s, Harold Mirisch had seen at first-hand how successful series films could be at the box office. Meanwhile, at Harvard and Lockheed

---

[7] Henderson, 2014: 55.
[8] Bordwell, Thompson and Staiger, 1985: 330.

during the Second World War, Walter Mirisch had learned the economies of ensuring continuity of production, rather than batch production, a lesson reinforced by his early experience as a producer at Monogram. During the so-called studio era, the majors had both on-screen and behind-the-camera talent on long-term contracts, even renting them out on occasion to their rivals. Stars, screenwriters and directors were virtually studio assets, the properties of the big five vertically integrated film businesses. In the disintegrated world of independent production companies, talent was freelance but now the films themselves became crucial properties – each company building up its own back catalogue (vitally valuable for sale to syndication for the new medium of television). The Mirisch brothers, with their previous experience on Poverty Row, had already learned how to operate at much lower budgets than many of their rivals. Their years at Monogram and subsequently Allied Artists, with its own TV division, not only accustomed them to tight budgets and schedules but also to series production, not least through the *Bomba* films, which Walter had initiated and produced.

The Mirisch Company strategy was ultimately an attempt to re-institute aspects of continuous production through the making of cinema sequels and TV series. When he arrived at Monogram in 1945, as Walter recalld in his autobiography, 'We were constantly attempting to determine whether we were operating in the most cost-effective way possible.'[9] To instil such cost-effectiveness, Mirisch applied the scientific management skills he had learned at Harvard and Lockheed to film production. One such skill was the ability to ensure production remained, whenever possible, continuous.

A decade before co-founding the Mirisch Company, Walter Mirisch went from being a salaried staffer at Monogram to a freelance producer, paid a fee for each production. As previously cited, Walter 'understood the value of the series pictures to their producers. They provided a minimum subsistence income to producers who were trying to survive in a most unstable profession'. Recognizing the insecurities of one-off productions, Mirisch 'started to look for a subject that could become a series and that would provide a minimum income for me while I was searching for better films to do.'[10] Mirisch launched the series with *Bomba, the Jungle Boy* and Steve Broidy, company president, who agreed they should produce two films a year, the first being shot for $85,000 in eight days. The series deployed considerable stock footage, a strategy the Mirisch Company would deploy repeatedly later.[11] Mirisch received a fee of $2,500 for the film, plus 50 per cent participation in profits, once overheads and other Monogram expenses had been deducted.

Like Harold Mirisch, Broidy's background was in theatres – he had run the Boston Monogram Exchange in the 1930s before becoming national sales director for the company in 1940. On his appointment as president, late in 1945, Broidy stepped up Monogram's reliance on series production. In June 1949, *Variety* announced that the company's ten current film series constituted an industry record. Broidy was adamant

---

[9] Mirisch, 2008: 25.
[10] Ibid, 27–8.
[11] Ibid, 34–5.

that 'This policy has proven immensely popular with exhibitors and the theatre-going public through the years and we intend to continue along the line which has proven so successful'.[12] In 1955 Harold Mirisch's perspective on series films was equally clear. 'While "big" pictures are being stressed under AA's production policy, Mirisch said that the company's "series" pictures such as *The Bowery Boys* would be continued for "unquestionably there's a definite distributor desire and need for these films."'[13] Furthermore, AA's corporate parent, Monogram, had been one of the first companies to recognize TV as a market for features, selling its back catalogue to television in 1951, several years before the majors began doing deals with the networks.

Mirisch series

The three films which launched Mirisch mini-franchises, *The Magnificent Seven*, *The Pink Panther* and *In the Heat of the Night* were released in 1960, 1963 and 1967 respectively, each project inaugurating a new contract with UA. In fact, before 1960, the company was already committed to series production, both through its TV subsidiary and by exploring the potential of cinematic sequels. Only a matter of months after the formation of the Mirisch Company on 1 September 1957, the William Morris Agency had submitted the pre-publication manuscript of James Michener's novel, *Hawaii*, to a number of possible purchasers including Mirisch, with Fred Zinnemann attached to direct an adaptation. 'Fred became convinced that the script had to be done as two films. . . . He wanted to shoot both films continuously. . . . In a sense it would have been a theatrical miniseries.'[14] This was twenty years before the advent of TV miniseries and more than fifty before *The Lord of the Rings* trilogy (Jackson, 2001–3).

Zinnemann and screenwriter Daniel Taradash started work on a screenplay in 1960, but after a year, still struggling with the structure of the novel and its unwieldy chronology (from colonization to independence) and huge ensemble cast of characters, the pair proposed a four-hour feature to be shown in two parts. Harold Mirisch wrote to Arthur Krim enclosing a press release about the ambitions of *Hawaii*, 'After close analysis of the structure and content of Michener's novel, Zinneman and Taradash have reached the conclusion that there is a necessity to tell the entire story contained in the book.' According to Harold Mirisch and United Artists, 'this basic decision to tell the complete story contained in the 946-page best seller will result in the first major American film ever to be shown in two parts'. The two films were envisaged as being exhibited in 'road show' form.[15]

When UA vetoed this idea, first Taradash and then Zinnemann left the project and were replaced by screenwriter Dalton Trumbo and George Roy Hill, who had

---

[12] *Variety*, 28.6.49: 5; See also Edwards, 2011: 386–400; and Yannis Tzioumakis, *American Independent Cinema: An Introduction*, 77–82.
[13] *Variety*, 13.7.55: 4.
[14] Mirisch, 2008: 134, 218–19.
[15] Harold Mirisch Letter, 12.4.61, United Artists Collection, Wisconsin, Box 5–10.

just directed *Toys in the Attic* for Mirisch. The Mirisch Company resolved to focus the (initial) film on the first half of the book, which dramatizes the period between 1820 and 1841. Shot on location not only in Hawaii itself but also in Tahiti, Norway and New England, the film was budgeted at $10 million and eventually cost another $4 million. But the second half of the novel remained to be exploited. 'I had always felt that if *Hawaii* was successful, we should make a follow-up film utilizing the excised material.'[16] The subsequent film, *The Hawaiians*, starring Charlton Heston, picked up the story from the second half of Michener's book, with the development of the islands in the twentieth century. *Variety* variously referred to it as 'the Mirisch freres' sequel', 'The Hawaiians' and 'sequel to the earlier "Hawaii"' but also as 'not strictly a sequel'.[17] This belated follow-up was finally released in 1970 but had little of the first film's success at the box office or with the critics. If evidence is needed to demonstrate its status for Mirisch, as an essentially secondary sequel, it is the assignment of TV regular, Tom Gries, to direct. At an Xmas 1969 party in Hollywood, Charlton Heston was reportedly 'Talking the third "Hawaii" pic' but this joke only reaffirms the serious role sequels played in the Mirisch strategy.[18] A letter from Alan A. Benjamin regarding *Hawaii* and *The Hawaiians* also mentions a 'THIRD PICTURE (Based upon the Michener Property, HAWAII, if produced.)'.[19]

Mirisch TV series

Even earlier, in January 1958, Yul Brynner and Walter Mirisch signed a deal with UA which contracted them to providing both film and TV productions including series.[20] In early 1959, Mirisch signed another deal with NBC, to produce two series for the network, *Wichita Town* and *The Iron Horseman* (NBC, 1960).[21] In the event *Wichita Town*, a disguised spin-off from the feature Walter had produced for AA, *Wichita*, also starring Joel McCrea, ran for just a single season while *The Iron Horseman* only appeared as a pilot. (Mirisch's *Gunfight at Dodge City* later featured the character, Bat Masterson, who had previously appeared in *Wichita*. Similarly, *Hour of the Gun* was a continuation of the story of Wyatt Earp which Sturges had initiated in *Gunfight at the OK Corral*.)

As Mirisch recalled, 'Because of the success of our earlier film, Wichita, I suggested a show revolving around a marshall in the city of Wichita and his deputy, rather in the same vein as Gunsmoke.'[22] Joel McCrea, star of both the original *Wichita* (which Walter Mirisch had produced for Allied Artists) and the Mirisch Company's own *Fort*

---

[16] Mirisch, 2008: 291.
[17] *Variety*, 4.11.68: 2; 21.5.69: 28; 4.10.68:19.
[18] *Daily Variety*, 22.12.69: 2.
[19] Alan Benjamin Letter, 28.1.71, UA Collection Addition, Box 5, File 10.
[20] 'Brynner, Mirisch Pledge UA TV Tie', *Variety*, 1.1.58: 23.
[21] 'Mirisch-NBC Team on 'Wichita' and 'Horseman'', *Variety*, 11.3.59: 32.
[22] Mirisch, 2008: 92.

Massacre and *The Gunfight at Dodge City*, agreed to the idea, in order to help secure his son, Jody, a regular role as deputy. *Wichita Town* was pitched by McCrea's agent at William Morris to NBC president, Robert Kintner, who agreed to twenty-six episodes without a pilot. According to Kintner, 'The theory of NBC is basically to create what we call a schedule of meat-and-potatoes.'[23] As Balio explains, 'if the Kintner era meant more film and less live work, it also meant more outside program procurement and less in-house production. Kintner explicitly advocated that his new network follow the example of ABC by cultivating good relations with a few reliable program producers and establishing durable licensing arrangements with them.'[24] By the time Mirisch was pitching NBC its own 'potatoes', *Wichita Town* and *The Iron Horseman*, the networks were wall to wall with Westerns. Indeed, In the 1958–9 season, seven of the top ten series were Westerns.[25]

Mirisch was partnered with Four Star, a reliable TV production company, and Walter appointed his long-time editor, Richard Heermance, to run the Mirisch TV arm. Daniel Ullman, who had scripted *Gunfight*, wrote several episodes of the series. Each episode was budgeted at $35,000 to $40,000 and was in black and white. 'I read all the material, gave notes, ran dailies and first cuts, but principally left production to our creative team.'[26] It was sponsored by Proctor and Gamble, scheduled at 10.30 pm, a late slot for a series initially aimed at primetime and the sponsor was entitled to have a say. James Coburn appeared in the opening episode. The ratings were disappointing and the series was cancelled.

Meanwhile, Mirisch

> came up with an idea for another show, which would be a sitcom. Peter Lind Hayes and Mary Healy were attractive speciality entertainers, and I proposed the idea of casting the two of them as a married couple who had been successful in show business and had determined that, to bring up their family, they needed to get away from the bright lights of Broadway and move to the country.[27]

Peter Loves Mary was also produced with Four Star for NBC but again only ran for a single season. NBC financed a pilot for *The Iron Horseman*, but this was not picked up for a series. Mirisch turned his attention back to the big screen, but the experience of these productions was not wasted. Meanwhile, if the small screen was suffering a surfeit of Westerns, the big screen could still accommodate more and Coburn soon reappeared in one of the company's most iconic films, *The Magnificent Seven*.

Christopher Anderson makes the case that while the studios 'phased out the standardized production' of movies in the 1950s, they integrated those business practices to television production, 'Supplying television programs to the networks',

---

[23] Robert Kintner, quoted in Tino Balio (ed), *Hollywood in the Age of Television*, Routledge, 1990, 53.
[24] Balio, 1990: 54.
[25] Ibid, 79.
[26] Mirisch, 2008: 93.
[27] Ibid, 94.

Anderson says, 'offered a new rationale for standardized, studio-based production'.[28] UA, as one of 'the little three', was able to outsource production to independent companies, and its familiarity with lower budget, factory-like B pictures was easily adapted to telefilm production. By 1960, 87 per cent of American families owned a TV set.[29] In August that year, Walter Grauman was appointed as producer/director in charge of TV development for Mirisch.[30] In the spring of 1961, NBC and UA's television subsidiary, Ziv-TV, co-financed Mirisch's production of a pilot for a series spun off from *Some Like It Hot*.[31]

The previous spring Mirisch, together with Ziv-UA and Wilder's associate, William Schorr, had begun to develop the idea for a *Some Like It Hot* series. Grauman was set to direct the pilot, from a script by Herbert Baker. (Wilder and Gary Cooper, whose Ashdown Productions had produced the film, were to take 20 per cent of any income, with the rest split between Mirisch and Ziv.) Baker's conceit was that Lemmon and Curtis reprise their roles for an afternoon, in a hospital ward set, where their characters, Jerry and Joe, have plastic surgery to evade capture by the mobsters who are still on their trail. On recovery from the anaesthetic the pair were revealed, when the bandages come off, to have been transformed into Vic Damone and Dick Patterson. Joan Shawlee reprised her role as Sweet Sue, Mike Mazurki and Sandra Warner also replayed their previous parts. The pilot was recorded at NBC studios in March 1961 but was apparently never broadcast.[32] Nevertheless, that such a singular film was ever considered a viable source for a series is an indication of just how seriously the Mirisch Company took the reproducibility of its productions.

Such viability took many forms. The original *Magnificent Seven* was released in November 1960. It was re-released in 1961 and again, on double bills, in 1962. Meanwhile, in 1961, Mirisch had proposed a ninety-minute TV movie and a subsequent series to NBC. Sam Peckinpah was to be executive producer and John Sturges agreed to direct five episodes. UA refused to sign up to the deal, however, and instead *The Magnificent Seven* set a record for the fastest post-theatrical. A feature film to appear on TV when it premiered on Sunday, 3 February 1963, and was a huge, small-screen hit. In January 1964 the first cinematic sequel, *Return of the Seven*, was announced.

However, by 1962, the company's initial lack of success with TV series had temporarily discouraged Mirisch from pursuing small screen commissions. Instead, Grauman was appointed director on *633 Squadron* (itself the pilot or progenitor for a subsequent cinematic cycle) and *Variety* reported that Mirisch had 'No TV Plans'.

> Big impact television formerly had at the boxoffice [sic], when people stayed home to keep their sets on regardless of programming, no longer accrues, Mirisch asserted. 'The tv situation no longer is cause for any havoc in attendance,' he said.

---

[28] Anderson, quoted in Menne, 2019: 131.
[29] Maltby, 2003: 163.
[30] *Daily Variety*, 16.8.60: 6.
[31] 'MCA's Hot Title Sale', *Daily Variety*, 19.4.61: 3.
[32] Laurence Maslon, *Some Like It Hot: The Official 50th Anniversary Companion*, Pavillion, 2009, 155–61.

'The whole answer to tv situation lies in the quality of film product.' Mirisch Co. has no tv plans 'for the moment.'[33]

As the firm refocused on the big screen, lessons had nevertheless been learned from its smaller sibling.

The Television effect

When the focus was on features, Mirisch movies made much of the inferiority of television or, in Mann's terms, 'sought to put television in its place'.[34] In *The Apartment*, Bud switches channels between indistinguishable Westerns and interminable sponsor's messages. In *The Party* when the director tells Sellers' actor character, Bakshi, 'You're through. Washed up. I'll see you never work on another picture' His immediate response is 'What about television?' In *Kiss Me, Stupid*, the two songwriters, watching Dino perform their song on TV, through a shop window, can only consider the Nielsen ratings. The medium is a wasteland, a final fallback, a crude money machine. Indeed, this is yet another example of the extent to which Mirisch films occasionally addressed the company's own culture.

In 1964, there was another abortive announcement, this time for a multi-picture deal with Janet Leigh, including a sitcom, *This Is Maggie Mulligan*, but nothing came of it beyond a pilot.[35] In 1965, *Variety* reported that

> United Artists seems to be staging a one-company campaign to revive the concept of the 'series film,' so popular in the 1930s and 1940s with such then-continuing characters as 'The Hardy Family,' 'Tarzan,' 'Charlie Chan,' et. al. Although the series concept has since become the backbone of tv programming, UA has presently got the makings of several in the works.[36]

At Monogram, *Charlie Chan* had been one of the studio's most successful series, while *Tarzan* itself had been the inspiration for Walter's *Bomba* series. The article went on to identify the James Bond series and the second Beatles film, before discussing the two nascent franchises then being produced by the Mirisch Company. If series were proving the 'backbone' of network TV, they could also provide continuity and a risk avoidance strategy for feature film independents, wrestling with the inherent insecurities of the 'one-offness' of the package-unit system.

By the end of the first twenty-picture deal with UA, only five Mirisch productions had earned a profit – including *The Magnificent Seven*.[37] Among the second twenty,

---

[33] 'All 20 Pix For UA; Half Definitely To Be Made In US.; No TV Plans "At Present"', *Variety*, 21.9.62: 1.
[34] Mann, 2008: 26.
[35] 'Mirisch Prepping TV series With Janet Leigh', *Variety*, 19.6.64: 1.
[36] 'Sequel Trend May Bring Return To "Series Films" of 1940 Vogue', *Variety*, 24.2.65: 7.
[37] Balio, 1987: 177.

The Pink Panther seemed such a guaranteed hit that the Mirisches had a sequel in the works before the original was released, a repurposed stage play transformed into an episode in the Clouseau series. The last twenty-eight-film-deal included more sequels. 'Exploiting the blackpix trend and the Academy Award honors won by *In the Heat of the Night*, the Mirisches had produced two sequels starring Sidney Poitier.... At best, the two pictures just about broke even.' According to Balio, of the final fourteen films owed to UA, all lost money except for *Fiddler on the Roof* and the final *Magnificent Seven* sequels.[38] (This seems to be a mistake, as *Mr Majestyk* apparently earned a healthy return on its budget.)[39]

While *The Magnificent Seven* had been the first Mirisch production to eventually spawn a sequel, the first Mirisch sequel to reach the screen was actually *A Shot in the Dark* – the follow-up to *The Pink Panther*. The script of the original initially centred on the jewel thief, played by David Niven, but 'the Clouseau character really took over and it became the centre of the film'.[40] By Henderson's definition, *A Shot in the Dark* is a spin-off rather than a sequel, as 'the spin-off tends to follow characters which were either previously subsidiary or parts of an ensemble'.[41] *The Pink Panther* took its title from the name given to the jewel that the Niven character was attempting to steal. In the sequel, Sellers' detective character took centre stage, but *The Pink Panther* remained in the audience's memory. There followed a four-year gap before *Inspector Clouseau* (1968), this time starring Alan Arkin (both Edwards and Sellers were temporarily unwilling either to work together or resuscitate the series) as the bumbling detective. *Life* magazine, in 1966, wrote of this second sequel, that

> *Inspector Clouseau* is, in its little way, a historic film, proving not only that the title character is now so well established that his name alone can lure us into the theatre, but that his spirit can survive delightfully unscathed the migration from Peter Sellers, in whom it resided so comfortably in *The Pink Panther* and *A Shot in the Dark*, to Alan Arkin.[42]

But the film flopped critically and commercially. By the time of Sellers' return to the role, Mirisch had lost its copyright on the character, which had reverted to UA.

By 1964 the average weekly cinema attendance in the United States was half that of what it had been in 1957 and consequently, companies that had seen their box office figures falling seized on anything that might maximize their revenues.[43] One such strategy was, of course, revisiting past successes, hence that *Pink Panther* sequel. Sequels not only reduced the risk but also some pre-production costs necessary for hiring freelance crews, finding locations, casting, hiring costumes and so on. Even the

---

[38] Ibid, 192, 194.
[39] Mirisch, 2008: 326.
[40] Walter Mirisch, quoted in Balio, 1987: 176.
[41] Henderson, 2014: 5.
[42] *Life* magazine, cited in Mirisch, 2008: 169.
[43] Maltby, 2003: 570.

theme music of *The Magnificent Seven* belatedly won an Oscar nomination – for its reuse in the first sequel! The imperative to minimize risk encouraged this increased reliance on remakes, sequels, series and spin-offs. Not only is *The Magnificent Seven* a remake of *Seven Samurai* (Kurosawa, 1954) but it spawned three cinematic sequels and, eventually, a TV series. Similarly, *The Pink Panther* functioned as a live-action film and an animated TV series but also inaugurated a cinematic series or franchise which continues to this day. The first sequel, *A Shot in the Dark* (an adaptation of a play which had initially been acquired as a vehicle for Marilyn Monroe, entirely separate from *The Pink Panther* series), was adopted for the Clouseau character. Subsequently, as *Variety* reported,

> Mirisch Corp. prexy Harold Mirisch said the company is 'determined to do a third picture to continue the Inspector Jacques Clouseau series'. Mirisch, noting the enormous success of the Bond film series, said this has 'inspired us to pursue the idea of our own series', also revealing the imminent production of 'Return of the 7', a sequel to its earlier successful 'The Magnificent Seven'.[44]

Mirisch pointed out that *A Shot in the Dark* reversed the usual ratio of sequel grosses by taking more at the domestic box office than the original film.[45] Clearly, the Mirisches calculated the grosses of such sequels extremely carefully.

A second TV initiative

Finally, in 1965, Lee Rich signed up with Mirisch to relaunch a TV subsidiary, Mirisch-Rich. Rich attributed this decision to the autonomy Mirisch allowed him over production decisions. 'This is going to be my business and I will be involved in the final decisions. If I make it, it will be on my own. And if I fail it will be on my own. My stuff will be commercial. I'm not out to change the world.'[46] Once again autonomy was a crucial consideration, but the emphasis was not on programme quality, or topicality, but simply on audience size. One of the first decisions Mirisch-Rich Television Productions made was, whenever possible, to include TV series rights in any film contracts and IP acquisitions it signed. As *Variety* reported, 'Rich said he thought most theatrical film properties could be converted into series; that the Mirisch brothers agree with him.'[47] But if most movies might be spun off into small screen series, it had also dawned on Mirisch that such films often had the potential of spawning cinematic sequels. After all, *A Shot in the Dark* had already been released before Rich was hired,

---

[44] *Variety*, 24.2.65: 7.
[45] *Variety*, 20.1.65: 4, 20.
[46] 'Advertising: A Chip off an Agency Family', *New York Times*, 16.4.65: 56.
[47] 'Mirisch To Parlay Pix and TV: To Seek Video Rights to Film Plots Acquired', *Daily Variety*, 24.6.65: 1.

and the first meetings about *Return of the Seven* began in 1963.⁴⁸ In June 1965, just months after Rich's arrival, *Variety* reported the signing of Sidney Poitier to star as Virgil Tibbs in an adaptation of the novel, *In the Heat of the Night*, adding that 'Mirisch also has acquired tv rights to the Tibbs character for potential use in a tv series under the banner of Mirisch-Rich Productions.'⁴⁹

By the spring of 1966, the success of this new Mirisch-Rich strategy was undeniable.

> The Mirisch Brothers had good reason to ring April 1 on the calendar. It marks the end of one full year in tv for the picture producers and with a record unmatched by any producing company in tv. Three shows, its entire output for the year, sold and on network schedule next fall. It was a spectacular comeback from six years ago when the Mirisches fielded two shows that lasted only one season and took them out of tv.⁵⁰

The three series were *Rat Patrol* (ABC) and *Hey Landlord* and *The Super Bwoing Show* (both NBC), which span off into animated series, *Super Six* and *Super President*. 'This time we're in it for good and are firmly established', said Mirisch. 'We hope to be a major factor in the television business as we are in pictures.'⁵¹

The economies of series production were undoubted. On action series like *Rat Patrol*, for instance, scripts were minimal, according to its star Christopher George,

> Most actors want to see how many lines they have in a script. We try to see how much we can cut out. That's because ours is an action series, and so we try to keep the dialog at a minimum, unless it pertains to the action. In combat, you don't take that much time to sit around and philosophise about everything.⁵²

Subsequently, Rich admitted of the minimal plots and dialogue that 'standard practice when filming "Rat Patrol" was "to blow up another tank" whenever plot problems came up.'⁵³

Rich remembered the writing and casting of *Hey Landlord* as equally streamlined.

> I knew Garry Marshall and Jerry Belson from the days on the Van Dyke Show when they were writing for Van Dyke. And they came to me with this idea . . . very funny, the idea was the story of people living in an apartment house with a landlord, a young guy as a landlord, and it was a very good idea, the scripts were very funny but the casting, the leads were horrible.

---

⁴⁸ Mirisch, 2008: 237.
⁴⁹ '16 United Artists Mirisch Films Blueprinted to Cost $73,000', *Variety*, 16.6.65: 18.
⁵⁰ 'Mirisch Bros. Strike It "Rich" on TV With Sale of All 3 Pilots for '66-'67', *Variety*, 30.3.66: 36.
⁵¹ *Variety*, 30.3.66: 36.
⁵² 'Perils of "Rat Patrol"-ing; Computer Spills "Blood"', *Daily Variety*, 29.3.67: 13.
⁵³ 'More Heat Than Light Shed in Second TV Academy Session On Video Violence', *Daily Variety*, 18.9.68: 1, 13.

(Norman Jewison almost walked away from producing *The Landlord* because of his concern over the similarities of the two titles.) Garry Marshall recalled his co-writer, Jerry Belson saying,

> You know, we could make a show – why do we need to write these other people's shows?' and then we created a show. Quite a flop. It was called Hey Landlord. It was a forerunner of Happy Days, actually. Two guys living in the Bronx, we didn't cast it very well, we didn't write it very well, but we learned how to make a show. . . . We wrote and wrote and wrote and the rating would be zero, nobody watched.[54]

Quincy Jones, who wrote the theme music for the series, recalled just how much of an assembly line the production process was.

> It was a job, you know, and everybody else on it, it was a job for everybody else too. The guys used to sit up in the middle of the night writing the scripts. I used to stick around sometime to watch them write and it was funny. . . . They were writing things down to throw it up to Garry or somebody, and he'd say 'funny', throw it in that pile, 'not funny', over here, 'funny'. No laugh or anything. Just throwing material. Amazing process, because every week they had to hammer that stuff out.

Later that year *Variety* reported on what appeared to be further small screen success. 'Mirisch-Rich Productions, which sold its first four vehicles, appears on the way to a fifth sale, on "Sheriff Who," for NBC-TV.'[55] Marshall recalled *Sheriff Who*'s genesis as a kind of anti-Western.

> We were trying to invent the wheel . . . so we said, 'let's not do issues, let's do what ((Jerry)) 'Belson used to like to call "the comedy of attack", and we would find things to attack, so one of the things we wanted to attack was violence, so we did a show about the most violent man in the world, it was a kind of cartoon, kind of satirical show, this was before Blazing Saddles, before anything, and we did this crazy western, that nobody understood. . . . We did this pilot which was great and was satirical about this mean man – so mean that he looked stupid – that was the point to the show – but they thought it was a statement about violence and nobody understood it. A few critics saw it and thought it was great, but nobody else – they wouldn't put it on.

The failure of *Sheriff Who?* was decisive for Lee Rich. Asked why he left Mirisch-Rich and went back to advertising, he replied,

> We did a pilot called Sheriff Who, a pilot that everybody who looked at that pilot said it was the best pilot they'd ever seen. And the idea was great – You killed

---

[54] http://www.emmytvlegends.org/interviews/shows/pink-panther-the
[55] 'NBC-TV Eyes Badge for Mirisch-Rich "Sheriff Who?"', *Variety*, 17.5.67: 42.

> a sheriff every week. It was just a tremendous pilot and I took it to New York and I couldn't sell it, I just couldn't sell the damn pilot and I was so frustrated coming back to Los Angeles because this was so good; really, so good it's become a classic.... Each week you killed another sheriff. Each week we'd have another sheriff. And it frustrated me so much that I couldn't sell it.... And I had a contract that was backed by UA and unfortunately, then Harold passed away and the other Mirisches were not interested in television at all. And I didn't want to be there. Arthur Krim came to me and said why don't you stay on, we'll put you in the movie business but I said no.

In fact, Harold Mirisch died in December 1968, well over a year after Rich left the company.

But whether their shows were ratings hits or not, the TV industry was less than conducive to independents. Short runs, swift cancellations, advertiser caution and escalating budgets meant breaking even, let alone making a profit, was almost impossible for those producers not inside the vertically integrated broadcasters, ABC, NBC and CBS. As Rich put it,

> Sooner or later, there will have to be some massive change. I don't know what it will be, but it can't continue this way. The advertiser, network and producers don't want to change shows every year. But tv has become so costly the advertisers don't want to take a long-term deal with a series and be stuck with a turkey. So, the networks turn to you, the producer, and tell you this is why deals aren't made for an entire season – but I can turn to nobody.[56]

When series were cancelled quickly there were not even enough episodes to sell into syndication or to foreign broadcasters in order to cover costs.[57] To square this circle, Rich had arranged that the first season of *Rat Patrol* was filmed in Spain, which saved money on locations, equipment and crew. But this in turn had led to trouble with the Hollywood unions and the show returned to the United States for its second and final season when a combination of budget overruns, controversies over TV violence and shifting tastes led to its cancellation.

It is worth quoting at length from *Variety* here, to explain Rich's decision to quit television and Mirisch's to effectively abandon the medium for a second time.

> Rich, meanwhile, said he was leaving the production field because an indie 'can take no short cuts like a major studio, which needs shows to fill a stage, to absorb the overhead. A major can offer a performer a movie in addition to his series – something I can't do. A major has more flexibility. At the same time, because the nets have scheduled so many hours of prime time for feature films, there is less

[56] *Variety*, 13.4.66: 32, 53.
[57] 'Lee Rich Calls for All-Industry "Crisis Meeting" to Find Way Out Of TV's Red-Ink-Stained Maze', *Variety*, 13.4.66: 31, 53.

available time on the air for producers. In addition, the networks are doing more and more of their own shows, their own programming, and this can do nothing but force the indie out of tv.'[58]

Part of the problem was that the networks retained most slots in primetime for their own in-house productions. This situation was only finally eased, if not altogether ended, by the Prime Time Access Rule of 1970, one of whose beneficiaries, ironically, was Lee Rich's new company Lorimar, which had launched in 1969. (Another was MTM, founded in 1970, about which I have written at length elsewhere.[59]) Among the huge hits Lorimar produced were *The Waltons*, *Dallas*, *Knots Landing* and *Falcon's Crest*.

Cinematic sequels

It is striking that it was precisely at this point, in 1967, that the Mirisch Company, in retreat from TV series, reinvested in cinematic sequels, releasing *Return of the Seven* and *In the Heat of the Night* that same year, *Guns of the Magnificent Seven* in 1969, *The Hawaiians* and *They Call Me MISTER Tibbs* in 1970, *The Organization* in 1971 and *The Magnificent Seven Ride* in 1972. It was also in exactly that same month, May 1967, when Rich's departure and the company's withdrawal from TV was announced, that production began on *Attack on the Iron Coast*, the first of the six films in Mirisch's British Second World War cycle, which is discussed in Chapter 7.

Another important imperative on sequel production may have been, 'the insatiable demand of network television for feature films. As the number of movie nights increased and as rental prices skyrocketed, Hollywood became complacent. The thinking became that if a picture didn't make it in the theatrical market, it would break even or earn a profit from the network television sale'.[60] Sequels or film series proved attractive acquisitions for the new medium, as they provided a more efficient solution to scheduling slots than individual films. Subsequently – and not surprisingly – syndication rights for TV series became not only extremely valuable economically for the Hollywood studios but also hugely influential aesthetically. Ageing film stars, filmmakers and family film genres could be conveniently relegated to television, while new talent could also be 'screen-tested' on the small screen.

The Mirisch strategy saw most films as, among other things, potential pilots – not unlike television pilots – of cinema series. More specifically, certain films performed the same function that pilots performed in television – as blueprints for characters, situations and story arcs – that could be reprised by sequels. And, reversing that process, a film could also be deployed as the source material for a television pilot and, ideally, a TV series spin-off of its own. Such synergies between film and television thus

---

[58] 'Mirisch Corp. In agonizing TV "Reappraisal"', *Daily Variety*, 25.5.67: 10.
[59] Feuer, Kerr and Vahimagi (eds), *MTM: 'Quality Television'*, London: BFI, 1984.
[60] Balio, 1990, 260.

include not only the possibility of spinning off films from TV series and TV series from films but also that of interchanging the narrative grammar of those respective media, so that a film package could lead to cinematic sequels in just the same way that a small screen pilot could spawn a TV series. The simultaneous production of films and TV programmes at the Mirisch Company, and an inevitable awareness that the small screen was an increasingly important destination for feature films was an additional imperative for finding properties with potential as series.

Henderson notes the ironic impact of independent production itself on serialization. The institutionalization of short-termism seems to have helped seed a desire for securing the future, which, in turn, favoured sequels.[61] Staiger describes 'the industrial shift away from mass production and towards film-by-film financing and planning'.[62] If an impetus towards film-by-film rather than firm-by-firm production was characteristic of the independent package producers, including Mirisch, then one way of resisting this intrinsic 'one-off-ness' was to think in terms of series of films – whether cycles, star vehicles or sequels. In such cases, while each individual film might require a unique contract with cast and crew, it would also be replicable for future films in the cycle, future vehicles with the same star, and future sequels that were equivalent to episodes in a cinematic series. Another characteristic of the package-unit system Staiger notes is profit-sharing, whereby major stars received a percentage of the profits in addition to their fee.[63] One perhaps unforeseen side effect of the 'star-replacement strategy' operated by the Mirisches is exemplified by the casting changes in the three *Magnificent Seven* sequels and the replacement of Sellers with Arkin as the titular *Inspector Clouseau*, which neatly side-stepped such profit-sharing – whether or not this was the actual reason for replacing a recalcitrant star. Sequels were a way of squeezing cinematic assets dry – by recycling not only characters, but also plots and even occasionally dialogue. Thus, the title of the sequel, *They Call Me MISTER Tibbs* is actually a line of dialogue from its predecessor, *In the Heat of the Night* and was used as such in the trailer. Poitier's contract also paved the way for further films in the series. 'In the deal we had made with Sidney (Poitier) for *In the Heat of the Night*, he agreed to give us an option for two more pictures if we chose to make Virgil Tibbs movies.'[64]

In 1970 the Hollywood trade press reported, 'Upcoming triple feature – "The Magnificent 7" and its sequels "Return of the etc" and "Guns of-" by the Mirii, being readied for UA theatre package billing, despite the fact that two "Sevens" will have been seen on tv by release time.'[65] In 1972 the fourth and final film in the series was released (*The Magnificent Seven Ride*) and in 1975, Walter Mirisch signed a deal with Universal TV and CBS-TV for an hour-long pilot for *The Magnificent Seven*. In fact, the long-awaited *Magnificent Seven* TV series did not appear until 1998 and ran on CBS for two seasons until 2000. It is credited to Trilogy Entertainment, MGM Television and The

---

[61] Henderson, 2014: 46.
[62] Bordwell, Staiger, Thompson, 1985: 332.
[63] Ibid, 334.
[64] Mirisch, 2008: 293.
[65] *Daily Variety*, 17.11.70: 2.

Mirisch Corporation. Walter Mirisch even got an executive producer credit on the recent remake, *The Magnificent Seven* (2016), though this time there was no corporate credit.

Both aesthetically and financially, a law of diminishing returns tends to operate on sequels, including Mirisch's, but the company proved adept at averting major losses by minimizing budgets and maximizing the long tail of their series films. That all three series proved iconic enough to eventually spin-off successful TV series – only the first of which was produced by Mirisch – is one thing. That two of the company's three film series were largely filmed outside America and found a huge audience beyond the US box office is even more striking. According to *Variety*, by 1975 the four 'Seven' films had generated world rentals theatrically of about $25,000,000 and, strikingly, 'foreign rentals always outran domestic performance'.[66] *The Magnificent Seven* itself is reported as having taken about $2,400,000 in the United States and Canada and 'a whopping $11,300,000 in the foreign market'.[67] *Return of the Seven* in 1966 cost $1.78 million to produce. The film took about $1.6 million profit of $3.2 million gross domestically and another $3.4 million internationally and came seventieth in the annual rankings by box office takings.[68] In 1967 Mirisch announced *Quest of the Magnificent Seven*, which was finally produced two years later, on a budget of 1.36 million, and released as *Guns of the Magnificent Seven*. It took $1.5 million in rentals in the United States but an additional $2.5 million abroad.[69] (*Variety* reports foreign rentals as $2,200,000.) *The Magnificent Seven Ride* had earned only $70,000 domestically and international box office figures were unavailable at the time of *Variety*'s report.

Such sequels succeeded in re-promoting the original, which was regularly re-released on double and treble bills with the new entries. Of the three *Seven* sequels only *Return of the Seven* made a slight domestic profit, just $37,000 on its initial release. *Guns of the Magnificent Seven* lost $605,000 and *The Magnificent Seven Ride* $21,000. However, network television and subsequent syndication netted *Return of the Seven* an extra $2.23 million, *Guns of the Magnificent Seven* $1.16 million and *The Magnificent Seven Ride* $1.05 million. According to Hannan, taking theatrical release and television sales together, the first sequel was sitting on a profit of $588,000, the second $595,000 and the third $236,000.[70] Domestic profits were transformed by TV sales, just as the international theatrical market increasingly rivalled and sometimes outweighed domestic takings. 'The average price of a theatrical movie rose from $100,000 for two network runs in 1961 to around $800,000 by the end of 1967.'[71] *Hawaii* had cost over

---

[66] *Variety*, 24.12.75: 1.
[67] Ibid.
[68] Brian Hannan, *The Making of The Magnificent Seven*, McFarland and Company, 2015: 218.
[69] Ibid, 218–19.
[70] Ibid, 228.
[71] Barry Litman, 'The Economics of the Television Market for Theatrical Movies', in Gorham Kindem (ed), *The American Movie Industry: The Business of Motion Pictures*, Southern Illinois University Press, 1982, 316.

$14 million but only grossed $19 million, while *In the Heat of the Night* cost $2 million and initially grossed $16 million.[72]

Of course, not all box office hits, let alone all films, lent themselves to sequelization – 'because the conclusion of the original largely precluded future continuation, as with the tragedies *West Side Story* (1961) and *Doctor Zhivago* (1965)'.[73] Henderson notes that road-show-era hits, like *The Magnificent Seven*, often used large ensemble casts. For any sequel to a multiple-star film, 'Given that the majority of these stars were no longer under long-term contract, reassembling all or even some of them presented a major logistical headache'.[74] For *The Magnificent Seven*'s sequels, the death of the majority of the ensemble in each episode facilitated rather than frustrated such a reassembly, as new 'sevens' could be easily – and more economically – recruited. Other projects with a previous existence on the page or stage or, indeed, real life, like *Cast a Giant Shadow*, were unextendible too, but clearly Mirisch was quick to identify and exploit opportunities where they existed.[75] The protagonists of *The Great Escape* are almost all dead at the end (though a semi-sequel was produced, but not by Mirisch). A high casualty rate among an ensemble cast is also, of course, true of *The Magnificent Seven*, but did not prevent Mirisch from recruiting replacements for the fallen gunmen after each of the films in the series. There are, after all, only three survivors of the original seven in the first film and only one of the original actors opted to reprise his role. Indeed, the disposability of the actors in the series was one characteristic of the *Seven* films (and is even referred to, obliquely, in *Return from the Ashes*).

There was a recession in Hollywood in 1969 and in response 'the majors learned to offset the risks of production by adopting defensive production and marketing tactics. During the seventies, the majors themselves increasingly relied on sequels and series. Sequels solved a major promotion problem for the studios – how to make known to an audience what a film is about'.[76] Even Wilder's *The Private Life of Sherlock Holmes* prompted press conjecture: 'could this be the start of a new "Bond" series for UA?'[77] As late as 1971 Mirisch and UA were still weighing up the television futures for potential spin-offs from their three cinematic series. 'UA is keeping in mind tv series possibilities for "Magnificent 7," "Tibbs" and "Clouzot" [sic] (Clouseau is the character's name in the films) – when the features are saturated which doesn't seem imminent.'[78] In the event, the first such series had to wait until long after the demise of the company, the second was only produced once the rights to the project had reverted to UA and only Clouseau (and *Pink Panther*) spin-off animations made it to the small screen, accredited, albeit only partially, to Mirisch.

[72] Balio, 1987: 181, 187.
[73] Henderson, 2014: 62.
[74] Ibid.
[75] Ibid.
[76] Balio, 1990: 261.
[77] *Variety*, 22.12.69: 2.
[78] *Daily Variety*, 27.12.71: 2.

Sequels and memory – remembering and forgetting

Eventually, three sequels to *The Magnificent Seven* were made but Sturges, McQueen and Wallach (who was invited back to play the uncle of the Calvera character) all turned down the idea of reprising their roles. Brynner alone agreed to take part again – and he only signed up for the first sequel, in which Robert Fuller was cast in the McQueen role as Vin. The role of Chico, played by Horst Buchholz in the original, was taken by Julian Mateos and that of Petra, previously played by Rosenda Monteros, by Elisa Montes. George Kennedy replaced Brynner as Chris in the second sequel; the third and final sequel recast the lead yet again, this time with Lee Van Cleef. Perhaps the gap between episodes erased or at least blurred the memories of audiences about the identities of the survivors. But advertising was able to refresh viewer memories. The trailer for *Return of the Seven* begins with the words, 'They rode into screen history with *The Magnificent Seven*. Now they ride on to greater adventure in *Return of the Magnificent Seven*.'

In the first sequel, *Return of the Seven*, Chico is wounded trying to defend his village against (another) bandit attack. His wife, Petra, goes in search of Chris and finds him at a bullfight where, fortuitously, he has just bumped into Vin. Chris and Vin team up again and recruit another five men. Of this seven, the eventual survivors are Chris, Vin, Chico and Colby (Warren Oates). *Guns of the Magnificent Seven* followed, this time with another Mexican, Max, seeking Chris out to help rescue an imprisoned rebel leader. 'All I know is he's a friend and his name is Chris.' When Chris saves the life of a horse thief about to be hung, a gunman shouts, 'I know you, Chris. A lot of people know you. Mostly sheriffs!' Thus, Chris is by now famous, even infamous, but on the wrong side of the law. When Max approaches them after a shootout in town, he says, 'Hello Chris. You were magnificent.' Not only is Chris famous, therefore, he is also already 'magnificent'. Chris decides to accept the challenge. 'I need help. More men. Six men. Not enough to cause suspicion. Just enough to do the job.' Max replies 'My cousin says seven is a lucky number for you.' Audiences are thus reminded of the film's place in a series in which a Magnificent Seven gunmen will triumph, against the odds. Of the assembled seven only Chris, Max and another gunman, Levy, survive the final gunfight.

In *The Magnificent Seven Ride*, Chris is a newly married Marshall. Approached by an old friend, Jim, to help yet another Mexican village, he says, 'I've crossed that border three times to fight bandits. I ain't going down there again'. During the three previous films Chris did indeed cross that border three times (in both directions). However, when Jim reminds him of their exploits together – 'Remember that first time? Seven of us got 350 dollars. Fifty bucks apiece' – we recall that there was no Jim in the first *Seven* adventure – or indeed any other – nor any previous mention of another Mexican skirmish in the series. Furthermore, if such an escapade with Jim had taken place, then Chris would already have crossed that border four times. When Chris initially refuses his request for help, Jim prompts, 'Maybe some of the others?' But none of the names Chris mentions refer to anyone we have previously encountered in the series. The films re-echo, each time rather more faintly, the initial assembly of the heavily outnumbered team, the journey, a first successful skirmish with the enemy, a reversal, preparation for and then a final costly victory. If the series is the gift that keeps on giving, then part of that reproductivity seems to necessitate forgetting the previous production.

Indeed, the collective memory of the series became so blurred that there was virtually no reliable shared narrative of the seven left to exploit – or repeat. In future, such series would be far more rigorously and rigidly enforced, with a combination of blockbuster budgets and auteur authority (most successfully in *The Godfather* trilogy and the *Star Wars* franchise). Trilogies like *The Matrix*, or *Lord of the Rings* as well as the *Star Wars* films have been beneficiaries of a pre-production plan incorporating multiple episodes. This never seems to have been the case with the Mirisch sequels. Each one was itself a one-off, exploiting a familiar title or character or situation, but never as part of a self-consciously continuing strategy, within which several spin-offs had been simultaneously conceived. Instead, the *Panther*, *Seven* and *Tibbs* sequels were all spawned individually. Poitier had an option for sequels in his contract, but neither the writers nor the directors nor even fellow cast members were reunited in them. This was part of what was to change as franchises subsequently became more imbricated in the economic logic of production.

In Mirisch sequels, characters (and actors) change inexplicably from one film to the next. Ironically, in the unsold pilot to *Some Like It Hot*, Mirisch had prematurely played with this idea, by using the plot device of plastic surgery to transform the leads from Jack Lemmon and Tony Curtis into Vic Damone and Dick Patterson. In the company's subsequent cinematic sequels, on the other hand, in which one actor is casually replaced with another, no such deus ex machina is summoned to post-rationalize the changed cast or character. Hence the apparently unproblematic recasting of Chris, Vin, Chico and Petra. Colby is one of the three survivors in *Return*, but in *Guns of the Magnificent Seven* that name is given to a villain, played by an entirely different actor – though no mention is made of Chris's former comrade with the same surname. Similarly, the Clouseau character was married in *The Pink Panther* but is living in a bachelor apartment in the sequel, *A Shot in the Dark*, with no mention of his former marital status. At the end of *The Pink Panther*, Clouseau was sentenced to jail, but in *A Shot in the Dark* that jail sentence too seems to have been forgotten.

In the Heat of the Night was released in 1967 and by the following year Sidney Poitier was, albeit briefly, America's top box office star and the film made waves for its depiction of racism and for Tibbs' literal refusal to turn the other cheek in the face of racial violence. By comparison, however, *They Call Me MISTER Tibbs* and *The Organization* must have seemed anachronistic in their avoidance of race and racism and in the perhaps well-intentioned colour-blindness of their focus and framing narratives. But these sequels aren't merely bleached in comparison with their predecessor and progenitor, they seem to have been virtually brainwiped. The discontinuities identified earlier in the *Seven* and *Pink Panther* films become biographical in the Tibbs trilogy. *In the Heat of the Night* (1967) tells us that its protagonist, police detective Virgil Tibbs works for the Philadelphia force and that he is unmarried. In the sequel *They Call Me MISTER Tibbs*, however, Tibbs is working for the San Francisco force ('We've got 12 good years invested in you', notes his police chief boss) and is married with two children, one of whom, his son Andy, appears close to adolescence.[79]

Series, IP and cinema's 'long tail'

Henderson notes that from the mid-fifties to the mid-seventies 'the role of the Hollywood sequel was in flux . . . neither what it had been in the years of vertical integration, nor what it would go on to become in the late 1970s, as horizontal integration became a fact of Hollywood life'.[80] This perhaps explains the less than assembly-line smoothness with which sequels, specifically those produced by Mirisch, whose output deals with UA precisely correspond with this period, were characterized. These sequels were, in general, afterthoughts. Nevertheless, Mirisch was experimenting with series and sequel forms throughout the 1960 and into the 1970s, in that transitional period before the Movie Brats. Theirs was a transitional cinema, appropriate to a transitional company. Mirisch was one of the companies that re-invented the sequel, well over a decade before *Jaws, The Godfather* and *Star Wars* made it famous as a long tail strategy for the studios in the 1970s. And it showed the way in which film franchises, cinematic series and sequels could provide synergies between film and television, with productions like *The Pink Panther* and *The Magnificent Seven* – not to mention *Wichita Town, Rat Patrol* and even that unlikely pilot for a *Some Like It Hot* series. The Mirisch companies helped pioneer the monetization of their films as potential prequels or pilots (both in the cinema, through sequels and on television as spin-off series). They were thus among the first of the post-Paramount Decree independents to see the long tail, bi-media potential of sequels.

As an independent set up in 1957, the Mirisch Company came into existence barely two years after the first deals were done between the major Hollywood studios and TV networks in 1955. This meant that Mirisch was structured to be able to produce both feature films and television series – from the outset. It did not have to adapt or transform itself to turn from one medium to another. It was always already prepared to produce for both media, either single films or series 'episodes'. Furthermore, the capacity to produce TV series meant that the Mirisch Company and its successors had in their DNA, or institutional infrastructure, the ability to produce episodic narratives on an assembly line. This may have begun as a capacity to make episodic television, with recurring characters and situations, but inevitably raised the possibility of applying the same 'repetition with difference' framework to cinematic storytelling. The industrial framework for fully fledged film franchises may only have arrived in the 1970s and 1980s, and perhaps needed the authorial imprimatur and box office impetus

---

[79] Henderson, 2014: 4.
[80] Ibid, 56.

provided by major filmmakers like Coppola, Lucas and Spielberg to gather momentum – and respectability. However, it was in the late 1950s and 1960s that the seeds for that New Hollywood were sown and a new imperative towards synergy emerged from the ashes of the studio era, ushering in new forms of series production for the big screen. The Mirisches were on the crest of that wave.

7

'You can't kill a squadron'
The Mirisch Second World War film cycle

In the late 1960s the Mirisch Company produced a 'cycle' of six 'British' Second World War films, through two subsidiaries, Mirisch Films Limited and Oakmont Productions. They were all based on the blueprint of *633 Squadron*. both cinematically (sharing narrative and iconographic similarities) and industrially (produced on the same financial model, with virtually identical budgets and schedules and often sharing crew members and studio facilities too). The six which followed *633* were *Attack on the Iron Coast* (1968), *Submarine X-1* (1968), *The 1000 Plane Raid* (1969), *Mosquito Squadron* (1970), *The Last Escape* (1970) and *Hell Boats* (1970). This cycle can be understood as another attempt to deploy Taylorist scientific management of cinematic resources and Fordist continuous production, in a post-Fordist film economy, to resolve the apparent contradiction between the industrial consequences of the end of mass production and the so-called package-unit system of one-off productions, with a desire to maximize output and minimize costs. In the wake of 1948 anti-trust legislation and the demise of the vertically integrated studios with their cinematic assembly lines and the rise of independents, this cycle attempted to square the circle of individual film packages, when every film production was a one-off, with 'a program of pictures', made to a formula including American star, producer and director, British supporting cast and crew, British subsidy, British or international studios and locations (each with subsidies, support, deals and discounts of their own), on a budget of approximately $1 million each. Setting the cycle in the 1940s, when mass production and consumption were at their peak, may have helped conceal the contradiction.

Applying Harvard to Hollywood

In August 1944, *Factory Management and Maintenance,* of which Walter Mirisch was already an avid reader and to which he was soon to be a contributor, published an article about Lockheed. That article, about Lockheed's work simplification program, on which Mirisch had by then been employed for a year, began by announcing 'Proposals for improvement made by employees at Lockheed Aircraft Corporation, Burbank Calif., are saving enough man hours annually to build 1000 big bombers' and that 'Work simplification means an analysis of any job, step by step, to find some part of it that can be improved.'[1] The idea of 1,000 American bombers – and of work simplification – was to stay with Mirisch for over twenty years, feeding into the plot, title and mode of production of the one US production among the six, otherwise 'British', films in the cycle that followed 633.

The following month's issue included an article entitled 'Scientific Management in a Post-War Plan'. which sought to obtain

> approximately a 50% increase in production . . . and to accomplish this with as small an increase in productive personnel as possible. The only way in which this can be done is to abandon the standard batch method of manufacture and to devise continuous methods of production. . . . There is but one objective . . . a continuous manufacturing cycle which will initiate an unexcelled product under constant scientific control.[2]

The shift from the 'standard batch method' to the 'continuous manufacturing cycle' through the provisions of scientific management, maximizing production while minimizing personnel, combines characteristics of the package-unit system, which the Mirisch Company deployed, with aspects of the 'continuous manufacturing cycle' associated with assembly-line production. What better way to test the wartime proposal of a 'continuous manufacturing cycle' in post-war Hollywood, than on a cycle of Second World War films?

Walter Mirisch almost certainly read both articles and may have written the first, as it concerned his current employer and the specific system he was charged with overseeing. If scientific management was what he had learned at Harvard, then at Lockheed, as a managing engineer, his responsibility was solving problems and maximising output. Later, at the Mirisch Company, it is perhaps unsurprising that several films dramatize engineering problems and their solutions, including the Second World War cycle, *The Great Escape* and *Gray Lady Down*. This book attempts to reverse engineer such films to reveal how these ideas ended up onscreen. Two months later, Mirisch's first signed article appeared in the same journal.[3]

Cinematic cycles

Klein usefully defines cinematic cycles as follows: 'A film cycle can come into existence only if its originary film, the first film released in the cycle, is financially or critically successful, addresses a topic of contemporary social interest and has a set of central semantics, including images, characters and plot formulas that are

---

[1] 'To Get Ready For Lower Unit Costs Take Advantage of Work Simplification Methods: Case of Lockheed Aircraft Corporation', *Factory Management and Maintenance*, August 1944: 129.
[2] 'Scientific Management in a Post-War Plan', 1944: 96–101.
[3] 'Measuring Drafting Output', 1944: 101.

recognizable enough to be repeated in several more films.'[4] (Klein's reference to recurring 'characters' – rather than character types – seems to me to identify such films with 'series' rather than 'cycles'.) Where Klein's definition insists on a complex of determinants, Nowell distinguishes between two explanatory frameworks for such cycles, 'Where the socio-symptomatic principle offers production trends as side effects of extra-industrial phenomena, the one-hit principle presents them as medium-term by-products of an important intra-industrial event. It suggests that trends result from attempts to emulate the economic achievements of a single film through the crafting of similar pictures.'[5] Klein's terms for these are the 'topic of contemporary social interest' hypothesis and the 'originary film' hypothesis. For Klein, a film cycle repeats the same images and plots within a short period of time. As if to test this, Stanfield 'tracks the emergence, consolidation, and dissolution of the short cycle of hot rod movies that was exhibited from 1956 to 1958'[6] The Mirisch Second World War cycle was produced and released equally rapidly – the first of the six which belatedly followed the originary film began shooting in May 1967 and the final film in the cycle opened in California in June 1970. In this chapter I discuss the emergence, consolidation and dissolution of that cycle.

The 'originary' film for the Mirisch cycle was *633 Squadron*. Mirisch had acquired the rights to Frederick Smith's novel shortly after its publication in 1956, initially for John Sturges to direct, though it took almost a decade, and another director entirely, to reach the screen. *633 Squadron* was produced by the Mirisch Company for UA and released on 4 June 1964 (two days before the twentieth anniversary of D Day which contributed to its 'topicality') and certainly tapped into a moment of nostalgic nationalism at the British box office, despite its North American hero. As Walter Mirisch described it,

> we had the extraordinary experience of earning almost the entire cost of the film out of the Eady Plan receipts in the UK, so the film was practically cost-free when it began distribution throughout the rest of the world. In fact, it was so successful that it led me to propose a program of pictures to United Artists, which would all comply with the Eady Plan requirements, would all be made in the $1 million cost bracket, and would all have a military theme, which appeared to guarantee a reasonably good playoff in the very patriotic UK of those years. . . . Each of the films had a recognizable American personality in the lead, they were Eady pictures, and they all had American directors.[7]

---

[4] Amanda Ann Klein, *American Film Cycles: Reframing Genres, Screening Social Problems & Defining Subcultures*, University of Texas Press, 2011, 61.
[5] Richard Nowell, 'Hollywood Don't Skate: US Production Trends, Industry Analysis and the Roller-Disco Movie', *New Review of Film and Television Studies*, 2012, 76.
[6] Peter Stanfield, 'Cycles of Sensation, "Intent to Speed: Cyclical Production, Topicality, and the 1950s Hot Rod Movie"', *New Review of Film and Television Studies* vol 11, 2013: 1.
[7] Mirisch, 2008: 204.

Subsidies and subsidiaries

The 'Eady Plan', established by the Cinematograph Films Act and administered by the British Film Fund Agency, became mandatory in 1957, just as the Mirisch Company was established. Previously, a voluntary system negotiated by Sir Wilfred Eady of the Treasury had run from 1950 to 1957. The Mirisch brothers, having seen the benefits of the scheme while at AA, successfully qualified for Eady 'subsidies' for several of their 'British' films (almost a sixth of their entire UA output) – including *Stolen Hours, Return from the Ashes, 633 Squadron, A Shot in the Dark, Inspector Clouseau, Attack on the Iron Coast, Hell Boats, Mosquito Squadron, Submarine X-1, Sinful Davey* and *The Private Life of Sherlock Holmes*. Smith's novel, *633 Squadron*, appeared in paperback just as the company was looking to acquire its first properties. Mirisch had founded a British subsidiary, Mirisch Films Limited, in 1957. Oakmont Productions, Inc. filed its Articles of Incorporation in the State of California on Friday, 20 May 1966, according to public records filed with the California secretary of state. In December 1966 Mirisch also joined the British Film Producers Association.[8]

To be eligible for Eady funds, producers were required to complete a form entitled 'Evidence of British Nature of Film', which was assessed by the Board of Trade, according to criteria drawn from the Films Act 1960. The Act stipulated, among other things, that (a) the maker of the film was, throughout the period of its production, either a British subject or a citizen of the Republic of Ireland or a company registered there or in the UK; (b) the studio, if any, used in making the film was in the UK, a Commonwealth country or the Republic of Ireland; and (c) that not less than the requisite amount (normally 75 per cent) of labour costs represents payments paid or payable to British subjects or citizens of the Republic of Ireland or persons ordinarily resident in a Commonwealth country or the Republic of Ireland.[9] (A highly paid American star and/or director was excluded from the calculation of this percentage.)

In 1966 a *Variety* headline announced, 'Estimate 80 per cent of Brit. Pic subsidy now goes to American companies'.[10] Indeed, British-based subsidiaries of Hollywood businesses were eligible for funding to make films with largely British casts and crews, in British studios and locations, even if produced and/or directed by and starring Americans. This production paradigm proved particularly attractive to the Mirisch Company. Furthermore, as Stubbs suggests, 'one model quickly emerged as the archetype for British runaway production: adventure films set in Britain's past'.[11] An obvious setting for such historical 'adventures' was the Second World War. Indeed, as Murphy acknowledges, 'The most consistent supplier of war films in the sixties was the American Mirisch Corporation which made 633 Squadron, Hell Boats, Attack on the

---

[8] *Variety*, 14.12.66: 12.
[9] Jonathan Stubbs, 'The Easy Levy: A Runaway Bribe? Hollywood Production and British Subsidy in the Early 1960s', *Journal of British Cinema and Television*, 2009, 8.
[10] *Variety*, 26 1.66: 1.
[11] Stubbs, 2009: 7.

Iron Coast, Submarine X-1 and Mosquito Squadron.'[12] Spicer refers to thirty British war films made between 1968 and 1981, citing 'the special mission film', a sub-category for which the highly successful *The Guns of Navarone* (Lee Thompson, 1961) had set the pattern. Spicer specifically identifies *Hell Boats, Attack on the Iron Coast, Mosquito Squadr*on and *Submarine X-1*, along with *Where Eagles Dare* (Hutton, 1968), as special mission films. In fact, six out of the eleven 'special mission' Second World War films made in this period were Mirisch productions.[13]

Of course, *633 Squadron* wasn't the sole precursor for this cycle. Mirisch itself had produced the hugely successful *The Great Escape*, while other high-profile Hollywood 'British' Second World War films of this period include *The Guns of Navarone*, based on an Alistair MacLean bestseller, and *Where Eagles Dare*, which MacLean scripted. (Mirisch's own MacLean adaptation, *The Satan Bug*, was not a Second World War story and had not been a success.) *The Last Escape*, a title originally registered for *The Great Escape*, seems to have originated as a pitch for a TV series, indeed, its director, Walter Grauman, had previously been Mirisch's TV head. The first *Variety* reference to what became the TV series, *Rat Patrol*, was a report that 'Rich and the Mirisch brothers are developing "The Trojan Horse", hour-long adventure series which takes place behind the German lines in World War II, for CBS-TV.'[14] This series never materialized, but the plotline of *Last Escape* is precisely a Second World War adventure behind enemy lines. (The Trojan Horse motif also provides a key plot device in both *Attack on the Iron Coast* – in which a British ship masquerades as a German naval vessel – and *Hell Boats* – in which a captured German ship is allowed into a heavily guarded enemy dock, its British crew disguised as Germans. *The Last Escape* even begins with its American hero in a German uniform.)

Like *633 Squadron*'s release, on the eve of the twentieth anniversary of D Day, the subsequent cycle coincided with the run-up to the thirtieth anniversary of the September 1939 declaration of war in Europe. Furthermore, the first film in the cycle, *Attack on the Iron Coast*, was greeted in *Variety* thus: 'With the 24th anniversary of the Normandy invasion – D Day – looming (June 6th) United Artists has an exploitation peg for its latest Mirisch Film presentation.'[15] Walter Mirisch, given his wartime work at Lockheed Aircraft Corporation, was putting down an early marker registering the company's appetite for aerial adventures. Indeed, barely a year into the company's existence, *Variety* announced two flying features – *The Proving Flight* and *633 Squadron*, though the former was never made.[16] The company also developed *Death Where Is Thy Sting?* (aka *The Bells of Hell Go Ding a Ling a Ling*) in the mid-sixties, the story of First World War flyers, though this was abandoned after only a few days shooting, due to the illness of its star, Gregory Peck. *The Great Escape*, of course, is about air force POWs.

---

[12] Robert Murphy, *Sixties British Cinema,* London: BFI, 1992, 260.
[13] A. H. Spicer, 'Secret Histories and the Dirty War: The 1970s Second World War film', in *'Going to War: Film History and the Second World War', Imperial War Museum, October 2010,* London, 22–23 October 2010 http://eprints.uwe.ac.uk/22267) Spicer, 2.
[14] *Daily Variety,* 20.5.65: 1.
[15] *Variety,* 20.3.68: 6 Reviews.
[16] 'Mirisches Set $10 Mil Theatre, TV, Film Production For 2nd Year', *Daily Variety,* 11.9.58: 1.

A narrative blueprint

In *633 Squadron*, a Norwegian resistance officer, Lieutenant Erik Bergman, travels to England to report the location of a German V-2 rocket fuel plant, and 633, led by Wing Commander Roy Grant, an American serving in the RAF, is assigned to destroy it. The factory is in a seemingly impregnable location, beneath a cliff at the end of a fjord protected by anti-aircraft guns. The only way to demolish it is by bombing the cliff until it collapses. The squadron trains in Scotland, where the terrain is similar to the fjord. Grant is introduced to Bergman's sister, Hilde, and they are attracted to each other, despite Grant's aversion to wartime relationships. The Norwegian resistance is tasked with destroying German anti-aircraft on the eve of the attack. When German reinforcements arrive, Bergman returns to Norway to recruit more men but is captured, taken to Gestapo headquarters and tortured. Bergman must be silenced before he breaks, so Grant and his newly married co-pilot, Bissell, fly in to bomb the building. Though they are successful, their shot-up Mosquito crash-lands and Bissell is blinded. Hilde thanks Grant for ending her brother's suffering. Air Vice-Marshal Davis decides to move up the attack to the next day. However, the resistance fighters are ambushed and killed, leaving the anti-aircraft intact. Grant is given the option of aborting the operation but decides to press on. The factory is destroyed, apparently at the cost of the entire squadron. Grant crash-lands, but his navigator, Flight Lieutenant Hoppy Hopkinson, pulls the wounded wing commander from the burning wreckage. Back in Britain, Davis tells a fellow officer, who is aghast at the losses, fearing they are all dead, 'You can't kill a squadron.'

Indeed, the six films that followed 633's success all resuscitated aspects of it. The narrative template for the cycle, loosely based on *633 Squadron*, is as follows. A North American officer, serving with a British unit, but haunted by the failure of a previous raid and consequent casualties, is recruited to lead a dangerous (probably suicidal), vital (the war may hinge on it), top secret (British) mission on an all-but impregnable target. The hero trains his volunteers for their mission with ruthless efficiency (in *Hell Boats* the sailors are told 'don't stop for survivors', and in *1000 Plane Raid*, an overly compassionate colleague is informed, 'If you want to apply for the Chaplain's job, do so in the proper manner'), in a race against time and despite being under-resourced, before the target (usually a new and deadly Nazi weapon) becomes operative, while struggling to convince sceptical officers of the viability of the plan.

The raid is planned, scheduled and budgeted in meticulous detail (specifying precise quantities, times and so on, with much made of logs, maps, stopwatches and models). Meanwhile, the hero conducts an affair with the sister/wife of a British officer, a female fellow officer or the mistress of a German officer. (In *633 Squadron,* the sister, in *Mosquito Squadron* and *Hell Boats*, the wife, in *The 1000 Plane Raid*, a female officer, in *The Last Escape*, a German woman.) This affair provides an excuse for a briefly exposed female breast in *Hell Boats* and *The 1000 Plane Raid*. The Nazis attempt to destroy the mission before it has even been launched. In both *633 Squadron* and *Mosquito Squadron* the airfield from which the raid is to be launched is attacked by the Luftwaffe, on the eve of the operation; in *Submarine X-1*, German paratroopers find and attack the midget submarine base, but are rebuffed. In *The Last Escape*, the American commander's unit is wiped out in the opening sequence, forcing him to join up with British Commandos. Meanwhile the Resistance fights bravely but is swiftly disposed of with no survivors – whether Norwegian in *633 Squadron*, Sicilian in *Hell Boats*, or French/Arab in *Massacre Harbor*.

During the attack itself, promised military support is cancelled at the eleventh hour (the Norwegian Ling is massacred in *633 Squadron*, the RAF are unable to offer air support in *Attack on the Iron Coast* and only arrive extremely belatedly in *Hell Boats*) making the raid even riskier, but the heroes go-ahead anyway, blithely disobeying orders ('permission to abort' is given but ignored in *633 Squadron* and *Attack on the Iron Coast*). A senior officer joins the raid at the last minute (*633 Squadron*, *Attack on the Iron Coast*, *Hell Boats*, *Submarine X-1*). Some prisoners are taken by the enemy and imprisoned within the target, but the hero must go-ahead with the raid anyway. The operation is a success but at a high price. None of *633 Squadron's* planes return to England; only one boat makes it back to Malta in *Hell Boats*; only one of the three midget subs gets back to Scotland in *Submarine X-1*; The hero, played by Lloyd Bridges, is killed in *Attack on the Iron Coast*. In *Mosquito Squadron* all the planes are destroyed in the raid, though the resistance ensures McCallum gets home safely to his, conveniently widowed, sister-in-law. The last lines of dialogue in *633 Squadron* are 'They're probably all dead'. To which the commandant replies, 'You can't kill a squadron'. Like the squadron, a cycle can be resuscitated, recast, literally re-crewed.

In *Attack on the Iron Coast*, Lloyd Bridges, who led a failed, and hugely costly, previous attack, must lead a Commando raid on an occupied French Port. In *Submarine X-1*, James Caan, one of the few survivors of a failed attack on a German battleship, the Lindendorf, must find a way to destroy it in a Norwegian Fjord; in *The 1000 Plane Raid*, Christopher George must lead a massive daylight raid on a fighter plane factory in Marstenberg, Germany; in *Mosquito Squadron,* David McCallum must destroy the V-1 rocket base and free French resistance prisoners; in *The Last Escape*, Stuart Whitman must go behind enemy lines to kidnap a German rocket scientist before the war ends; in *Hell Boats*, James Franciscus must lead a torpedo boat raid on a Sicilian port, where the Nazis have concealed the base for their Fritz X Glide Bombs. To successfully accomplish their missions, the heroes must destroy their targets, even though their fellow officers may be being held prisoner there (in *Mosquito Squadron* and *Submarine X-1*). The heroes accomplish their mission, against the odds, despite high casualty rates. *The Last Escape* departs from this formula in several respects. The unit is already in action at the very start when American troops behind enemy lines are attacked and all except their leader are killed. He joins forces with the British paratroopers that his unit was due to meet up with, but their Major is killed in their first action (saving the life of a young, inexperienced officer). There is an equally inexperienced young flyer in *The 1000 Plane Raid*, a scared sixteen-year-old seaman in *Attack on the Iron Coast*, and a nervous young diver in *Submarine X-1*.

Cycles and corporate self-expression

According to Klein, 'Any film or film cycle, no matter its budget or subject matter, has the potential to reveal a wealth of information about the studio that made it'.[17] One such revelation is such films' on-screen (and the company's off-screen) stress on efficiency, tight budgets and schedules and training. As Wing Commander Grant is told in an early scene explaining his appointment to lead the mission, 'Since you took over, the squadron has attained a high degree of efficiency.' Such 'efficiency' (a curious choice of words when 'effectiveness' or 'success' might have been expected) is the watchword not only for the squadron's mission, indeed for all the missions of the subsequent cycle, but also for the very production of the films which depict them. The schedule is paramount. 'The factory will be shipping fuel in 18 days. Your special bombs will be ready in 17.' The task can only be accomplished with scientific precision, as Grant explains, 'We will drop the bombs within fifty yards of each other, at ten second intervals. . . . The geologists calculate that ten bombs of their size, exploding in this pattern, will break loose the overhang.'

Klein notes that film cycles can appeal to 'the periodic upswelling of a sentiment – such as the predictable resurgence of patriotism during times of war', though of course, while the US was then at war in Vietnam, the UK was not.[18] Stanfield quotes *Variety*'s coverage of a cycle produced during the Korean War, noting that 'Reports from the field indicate that exhibs are convinced that the wide excitement of the public over Korea and its military events is reawakening a taste for battle scenes'.[19] *Variety* also noted at the time that the latest 'and perhaps most topical' was the 'airplane cycle' – a group of films that was 'tied in with the current situation in Korea' and elsewhere with the technical development of 'particular planes and training of fliers'.[20] Walter, having produced a Korean cycle at Allied Artists, may have calculated that comparable films could also tap into British Second World War nostalgia (among the older generation) and curiosity (among younger cinemagoers).

Just days after *Variety*'s report on US domination of British subsidy receipts, on 29 and 30 January 1966, a meeting took place between UA executives and the three Mirisch brothers about their future production plans.[21] The discussion included *Death Where Is Thy Sting-a-ling-a-ling* (item 15) and *The Cruel Eagle* (an ultimately unmade project, based on another novel by Frederick E. Smith, author of *633 Squadron*) (items 12 and 14). The memorandum of the meeting records, under the heading, 'PROGRAM OF LOW BUDGET EADY PLAN PICTURES' that 'United Artists agreed that the Mirisches may set up a unit in England, initially for the production of four pictures, at budgets of $1,000,000 or less. By necessity these are to be disciplined pictures all produced under

---

[17] Klein, 2011: 20.
[18] Ibid, 90.
[19] 'Korean Situation Cues Circuit War-Pix Buys In Sharp About-Face', *Variety*, 26.7.50, 3. See also 'Pix Biz Spurts with War Fever': Film and the Public Sphere – Cycles and Topicality by Peter Stanfield, 2013: 217.
[20] 'H'wood's Head in the Clouds', *Variety*, 26.7.50: 11.
[21] See Interoffice memorandum 3 February 1966 in UA Collection Addition, Box Five, Folder 4–5.

the Eady Plan. All of the pictures are to be "service" pictures and all are to be produced in color.' UA agreed that three people would make up the nucleus of the company in England. 'These three people would consist of a production man, a story idea man, and a producer or producer-director. The Mirisches are to start looking for story material as soon as possible.'[22] In the event, only one book is listed among the cycle's sources – *The 1000 Plane Raid* by Ralph Barker, originally published in 1965 as *The Thousand Plan*.

If the Eady quota system proved an external enabler of and incentive for such a cycle, Mirisch's contract as a supplier for United Artists, obliged to provide the distributor with a final twenty-eight films between 1968 and 1974, provided another imperative for it. A team based in England was swiftly appointed. John C. Champion was employed to storyline and produce the cycle, having worked with Blake Edwards as co-writer earlier in his career. (Edwards was then contracted to Mirisch, on his own Second World War film, *What Did You Do in The War, Daddy?*). Champion also had the experience of co-writing and producing aerial films including *Dragonfly Squadron* (Lesley Selander for Allied Artists 1954), which was part of the Korean-War cycle cited by Stanfield[23] when Walter was head of production at AA. Champion's colleague, Irving Temaner, had already been associate producer on two 1967 Mirisch productions, *How to Succeed in Business Without Really Trying* and *Fitzwilly*. Champion produced *Attack on the Iron Coast* and *Submarine X-1*, on which Temaner served as executive producer, while a British associate producer, Ted Lloyd, was hired to do the leg work and tick any Eady-obligatory boxes. Then, with Mirisch concerned about inefficiencies in budgetary control and scheduling, Champion was replaced by Rachmil on *The 1000 Plane Raid*, *Mosquito Squadron* and *Hell Boats*, while Temaner oversaw *The Last Escape*. Champion had moved to London in early 1967 to oversee the first four films, but Rachmil, executive producer of *633 Squadron,* and having since become a VP at Mirisch, soon took over.[24] Champion left Mirisch in July 1967.[25] As *Variety* reported, 'Next on producer Lew Rachmil's slate for Mirisch-UA will be "Mosquito Squadron," to be filmed in England. Boris Sagal will direct pic, sequel to "633 Squadron."'[26]

Why a Second World War cycle?

What persuaded Mirisch of the viability of such a cycle? According to *Variety,* Champion, who oversaw the outlines for the six films, was confident there was an audience.

> World War II continues to be a prime plot lode for both pix and tv, with at least 17 features now on the planning board at five major film companies. In particular,

---

[22] Interoffice Memorandum 3 February 1966, UA Collection Addition, 1950–1980.
[23] 'Pix Biz', op cit.
[24] 'Rachmil Promoted to Mirisch V.P.O', *Daily Variety*, 26.5.66: 1.
[25] 'John Champion Departs Mirisch', *Daily Variety*, 21.6.67: 1.
[26] 'Mosquito' Rachmil Sequel to '633', *Daily Variety*, 26.3.68: 1.

writer-producer John C. Champion's entire six-pix program with The Mirisch Corp.-United Artists will be devoted to that war ... Champion ... is plotting his entire Mirisch film slate on World War II stories, on the theory that young audiences – the bulk of the film market – include many potential draftees who are curious about war. At the same time, however, use of contemporary strife (Vietnam, etc) is too close to personal and political disagreements. Thus, going back to 'somebody else's war' gives the desired remoteness, while satisfying youthful curiosity.[27]

A few days later, *Variety* reported, 'The popularity of war films is going to increase, not decline', avers writer-producer John C. Champion ... 'There has not been a time, within human memory, that a war has not been fought somewhere in the world. Also, we must bear in mind that as long as the youth of America must serve in the armed forces, they are going to be keenly interested in learning anything they can about what war is like.'[28] Champion's confidence seems to have been based on an assumption that the cycle's box office destination was primarily the US, not the UK. In fact, the cycle was to suffer commercially for two reasons. While America was at war, Britain was not, no longer had conscription, nor had the new majority cinemagoing generation in the UK either experience or expectation of going to war. Meanwhile, by the end of the decade, the American cinemagoing demographic was increasingly anti-war (i.e. against the war in Vietnam) which made films celebrating the military out of synch with the times and perhaps both historically and geographically too distant for the identification Champion predicted.

Stanfield describes such cycles as 'For the most part ... the product of new independent companies that exploited the gap in the market left by the major studios which were abandoning the production of genre films or programmes to concentrate their resources on fewer, more expensive features.'[29] Mirisch was one such independent, but for its subsidiaries, Mirisch Films Limited and Oakmont Productions, the cycle proved little more than an Eady-extraction vehicle. For Klein, 'Film cycles thrive in a low-budget, B-film environment because much of the work (and, by extension, much of the cost) has been completed before production even begins: actors know their motivations from previous films, scriptwriters recycle dialogue and plot formulas, and set designers reuse or reconstruct soundstages.'[30] For Klein, films in cycles stand in opposition to so-called 'quality cinema' - which is often, by association, equated with bigger budgets.[31] Instead, cycle films exemplify what she refers to as 'slavish repetition'. I will return to the question of repetitiousness and the formulaic later. Walter Mirisch had produced the *Bomba the Jungle Boy* series at Monogram. 'I was screening stock film, generally from the libraries of other studios ... we would determine what we

---

[27] 'Poised Pix Pegged on World War II, Including Champion's 6 For Mirisch-UA', *Daily Variety*, 10.4.67: 4.
[28] 'Champion Sees War Pix Popularity on the Increase', *Daily Variety*, 10.8.67: 3.
[29] Stanfield, 2013: 45.
[30] Klein, 2011: 91.
[31] Ibid, 8.

wanted to use and write sequences around the stock material.'[32] The cost-effectiveness of recycling stock footage and, indeed, exploiting Mirisch's own back catalogue, played an important role in the Second World War cycle.

Producing the cycle

Champion's skeletal plots were developed by numerous writers, through several drafts. Indeed, the writing process of the six films reveals the speed with which they were prepared. The first film in the cycle, *Attack on the Iron Coast*, began with a story by Champion which was then drafted into a screenplay by Herman Hoffman (who had written episodes of *Attack* star, Lloyd Bridges', TV series, *Sea Hunt*).[33] The second film, *Submarine X-1*, also began as 'an idea by John C. Champion', 'based on an idea by Charles M. Warren' (himself an ex-Second World War naval commander) and this was the basis of a screenplay by Edmund H. North, *The X-Men*.[34] *Variety* reported that Mirisch had previously tried to spin-off a submarine movie into a TV series. *Run Silent, Run Deep* (Wise, 1958) had been directed by Mirisch contract director, Robert Wise, for rival indie, Hill-Hecht-Lancaster, and dramatized a sub-commander's obsession to sink an enemy destroyer, and though the series was aborted, it may have provided a seed for the film.[35] North rewrote this screenplay in May 1967 as *The Iron Men*, but by August 1967 it had been completely redrafted and retitled once again, this time by Donald Sanford and Guy Elmes as *Submarine X-1*.

The third film in the cycle, *The 1000 Plane Raid*, was overseen by Lewis Rachmil (and Walter Mirisch) in LA and began as an adaptation of Ralph Barker's novel. This resulted in *The Big Raid*, a treatment by Robert Vincent Wright, submitted on 21 November 1966. By 11 January 1967 this had been transformed into Sanford's screenplay *The Big Raid* and subsequent redrafts followed on 27 January and 10 February and late into December 1967. Between the multiple revised drafts dated December 1967 the logistics scene discussed later was inserted.[36] It seems likely that it was then that Walter Mirisch's experience at Harvard and Lockheed made a direct impact on the script. Harold also had an interest in the story. On 27 August 1942 he had sent a telegram to RKO Albee Theatre, announcing that 'Pathe News Number One Released August Twenty Eighth Has Four Minute Story of Thousand Plane Raids Over Germany Have This In Newspaper Ads Using Following Lines Quote First Pictures RAF Over Europe In Pathe News Unquote Regards H. J. Mirisch.'[37]

---

[32] Mirisch, 2008: 34–5.
[33] Walter Mirisch Papers, Wisconsin Historical Society, Box 24.
[34] Ibid, Box 25.
[35] *Variety*, 30.3.65: 36.
[36] Sanford Screenplay, Walter Mirisch Papers, Wisconsin Historical Society, Box 47.
[37] Western Union Telegram, Harold J. Mirisch Film Bookings 1942–43, University of Iowa Digital Library.

Despite the number of drafts – and screenwriters – involved in scripting the cycle, the speed with which these six scripts were completed remains striking. Donald Sanford, whose name is on *Submarine X-1*, *The 1000 Plane Raid* and *Mosquito Squadron*, reveals the pace of their production in a letter to Champion.

> Dear John, . . . If we have set some kind of record for turning out what I believe to be a damn fine screenplay in next to no time, the major credit should go to you. The fact that you were available on a day and night, seven-day-a-week basis, for story conferences, rewriting, guidance, frequent pep talks, etc etc., kept the work on target and moving.[38]

The production cycle was continuous.

The fourth film in the cycle, *Mosquito Squadron*, saw Champion replaced as supervisor by Rachmil. At this point, Guy Elmes' screenplay, dated 15 November 1967, was read for 'general background' but Rachmil and director, Boris Sagal, wanted 'a wholly new story line'.[39] Rachmil was less than impressed with the set-up in London, writing to Sanford,

> This picture is a problem to me in that as I write this I still do not have sufficient aircraft to make the picture. A lot of promises were made and a lot of people believed them without checking. I started smelling something wrong the second day I was here and have since fired the coordinator of aircraft, hire [sic] a new man and on top of that hire a technical advisor from RAF . . . No leading man yet for the film.

Sanford replied, 'Thanks for your comical letter – are there any medical benefits under the Eadie [sic] plan? Like free Maalox, for instance . . . Seriously, though, I tip my toby to you – I wouldn't be a producer, not no-how I wouldn't.'[40] Sanford's story outline is dated 4 March 1968 and his first script on 6 March that same year. The final draft screenplay is dated 7 May 1968 with additional revisions on 14 June. The files for the film include the note, 'Suggested screenplay credits – Screenplay by Donald S. Sanford, Donald and Derek Ford, Story by Joyce Percy'. Sanford replied, 'Please be advised that I do not believe the division of credit as presently determined, accurately represents my contribution to the final screenplay.'[41] *The Last Escape*, initially entitled *Escapeline*, had a late revision by Philip Saltzman, a TV screenwriter, but is credited to Herman Hoffman (who also scripted *Guns of the Magnificent Seven*) and seems to have been through comparatively few drafts. The resulting film is seriously underwritten. The

---

[38] Letter to John C. Champion, 8.5.67 in Walter Mirisch Papers, Wisconsin Historical Society, Box 42.
[39] Letter from Mary Dorfman, Screen Credits Secretary, Writers Guild of America, 25.9.68, Walter Mirisch Papers, Wisconsin Historical Society, Box 42, File 2.
[40] Rachmil letter 17.5.68. Sanford replied on 27.5.68 Walter Mirisch Papers, Wisconsin Historical Society, Box 42, File 2.
[41] 23.9.68. Letter from Mary Dorfman, Screen Credits Secretary, Writers Guild of America, 25.9.68. Box 42, Walter Mirisch Papers, Wisconsin Historical Society.

story for the last film in the cycle, *Hell Boats*, for which an early title was *The Die Hards*, is credited to S.S. Schweitzer, with the final screenplay attributed to Anthony Spinner and two of BBC TV's *Z Cars* writers, Donald and Derek Ford.

Attack on the Iron Coast, started shooting in London on 15 May 1967, had a seven-week production schedule and wrapped at the end of June 1967 on a budget of just over $1 million.[42] *Submarine X-1* began filming on 17 July 1967. *The 1000 Plane Raid* started shooting – in California! – on 16 January 1968. *Variety* reported it would be scored within eight weeks – quite a fast turnaround.[43] *Mosquito Squadron* began filming on 10 June 1968 in London. *The Last Escape* began filming on 22 July 1968 in Munich. *Hell Boats* started shooting on 12 August 1968 in Malta. *Attack on the Iron Coast* was released in the United States on 5 June 1968. *Submarine X-1* was released on 22 March 1968 in the UK, but not until August 1969 in the US. *The 1000 Plane Raid* was released in the United States in July 1969. *Mosquito Squadron* was released on 17 January 1970 in the UK and 1 July 1970 in the US. *The Last Escape* was released on 6 May 1970 in the United States. *Hell Boats* was released in the UK on 22 November 1970 and in the US on 10 June 1970.

That this was very much a continuous production cycle is also evidenced by the continuity of employment it offered key crew members. Paul Beeson shot four of the films – *Attack*, *Submarine*, *Mosquito* and *Hell* consecutively; *The 1000 Plane Raid* was shot by William W. Spencer, *The Last Escape* by Gernot Roll (who later shot *Heimat*). John S. Smith edited *Submarine*, *Mosquito* and *Hell*; Bill Andrews was the art director on *Attack*, *Submarine* and *Mosquito* and Anthony Waye was the assistant director on *Attack, Submarine, Mosquito* and *Hell* (but not the two made in Germany and the United States, as that would have required additional permits – and expense).

The three British-based films – *Attack*, *Submarine* and *Mosquito* – were all made at Borehamwood Studios and on location. The romantic scene filmed at Tykes Water Lake in Aldenham County Park in *Mosquito Squadron* was the same location as for a similar scene in *633 Squadron*. Similarly, the RAF base sequences for *Mosquito Squadron* were filmed at RAF Bovington, also the base for *633 Squadron*.[44] The Bowie Organization made the special effects models for the three British-shot films; for *Mosquito Squadron*, the model work was done at Malta Film Facilities, because of Malta's reliable blue skies and this studio subsequently became the base for *Hell Boats*. The other two films – *1000 Plane Raid* and *The Last Escape* – were filmed in California and Bavaria respectively. *Raid* was shot at Santa Maria airport in California and at the Samuel Goldwyn Studios. *Escape* was filmed at Bavaria-Geiselgasteig Studios (where Mirisch had already shot *One, Two, Three* and the studio sequences of *The Great Escape*).[45]

On *Hell Boats*, Rachmil was impressed by the facilities in Malta. 'We have worked without interruption for two months, thanks to the excellent Maltese weather, and the

---

[42] *Daily Variety*, 5.7.67: 1 and *Variety*, 12.4.67.
[43] *Variety*, 26.3.68: 1.
[44] Howard Hughes, 'History of Oakmont Films', *Cinema Retro*, 25: 42–3.
[45] '"The Last Escape," Mirisch-UA World War II yarn is lensing at Munich's Bavaria-Geiselgasteig Studios and various nearby locations', *Variety*, 11.9.68: 15.

film will be completed ahead of schedule in mid-October at a cost appreciably lower than we had originally anticipated.'[46] *Variety* reported that,

> Among the moneysaving factors on the pic . . . have been the extensive cooperation extended by the Maltese government, the R.A.F. and the Admiralty in offering their establishments for unit filming. The R.A.F. even loaned the company its Air-Sea Rescue Boats, which have been converted into WWII MTBs. Arrangement with the authorities was made contingent on the guarantee that the disguise could be dismantled in five minutes, should the boats be required in an emergency. Location shooting has been completed, with three weeks of interior filming still to go at the Malta Film Facilities. According to Rachmil, 'our decision to film "Hell Boats" in Malta was motivated by the availability of the huge and, in a way, unique film tank at the studio. Not only is this the largest film tank in the world, but it is situated by the sea so that the natural horizon, rather than artificial skybacking, can be utilized. Because of the tank's size (it holds 3,500,000 gallons of water), we will be able to attain a degree of realism not possible anywhere else.'[47]

Calculating probabilities

Given Walter Mirisch's training at Lockheed, it is striking that not only *633 Squadron*, but also the two flying films in the cycle – *Mosquito Squadron* and *The 1000 Plane Raid* – concern themselves explicitly with computing 'the probabilities of hitting targets and the amount of tonnage required to fall on a given target to yield a statistical probability of destroying it'. Significantly perhaps, *The 1000 Plane Raid* was a departure from the cycle, the only one of the six films not filmed in Europe, presumably preventing it from qualifying for British or European subsidy. Nevertheless, filming in California allowed it to be closely supervised by Walter Mirisch. Dialogue which was only inserted into the final draft of the screenplay includes the following exchanges between Colonel Brandon (Christopher George) and the assembled officers hearing his plan (Figure 10).

> A strike of this magnitude will require a minimum of thirty fully operational airfields, plus an additional thirty airfields for the required British fighter support. Estimated bomb tonnage needed: 3500 tons. Total fuel: One million 850,000 gallons minimum. 50 Calibre ammunition. Five million rounds. Oxygen. 'We'll study your logistics later, colonel.' Collision due to pilot error will cost 1% of our force. Navigational error: one half of one percent.

---

[46] 'Lewis J. Rachmil: Malta Aid Keeps UA Film Ahead', *Variety*, 23.10.68: 11.
[47] Ibid.

Figure 10 The thousand plane raid plan being 'pitched' to top brass in *The 1000 Planes Raid*.

There is a similar scene in *Submarine X-1* when James Caan's Commander Bolton unveils the midget submarine to his men.

> The X Craft gentlemen. 51 foot long. Beam – 8 foot six. Draft – 7 foot six. Weight – 35 tons, maximum diving depth – 300 feet, surface speed – six and a half knots. Submerged – 5 knots. Range – 1400 miles at 4 knots. 4 men to a crew. She carries two, 4000 pound charges of amatol – enough to blast open the hull of any battleship afloat.

Scientific management is applied to the scheduling of these missions too: In *The 1000 Plane Raid*, Wing Commander Brandon asks Cotton: 'When do we hit Marstenburg?' 'On the 19th'. 'That's less than three weeks. How the hell are you going to get a thousand planes assembled, fitted, fuelled, armed and ready to go in less than three weeks?' 'By telescoping your timetable, Colonel.' Similarly, in *Attack*, Bridges is told, 'Postponement is out of the question, we've got to move within six days or not at all . . . . They've given you the green light.'

Familiarity breeds content

The choice of storylines for the cycle evidences a cautious preference for the already familiar, both with potential audiences and producers. Not only are most of the films based on actual operations but also, in several cases, those very operations had already provided the bases of previous films. Thus, *Attack on the Iron Coast* was based on Operation Chariot, the naval raid on St Nazaire (the codename in the film is Operation

Mad Dog), which had already been the basis for *Gift Horse* (Bennett, 1952); *Submarine X-1* was loosely based on Operation Source, the attack on the Tirpitz, which had been previously filmed *as Above Us the Waves* (Thomas, 1955) *The 1000 Plane Raid* was based on the RAF (not USAF)'s Operation Millennium air raid on Cologne (thus, as in *The Great Escape*, a British wartime exploit was literally recast for the American market). *Mosquito Squadron* was loosely based on Operation Jericho, but misleadingly marketed as a sequel to *633 Squadron*. *The Last Escape* was inspired by Operation Paperclip; *Hell Boats* was based on Operation Ruthless, planned by wartime naval officer, Ian Fleming. And such recycling had started with *633 Squadron* with its echoes of *The Dam Busters* (Anderson, 1955).

Walter Mirisch was adept at applying such logistics (perhaps deploying his very own Gantt Charts) and the cycle provided a perfect laboratory for experiments in the scientific management of film production. As Klein suggests, 'for a cycle to form, it needs to repeat the same images and plots over and over within a brief window of time.'[48] It is worth pausing to identify some of this cycle's characteristic imagery, including uniforms, maps, stopwatches, models, pointers, charts, logbooks, navigational devices, cockpits, observation decks, explosions, air raids, uniforms, mosquitos, tanks, jeeps, armoured cars, anti-aircraft guns, machine guns, fuel depots, midget submarines, motorized torpedo boats, control towers, briefing rooms, country houses requisitioned for wartime use, fjords, mountain ranges, dockyards, officers' quarters as well as such civilian sites as river banks, fields, country roads and village pubs. Sometimes, however, such imagery proves prohibitively expensive and alternative sources present themselves.

In *The 1000 Plane Raid* the crews run out of spare parts, so Brandon advises his Sgt to 'Cannibalise the Can Do. Strip everything you need out of her for the other aircraft.' Similarly, in *Hell Boats*, an officer asks his new commander, 'What about spare parts, sir? Ship carrying our supplies was sunk.' 'Well, there are two boats at the bottom of the harbour. Strip those boats of everything usable and you'll have all the spare parts you'll need.' This is not just recycling, it also reflects the way these films themselves recycled footage from other movies, cannibalizing their predecessors for dramatic aerial sequences, explosions, air raids and otherwise prohibitively expensive and time-consuming footage. Salvage, meanwhile, was not simply an economic strategy whose use in wartime could be replicated in cyclical production. It was also the title of a seven-minute newsreel which Harold Mirisch himself had recommended for bookings at RKO.[49]

As Klein insists, 'The originary film must have a set of images that are recognizable enough to be easily duplicated in several more films' (Klein, 11). Sequences from *633 Squadron* are literally duplicated (reprinted and inserted) in *Mosquito Squadron*, *The 1000 Plane Raid* and *The Last Escape* (and, later, *Midway*) and *633*'s theme music is also reused in several of the films. That 'a set of images' from *633 Squadron* is 'easily duplicated' in subsequent films in the cycle is evidenced by the way the Luftwaffe raid

---

[48] Klein, 2011: 80.
[49] Letter to George French, Harold J. Mirisch Film Bookings 1942–43, Iowa Digital Library, 25.9.42.

on the RAF airfield sequence is reused in *Mosquito Squadron*. But *Mosquito Squadron* not only recycles actual footage from *633 Squadron*, it also recycles the entire pre-title sequence, complete with Frank Cordell's theme music, from *Operation Crossbow* (Anderson, 1965); furthermore, it reproduces documentary archive footage of the bouncing bomb. Plots are equally ransacked. In *633 Squadron*, the commander's friend is captured in Norway, and he falls in love with his sister. In *Mosquito Squadron*, the Squadron Leader's (McCallum) best friend has been captured in France, and he falls in love with the latter's wife. Subsequently both men are assigned to bomb the buildings where their friends are being held. In both films there is an airman with a metal hand. *The Last Escape*'s aerial sequences are also recycled from *633 Squadron*; both films were directed by Walter Grauman.

More striking, perhaps, these six Mirisch films are also, in one sense, *about* simulation/imitation and repetition. These twin themes are introduced in *633 Squadron* when Wing Commander Roy Grant tells his men, after demonstrating how to fly over the rehearsal target in Scotland, 'Try and match that. Speed 295 dead on. Altitude 200 feet and keep it low.' The instruction is to imitate as precisely as possible the action of the leader. This is, essentially, an attempt to make war and, more specifically, military strategy, into a quantifiable, calculable and repeatable operation. This is the very same ethos Mirisch imbibed both at Harvard Business School and subsequently at Lockheed.

Production and reproduction

The first film in the cycle, *Attack on the Iron Coast*, includes one officer describing another, 'Pushing his men ruthlessly, training them under simulated battle conditions'. But where there is simulation there is also dissimulation – in the same film, the captain explains that, 'We've had sweepers visit this area a number of times during the past few weeks. The idea was to let Jerry think we were sweeping regularly.' The training which takes up a large proportion of the running time of the film is a series of rehearsals for the raid itself, indeed, a kind of dress rehearsal (ducking, climbing, running while wearing blindfolds in preparation for a moonless night attack). When they finally approach the target port in the minesweeper, Major Wilson says, 'Time to start the minstrel show' and begins blackening his face to remain unseen in the dark. Below deck his second in command says to the men, 'Come on girls. A little faster with your make-up.'

In *Submarine X-1*, the commander is told, 'I'm assigning you to command a training programme. Top secret training of selected volunteers.' This training involves diving and unscrewing bolts and cutting through nets while underwater. (The commander himself shows how this should be done and also demonstrates a stranglehold which he later deploys to kill a German paratrooper attacking the submarine base.) As in *633 Squadron*, the training takes place in Scotland (the actual attacks are on Nazi bases hidden away in Norwegian Fjords) but all the location filming was done in Scotland – both the training simulation and the 'real' raid! In *Hell Boats* the commander tells his men, 'On the basis of what I saw on our last operation, our chances of survival on this one are nil. Now since I don't like committing suicide, you're going to spend every moment you're not out on a combat mission in training. You'll work until this flotilla satisfies me that it is capable in every respect of carrying out the job we were selected for.' Training for an assault on an apparently impregnable target is crucial and much of the film's running time is devoted to it. The unit capture a German E Boat, shoot it up to make it appear to have been heavily damaged in a British assault, fake a radio message about it being attacked and then pretend to be wounded Germans (wearing German naval uniforms and putting red paint on their faces to simulate wounds) before navigating the boat into the German base in Sicily. In *The Last Escape*, the opening narration describes Stuart Whitman's character 'posing as a Wehrmacht Major' as, once again, the characters are dressing up, performing roles to succeed in their mission.

The films in this cycle can thus be said to document their own 'rehearsals', and foreground their own budgets and schedules, equipment lists and 'crews'. They function as virtually their own 'making ofs'; indeed, 'in some ways their mission is an allegory for the task of the film's producer and casting director'.[50] In his book about one of the key 'special mission' films, *Where Eagles Dare*, Geoff Dyer suggests that 'Pre-mission briefings are always addressed to the audience as well as the actors gathered around to listen, sitting or standing . . . who are effectively our surrogates, eager to know what we and they are in for'.[51] The films in the cycle (and others like them) function as allegories for filmmaking in which the unsung heroes are arguably the producers themselves, who plan the missions on which the war will turn, given projects to undertake on limited budgets and schedules, with minimal resources, training their crews to accomplish their missions.

Indeed, the protagonists each pitch the plans for their respective 'raid' in a formal presentation. (The pitch in *The 1000 Plane Raid* is at 'Pinetree', almost Pinewood, the heart of the British film industry.) The preparation for such raids often involves watching films. In *633 Squadron* they watch rushes of their own Scottish training flights; *Attack on the Iron Coast* begins with Lloyd Bridges watching footage of the tragic failure of the operation he previously planned and led; in the same film, German officers are shown watching a stag film of a woman undressing; in *Mosquito Squadron* the Luftwaffe drop a can of film showing Mosquito crews now held prisoner – in the very building which is the target of their raid.

Qualifying for Eady, with predominantly British casts and crews (but American leads and American producers and directors), involved rather transparent plot devices to motivate the American presence in the films. Thus, in *The 1000 Plane Raid*, we hear, 'You have a way with Americans, I'm told.' Wing Commander Howard: 'Americans?' '103rd Heavy Bombardment Group at Steeple Bassington, to be exact. You'll fill them in on enemy fighter tactics. You'll be interested to know that other RAF fighter pilots are being posted to American bomber groups. Sort of lend-lease in reverse.' Since the film was loosely based on an exclusively RAF action, here fictionalized as an American

---

[50] Geoff Dyer, *'Broadsword Calling Danny Boy': On Where Eagles Dare*, Penguin, 2018, 107.
[51] Ibid, 4.

operation, this recasting of the conflict could hardly hope to go down well with British audiences. (Even *The Great Escape* had almost equal numbers of British and American escapees.) In *Hell Boats*, the commander, looking through the hero's paperwork before meeting him asks, 'What's this? He's American!' 'English mother, Sir.' 'Have him sent in. Oh, er, he doesn't chew gum, does he?' In *Attack on the Iron Coast* Major Wilson is a Canadian working with the RAF, Royal Navy and Army. In *Hell Boats* it is implied that the British commander is impotent, as explanation for the American hero's affair with the former's frustrated wife. The casting of American leads (and hiring of American directors, producers and, in several cases, screenwriters) is a crucial aspect of this strategy. The cycle's stars were essentially B Movie leads or identified with small screen series. Such TV-friendly casting reduced costs, while easing eventual sales to the networks.

The end of the cycle

Nowell argues that 'the duration of a production trend is also determined by the presence or absence of those conditions which lead trends to unfold in the first place'.[52] He goes on to suggest that 'Just as a solitary hit tends not to cement confidence in production, so a single flop provides inconclusive evidence of commercial impotence. A solitary box office failure can just as well indicate an unappealing marketing campaign, a poorly timed release, intense competition from other films and other free-time activities, or a combination thereof.'[53] What, then, explains the end of the cycle? Certainly, Mirisch had only intended to produce 'a program of six films' and this was all that United Artists agreed to support. Furthermore, as *Variety*'s reviews and UA's feedback makes it clear, none of the six were successful at the box office. They may have received substantial subsidy via Eady, but this alone could not guarantee profitability.

However, as with *633 Squadron*, Eady contributed to recouping their costs, budgets were kept low and all six films were released on double bills, avoiding the necessity to be major attractions themselves. In the UK at least, *Attack on the Iron Coast* was released with *Yellow Submarine* on 4 August 1968; *Submarine X-1* was released on 9 February 1969 with *The Thomas Crown Affair*; after a West End opening in November 1970, *Mosquito Squadron* was programmed with *The Private Life of Sherlock Holmes* on its general release 18 January 1971; *The 1000 Plane Raid* (6 July 1969) opened on double bills with *Guns of the Magnificent Seven* (no London area release according to *Cinema Retro*); *Hell Boats* was programmed together with *Master of the Islands* (aka *The Hawaiians*) 22 November 1970; in summer 1970, *Variety* reported that a double bill combining *The Last Escape* and *Mosquito Squadron* replaced Mirisch's, *The Hawaiians* in New York.[54] The November 1970 UK releases of *Hell Boats* and *Mosquito Squadron*

---

[52] Nowell, 2012: 90.
[53] Ibid, 91.
[54] *Variety*, 8.7.70 and 19.8.70.

coincided with the British TV premiere of *633 Squadron* on 17 November 1970 'which achieved a then-record audience for a film on the BBC'.[55]

The last two films in the cycle departed from the formula in several ways. *Hell Boats* was a departure in that it added production values by being entirely – and comparatively expensively – filmed in Malta, despite reducing production costs through arrangements with Maltese and British officials. *The Last Enemy* was filmed entirely in Germany, perhaps profiting from newly introduced German studio discounts. *The Last Escape* is probably the worst of the six films, but it completes the circle, being directed by *633 Squadron*'s Walter Grauman and recycling footage from that film. The cycle was out of sync with its conditions of existence. The extent to which this is the case is perhaps epitomized by the fact that *Hell Boats* was filming at precisely the same time as Ken Loach's *Kes* and the surreal double bill of *Attack on the Iron Coast* with *Yellow Submarine* (Dunning, 1968), which could hardly have been better designed to reveal the anachronism of the cycle.

Discussing *M*A*S*H* (Altman, 1970), *The Dirty Dozen* (Aldrich, 1967) and *Kelly's Heroes* (Hutton, 1970) as films about 'failure', characteristic of the New Hollywood, and as an accommodation with late 1960s counter-culture, Robnik reads these three war movies too as 'allegories of production'.[56] 'The film conceived as a special mission and norm-defying event, carried out by a package-team of maverick experts with non-standardized skills and no institutional ties – this is the logic of flexible production that is allegorized by the successes of the undisciplined in New Hollywood´s war movies'.[57] By comparison, Mirisch's cycle consisted of six films which were low budget, old Hollywood programmers, maintaining continuity of production for an independent supplier, requiring a constant cash flow, but lacking the 'talent' behind the camera or the star power in front of it to 'authorize' such a counter-cultural critique. (Mirisch's unmade First World War project, *The Bells of Hell Go Ding a Ling a Ling*, might have come closest in spirit, but Altman, without a green light to shoot Roald Dahl's screenplay, ultimately made the anti-war *M*A*S*H*, instead.)

The cycle of six Second World War films was probably the most calculated of all Mirisch production decisions and yet, ironically, none of them were particularly successful. The calculation constrained costs, but also creativity, which kept the charisma of star power and significant writing or directing talents out of the equation. Mirisch did, however, ensure that three of the four directors hired had seen active service and had significant experience of the efficiencies of TV production. Discussing *Mosquito Squadron*, for instance, Patrick Tull, who played Flight Lt. Templeton, recalled 'Boris Sagal shot very quickly. He knew what he wanted and there wasn't much mucking around. Boris came from television, anyway, so he was used to working very fast . . . But you know the Mirisch brothers, they never wasted a penny. They were

[55] *Cinema Retro*, 9: 26 2013, 41.
[56] Drehli Robnik, 'Allegories of Post-Fordism in 1970s New Hollywood: Countercultural Combat Films, Conspiracy Thrillers as Genre-Recycling', in Thomas Elsaesser, Alexander Horwath, Noel King (eds), *The Last Great American Picture Show. New Hollywood Cinema in the 1970s*, Amsterdam University Press, 2004, 333–58.
[57] Ibid, 344.

smart enough to know it was always cheaper to rent than to own a single piece of equipment. They rented everything.'[58] Another member of the cast, Nicky Henson, added, 'The Mirisch brothers made the film because they had all this previous flying footage from 633 Squadron.'[59]

By the end of the sixties, the financial context in Britain had changed dramatically. The Films Act, 1966, extended statutory provisions to encourage British film production, including the Eady Plan, only until the end of 1970. Meanwhile, UA was having second thoughts about the viability of funding programmers. In March 1969, just as production of the cycle was coming to a head, Transamerica circulated to its executives and those of its subsidiaries, including UA, copies of Peter Drucker's latest book, *The Age of Discontinuity*.[60] This letter was accompanied by some extended 'Remarks' by John Beckett, chairman of the Board of Transamerica. Ironically, Beckett's fetishizing of 'hard data', his conviction that 'It is only by quantifying decisions that we can weight the arguments for and against' echoed Walter Mirisch's assumptions at Lockheed, articulated in *Factory*, but one victim of such data-driven decision-making was UA's relationship with the Mirisch Company itself.[61] As Krim put it, in a response to what he saw as Transamerica interference,

> the vagaries of the business simply do not and will never fit into the TA emphasis on prognostication, per annum growth, patterns of return on equity, or other guidelines applicable to other operations of TA. This, coupled with the new accounting guidelines, portends severe uncertainties in the future. The TA directors should understand this. It would be folly to interpret the theatrical results as typical or automatically *redoable* (my italics) merely by application of formulas or artificial prognostifcations.[62]

The late Harold Mirisch, who died on 5 December 1968, had favoured a comparably experiential approach to the intrinsic 'un-redoability' of films. The Harvard and Lockheed trained Walter, on the other hand, might have shared Drucker – and Beckett's – approach of applying managerial and narrative formulas to B filmmaking and, ironically, that very calculation, that commitment to scientific management, probably proved, in this instance at least, to be a strategic mistake.

In a hand-written table, the negative costs and domestic and foreign box office takings are reported for some of those twenty films, including four of the six films in the cycle. (There are no figures for *633 Squadron*, or the first two films, *Attack on the Iron Coast* and *Submarine X-1*.) *The 1000 Plane Raid* is recorded as having cost $1,116,000 and earned only $100,000 at the US box office and $700,000 at the foreign box office. *The Last Escape* is recorded as having cost $995,000 and earned a total of

---

[58] *Cinema Retro* 28: 54.
[59] Ibid, 29: 44.
[60] Peter Drucker, *The Age of Discontinuity*, New York: Harper & Row, 1968.
[61] cited in Balio, 1987: 319.
[62] *UA 70–73 Background Report*, United Artists Collection Addition, Box 5, Folder 4 Wisconsin Historical Society.

$550,000. *Mosquito Squadron* cost $1,130,000 and earned a total of $850,000. *Hell Boats* cost $1,368,000 and earned a total of $650,000. Some of the remaining films of the twenty record totals inclusive of TV sales but this is not the case for any of the films in the cycle.[63]

Calculation over cost control, the securing of subsidies, studio discounts and negotiated access to equipment and locations, a continuous production cycle and minimal differentiation may all have proved successful. But to work with audiences the films needed to be seen in cinemas and to engage those who saw them. In fact, despite a product shortage, there turned out to be little appetite for what were viewed as British 'B' war movies in the US, nor for such cynical and yet anachronistic fictions, with their minor American stars, in the UK.

Within weeks, UA's David Picker was acknowledging that such films had no audience and that there was little, if any, point in making them, let alone releasing them.

> Not only is there no longer an 'audience base' for such films in the cinema, said Picker, but the tv market is narrowing, and the 'programmers' which used to have network sales as prime insurance against costs (upwards of $600,000) now can't compete with the 'premiere' cheapies the webs are buying. The overall result, according to Picker: 'You can lose the total cost of a picture very, very easily.' What is United Artists doing about the situation? First off, Picker says, it has stopped making programmers (comparatively recent examples include '1,000 Plane Raid,' and 'Mosquito Squadron').[64]

Finally, however, it is worth remembering that it was the 'originary' film for the cycle, *633 Squadron*, which ironically helped inspire the iconic 'trench run' sequence in *Star Wars*, perhaps the film that did most to launch the franchise culture characteristic of today's Hollywood. For Mirisch, *633 Squadron* provided not just an iconographic, but also an industrial blueprint for a cinema that could, albeit briefly, square the circle of post-Fordist, one-off package-unit production with Fordism's continuous production cycle. The following decade, *Star Wars*, in turn, initiated the blockbuster era that helped bankroll the vertically re-integrated film industry and the very franchises and cycles that characterize so much of that industry's output today.

---

[63] 'Mirisch Second 20 Picture Deal', United Artists Collection Addition, Wisconsin Historical Society, Box 5, Folder 5.
[64] 'Flops' Loss-Cutting', *New York Times*, 26.8.70: 3, 6.

8

The border jumpers

'Lend lease in reverse' – The Mirisch Company and transnational cinema

Running away from Hollywood

Two recent books about the history of Hollywood location shooting and so-called 'runaway production' share an implicit acknowledgement of the role the Mirisch brothers played in that story[1]. The cover of *Hollywood on Location* is a production still from *Man of the West*, a Mirisch production. The first case study in *Runaway Hollywood* is of *Moby Dick*, which was made by Moulin Productions, the earliest independent the Mirisch brothers were involved in running. (Neither volume recognizes the Mirisch role in the acceleration of this trend.) The former film exemplifies location shooting within the United States, the latter filming abroad. Location filming, in both senses, came into its own once the majors had to divorce their production studios from their theatrical holdings, at a stroke removing their previously guaranteed market and thus threatening the viability of long-term studio staff contracts. Independent production companies and the freelance casts and crews they employed emerged to fill the gap. Studio overheads became increasingly unaffordable and both American and foreign locations became more attractive. Mirisch productions were made in the studio, on domestic locations and abroad but the implicit slur of 'runaway' was of avoiding US prices and US labour in favour of cheaper locations and crews outside Hollywood and often outside the United States altogether. Mirisch made many of its films abroad into the late 1960s, with important, successful exceptions like *In the Heat of the Night* and *The Thomas Crown Affair*, but international locations began being priced out of mid-budget productions by the studios and became less popular with many auteur filmmakers in the New American Cinema of the 1970s.

Moby Dick had been shot in Ireland, Wales, Portugal, Spain and at Associated British Picture Corporation's Elstree Studios in England. Huston had filmed the exteriors of

---

[1] Daniel Steinhart, *Runaway Hollywood: Internationalizing Postwar Production and Location Shooting*, University of California Press, 2019, and Joshua Gleich and Lawrence Webb (eds), *Hollywood on Location: An Industry History,* Rutgers University Press, 2019.

his previous Moulin production, *Moulin Rouge,* in Paris and then recreated Parisian interiors at Shepperton Studios. This had qualified it as 'British' under the quota system, thus eligible for Eady funds. Subsequently, Huston and Harold Mirisch agreed with ABPC that the latter provide studio space and technical support and thus ensure *Moby Dick* qualified for the quota too. Production manager Cecil Ford was British and repeatedly proved a crucial member of the production team for the Mirisches. In Las Palmas, meanwhile, Spanish requirements necessitated the recruitment of crew members from the local union.

This transnationalism extended to the status of the film in exhibition. As Huston admitted, 'I would hate to see Moby presented anywhere else but in England as anything but an American picture.'[2] Huston avoided a prestigious Cannes premiere, where its nationality as an entry would have proved uncomfortable and premiered it instead in New Bedford, Massachusetts, where it was set, though not shot. Allied Artists subsequently produced Wilder's *Love in the Afternoon* at the Studios de Boulogne, where several Parisian interiors, including the Ritz Hotel and the Opera, were recreated, with a few authentic exteriors filmed on location around Paris.

Between the making of Moulin's two Huston films, Allied Artists had signed a deal with 20th Century Fox to co-finance three CinemaScope films in Technicolor, one of which Walter Mirisch produced himself. This was *The Black Prince* (director, Henry Levin) (aka *The Warriors*) starring Errol Flynn and scripted by AA regular, Daniel Ullman. Fox co-funded with Associated British Pathe, AA's UK distributor, and the latter's Elstree studios were rented for the film, including MGM's exterior castle set for *Ivanhoe*, which remained on the back lot. The film failed at the box office, but Mirisch was sheltered from losses by the investments of Fox and A-B Pathe. Indeed, the combination of reduced cast, crew and studio costs, and the attractions provided by local subsidy and 'international' locations and subject matter proved an appealing recipe that the Mirisches would soon repeat with their own production company.

Mirisch production outside America

In fact, thirty-two of the seventy-five films subsequently produced by the Mirisch Company were made either entirely or partially outside the United States – in neighbouring Canada and Mexico, but also in Spain, Italy, France, Switzerland, the UK, Israel, Austria, Germany, the former Yugoslavia and elsewhere. Mirisch shot thirty of its sixty-eight films for United Artists, wholly or partially abroad, many of them international co-productions, benefitting from foreign subsidies and frozen funds (at least thirteen Mirisch films received the UK's Eady Levy monies, for instance, which were exclusively earmarked for *British* productions). And the company also remade foreign films – two of its most iconic and quintessentially *American* movies – *Some Like it Hot* and *The Magnificent Seven* – were essentially remakes. The former was

---

[2] John Huston, quoted in Steinhart, 2019: 60.

adapted from *Fanfare d'amour* (Pottier, 1935) and *Fanfaren der Liebe* (Hoffman, 1951), respectively French and German comedies, while *The Magnificent Seven* was based on Akira Kurosawa's *The Seven Samurai* (1954).

Non-American IP

Border jumping was thus, perhaps prematurely, always among the company's business strategies. Let us begin by identifying those Mirisch films based on what we might call *non-American* IP. Besides *The Magnificent Seven* and *Some Like It Hot*, Mirisch acquired and adapted non-English language plays – *One, Two, Three* was based on Ferenc Molnar's *Egy, kettő, három*; *Irma La Douce* was based on the 1956 French stage musical *Irma La Douce* by Marguerite Monnot and Alexandre Breffort (the film dropped the songs), *Kiss Me, Stupid* was based on the play *L'ora della fantasia* (*The Dazzling Hour*) by Anna Bonacci, which had already inspired the Italian film, *Wife for a Night*, aka *Moglie per una notte* (Camerini, 1952), starring Gina Lollobrigida, while *A Shot in the Dark* was adapted from a play by Harry Kurnitz, itself based on Marcel Achard's *L'idiote*. The company also adapted foreign language fiction – thus *Town Without Pity* was based on the novel *Das Urteil* (*The Verdict*) by Manfred Gregor and *Return from the Ashes* was adapted from *Le Retourne des cendres* by Hubert Montheilhet. This is without even mentioning the many British books and literary heroes and anti-heroes which the company adapted, from Conan Doyle characters (*The Private Life of Sherlock Holmes*) to Count Dracula (*Dracula*), from the aerial heroics of *633 Squadron* (based on a British novel) and *The Thousand Plane Raid* to the mass POW break-out of *The Great Escape* (the latter pair both based on non-fiction).

One, Two, Three had an American and German cast and starred James Cagney (as an American Coca Cola executive based in Berlin) and Horst Bucholtz (as an East German communist). It was shot in Berlin and was a co-production between The Mirisch Company and Bavaria Film. Co-writer and producer/director, Billy Wilder, had been born in Galicia, like the Mirisches' father. (Wilder's co-writer, as with all his Mirisch films, was the Hungarian I. A. L. Diamond.) The story is equally transnational. *Irma La Douce* had an all-American cast, but its exterior establishing shots, particularly those seen over the opening voice-over, were filmed in Paris, while the rest of the film was shot at the Samuel Goldwyn Studio, adjacent to the Mirisch production offices.

A Shot in the Dark was filmed in England and France. The cast was largely British, with French and German support. The story takes place in Paris. It was produced by Mirisch's British subsidiary, Mirisch Films and received Eady Levy funds. *Town Without Pity* is set in Germany and was written and directed by Germans (though its star, Kirk Douglas, insisted Dalton Trumbo was hired to do rewrites), and featured an American and German cast (playing occupying Americans and German citizens). It was shot in Germany, but the studio sequences were filmed in Austria and the key lakeside scene, in France. It was a Mirisch Company production in association with the German company Gloria-Film GmbH. *Return from the Ashes* was set in France, shot in the UK, directed by an Englishman, written by an American and starred a Swede, an Austrian and an Englishwoman as three civilians in post-war Paris. It was produced by the Mirisch Corporation in association with Thompson's British-based Orchard Films. It too was a recipient of Eady funds, evidence of the decline of Hollywood as a geographical centre of production, despite its continuing role in finance and distribution. The employment of transnational talent – both behind and in front of the camera – eased the global circulation of such films, most visibly with European stars like Horst Bucholtz, Max von Sydow, Alain Delon, Peter Sellers, Elke Sommer, Julie Andrews, Ingrid Thulin and Maximilian Schell.

Border jumping

The very first book the company bought seems to have been *The Border Jumpers* (adapted as *Man of the West*) and the title is an appropriate one, for border jumping was to become a characteristic Mirisch strategy. In that novel, the border in question in the novel (though not reprised in the film) is the one between the United States and Mexico, and it was to reappear in many subsequent Mirisch films including *The Magnificent Seven* and its three sequels, as well as *Cannons for Cordoba*. Meanwhile *The First Time* features an illegal crossing between the United States and Canada over the Peace Bridge (where Mike tells his two friends 'Look I'm standing in two countries at once'), and *The Great Escape* depicts prisoners escaping Germany (Danny and Willie steal a boat and row to a port, where they board a Swedish merchant ship; Sedgwick steals a bicycle, then hides on a train to France, where French Resistance fighters help him reach Spain), *Cast a Giant Shadow* dramatizes the battle for Israel, and *Fiddler on the Roof* shows the struggle of the Jews in Russia; Both *Hawaii* and *The Hawaiians* concern colonialism, while other productions feature globalization – including *One, Two, Three* and *Avanti* (Figure 11).

Mirisch deployed transnational business strategies including adapting 'foreign' films, books and plays which are reflected in the locations, funding, casts, crews and marketing of the company's films' stories and styles. Indeed, if Mirisch films were often transnational productions, they were also transnational products. Such films travelled light and spoke in an international visual language, where dialogue – and thus dubbing or subtitles – was often kept to a minimum. Whether they were Westerns like *The Magnificent Seven* or slapstick comedies like *The Pink Panther*, the transnational Mirisch signature style was either landscape, action and laconic dialogue in the former or physical comedy and visual gags in the latter. This reduction of the classical reliance on plot, characterization and dialogue, notably in Blake Edwards' comedies, found its peak – or nadir – in *The Party*, whose sixty-eight-page screenplay was extended to feature-length largely through improvisation by its star, Peter Sellers and indulgence by its director.

Similarly, the Mirisch-Rich TV series, *Rat Patrol*, minimized dialogue and emphasized action sequences and stunts. As its star, Christopher George put it, '. . . ours is an action series, and so we try to keep the dialog at a minimum, unless

Figure 11 *Avanti* poster.

it pertains to the action. In combat, you don't take that much time to sit around and philosophize about everything'[3] Producer Stan Shpetner described the series as 'bigger than life missions or capers . . . The key to the series is – they are in constant jeopardy from start to finish. . . . There is a cinematic excitement about what you see happening on the screen. . . . These are not stories of deep, personal, psychological conflicts'.[4] Such 'cinematic' aspirations help to explain the decision to produce a three-parter and subsequently release a compilation of these three episodes as a movie, *Massacre Harbor*, in foreign markets.

---

[3] Quoted in *Daily Variety*, 29.3.67: 13.
[4] *Daily Variety*, 29.6.66: 8.

According to the *New York Times*, Harold Mirisch claimed, 'If you take all our films' he said, 'you will find that at least 55 per cent of our take, maybe 60 per cent has come from American audiences.' According to Mirisch, *The Apartment* cost $2,800,000. Of the $10,000,000 it grossed, almost $5,500.000 was from the US. *Some Like it Hot* took in $13,000,000 on an investment of $2,800,000. More than $7,600,000 was from the American market. However, he admitted, 'Westerns . . . are a notable exception. In this field, the European market very often outgrosses the domestic market.' The Magnificent Seven, which had all the earmarks of a flop when distributed in the United States, has done very well abroad. The domestic gross of 2,400,000 was more than doubled abroad.[5]

Nevertheless, much of Mirisch's reputation was initially built on its early deployment of naturalistic settings in American locations – from *Some Like It Hot* to *The Apartment* (though both were also partly shot in the studio), from *West Side Story* to *Two for the Seesaw* and later *In the Heat of the Night* and *The Landlord*. That naturalism was later replaced by a cost-cutting minimalism in settings on films like *The First Time* and *Halls of Anger* and an over-the-top, anti-realism in *The Party* or *Gaily Gaily*. Crudely, Mirisch's most 'literate' or 'serious' productions often worked better at home; its most popular, more visual ones – comedies and action movies, often fared better abroad. However, the international market remained crucial, even for those films which did better domestically. As *Motion Picture Daily* reported, 'Billy Wilder, Jack Lemmon, I. A. L. Diamond and Harold Mirisch went on a nine-city European publicity tour for Some Like it Hot stopping off in London, Paris, Vienna, Rome, Zurich, Munich, Berlin, Copenhagen and Brussels starting in London May 4th, 1959.'[6]

A studio without walls

Part of the explanation for this appetite for border jumping was conjunctural. Politically, the Paramount Decision and the post-war reopening of the global market, combined with the wartime development of lightweight location equipment, meant that by the late 1950s Hollywood was no longer the default production hub. This only compounded the impact of the 1944 De Havilland decision, which had reshaped contracts for casts and crews. In 1957, the year the three Mirisch brothers founded the Mirisch Company, Industry analyst Dorothy Jones published a report entitled 'Hollywood's International Relations', which recalled, 'There used to be a saying in Hollywood that any place or anything under the sun could be recreated on the back lot. Producers had reasoned: Why go to tremendous expense and become embroiled in the many difficulties inherent in taking a production unit abroad if it can be shot just

---

[5] 'Hollywood Birthday Mirisch Company', *New York Times*, 30.9.62: X7.
[6] 'Wilder, Lemmon Will Tour Europe For "Hot"', *Motion Picture Daily*, 1.5.59: 3.

as well or better on the back lot?' But, Jones noted, this era was now over.[7] The back lot was slowly becoming history, just another stop on the studio tour.

Also in 1957, the Hollywood Film Council of the American Federation of Labor (AFL) published labour historian Irving Bernstein's *Hollywood at the Crossroads*, an investigation of what Bernstein called 'American-interest films produced abroad'. Using data from *Hollywood Reporter*, Bernstein reported that 314 features had been filmed abroad between 1949 and 1957 which constituted 5 per cent of Hollywood's output in 1949 and 15 per cent in 1956.[8] The term 'runaway production' had been coined by the IATSE and AFL unions in 1949 in condemnation of the loss of American jobs resulting from filming abroad.[9]

In 1960 Walter Mirisch himself, as editor of the *Journal of the Producers Guild*, devoted a special issue to runaway production, to which Harold Mirisch contributed an article on the subject.[10] The Mirisch Company even commissioned its own report on the pros and cons of filming overseas – though whether the conclusion – that filming in America often worked out better, both financially and aesthetically – was simply for the press and the unions, remains uncertain.[11] What is certain is that the company continued making many of its films abroad. That same year, announcing fourteen films to be made over the following eighteen months, at a cost of $45,000,000, Harold Mirisch confirmed that eleven of them would be made in Hollywood. He explained to the *New York Times*:

> It takes so much longer to make pictures abroad that by the time you have finished you would have been better off to make them in Hollywood . . . There are a few stars who are abroad for tax gimmicks. I don't think we need use names, but they are only a few. With very few exceptions I think the top stars are mainly concerned with making good movies and having good directors. The only time I can see making movies on foreign locations is when there are strong artistic reasons for a foreign locale. . . . When we made Moby Dick abroad we got a subsidy. We would have been wiser to make it right here in Hollywood. The subsidy we got did not begin to make up for what we lost in shooting time. . . . We have technicians and craftsmen here who are the best in the world. You pay them more, that is true. But they give you quality. If the producer and director know their business they save in time much more than you can save yourself by cheap foreign wages. . . . So far as the Mirisch Company is concerned we are not running away from Hollywood. This is where the pictures are put together, from talent agents to film editors. This is the center of the movie world and this is where we will make movies.[12]

---

[7] 'Hollywood's International Relations', *Quarterly Review of Film Radio and Television* vol 11 no 4, Summer 1957: 370.
[8] Irving Bernstein, *Hollywood at the Crossroads*, AFL, 1957, 48–50.
[9] 'IA Backs AFL Film Council on "Runaway Foreign Production"', *Hollywood Reporter*, 18.2.49: 4.
[10] Harold Mirisch, 'Why Runaway?', *Journal of the Producers Guild* vol 6 no 7, December 1960: 13–14, 30.
[11] 'Hollywood Sees a Rise in Filming', *New York Times*, 8.10.62: 18.
[12] 'Hollywood Paean Producer Praises the West Coast as Best Place to Make Films', *New York Times*, 21.8.60: X7.

Independent production companies, without studio facilities of their own to work in, were, by 1957, producing 40 per cent of Hollywood features and increasingly preferred shooting on location to the – often exorbitant – rental rates charged by Hollywood studios.¹³ According to *Variety*, however, by the end of the 1950s the economic advantages of shooting abroad had reduced and the early 1960s saw a return to domestic locations and filmmakers, like William Wyler, returning from shooting epics abroad were happier making domestic films, like *The Children's Hour*.¹⁴

Why runaway?

The determinants of this wider development – and Mirisch's pioneering of it in particular – are both political and economic. Gleich notes that 'United Artists was the least likely major company to shoot in Hollywood' without explaining that it was also the only major without a studio to shoot in and that it funded independents to make its productions.¹⁵ Furthermore, those independent production companies, exemplified by the Mirisch Company, whose films it financed and distributed, were also without studios of their own, so the decision of where best to shoot was never impacted by any consideration of amortizing overheads. Like any successful independent, with neither a studio nor theatre chain of its own, the Mirisch Company's strategies for survival included both off-shoring and off-shelfing. By off-shoring I am referring to runaway productions, using cheaper foreign facilities, casts and crews, and foregrounding lavish locations in Technicolour and VistaVision or Cinemascope – while exploiting tax incentives, thawing frozen foreign revenues and tapping local subsidies. And by off-shelfing I mean shaving development costs, writing off marketing expenses as pre-production costs on book, story and play rights, while increasing the bankability of any film – and the familiarity of its story – in at least one foreign market – its literal and literary location. Indeed, such productions outsourced labour, locations and literary pretexts (whether plays or prose, fiction or non-fiction). And foreign rights or locations could lead to subsidy. 'While blocked earnings were responsible for the first wave of runaway production, the availability of subsidization was the cause of its perpetuation and development into a second wave.'¹⁶

Another part of the explanation for border jumping is ideological. First there is the drive for so-called authenticity – filming in the actual locations where the story was set. This coincided with the avowed social realism of style and subject matter exemplified by those black and white essays in Hollywood art cinema – *The Apartment, Town Without Pity, Two for the Seesaw* and even the opening sequence of the otherwise

---

[13] Joshua Gleich, 'Postwar Hollywood, 1947–1967, Part One: Domestic Location Shooting', in Gleich and Webb (eds), 83.
[14] 'Home Is Where You Shoot: But O'Seas No Longer Cheap', *Variety*, 15.6.60: 3, 16.
[15] Gleich, 'Postwar Hollywood, 1947–1967', in Gleich and Webb (eds), 91.
[16] Thomas Guback (ed), *The International Film Industry: Western Europe and America Since 1945*, Indiana University Press, 1969, 166.

melodramatic *Return from the Ashes*. According to Gleich, 'Authenticity and spectacle were real enough attractions for audiences, but they also operated as a figleaf for the economic priorities of the studios'.[17]

Hollywood on Location notes that the semi-documentary genre had all but disappeared by 1948 'ending Hollywood's post-war experiment in extensive location shooting', adding that it was films such as *Bonnie and Clyde* and *The Graduate* which 'heralded New Hollywood's rapid shift to shooting largely on location by the early 1970s'.[18] But of course this is to ignore the number of location-shot films made in the 1950s and 1960s. Instead, the book details the ways in which first unit crews shot exteriors abroad but returned to US studios for the bulk of filming.[19] But since Gleich cites Siegel's *The Line Up* (1958) as an example, it is worth mentioning that the same director's *Riot in Cell Block 11* and *Invasion of the Body Sna*tchers, as well as Phil Karlson's *Phenix City Story*, were also all partly shot on location – and all at Allied Artists, under the supervision of then production head, Walter Mirisch.[20] It is also striking that of the five filmmakers who directed location-shot documentaries as part of the war effort (Capra, Ford, Huston, Stevens and Wyler), three subsequently deployed their credentials for authenticity working for Mirisch.

Second, there is the issue of soft power, which Godard famously called cocacolonization (particularly appropriate given the setting of *One, Two, Three*, in the Berlin HQ of that very company). As Walter Mirisch himself put it in 1960,

> 'American films must continue to fill the screens of the world. The moving picture is the greatest instrument for influencing the minds of men [*sic*] that has ever been devised. We do not wish to impose our way of life on any other people, but we do wish to spread the view of the American way of life, not as a message, but as the normal, honest background for our entertainment and storytelling.'[21]

Mirisch's liberalism led the company to produce politically liberal films like *In the Heat of the Night* and *The Landlord*, but that on-screen liberalism was balanced with a neo liberal business model off-screen.

In the same issue of the *Journal*, Harold Mirisch argued that 'I do not believe there is any value in filming abroad merely for the sake of filming abroad . . . As a rule of thumb, it can be stated that if the story is about Hong Kong, Israel or Paris, it must be made overseas. Or at least those parts of the film dealing directly with the locale must be done away from Hollywood.'[22] The article provides a calculus for the pros and cons of runaway filmmaking. Harold uses his own past production experience outside the United States as his examples.

---

[17] Gleich and Webb, 'Introduction', in Gleich and Webb (eds), 12.
[18] Joshua Gleich, in Gleich and Webb (eds), 73.
[19] Ibid, 74.
[20] Ibid, 82.
[21] Mirisch, 'Make Way for Tomorrow', 1960: 24.
[22] Mirisch, 'Why Runaway?' 1960: 13–14.

Perhaps labor was cheaper. But shooting schedules were longer. The two quickly averaged out, and in the bargain we forfeited the unparalleled services of Hollywood's technicians. Perhaps lumber was cheaper, but Hollywood carpenters might be faster. Perhaps actors would work for less, but you had to reach out over all Europe to 'import' them to wherever you were shooting and pay living expenses while they were working.

He concludes that 'There are pictures, however, which should be made overseas. The standard by which these pictures can be identified is simply this: If it is not made overseas, is it therefore impossible to make this picture?'[23]

Thus, *Irma La Douce* included only some background footage shot in Paris, with the rest of shooting on a studio set in Hollywood. 'We're reversing runaway by bringing Paris to Hollywood,' as Harold Mirisch put it in 1962. Or as the *NYT* reported, 'One reason that Hollywood is once more finding favor with producers is that costs are rising abroad. Technicians there are no longer willing to work for the small wages they accepted originally. Harold Mirisch: "Now as soon as they find out you are an American, they clobber you."'[24] However, as director John Huston recalled, 'If I have a trademark at all, it's that I prefer to make my movies where they happen.' In the 1963 edition of the *Journal of the Screen Producers Guild*, edited by Walter Mirisch, Huston wrote, 'Story needs and not economics should dictate where a picture should be filmed. I have never saved money by shooting on location. The cost is just as much in the long run. You take people to another country, support them, incur travel expenses and consume time.'[25]

The politics of runaway production

Among the many motivations for this exodus was the attempt to free frozen or blocked revenues abroad that could not be extracted but could still be spent there on a specific production or on film infrastructure or even on acquiring foreign story properties or film rights. Most significant of these was the investment of such funds in the production of Hollywood movies filmed abroad.[26] There were significant incentives to such productions too – from national subsidies like Eady, to cheaper below-the-line cast and crew costs. Meanwhile, protectionist opposition to international productions often overlapped with anti-communism, with accusations that there was something un-American about filming abroad in the first place, or more specifically that films shot elsewhere often involved hiring HUAC blacklistees and working with allegedly

---

[23] Ibid.
[24] *New York Times*, 8.10.62: 18.
[25] John Huston, 'Home Is Where the Heart Is – and So Are Films', *Journal of the Screen Producers Guild* vol 10 no 3, March 1963: 4.
[26] Daniel Steinhart, 'Postwar Hollywood, 1947–1967, Part Two: Foreign Location Shooting', in Gleich and Webb (eds), 103.

communist unions.²⁷ The premiere of *Moulin Rouge* had been picketed by the American Legion as both Huston and star, Jose Ferrer, were seen as un-American, left-wing or communist sympathizers. Eventually, Ferrer, Huston and Moulin Productions were pressured to be joint signatories of a letter expressing their willingness 'to eliminate Communist influence throughout America'.²⁸

In Britain, Mirisch's subsidiaries, Mirisch Films and Oakmont Productions, both became beneficiaries of Eady funding. In Spain, Franco's Ministry of Information and Tourism, despite its suspicion that visiting Hollywood companies were 'penetrated by Judaism and communism' prioritized United Artists as the number one American film operation there and, of course, the Mirisch Company had an exclusive contract with UA. In 1963 the Franco regime added a new incentive to entice foreign film companies to the country, establishing free licensing arrangements for films whose budgets exceeded $1.65 million.²⁹ By 1968 the city of Almeria was proclaiming itself 'the Movie Capital of the World' and subsequently *Guns of the Magnificent Seven* and *The Spikes Gang* were both shot there.³⁰ In Germany, *One, Two, Three*, *Town Without Pity* and *The Great Escape* all seem to have received aid of one kind or another.³¹

Rat Patrol

Perhaps the most revealing example of this process and of the problems associated with it is *Rat Patrol*. *Rat Patrol* (ABC 1966–8), a TV series, co-produced by Mirisch-Rich Productions, Tom Gries Productions and United Artists Television, exemplified transnational television. It had an international setting and storyline (a Second World War allied commando unit, operating behind enemy lines in North Africa); it was an international production, shot in Almeria, Spain, causing union disputes back in Hollywood about its status as a 'runaway' production, but was post-produced in the United States; it starred an international cast (three American and one British lead, plus international as well as American guest stars and support) and crew (American, Spanish and British). It was screened on TV in the US, UK, Spain and Latin America (*Comando en el desierto*), France (*Les rats du desert*), Italy (*Pattuglia del deserto*) and even the Soviet Union (*Крысиный патруль*). It was not only a hit at home (number one in the Nielsen ratings among shows launched in 1966), but also travelled well – being controversially scheduled in primetime by the BBC in the UK, before being equally controversially dropped. It had a transnational historical setting – the Second World War (rendering it immune from association with the contentious, contemporary, war

---

²⁷ Ibid, 103–4.
²⁸ quoted in Steinhart, 2019: 65.
²⁹ Neal Moses Rosendorf, 'Hollywood in Madrid': American Film Producers and the Franco Regime 1950–1970', *Historical Journal of Film, Radio and Television* vol 27, no 1, 2007: 81, 88.
³⁰ 'Almeria – Movie Capital of the World, Says Here', *Hollywood Reporter*, 15.2.68.
³¹ 'Escape' From Tax Rap, John Sturges' 'The Great Escape' has been classified 'Wertvoll' (valuable) by board of valuation in West Germany. Rating gives the Mirisch-UA release a special tax consideration in all West German theatres', *Daily Variety*, 10.10.63: 4.

in Vietnam) – yet sat comfortably within the action-adventure generic formulas of sixties series television. And, as a series set during Second World War, it was inherently accessible around the world.

The reasons for the decision to shoot *The Rat Patrol* abroad include: budget – 'Estimates vary – ranging between 50% to 60% below Stateside costs', setting and location – 'the proximity of desert, Moorish-type villages, unlimited arid topography and scenic landscapes – sea, mountains, subtropical vegetation – all within a half-hour of the filming unit's base', and climate – '958 hours of summer sunshine, 790 hours of spring sunlight, 665 sunny hours in autumn and 525 hours of location winter shooting'.[32] The series can be characterized not only as transnational TV drama but also as an early example of transmedia storytelling and media convergence, as it was seen both on the small screen and in cinemas, when three consecutive thirty-minute episodes (*The Last Harbor Raid*, ABC-TV: 19 December 1967, 26 December 1967 and 2 January 1968) were re-edited as a ninety-minute feature, for international release, as *Massacre Harbor*, screened in countries including Japan, Denmark and Sweden, but not the United States.

Runback

Why, then, was such transnationalism short-lived? Steinhart concludes that 'Starting in the mid-1960s, the takeover of studios by conglomerates like Gulf + Western, Transamerica and Kinney led to cost-cutting measures that included a reduction in costly foreign location shoots.'[33] Gleich and Webb offer another explanation: 'Independent companies such as BBS, American Zoetrope, and Lions Gate were at the forefront' of using small often non-union location crews while older, more established indies abided by traditional union customs and practices.[34] This industrial context found its textual form in the American road movie, characteristic of so many 1960s and 1970s indie films, but not those of the Mirisch Company.[35] *The Spikes Gang*, for instance, has the pessimistic storyline (all three young leads die violent deaths, echoing *Easy Rider*) and the picaresque structure of many road movies, but it is a Western, with neither the characters, performances, dialogue, visual style nor contemporary resonance to qualify it as canonical.

Rat Patrol returned to Californian locations for its second series (following intense union controversy about its erosion of US-based jobs) and the fourth of *The Magnificent Seven* series was also the first to be made entirely in the United States. This latter decision 'becomes significant when it's recalled that the first in the series was filmed in Mexico, and the next two were made in Spain'. According to *Variety*,

---

[32] *Variety*, 19.10.66: 43.
[33] Steinhart in Gleich and Webb, 119.
[34] Gleich and Webb, 132.
[35] Lawrence Webb, 'The Auteur Renaissance, 1968–1979', in Gleich and Webb, 140.

Walter Mirisch took some pains to pooh-pooh the idea that his film represents a 'runback' trend, and he stressed that a principal consideration in the decision to shoot in the U.S. was the availability of a setting, which would have had to be constructed overseas. Nonetheless, Mirisch disclosed that the film's budget of 'around $1,000,000' is less than that for any of the three previous pix, and that a principal reason for this will be the brief thirty-day schedule, something he thinks can be accomplished because 'American crews are accustomed to shooting more quickly.' Although he admitted that the shorter shooting schedule represents a certain 'willingness to compromise' on quality, Mirisch also noted that domestic production provides an opportunity for tighter control over both quality and budget, and that overseas shooting offers a choice between settling for a less-than-adequate supporting cast or 'sending a great many people abroad at considerable expense'. . . . (Mirisch) stressed the needs of his individual production – fewer horses and riders this time, the goal of a summer release date. But all in all, some might conclude that the US unions may have had a point all along, and that high costs in the past were more related to producers' decisions than to domestic crew sizes or wage scales. If the producers and production companies agree – as Mirisch and UA seem to have done, at least in part, – it could be that the 'Magnificent Seven' are the vanguard of a ride into 'runback' era.[36]

But if *Ride* retreated to the United States, a majority of the company's final productions for UA were filmed abroad – *Cannon for Cordoba* (Mexico and Spain), *The Private Life of Sherlock Holmes* (UK), *Fiddler on the Roof* (Croatia and UK), *Avanti!* (Italy), *Scorpio* (Austria, UK, US, France) and *The Spikes Gang* (Spain). The transnational strategy was never entirely abandoned, but nor was it ever navigated as successfully in Mirisch's post-UA years.

---

[36] 'Seven Ride' Shoots in California Previous Three in Mexico and Spain—Comments of Walter Mirisch', *Variety*, 23.2.72: 3.

9

The children's hour – Why the Mirisch brothers never worked with the movie brats

The French New Wave and the American New Wave

The most popular book on the movie brats, Peter Biskind's *Easy Riders, Raging Bulls*, provides a sketch of the Mirisch Company in the late 1960s. Biskind's source was Hal Ashby's subsequent associate, Charles Mulvehill.

> By the time Ashby was editing Jewison's *The Russians Are Coming! The Russians Are Coming!* at the Mirisch Company for UA on the old Goldwyn lot, Mulvehill, who was only a kid, was head of production. Harold Mirisch was considered the only one of the Mirisch brothers with any brains. When he died suddenly, the bottom dropped out of the company. 'There was nothin' going on,' says Mulvehill. 'I was the head of nothin' going on.'[1]

There are several problems with this account. Charles Mulvehill was not head of production, indeed he never occupied any senior position at the Mirisch Company. He was credited as the production associate on *How to Succeed in Business Without Really Trying* in 1967, and as the location manager on *Some Kind of a Nut* in 1969 and *The Hawaiians* in 1970. Harold Mirisch died in December 1968. In 1966 the Mirisch Company had several films in progress, including post-production on *Cast a Giant Shadow*, *The Russians Are Coming, The Russians Are Coming*, *Hawaii*, *The Fortune Cookie* and *What Did You Do in the War, Daddy?* (the latter pair only wrapped in January 1966) and shooting on *The Return of the Seven*, *How to Succeed in Business Without Really Trying*, *In the Heat of the Night*, *Hour of the Gun* and *Fitzwilly*. There was clearly a great deal going on at Mirisch, indeed Mulvehill even worked on one of the films. And since eight Mirisch productions were released in 1969 and nine in 1970, it seems odd, to say the least, to accuse the company of idleness. Harold's sudden death from a heart attack in December 1968 could hardly have impacted on the productivity of Mirisch quite so catastrophically. He had, furthermore, been increasingly absent from the company since his first heart attack in 1961. I will leave the question of the surviving brothers' 'brains' to the reader.

[1] Peter Biskind, *Easy Riders, Raging Bulls: How the Sex 'n' Drugs 'n' Rock 'n' Roll Generation Saved Hollywood,* Bloomsbury, 1998, 172.

It is often suggested that the so-called American New Wave or Hollywood Renaissance was inaugurated by the 1967 release of *Bonnie and Clyde* and *The Graduate*. Much is made of the fact that the screenplay of *Bonnie and Clyde* was first offered to Truffaut and Godard, this New Wave association somehow evidence of the film's status as an exemplar of an American cinematic modernism. Curiously, few recall that Godard had dedicated *A Bout de Souffle* to Monogram (whose head of production, from 1951 to 1957, was one Walter Mirisch, and whose vice president was then Harold Mirisch) and that, in 1960, the year of the latter film's release, Godard wrote a paean to Anthony Mann's *Man of the West* – the very first film the Mirisch Company produced.[2]

Besides *The Graduate* and *Bonnie and Clyde*, there was, however, an equally significant film released in 1967. A film which, like both *Bonnie and Clyde* and *The Graduate*, was nominated for Best Picture. That film was *In the Heat of the Night* – but, while its director, Norman Jewison, was never high in the auteur canon, nor a movie brat, it was 'his' film which won the Best Picture Oscar for 1967. Indeed, while *The Graduate* and *Bonnie and Clyde* continue to be celebrated as auteur triumphs, pioneers of the Renaissance, *In the Heat of the Night* can claim to have been a trailblazer too. *Bonnie and Clyde* and *The Graduate* were white films, barely connected to the Civil Rights movement beyond a reflex of youthful rebelliousness, safely defused within the distant rural past and white middle-class suburban present respectively. They might embody middle-class twentysomething angst and chicly romanticized period banditry, but they had little to do with that year's racial tensions. Neither could have contained lines like, 'There's white time in jail and there's coloured time. The worst time you can do is coloured time'. Let alone the iconic moment when Sidney Poitier slaps a white man.

The slap which Sidney Poitier's Lt Tibbs gave the white planter, Endicott, proved far more radical, indeed explosive, than any scene in its Oscar competitors. Of course, the extent to which white liberal tolerance of Poitier as the acceptable face of African Americans explains the actor's appeal, as the exception that proves the racist rule, remains controversial. Quinn, in her excellent study, *A Piece of the Action: Race and Labor in Post-Civil Rights Hollywood*, argues that 'Poitier was an isolated black creative in overwhelmingly white production contexts and these racial employment relations were mirrored by his predicament on-screen as an isolated black professional in a white world'.[3] Poitier himself was at pains to depict the constraints in which he was forced to operate. 'The guys who write these parts are white guys, more than not, they are guys in a business and they are subject to the values of the society they live in. And there are producers to deal with who are also white. And a studio with a board of directors, also white'.[4] The only way around this for Poitier was to become a filmmaker himself, and he duly became 'the most commercially successful black film director and producer'[5] not least because while working on *They Call Me Mister Tibbs*, the director,

---

[2] Godard, 1959. Reprinted in *Godard on Godard*, New York: Viking Press, 1972, 117.
[3] Eithne Quinn, *A Piece of the Action: Race and Labor in Post-Civil Rights Hollywood*, Columbia University Press, 2020, 26.
[4] Poitier, quoted in ibid, 55.
[5] Quinn, 2020: 133.

Gordon Douglas, 'turned over the directorial reins to Poitier' because the star 'plans in the future to produce and direct films himself'.[6] It is unlikely that such a delegation of responsibility would have been allowed, let alone reported on, without the knowledge and probable encouragement of Poitier's close friend, Walter Mirisch.

The Slap

Quinn suggests, 'Tibbs stands as a misleading departure from actual black experiences of employment in the North and in Hollywood. But he is representative of Sidney Poitier – occupying the exciting yet burdensome and precarious role of being the singular, immaculate black film star in a white world' (Figure 12).[7] She asserts that 'there was no sense on the part of producer Walter Mirisch or director Norman Jewison that they had a responsibility to employ any blacks for the film production . . . Walter Mirisch was not a creative producer, nor was he pursuing a liberal-reformist project . . . With no particular connection to problem pictures or to race as a theme beyond seeing its marketability as the 1960s progressed.'[8] This is a strong statement, but the evidence of anti-racism in pre-*Heat* Mirisch films including *Fort Massacre*, *The Magnificent Seven*, *West Side Story*, *The Fortune Cookie* and *Hawaii* – not to mention post-*Heat* productions including *Halls of Anger*, *The Landlord*, *Fiddler on the Roof* and *Mr Majestyk* – undermines such sweeping generalizations. (Other 'problem pictures'

Figure 12 The slap, from *In the Heat of the Night*.

---

[6] *Variety*, 4.7.70.
[7] Quinn, 2020: 52.
[8] Ibid, 42.

the company produced tackled issues as diverse as lesbianism, adultery, rape, divorce, conformism, capitalism and colonialism.)

Quinn's critique of Tibbs' – and Poitier's – exceptionalism is ambivalent. As she puts it, 'The implausibility of Tibbs being the "number one homicide detective" in Philadelphia of the mid-1960s is tempered by the extraordinary fact of Poitier as number-one bankable star on Quigley's list. Poitier in 1968 was also, even more exceptionally, the highest paid actor in the world.'[9] But such exceptionalism was not simply the consequence of racially invidious hiring decisions, neither by the director or producer or their staff nor indeed of the employment policy of the production company itself. The Hollywood unions in this period operated a system in and by which all existing members must be employed or offered a job *before* any new recruit could be employed. This closed shop ensured that union membership remained disproportionately white and male, while the unions themselves continued to be sexist and racist.[10]

Nevertheless, Quinn condemns the production – and by implication the production company – by stating that '*In the Heat of the Night* employed no black workers behind the scenes. Black musicians were brought in for the soundtrack – Quincy Jones wrote the universally lauded score and Jones got his friend Ray Charles to sing the famous title song'. Such criticism is particularly pertinent because 'workplace integration' was a major theme in the film' which underlines the fact that 'there was no equivalent impetus behind the scenes from the production company'.[11] However, this was by no means a matter which one production company could solve single-handedly or without risking the ire of the unions. The film could not have been exhibited in union theatres if it had employed non-union labour, and Quinn fails to acknowledge the extent to which the company did indeed strive to employ proportionate numbers of Blacks on- and off-screen in subsequent Tibbs features as well as *The Landlord* and *Halls of Anger*. Furthermore, while Norman Jewison claims that he brought the novel to Mirisch, this is untrue. Poitier's agent, Marty Baum, brought the novel to Walter Mirisch who in turn offered it to Jewison to direct.

The scene in which Tibbs first meets Rod Steiger's Gillespie reveals that the former earns more than the latter as a policeman, and 'suggests that workplaces in an enlightened North, such as Philadelphia's police department, were already well-integrated by 1967, with Blacks getting hired, promoted, and well-remunerated without facing individual and institutional discrimination'.[12] This ideological fiction within the fiction perhaps helps explain the conspicuous absence of race as an issue in *Heat*'s two subsequent Northern-set sequels. Quinn persuasively demonstrates that the Northerners, Tibbs himself and the Colberts (the murder victim and his widow, played by Lee Grant) are depicted as bringing enlightenment to a backward southern town,

---

[9] Ibid, 54.
[10] Ibid, 29. See also Derek Nystrom's *Hard Hats, Rednecks and Macho Men: Class in 1970s American Cinema*, Oxford University Press, 2009.
[11] Quinn, 2020: 41, 42.
[12] Ibid, 36.

with the implication that both Tibbs and the Colberts' already integrated northern factories had prospered without intervention or reform, so liberal laissez-faireism was the film's implicit message. If this is the case it is a failure which Mirisch's subsequent sequel, *They Call Me Mister Tibbs*, did much to rectify with its explicitly integrated casting just as, later, *The Landlord* did the same both on- and off-screen.[13]

For all its admittedly liberal compromises, *Heat* could not even be screened in much of the south. It has also been criticized, perhaps most famously by Richard Dyer in his book, *White*, for lighting which makes the white face the norm.[14] However, as Quinn points out, criticism of the male bonding scene in Gillespie's house, which has often been accused of privileging the white cop's facial features,

> fails to account for Wexler's innovative techniques in lighting Poitier . . . in other key sequences. In the pivotal police station scenes, the light is bounced off the ceiling and down onto the set in the manner of still photography, illuminating the actor's face and in the iconic Endicott greenhouse scene an umbrella light sends rounded rays of light that enhance Tibbs' expression as he slaps back. In both scenes, the dark-skinned Poitier's facial modulations are on display, using innovative techniques that later became standard.[15]

The Landlord

Mirisch's most innovative production in regard to both race and representation *and* aesthetics, however, is the all-but-forgotten *The Landlord*, in which Professor Duboise unforgettably remarks, 'You whiteys scream about miscegenation and you done watered down every race you ever hated'. *The Landlord* came out only a year after the first-ever Hollywood feature directed (and written) by a Black filmmaker – Gordon Parks's *The Learning Tree* (1969) – and just three years before the first Oscar-nominated Black screenwriters for *Sounder*, (Ritt, 1972), and *Lady Sings the Blues*, (Furie, 1972). Perhaps more significantly still, Hollywood movies about Black America, which immediately followed the assassination of Martin Luther King, including both *The Landlord* and *Halls of Anger* 'strained to make sense of a social climate characterized by heightened interracial mistrust. These studio pictures depicted race relations with a pessimism uncommon in Hollywood cinema and a fatalism about the prospects for true racial understanding'.[16] According to Sieving's seminal study, *Soul Searching: Black Themed Cinema from the March on Washington to the Rise of Blaxploitation*, *The Landlord* was both typical and outstanding. Typical because it showed race relations as perhaps irreparably damaged and outstanding because it was 'the product of a nearly

---

[13] *Variety*, 4.7.70.
[14] Richard Dyer, *White: Essays on Race and Culture,* London: Routledge, 1997.
[15] Quinn, 2020: 45–6.
[16] Christopher Sieving, *Soul Searching: Black Themed Cinema from the March on Washington to the Rise of Blaxploitation*, Wesleyan University Press, 2011, 112.

unprecedented close collaboration between leading film talent of both races'.[17] Like Quinn, however, Sieving is apt to credit UA rather than (or as well as) the Mirisch Company with any corporate kudos. Thus, he notes that 'UA's profile in 1970 as Hollywood's most racially diverse major studio, with regard to both production content and hiring record, earned the studio a featured spot in a special issue of the *Chicago Defender* on US businesses making noteworthy advances in race relations'.[18] In fact, of course, UA was not a studio as such, though it was a major distributor and financier. Thus, when Sieving is applauding UA for 'Amazingly' distributing *Halls of Anger*, *In the Heat of the Night* and *The Landlord*, he should also be crediting the Mirisch Company for producing them all. Indeed, it was Mirisch, not UA, which deserved recognition both for its 'production content' and its 'hiring record', such as it was. (UA hired no non-whites in key creative roles in the period.)

The Landlord was adapted by Black screenwriter, Bill Gunn, from a novel by Black writer, Kristin Davis. In fact, Jewison had initially wanted Erich Segal, of *Love Story* (Hiller, 1970) fame, to adapt it.[19] It was the directorial debut of the editor of *In the Heat of the Night*, Hal Ashby, who had already been working for the Mirisches for several years. Sieving details these relationships citing numerous exchanges between Marvin Mirisch and Norman Jewison. He concludes that once Segal was replaced by Gunn, working with a major like UA and an independent production company like Mirisch clearly necessitated compromise for all parties, and 'Gunn undoubtedly chafed under this system, which explains his move to independent filmmaking after 1970. But when he had the opportunity to work with sympathetic and enthusiastic collaborators, as he did on *The Landlord*, both he and they profited from the experience'.[20] This chapter is entitled 'Black Hollywood Meets New Hollywood' and in it the author acknowledges that:

> The filming of The Landlord represents the most significant point of collaboration between two groups that would play an enormous role in the formation of an artistically and economically viable system of production in 1970s Hollywood: the black actors and craftspeople who would serve as the backbone of the black movie boom and the white filmmakers who initiated an auteurist-based movement, roughly spanning from 1967 to 1977, known variously as the New Hollywood or the Hollywood Renaissance.[21]

In contrast to *Heat* and perhaps in response to dissatisfaction about the racial make-up of its crew, 'the makers of The Landlord also actively sought qualified blacks for the production craft positions' and with the appointment of Hal De Windt, as assistant to

---

[17] Ibid, 163.
[18] Ibid, 166; 'United Artist (*sic*) Showing Progress in 1970', *Chicago Defender*, 13.6.1970, 6A & 8A.
[19] United Artists Collection, 5–15.
[20] Sieving, 2011: 175.
[21] Ibid, 184.

the producer, shooting in sensitive Bedford-Stuyvesant locations was painless and he ensured that the crew was 'heavily integrated'.[22]

Finally, perhaps, it is worth noting that the film, appropriately enough, included several homages to Godard in general and *A Bout de Souffle* in particular. As Sieving puts it,

> *The Landlord*, formally the most audacious film of Ashby's career, adheres to the conventions of narrative and visual style developed by the practitioners of the auteur-driven European (in particular, French) art cinema of the 1950s and 1960s ... Godard seems to be Ashby's main source of inspiration, manifest both in Elgar's direct address 'interview' in the film's opening sequence and in the *Breathless* style jump cuts that highlight Elgar's journey by car away from the Brooklyn ghetto and back to midtown Manhattan.[23]

Penn and Turman

While Mirisch won the Best Picture award for *In the Heat of the Night* in 1968, both the producer of *The Graduate* – Lawrence Turman – and the director of *Bonnie and Clyde* – Arthur Penn – were available to the Mirisch Company earlier in the decade. William Gibson's play, *Two for the Seesaw*, was directed on Broadway by Penn, starred Anne Bancroft and Henry Fonda, and was a resounding success from January 1958 to October 1959. Penn had followed this up with his film, *The Miracle Worker* (1962), starring Patty Duke and Bancroft again (both of whom had starred in his Broadway production of the play). *The Miracle Worker* did reasonably at the box office and won almost universal critical praise, earning Penn an Oscar nomination for best director and winning awards for both Bancroft and Duke. Nevertheless, after the Mirisches acquired the screen rights to *Two for the Seesaw*, they remained unconvinced that Penn had the directorial experience and Bancroft the star presence the film required and assigned Robert Wise and Shirley MacLaine to their 1962 production instead.[24] Elizabeth Taylor and Paul Newman had initially been announced as the leads, but both dropped out.[25] Penn, of course, subsequently directed *Bonnie and Clyde*; Bancroft co-starred in *The Graduate*. In fact, Bancroft's signing to star in *The Miracle Worker* was itself initially announced as 'under the UA-Mirisch banner'.[26]

While Penn was being turned down for directorial duties by the Mirisches, or their UA financiers, the producer of *The Graduate* was actually working in the company's offices.[27] Laurence Turman and his partner Stuart Millar's production of *Stolen*

---

[22] Ibid, 185–6. In fact the film was largely shot in Park Slope.
[23] Sieving, 2011: 187–90.
[24] 'Mirisch, Seven Arts Set Two for United Artists', *Motion Picture Daily*, 34.59: 2.
[25] *Variety*, 6.1.60: 65.
[26] 'Improved Trend for Production', *Boxoffice Barometer*, 26.3.62: 16.
[27] Lawrence Turman, *So You Want to Be a Producer*, Three Rivers Press, 2005, 37.

Hours in 1962 was a co-production between their British-based Barbican Films and Mirisch Films.[28] *Stolen Hours* was shot in the UK in September–October 1962 and was released in the US in October 1963 and in the UK in April 1964. The pair's subsequent production, *The Best Man* (Schaffner, 1964) was also initially announced as a Mirisch-Turman-Millar co-production, with William Wyler to direct and was also released in April 1964, after both Mirisch and Wyler had departed the project.[29] Charles Webb's novel, *The Graduate*, meanwhile, had been published in August 1963 and Turman apparently bought the rights in October that year, while he was still busy promoting *Stolen Hours* for Mirisch. Nichols agreed to direct the film in March 1964.[30] Turman says it was turned down by every studio in Hollywood – and he mentions UA, though not the Mirisch Company itself.[31] Nevertheless, Turman had been working at Mirisch, at a desk next to Robert Wise, while the latter worked on *West Side Story* and *Two for the Seesaw*, and he was still there in January 1964.

UA had bought the rights to the musical and handed them to Mirisch in 1959 and Wise was already employed on it by November 1959.[32] *West Side Story* was in production from 1 August 1960, and filming finally ended on 14 February 1961 but post-production continued until almost the roadshow release that October. *Two for the Seesaw* was released in November 1962. It seems extremely unlikely that Turman would pitch his package – comprising Webb's novel with Mike Nichols attached as director – to every Hollywood studio, except the very company where he was currently working. But assuming he did, why would they have said no? This chapter attempts to explain why. In doing so it argues that the company was both traditional, retaining residual generic hierarchies and employing veteran talents and adapting often anachronistic material, while also exploring emergent themes and topics long before its younger movie brat peers.

In terms of their expression of late sixties rebellion, *In the Heat of the Night* and *The Landlord* deserve far more scrutiny than they generally receive. In their provision of career-defining roles for Sidney Poitier and Beau Bridges (as in previous Mirisch productions, for actors like Steve McQueen and Shirley MacLaine) the Mirisch Company helped rejuvenate Hollywood's on-screen demographics. A similar generational – and cultural – gear change was occurring off-screen too. On *The Landlord*, Mirisch employed ex-editor, Hal Ashby, as director (he went on to direct *Harold and Maude* (1971) *The Last Detail* (1973), *Shampoo* (1975), *Coming Home* (1978) and *Being There* (1979), to name only a few), Gordon Willis as cinematographer (he went on to shoot *The Godfather*) and Michael Chapman as Camera Operator (he later operated on *Jaws*, *The Godfather*, *Klute* (Pakula, 1971) and *Husbands* (Cassavetes, 1970) before being DoP on Ashby's *The Last Detail*, Scorsese's *Taxi Driver* (1976) and *Raging Bull* (1980) and Schrader's *Hardcore* (1979). Between them, they helped transform the look

---

[28] 'Stu Millar, Turman to Make "Flight" For Mirisch And UA', *Daily Variety*, 10.1.62: 1, 4.
[29] 'Millar & Turman Alone On "Best Man" Credits; Scratch Mirisch Bros', *Variety*, 1.1.64: 4.
[30] Mark Harris, *Scenes from a Revolution: The Birth of the New Hollywood*, Canongate, 2008, 26–7, 50; and *New York Times*, 15.
[31] Turman, 2005: 195.
[32] 'Bob Wise NY Bound to Seek "Side" Streets', *Variety*, 27.11.59.

of Hollywood filmmaking. Similarly, Haskell Wexler was cinematographer on *In the Heat of the Night* and went on to shoot *Faces* (Cassavetes, 1968), *The Conversation* (Coppola, 1974) and *One Flew Over the Cuckoo's Nest* (Forman, 1975), but Ashby was the only American Renaissance director – albeit one included in that group, if at all, as an afterthought – to have worked for the Mirisch Company. Why?

The Hollywood Renaissance

Krämer and Tzioumakis, in their recent anthology on the Hollywood Renaissance, identify a series of innovations associated with such films including an increased 'realism' regarding both subject matter and style (the latter derived from documentary filmmaking and European art cinema), an often left-liberal engagement with social reality, a self-conscious interest in style and in film as an art form (with the director as artist), a focus on mostly male, young and rebellious protagonists, a loosening of cause and effect in narrative construction, and a more explicit depiction of sex and/or violence.[33] Many 1960s Mirisch productions conform to such criteria – in the jaded realism of *Town Without Pity*, the radical social engagement of *The Landlord*, the fractured style of both the latter and *The Thomas Crown Affair*, the disaffected protagonists played by Steve McQueen (in *The Magnificent Seven* and *The Great Escape*), but also, and more radically, of female and Black protagonists Shirley MacLaine (in *The Apartment*, *The Children's Hour*, *Irma La Douce* and *Two for the Seesaw*) and Sidney Poitier (in *In the Heat of the Night* and its sequels) and Diana Sands, Marki Bey, Pearl Bailey, Louis Gossett Jr and Mel Stewart in *The Landlord*. There is a loosening of cause and effect in *The Landlord* too, and elsewhere a play with the norms of linear narrative, including occasionally ambivalent or open endings, and there is a more radical, candid depiction of sexual relationships in *The Children's Hour*, *Town Without Pity*, *The Apartment*, *Some Like It Hot*, *Two for the Seesaw* and even *Kiss Me, Stupid*.

Such candour, however, should not simply be confused with progressive representation. A female protagonist attempts suicide in *The Apartment* and commits suicide in *By Love Possessed*, *Town Without Pity* and *The Children's Hour*; in *Kiss Me, Stupid* one of the central characters is a prostitute; in *Gaily Gaily* and *Irma La Douce* almost all the female characters are prostitutes. In *They Call Me Mr Tibbs* the opening scene is of the murder of a prostitute. In *The First Time* the entire plot hinges on three teenage boys crossing the border to Canada to go to a brothel (which is a figment of the hero, Kenny's imagination) and mistaking Anna (Jacqueline Bisset) for a prostitute. In *Town Without Pity* Karin is raped and commits suicide. In *A Rage to Live* Grace is raped and becomes a nymphomaniac. All the women in the village in *The Magnificent Seven* hide in the hills to avoid being raped. Women are murdered in *Man in the Net*, *Return from the Ashes*, *They Call Me Mr Tibbs*, *The Organization* and *A Shot in the*

---

[33] Peter Krämer and Yannis Tzioumakis, *The Hollywood Renaissance: Revisiting American Cinema's Most Celebrated Era*, Bloomsbury Academic, 2018, xv.

Dark. On the other hand, the women's roles in *Two for the Seesaw*, *The Children's Hour* and *The Landlord* are significantly more three-dimensional and proactive.

Peter Krämer made another attempt to sketch the defining characteristics of American Renaissance cinema. The subject matter 'left the ideal of all-inclusive family entertainment far behind, mainly due to their prominent and graphic displays of sex and violence'.[34] A 'permissive' attitude to sexuality is exhibited in *Kiss Me, Stupid*, and prurient, rather than relaxed, scenes of partial nudity appear in *Avanti* and *Hawaii*; there is a critical depiction of race relations in *In the Heat of the Night*, *Halls of Anger* and *The Landlord*. But *The Landlord* is the only Mirisch film to really seriously attempt to represent the counter-culture. Walter Mirisch described *The Landlord* as 'Our attempt to make a non-establishment kind of film'.[35] (Previously, Mirisch, targeting *The Graduate's* enviable teenage and twentysomething audience, had opted for the execrably anachronistic *The First Time*, a putative teen 'comedy'.) The influence of European art cinema tropes on such films is again only visible in one or two productions, again including *The Landlord*. Meanwhile violence is never sensationalized or indeed aestheticized in Mirisch films in the manner of *Straw Dogs* (Peckinpah, 1971) *Bonnie and Clyde* or *Clockwork Orange* (Kubrick, 1971) Nevertheless, the company came perhaps closest of all its early 1960s rivals to accommodating art cinema. Having already adapted Kurosawa's *Seven Samurai*, the brothers subsequently announced that Fellini was to make a film for them.[36]

Between art cinema and blockbuster cinema

Denise Mann proposes that 'a definite paradigm shift occurred in the late 1940s and 1950', leading to 'two divergent but ultimately related trends: an art cinema and a blockbuster cinema'.[37] Mann identifies five categories of what she calls a post-classical era of self-conscious independent art films and Mirisch films fit into each of her five overlapping categories.[38] Black and white new American realist films (*Town Without Pity*, *The Apartment*, *Two for the Seesaw*); star-studded adaptations of significant literary or theatrical properties (*West Side Story*, *The Children's Hour*, *Two for the Seesaw*, *Hawaii*); stylistically ambitious, proto-postmodernist reversals of accepted A- and B-film genre formulas (*The Landlord*, *The Thomas Crown Affair*); films made by auteurs (Wilder, Wyler, Ford, Mann) including *The Apartment* and *Some Like It Hot*, *The Children's Hour*, *The Horse Soldiers*, *Man of the West*; politically and/or socially provocative films – *Kiss Me, Stupid*, *In the Heat of the Night*, *The Children's Hour*, *Some Like It Hot*, *Town Without Pity* and *Irma La Douce*.

---

[34] Peter Krämer, *The New Hollywood: From Bonnie and Clyde to Star Wars*, Wallflower, 2005, 87.
[35] Mirisch, 2008: 287.
[36] *Daily Cinema*, 24.9.62: 3.
[37] Mann, 2008: 2.
[38] Ibid, 12–13.

Nevertheless, if there was a reluctance to fully endorse an art cinema aesthetic, this was grounded in a resistance to a European sensibility, shared with Wilder. In 1959 Wilder told *Film Quarterly*, 'it is an absolute cinch to make a film so it will win first prize in some festival in Zagreb. It is much more difficult to make a film which has world-wide popularity. I have no interest in making arty films'.[39] The following year he explained this aversion. 'In Europe, you can shoot clouds. Then more clouds. Then still more clouds. For an American audience you photograph the clouds once and it is done. Next time you show clouds you have to have an airplane. And if you show clouds a third time, you have to show that plane explode or the audience wraps up the popcorn and goes home.'[40] It is tempting to see the place of a plane in this anecdote having been rehearsed in conversation with aviation film afficionado, Walter Mirisch. Wilder's co-writer, I. A. L. Diamond, agreed.

> In a way, I suppose, 'The Apartment' represents the 'old wave' of moviemaking. It was shot in a studio, using a script and professional actors. Every frame of film is in focus, there is not a single shot of drifting clouds, and no scene was photographed through a wet paper tissue. It is very simply a story designed to entertain millions, not to tickle the fancies of three judges at a film festival in Zagreb.[41]

Five years later, after the box office failure of *Kiss Me, Stupid*, Wilder remained unrepentant. After watching the work of some of his younger, more 'stylish' peers, he was quick to condemn them and their films.

> They are a bunch of arrogant artisans. Arty Schmarty. They compulsively keep reminding you how clever they are. All these gimmicks – the freeze camera, the runbacks, the hand-held camera, shooting a scene through a parking meter – that's the sort of stuff that classical picture-makers threw out 30 years ago. . . . I can't shoot a living room from the inside of the fireplace through the flames – not unless I'm shooting it from the viewpoint of Santa Claus. My purpose is to involve the audience, to make people care about the characters and story. I want them to forget there's a director; I don't feel a compulsion to remind them every five minutes how brilliant I am.[42]

Wilder's aversion to self-referential and reflexive filmmaking is in direct contrast to the art cinema tropes identified by Denise Mann, who discusses the 'self-referential and ideologically reflexive entertainment-business films of the period'.[43] Jeff Menne clarifies this development by characterizing what he calls 'New Hollywood textuality' as 'the crossing of New Wave form and sensationalized formerly verboten subject matter'.[44]

[39] 'The Old Dependables', *Film Quarterly* vol 13 no 1, Autumn 1959: 3.
[40] 'Wilder – And Funnier – Touch', *New York Times*, 24.1.60A.
[41] '"Apartment" With View', *New York Times*, 12.6.60A.
[42] 'When the Cookie Crumbled', *New York Times*, 7.11.65.
[43] Mann, 2008: 21.
[44] Menne, 2019: 70.

Mirisch films often attempted the latter, but, with the exception of *The Landlord*, rarely if ever dipped their toes into the former, though there are, perhaps, touches of it in the location realism of *The Apartment* and *Two for the Seesaw*. The latter pair both conclude as open-endedly as the more celebrated final sequence of *The Graduate*. There is, furthermore, a social realism implicit in the black and white cinematography of *The Apartment*, *Two for the Seesaw*, *Town Without Pity* and the opening, at least, of *Return from the Ashes*.

Interviewed in 1972 by Gordon Gow for *Films and Filming*, Walter Mirisch was more amenable to a sophisticated cinematic language:

> while there are fewer people going to the cinemas, there are more people reading about films than ever before in history. That is kind of a hidden asset we just haven't really mobilized properly yet. . . . And we've got to bring people in to see things that may be experimental in certain areas of photography or direction or acting or writing or what-have-you. Encouragement is necessary for the creators so that they can go on to use those devices and techniques in other films.[45]

When Gow mentions *The Thomas Crown Affair*, Mirisch replies, 'We did another film that was much more experimental than Thomas Crown and that was The Landlord. . . . It didn't succeed completely although I think it did succeed in many respects. . . . It was an attempt to use new methods in direction and editing techniques'.[46] At the time, however, Mirisch was less receptive to such experimentation. According to Ashby, beyond going over budget and schedule,

> The first thing the Mirisch Company came down on was the photography. It was too dark. They couldn't see the actors' eyes. I explained how I wanted the look of the ghetto footage to have the etched feeling it did so we would have a contrast to the so-called, blown-out, billowy, white-on-white sequences which we were shooting in a few weeks. 'But this is a comedy', Walter Mirisch said, 'and you've just got to see their eyes'.[47]

However, if the impetus towards an art cinema was thwarted, so too was the thrust towards blockbusters. A 1972 *Variety* analysis revealed that in 1971, 52 per cent of total US box office income had been earned by only fourteen blockbuster movies. Only one-third of 185 films released that year broke even.[48] Mirisch, however, produced few, if any, such blockbusters, beyond their Broadway and bestseller adaptations – *West Side Story*, *Fiddler on the Roof* and *Hawaii*. As Marvin Mirisch explained in 1972,

---

[45] Gordon Gow, 'Interview with the Mirisch Brothers', *Films and Filming*, March 1972: 40–4.
[46] 'Interview with Gordon Gow', *Films and Filming*, March 1972: 42.
[47] 'Breaking Out of the Cutting Room: Hal Ashby', *Action*, September/October 1970: 10.
[48] *Variety*, 30.11.72: 5–6.

'We're in a position of feast or famine now, in my opinion. There are fewer successful films percentage-wise than there were 12 years ago. But those fewer successful films do great – way up here.' (He raises his arms high). 'And the large number of failures now are way down to the floor. Whereas ten or twelve or fourteen years ago there were many more films which hit a medium kind of gross.'[49]

Mirisch remained in that middle ground, despite such shifts in the market.

Mirisch protagonists and 'defection'

Menne suggests that the years 1962–75 saw the establishment of a New Hollywood and identifies not just its stylistic tropes but also what he calls 'the most prominent, if undertheorized genre of late 1960s and early 1970s Hollywood the "defection" movie'.[50] But while, for Menne, the textual traces of this shift were a 'novelty' in 1967, in fact they can be detected much earlier in the decade. Indeed, a disillusion with narrative momentum, the dejection of protagonists, their defection from American (and Hollywood) norms and forms is evident earlier in Mirisch films like *The Magnificent Seven*, *The Apartment*, *Man in the Net* and *Two for the Seesaw* as well as in later ones like *The Thomas Crown Affair* and *The Landlord*. Similarly, Menne discusses border raider Westerns by Ford, Sturges and Mann noting 'first John Ford and then Anthony Mann were refashioning the genre's principles in a way that would comport with the changing Hollywood industry' without acknowledging that all three made just such films for Mirisch.[51]

The Landlord fits Menne's defection template too. But perhaps the alienation from corporate life depicted in *The Apartment* and from conventional life in *Two for the Seesaw* and *The Landlord*, appealed as properties or projects to the Mirisches precisely because of their own attempt to escape corporate roles, structures and strategies at AA, while also echoing their frustration at finding themselves instead at the whim of United Artists. Independent production was a relative autonomy, a dependent independence and however much they differentiated themselves from the vertically integrated corporations – 'the majors' – Mirisch still depended on them and could not afford to differentiate their product to the extent that the former would no longer finance or distribute or exhibit it. Their defection from and disaffection with corporate Hollywood (institutionally and textually) was always delimited by the very dependence which also enabled it.

Bud leaves Consolidated Life at the end of *The Apartment*, the hero drops out of the New York rat race for his art in *Man in the Net*, the heroine makes her living as a dancer in the beatnik milieu of *Two for the Seesaw*, and even Dick Van Dyke's bank clerk becomes a rebel in *Some Kind of a Nut*. These are all examples, perhaps, of

[49] *Films & Filming*, March 1972: 41.
[50] Menne, 2019: 25, 75.
[51] Ibid, 41, 45.

such disaffection, defection, a species of premature and somewhat half-hearted anti-capitalism. These are far from being fully fledged counter-cultural icons, just as the protagonists of *The First Time* or *The Spikes Gang*, are far from typical examples of rebellious late sixties teenagers. But they are all, more or less, disaffected, disenchanted with their ordinary lives, if both unconvinced and unconvincing about what they want instead.

Menne discusses Kirk Douglas' Bryna Productions as an exemplary independent, analogous with a 'guerrilla warrior' of the Cuban revolution era.[52] It is worth quoting Menne on the independent/guerrilla parallel at length here.

> A sign of how equivocal a figure it was appears in the rather unmotivated scene from ... *The Apartment* ... in which the company man C.C. Baxter is asked by a fellow carouser on New Year's Eve what he thinks of Fidel Castro. In this scene it would have been a year since the fidelistas had seized Havana, and the throwaway question suggests the unsettling fascination, I believe, not for ideological reasons per se but because they were an object lesson in organizational theory.[53]

But the question was asked because the carouser was married to one of the Bay of Pigs mercenaries, not one of the guerrillas. Furthermore, as Menne admits, *Lonely are the Brave* (Miller, 1962) 'does not address guerrilla war but simply resembles it'. A stronger case might have been mounted, however, if Menne had instead discussed *Cast a Giant Shadow*, which was explicitly about guerrilla warfare, and which was, of course, produced, with Bryna, by the Mirisch Corporation. Nevertheless, for Menne 'The bleak ending of *Lonely Are the Brave* is typical of that first wave of movies in the Hollywood Renaissance ... *The Graduate*, *Bonnie and Clyde* and so on'.[54] But the, at best, ambivalent endings of *Fort Massacre*, *The Magnificent Seven* ('We lost, we always lose'), *West Side Story*, *The Children's Hour*, *The Great Escape*, *Two for the Seesaw* and *633 Squadron* ('They're probably all dead') all preceded that *first* wave.

Mirisch films and tradition

Perhaps another way of gauging the difference of Mirisch movies on the cusp of the American Renaissance is to see them through the lens, not of an emergent, 'modernist' American cinema but of a residual, 'traditionalist' stream of filmmaking. In his book, *From El Dorado to Lost Horizons: Traditionalist Films in the Hollywood Renaissance 1967-1972*, Ken Windrum discusses four key categories of such cinema in the period – musicals, war films, 'naughty sex comedies' and Westerns.[55] He characterizes *How to*

---

[52] Ibid, 48.
[53] Ibid, 53.
[54] Ibid, 69.
[55] Ken Windrum, *From El Dorado to Lost Horizons: Traditionalist Films in the Hollywood Renaissance 1967–1972*, SUNY Press, 2020.

Succeed in Business Without Really Trying and *Fiddler on the Roof* as 'residual' musicals. He identifies two war film sub-genres – blockbuster action spectaculars on the one hand and smaller Second World War combat unit films on the other. *633 Squadron* and the subsequent six-film British Second World War cycle and *Massacre Harbor* may fit the latter category; *Midway* may more closely approximate the former, with *The Great Escape* occupying the middle ground. Certainly, the cast of *The Great Escape* combines a younger generation of (American) stars (McQueen, Coburn, Garner) with older (British) stars (Attenborough, Donald, Pleasance). Meanwhile, *Midway* famously recycled sequences from Windrum's exemplar of the genre, *Tora! Tora! Tora!* (Fleischer, 1970) as well as from *633 Squadron*.

The third sub-genre Windrum identifies is the 'naughty sex comedy' of which he suggests 'The form's foundational texts are the comedies of two directors', one of whom was Billy Wilder, and he names *Some Like It Hot, The Apartment, Irma La Douce* and *Kiss Me, Stupid* among those foundational texts.[56] Wilder's *Avanti* is seen as a late entry 'as the period was ending'.[57] Finally, Windrum's discussion of Westerns identifies 'revisionist efforts (that) began altering the mode's long-cherished (although endlessly mutable) paradigms' including psychological or adult Westerns like Anthony Mann's. Indeed, in his discussion of sexuality in these Westerns, he singles out how 'Julie London's striptease in *Man of the West* (Anthony Mann, 1958) set a precedent'.[58] Another Western trope he notes is how 'youthful characters, by their mere presence, also pose a challenge to aging protagonists' which illuminates the McQueen/Brynner rivalry in *The Magnificent Seven*, while *The Spikes Gang* exemplifies this when the three youthful protagonists (two of them cast following their successful appearance in *American Graffiti*) and the older villain, Lee Marvin, are all dead by the film's end.[59] Arguably, therefore, Mirisch produced some of the foundational and final works of this traditionalist cinema, against which the innovations of the movie brats could be measured.

Given the innovations of both form and content championed in Renaissance films, (though, as we have seen, for Mirisch, content almost always came first), the question is, why they never worked with the directors most associated with it, the so-called movie brats? I want to offer several answers to this question. Such answers are economic (most independents could not afford to develop new talent, unlike the majors); demographic (the age of the Mirisches themselves as well as of their directors and writers and their increasingly anachronistic, if understandable, commitment, as a family firm, to family films and the family audience); ideological (their ambition, as ex-B movie producers, to target respectable, 'adult', serious subject matter and source material – not exploitation genres like horror, fantasy, sci-fi and gangster films, evidenced by their early abandonment of all three of their horror and sci-fi projects – *The Haunting*, *King Kong* and *Gargantua*; the source of the recent Netflix hit, Shirley

---

[56] Ibid, 74.
[57] Ibid, 98–9.
[58] Ibid, 157.
[59] Ibid, 136.

Jackson's 1959 novel, *The Haunting of Hill House*, was acquired by Mirisch for Robert Wise but he ultimately directed it elsewhere as *The Haunting* (1963)).[60] And finally, political (as Hollywood liberals, they espoused a realist aesthetic – which prioritized reliable ready-made material – from page, stage, newspaper headlines and screen, respectable styles – black and white was assumed to be inherently more 'serious', and reputable, already established filmmakers).

The youth market

The final UA contract period from 1967 to 1974 witnessed the Mirisches producing a handful of half-hearted attempts to attract the youth market – *The First Time* (three frustrated boys leave their families for a weekend in Niagara to try to lose their virginity), *The Spikes Gang* (three frustrated boys leave their families for the life of outlaws and are all killed in the process), *Sinful Davey* (a belated attempt to tap the *Tom Jones* (Richardson, 1963) market), *Gaily Gaily* (Beau Bridges as a fictionalized young Ben Hecht), *Halls of Anger* (a school bussing story, co-starring a teenage Jeff Bridges) and *The Organization* (a Mr Tibbs sequel with a drugs theme). Meanwhile, the three *Magnificent Seven* spin-offs singularly failed to target the teen audience with sufficiently attractive on-screen identification figures. Both *The First Time* and *The Spikes Gang* evidence an about-turn from Mirisch's initial cinematic strategy – of differentiation from TV (in scale, style and subject matter) – to accommodation with it. The latter pair are so tame in terms of sex and violence that they would have had no problem at all being on network primetime. Of these 'youth market' ventures, only *The Landlord* (Beau Bridges again) pushes the envelope, stylistically and thematically. Why this relative resistance, if not outright refusal, to meet the changing imperatives of production and indeed reception?

First, an economic answer. Harold Mirisch had been adamant, in *Variety*, that trying out new talent was not viable for a small independent production company.

> The indies, said Mirisch, haven't got either the time or the resources to develop new talent. 'United Artists takes each picture from us on merit,' he commented. 'We can't invest in any large effort to tie up new people. Only the big studios, like 20th-Fox, can do that. And for an independent to have names under contract is dangerous. That means you start making films, often bad films, just to keep a certain performer busy.' The producer admitted that this policy stood in the way of new talent development. On the one hand, the indies cry for new (and less expensive) talent. On the other hand, they'll only use established box-office names.

---

[60] 'RKO vs. Mirisch "Kong"', *Variety*, 11.9.57: 7; 'Gargantua' To Be Mirisch's 9th Pic', *Daily Variety*, 3.3.58: 1; 'Gidding Winds Plots of 2 Mirisch Films', *Variety*, 27.7.60: 4.

Since there's been such a rise in the number of active independents 'delivering' films to studios, the demand for the handful of remaining top stars is great.[61]

Perhaps significantly, Harold Mirisch here conflates new talent with new on-screen talent. It may be that new directorial talent in particular, and off-screen talent in general, barely registered with him. Certainly, the one and only directorial debut Mirisch ever greenlit was Hal Ashby's, who only secured the director's chair after Harold's death. The end of the vertically integrated studio system also meant the end of long-term contracts with directors who had previously been attached for years to a single company. Directors like Michael Curtiz (who worked exclusively at Warners from 1926 to 1953), Billy Wilder (who spent seventeen years at Paramount), or John Ford (who worked for Fox for almost three decades) were forced to find new employers when the studio system came to an end, and all three worked for Mirisch – Ford, Mann and Curtiz each made one film for the new company, while Wilder spent seventeen years working there, making eight. The Mirisches also hired directors who had started out in television – people like Blake Edwards and Norman Jewison. What they almost never did was discover or promote *new* ones.

'Relationships with directors'

While some independents were co-founded by stars (Burt Lancaster's Hill-Lancaster and Kirk Douglas' Bryna are among the best-known examples – though both stars also appeared in Mirisch films), the Mirisch Company was built on its relationships with directors. Why did so many major studio-era directors sign on with them? The list of veterans also includes William Wyler, Robert Wise, John Huston and John Sturges. There are two answers – one was that the Mirisches focused on directors more than stars or screenwriters. The second was that they gave them considerable creative freedom. 'We felt we couldn't attract the stars without either outstanding material or directors with whom they were anxious to work. We obviously tried to develop material, but at the same time we continued to develop the relationships with directors.'[62] Indeed, the brothers announced their corporate ambition to: 'find the best filmmakers and provide them with the very best story material and most talented associates – enable the filmmaker to do the thing he most wants to do – concentrate completely on the films, on what appears on the screen and let a small, effective organization handle all the other complex matters that are part of making a movie.'[63]

However, Mirisch rarely 'found' such filmmakers, it either hired those already recognized as the best among their peers, or contracted undistinguished, or at best reliable, directors from television and Poverty Row. This is striking because the Auteur Theory's emergence almost exactly coincides with the creation of the Mirisch

---

[61] 'Majors Originated 'Outrageous Wages; Mirisch: Stars A Calculated Risk', *Variety*, 10.12.58: 4.
[62] Walter Mirisch quoted in Balio, 1987: 167.
[63] *Boxoffice*, 1.10.62: 8–9.

Company. While the Auteur Theory (or 'la Politique des Auteurs') can be dated back to an article by François Truffaut entitled 'Une certaine tendance du cinema français', the first article specifically about auteurism was André Bazin's 'La politique des auteurs'.[64] The formation of the Mirisch Company was first announced only a matter of weeks later. Bazin's article singled out John Ford and Anthony Mann as exemplary Western directors, whose mastery of their material could be measured against the classical conventions of the Western genre in which much of their work was done. Five of the company's first seven films were Westerns – two of them, *The Horse Soldiers* and *Man of the West*, directed by Ford and Mann respectively.

For those directors, like Ford and Mann, or Wyler and Wilder, or, indeed, Jewison and Sturges, whom the Mirisches most wanted to work with, the deals they offered were very sweet indeed. As Wilder put it, 'All the Mirisch Company asks me is the name of the picture, a vague outline of the story and who's going to be in it. The rest is up to me. You can't get more freedom than that.'[65] Jewison's long-time associate producer, Patrick Palmer, agreed: 'those who worked for the Mirisches were able to negotiate greater preparation time, at least mutual approval rights of cast, cameraman, editor etc. Mirisch would not just arbitrarily assign someone to a film. Personnel would be introduced to one another. If they felt comfortable with one another, then they would team up.'[66] Wilder himself has a good claim to be the first 'auteur' to be institutionally recognized as such. He was, after all, the first man in history to win the three top Oscars on one night, winning Best Picture (and therefore recognition as Best Producer), Best Director and Best Writer (with I. A. L. Diamond) at the 1961 Academy Awards for *The Apartment*.

However, it is not strictly true that the Mirisches did not at least try to work with new talent. In an article entitled 'Make Way for Tomorrow?' Walter stressed the need for 'fresh ideas, new forms, radical approaches. . . . I ask for a youthful outlook, for daring, for chance-taking and enterprise'.[67] That same year, *Variety* reported the Mirisch strategy as follows: 'While the Mirisch Co. will not undertake a campaign of talent building, the indie will assign secondary roles to new people. Walter Mirisch explained the company will have a continuing contractual arrangement with these newcomers and thus try to build them through its own films.'[68] But to finance such a radical strategy, Mirisch argued for an equally radical shift in the economics of the industry. And it seems to have been UA and the unions rather than the Mirisch Company itself which proved a stumbling block to such ambitions.

In his capacity as the president of the Screen Producers Guild, Walter gave a speech to the Theatre Owners of America convention in Los Angeles in 1960. In it, he proposed 'that we begin immediate steps to investigate and develop what I would call an American version of the British Eady Plan. . . . Think what such a plan could mean

---

[64] *Cahiers du Cinéma* vol 31, January 1954 and *Cahiers du Cinéma* vol 70, April 1957 respectively.
[65] Balio, 1987: 167.
[66] quoted in ibid.
[67] Mirisch, 1960: 21–4.
[68] *Daily Variety*, 16.8.60: 1.

for American producers and theater owners!'⁶⁹ His proposal was roundly rejected. Mirisch's proposal had been an attempt to address a serious problem in the industry blocking both new forms of filmmaking and a younger generation of filmmakers. By the following year, film graduates, frustrated at not being able to penetrate Hollywood, were resorting to jobs in industrial film units. Producer William Perlberg, in a speech to American Cinema Editors, claimed that while one graduate had secured a job as a script reader at Paramount and several more had found employment in TV, at Revue Productions, 'many of those top students have gone to work for Lockheed or Douglas in film units – or have gone into teaching visual aids'.⁷⁰ Perhaps the story caught Walter or Harold's eye. Harold knew Perlberg well, having booked the producer's *Song of Bernadette* into hundreds of RKO theatres. And Walter had, of course, worked at Lockheed himself.

New talent

The following year, Irvin Kershner, a USC Cinema Dept alumnus, was hired by Mirisch to make low-budget films.⁷¹ That makes Mirisch one of the first Hollywood companies to hire a director from USC to make films. However, none were made. Furthermore, in 1962 Kershner was already thirty-nine, having served in the Second World War as a flight engineer. Haskell Wexler (who went on to shoot *In the Heat of the Night* and *The Thomas Crown Affair* for Mirisch), had shot two of Kershner's early, low-budget films. Earlier that year, Mirisch vice president, Leon Roth, came up with 'A Proposal for the Formation of a Motion Picture Production Organization' to be run by himself and Kershner. *Boxoffice* reported the formation of Roth-Kershner Productions on the Goldwyn lot to 'develop a program of quality films to be made in association with the Mirisch Co for United Artists release'.⁷² The relative autonomy that UA allowed the Mirisch Company was, in turn, delegated to the producer-directors who worked for the company, or at least those employed on their prestige productions. But perhaps only in the case of *The Landlord* was such autonomy extended towards radical shifts in both the form and content of a film.

By the time the trade press was reporting on this initiative, however, United Artists, Mirisch's ultimate financiers – for all the latter's relative autonomy – was already rejecting it. In an Office Rushgram, UA's David Picker sent his boss, Arthur Krim, a confidential note on Roth's project which was 'strongly opposed to the proposals outlined in Leon Roth's brochure' concluding, 'Harold is strongly in favour of this idea and I think we have to discuss it right away'.⁷³ Part of Picker's rationale was that

---

⁶⁹ Mirisch, 1960: 21–4.
⁷⁰ 'Producer Perlberg Calls for NEW BLOOD', *Independent Exhibitors Film Bulletin*, 15.5.61: 12.
⁷¹ 'Independence with a Vengeance', *Film Quarterly* vol 15 no 4, Summer 1962: 19.
⁷² *Boxoffice*, 13.3.62: 16. See also Kershner's contributions to a discussion on 'Personal Creation in Hollywood: Can It Be Done?' *Film Quarterly* vol 19 no 3, Spring 1962: 16–34.
⁷³ Office Rushgram dated 9.3.62.

UA was itself 'trying to initiate a certain number of low priced but creatively exciting pictures' and Mirisch might steal their thunder, but he was also concerned that the proposal 'extends the Mirisch Company to an area where they have never been before and thereby gives even more credence to the current Hollywood shop talk that in order to make a UA deal you have to go with the Mirisches. Secondly, it removes UA from direct contact with exactly those creators who will be the Wilders and Zinnemanns of tomorrow'.[74] In fact, of course, at Monogram/Allied Artists the Mirisches had had precisely the experience of working with extremely tight budgets and of overseeing films by directors somewhat outside the industry's stylistic – if not demographic – mainstream – from Joseph H. Lewis to Don Siegel.

Perhaps significantly, Roth's proposal included several of the ambitions which Krämer and Tzioumakis identified earlier. The new company would employ filmmakers who are 'dedicated to film in the artistic sense'; would produce films deploying 'modern techniques of direction', films with a 'neo-realist style', films aimed not at the mass audience but at 'an audience'.[75] In October 1962 *Boxoffice* reported two Roth-Kershner productions in development, *Young Lucifer*, from Ursula Torday's novel to star George Chakiris, and *Dark Sea Running* from George Morrill's novel.[76] A few days later, Roth-Kershner signed Allan Marcus to write the screenplay of *Young Lucifer*.[77]

Nor was this the last Mirisch initiative to support newcomers to the industry. In February 1963, the company participated in a 'non-profit experiment' in which eleven 'young men', all students of USC's Cinema Department, were selected to work on a 35 mm short, *Off the Highway*, directed by Fred Zinnemann and starring Richard Widmark and Whit Bissell. While the key technicians were also studio employees, the students received on-the-job training, shadowing Hollywood professionals. The latter included 'Emmet Emerson of the Mirisch Company, and Joe Popkin of 20th Century Fox, who acted as production managers, Joe Edmondson, of Goldwyn Studios, was sound man; Sam Bedig, of Universal-International Studios acted as special effects technician; Jack Holmes of 20th Century Fox was film editor, and Terry Sanders supervising cameraman'.[78] Emerson went on to be production manager on *Hawaii* (which Zinnemann was originally to have directed), and assistant director on *Toys in the Attic* and *A Rage to Live*. The USC students included Mike Neyman, camera operator on the film, who recalled, 'After three days of shooting at Pear Blossom, Calif, we practically lived at the Mirisch Company cutting rooms at the Goldwyn Studios while our film was being cut'.[79]

The following month, Roth-Kershner Productions announced that they had contracted Robert Kaufman and Peter Barry to develop a screenplay entitled *The Only Way to Go*, a comedy about young married couples, to be made in association

---

[74] Office Rushgram, David Picker to Arthur Krim, 8.3.62.
[75] Krämer and Tzioumakis.
[76] *Boxoffice*, 1.10.62: 8–9.
[77] Ibid, 16.
[78] 'The Pros Show the Students How', *American Cinematographer*, February 1963: 92.
[79] Ibid, 110.

with the Mirisch Corp, with Roth to produce and Kershner to direct.[80] In December 1963 Kaufman's screenplay *In Training, Do Not Talk With Me*, was also acquired by Mirisch Corp and Roth-Kershner, though none seem to have been produced.[81] Instead, Kaufman went on to write the counter-cultural *Getting Straight* (1970) and write and executive produce *Love at First Bite* (Dragoti, 1979) the vampire comedy whose release coincided with, and commercially defanged, Mirisch's own *Dracula*. One of those USC students, Gary Kurtz, subsequently produced Lucas's *American Graffiti* and both the first and second *Star Wars* films; Kershner himself, meanwhile, directed the latter, *The Empire Strikes Back* (1980).

In 1967 Walter Mirisch re-stated the company's commitment to new talent, noting, 'In the years since the "B" picture vanished as a format for Hollywood films there have been constant complaints that filmmakers offer no opportunities for the development of new talent'. Mirisch differentiated his own company where, 'as producers who anticipate continuing to make the best films possible we also recognize the importance of finding new people to work with and we are delighted to have a hand in the development of such new talent'.[82] The article proceeds to list 'a few of the fresh new personalities who will join established stars in Mirisch pictures and who will bear witness to our continuing effort to add to the talent pool of the industry'. This continuing conflation of new talent with new on-screen talent is perhaps revealing. Nevertheless, the previous year's *Hawaii* had boasted the screen debut of an uncredited Bette Midler and a pre-*Bonnie and Clyde* Gene Hackman.

In January 1968 an internal UA memo from Sam Gelfman to David Picker notes,

> After sitting in on the meetings with the Mirisches, and further to our conversations about developing films with the newer, or younger talent, with perhaps experimental or questionable themes, subject matter, techniques, and styles, I wonder if you have thought about the possibility of setting up yet another Mirisch production company, or utilizing an existing Mirisch production commitment to encompass these films.... I don't believe that the Mirisches should do this on their own, but instead should be put together with a producer who's a little more 'hip', but who would be willing to work within such a framework.[83]

The man suggested for this role was David Balding, 'the first person, after all, to hire Mike Nichols to direct a play'.[84] The proposal seemed to Gelfman to be 'a good way to allow the Mirisches to maintain their relationships with the creative people who bring them questionable ideas, but which keep these problematical pictures within a realistic framework and set up an institutionalised way to ask big money creative types to take cuts in order to do these things for us'.[85] In 1969 UA itself placed an

---

[80] *Boxoffice*, 11.3.63: 37.
[81] *Boxoffice*, 23.12.63: 8.
[82] 'New Faces: Getting Full Chance', *Film Daily*, 16.10.67: 20.
[83] Office Rushgram, Sam Gelfman to David Picker, 8 January 1968, 1.
[84] Ibid, 2.
[85] Office Rushgram, 1968: 3.

ad in *Variety* stressing its commitment to taking risks and backing new talent.[86] In fact, while Mirisch never worked with the movie brat directors (except Ashby), UA proved equally hesitant to work with them – the first film school-trained director's film it released was *Carrie* (DePalma, 1976)!

Staff demographics

If we accept, at face value, Mirisch's commitment to trying out new on-screen talent, we still have no explanation for the company's aversion to new directors beyond their greater financial risk. In such comparatively conducive circumstances, why, other than United Artists' caution, did only one of these new directors – Hal Ashby (the eldest) – ever work for them? Or, to put it another way, why did the rest of the movie brats not work for the Mirisches? Let's start with the demographics of their key employees. When the Mirisch Company was formed in 1957 all three brothers had already had considerable careers in the industry. Howard was born in 1907, Marvin in 1918 and Walter in 1921. In 1967 they were sixty, forty-nine and forty-six respectively. By contrast, that same year, key 1970s studio executives, Richard Zanuck, David Picker and Robert Evans were thirty-four, thirty-six and thirty-seven respectively. (This is not a determinist argument: Roger Corman was only five years younger than Walter Mirisch – but he was also an early employer of Jack Nicholson, Peter Fonda, Martin Scorsese, Francis Coppola, Jonathan Demme and James Cameron.) Nevertheless, the transformations of 1967 were also too late for the Mirisch-contracted directors, except for a handful like Ashby, Jewison, Hill and Edwards, and even they were the eldest of their peer group. It was also, perhaps, too late for the Mirisches themselves, who had all come of age before 1945, before the vertical disintegration of the studio system, before the end of the Production Code, before directors began to emerge from film schools rather than rise up the craft hierarchy, while increasingly, for Mirisch, such directors now emerged through television.

Second, demographics – not just of their consumers but also of their casts and crews. Here are the names and birth years of the most frequent and/or famous Mirisch directors, with the number of their Mirisch films in parentheses:

Michael Curtiz 1886 (1)
John Ford 1894 (1)
William Wyler 1902 (1)
Billy Wilder 1906 (8)
Anthony Mann 1906 (1)
John Huston 1906 (1)
Thomas Carr 1907 (1)
Gordon Douglas 1907 (2)

---

[86] *Variety*, 28.5.69: 31.

Phil Karlson 1908 (1)
James Neilson 1909 (1)
Joseph Newman 1909 (2)
John Sturges 1910 (6)
Garson Kanin 1912 (1)
Robert Wise 1914 (2)
J. Lee Thompson 1914 (2)
Richard Fleischer 1916 (2)
Don Medford 1917 (1)
Paul Bogart 1919 (1)
David Swift 1919 (1)
Delbert Mann 1920 (1)
George Roy Hill 1921 (2)
Tom Gries 1922 (1)
Blake Edwards 1922 (4)
Walter Grauman 1922 (3)
Boris Sagal 1923 (2)
Paul Wendkos 1925 (4)
Bud Yorkin 1926 (1)
William Graham 1926 (1)
Norman Jewison 1926 (5)
Hal Ashby 1929 (1)
Michael Winner 1935 (1)

Curtiz, then, was the eldest and like *Man in the Net*'s male lead, Alan Ladd, was perhaps too old to engage the younger audience that was already dominating cinema going. Indeed, of those Mirisch directors, all but two were born in the silent era – and Ashby himself was only born in the year the talkies arrived. Even those three 'name' Mirisch multiple-film directors whose careers are most identified with the sixties and seventies – Norman Jewison, Blake Edwards and George Roy Hill – were all born in the 1920s, a decade or more before the movie brats. By the end of the 1970s 'the five highest grossing films of all time – *Star Wars, Jaws, The Godfather, Grease, Close Encounters of the Third Kind* – had all been made by directors under thirty-five years old'.[87]

> Most of the older generation – we can call them the studio generation – (were) born between the mid-1890s and the late 1910s. . . . The new generation of filmmakers, rising to prominence in the late 1960s and early 1970s (since the majority had started in television, we can call them the television generation) were born between the early 1920s and the mid-1930s.[88]

---

[87] Gilbey, xiii.
[88] Krämer, 83–4.

Here, in chronological order, are the names and birth years of the key 'directors' associated with the movie brats and New Hollywood:

Arthur Penn 1922
Robert Altman 1925
Sam Peckinpah 1926
Hal Ashby 1929
Mike Nichols 1931
Dennis Hopper 1936
Peter Bogdanovich 1939
Francis Ford Coppola 1939
Brian DePalma 1940
Martin Scorsese 1942
John Milius 1944
George Lucas 1944
Paul Schrader 1946
Steven Spielberg 1948

It is striking that Ashby, at forty in 1969, was among the youngest directors the Mirisches ever hired – while being one of the oldest filmmakers associated with the Hollywood Renaissance (almost twenty years older than Spielberg). Ashby first worked for the Mirisch Company as assistant editor on Wyler's *The Children's Hour* in 1961. (He had been assistant editor on Wyler's *Friendly Persuasion* in 1956 at Allied Artists.) He then worked for Mirisch as an editor on *The Russians Are Coming, The Russians Are Coming, In the Heat of the Night* and *The Thomas Crown Affair*. He was Associate Producer on *Gaily Gaily* and *The Thomas Crown Affair*, before getting his directorial debut on *The Landlord*. Rather than emerging from film school and talking his way into writing or directing a low-budget quickie, he worked his way up, the traditional way, from the cutting room to the directors' chair over almost two decades.

Consumer demographics

By 1957 39 per cent of Americans over fourteen attended cinema less than three times a year. By the early 1970s, 50 per cent of Americans over eleven went to the cinema less than three times a year.[89] Age was an increasingly crucial part of the demographics of cinema going. 'Nearly half of US filmgoers were between sixteen and twenty-four years old. Studios launched a cycle of "youthpix", films which offered subject matter unavailable on television.'[90] Krämer notes that a 1967 MPAA survey revealed that 'half

---

[89] Ibid, 43–4.
[90] Kristin Thompson and David Bordwell, *Film History: An Introduction*, McGraw Hill, 1994, 698.

of the United States population 16 years and older almost never goes to the movies'.[91] But 78 per cent of 16–20-year-olds were going to the movies once a month or more.

The Mirisch Company did try to attract the new youth audience. *The Magnificent Seven*, *West Side Story*, *Kid Galahad* and *Follow That Dream* (their two, albeit belated, Elvis vehicles), *Sinful Davey*, *The First Time*, *The Spikes Gang*, *The Landlord* and *Halls of Anger* and, of course, *In the Heat of the Night* all featured comparatively young actors/protagonists and themes which were probably expected to appeal to younger filmgoers. But none of them chimed with the youth audience as profitably as *The Graduate* or *Bonnie and Clyde*, *American Graffiti* or *Easy Rider*. Indeed, their attempts to target the teen market backfired. Here, for instance, is the late Roger Ebert's review of *The First Time*.

> The people who made 'The First Time' must have been born at the age of 40, about 30 years ago. This is a movie about three teenage kids and how one of them makes love for the first time – and not a single second of the movie, not one, is an accurate portrait of young men at that age. I gather the kids are around 16 or 17 years old. Yet they have the personalities of 13-year-olds, the emotions of 9-year-olds, the naivete of 6-year-olds, the mannerisms of child stars and the vocabularies of teenagers circa 1916. . . . The most serious fault of 'The First Time' is in its dialog. Speech after speech falls flat because the writer, director, and apparently even the actors, have no idea how teenagers talk and what they talk about. One of the young characters, describing something he approves of, says it's 'snazzy.' Maybe Bing Crosby would have called something snazzy on an old Paul Whiteman radio program.[92]

Despite such reviews, according to *Variety*, Walter Mirisch remained sceptical about what he referred to as 'the new rules of picture making'.

> We're not supposed to use any stars. Make only cheap pictures. Don't talk to anyone over 20 and get rid of all the studios. There's certainly much truth in them, but a lot of the present problems have developed from a terrible amount of mismanagement. . . . We've tried to make the films of general satisfaction that did the job and covered the table. Those films tended to bleach out. Audiences have become more and more fragmented, and, of course, the young audience is the easiest to reach. But I'm still interested in the stay-at-homes. For Mr. Nixon, they are the silent majority. For us, they are the stay-at-home majority. We think 'Fiddler' has that immense worldwide appeal to reach them.[93]

As Walter put it to *Variety*'s Army Archerd, 'The public is fed up with X and R films. The business has been built up by moviegoers who don't go to theatres to hear four-

---

[91] Krämer, 7.
[92] Roger Ebert Review, *Chicago Sun Times*, 9.5.69.
[93] 'Audiences Fragmented', *Daily Variety* 23.2.70: 11.

letter words.'⁹⁴ So much for the 'adult' films and filmgoers he had identified as the company's targets. Good management could only take a company so far.

Films without an audience

The young audience remained obstinately out of reach and big budgets did not necessarily help. In his audit of what went wrong during his absence from UA, Arthur Krim determined that the thirty-five films produced for UA in late 1968 or 1969, costing a total of $80 million, would lose in the region of $50 million.⁹⁵ Krim was obliged to satisfy UA's auditor and the Securities and Exchange Commission that the write-off value of those films still to be released was based on sound evaluation of their box office potential and was not an accounting ploy. Among those he discussed were *The Landlord* and *Cannon for Cordoba*. Of the former, he wrote,

> What was expected to be provocative material to the new modern film audience of 1968-69 in depicting black and white relationships in an urban setting, emerged as a film which we felt would be of limited interest to the audience of 1970 – an audience more and more sated with films of this genre. This is still a type of film we intend to continue to make but at one-quarter the cost. Unfortunately, at the time this film was programmed, unrealistic optimism about the potential audience for this type film prevailed.⁹⁶

Krim was equally pessimistic about *Cannon for Cordoba*.

> In 1970 there was a marked change in global acceptance of western and adventure film. The results of films of other companies . . . indicated a need for substantial downward revision in assessing proper budget costs for pictures in this category – even with the so-called big name action stars. This picture falls in that category. If programmed today, it would be considered acceptable only if it could be made at half its costs.⁹⁷

Krim also criticized the greenlighting of *Ned Kelly* (Richardson, 1970) which bears comparison with Mirisch's period youth movies. 'This is again a case of programming a film in a time of much greater optimism about the size of the so-called youth-oriented audience.'⁹⁸ Certainly, *Gaily Gaily*, *Sinful Davey* and *The Spikes Gang*, which were also aimed at that youth audience, suffered similarly disappointing returns. With *Sinful Davey*, as with *Ned Kelly*, the director 'handled the material in a very slow-paced

---

⁹⁴ *Daily Variety*, 30.10.70: 2.
⁹⁵ Balio, 313.
⁹⁶ Krim quoted in Balio, 1987, 314.
⁹⁷ Ibid.
⁹⁸ Ibid.

manner and we have not been able to persuade him to make the cuts necessary to improve the film'[99] (Indeed, Walter Mirisch and John Huston never forgave each other.) Criticizing another film as 'a minor American comedy with no overseas value' Krim noted how 'An old commitment to Dick Van Dyke, and what seemed to be a good idea for the American market, became an overpriced film with a has-been personality by the time of its release.'[100] Much the same applied to Mirisch's two late 1960s Van Dyke vehicles – *Fitzwilly* and *Some Kind of a Nut*.

Paradigm shifts

One way of trying to understand this anachronism is to compare this moment in Hollywood's history with a comparably transformative moment in American industrial history discussed by Malcolm Gladwell in *Outliers*. Gladwell argues of nineteenth-century industrialists born too late that their 'mind-set was shaped by the pre-Civil War paradigm'.

> In the 1860s and 1870s, the American economy went through perhaps the greatest transformation in its history . . . It was when all the rules by which the traditional economy had functioned were broken and remade. What this list says is that it really matters how old you were when that transformation happened. If you were born in the late 1840s you missed it. You were too young to take advantage of that moment. If you were born in the 1820s you were too old: your mind-set was shaped by the pre-Civil War paradigm. But there was a particular nine-year window that was just perfect for seeing the potential that the future held.[101]

Gladwell's paradigm can be applied to transformations and opportunities in the American film industry precisely a century later. Indeed, in the 1960s and 1970s Hollywood went through one of the greatest transformations in its history when many of the rules by which the traditional film industry – and cinema – had functioned were broken and remade. It really mattered how old the decisive people in Hollywood were when that transformation happened. If they were born in the 1950s they missed it. They were too young. If they were born in the 1920s they may have been too old: their mind-sets shaped by the pre-Paramount Decree 'classical Hollywood', studio system, family film, Production Code paradigm. But there was a particular window which was ideal for realizing the potential of what became the American New Wave.

Those born between, say, the first anti-trust case in 1938 and the final decision in 1948 were perhaps ideally placed to profit from that transformation. The first generation of filmmakers to come of age after the end of the vertically integrated studio

---

[99] Ibid, 311.
[100] Ibid, 314.
[101] Malcolm Gladwell, *Outliers: The Story of Success*, Penguin, 2009, 62–3.

system in the wake of the 1948 anti-trust decision, were those often associated with the movie brats, the so-called film school generation. Coppola joined the two-year graduate film programme at UCLA in 1960. (Roger Corman advertised for crew on the UCLA noticeboard – which was how Coppola got his first industry credit.) Lucas, Milius and Walter Murch all attended USC, Brian DePalma was at Columbia, and Scorsese was at the New York School for the Arts (later renamed the Tisch School of the Arts) in 1960.

Discussing the personal computer revolution of the 1970s Gladwell offers a more contemporary comparison. 'If you were more than a few years out of college in 1975, then you belonged to the old paradigm. . . . At the same time though you don't want to be too young. You want to get in on the ground floor, right in 1975, and you can't do that if you're still in high school.'[102] The Mirisch directors were all in their forties, fifties, sixties and even seventies by the 1960s. The movie brats (Ashby and a handful of peers aside) were mostly in their twenties and the oldest directors associated with the New Hollywood were in their forties in 1967.

Word may also have got around that directors were not irreplaceable at the Mirisch Company – and that Mirisch sometimes seemed to allocate them on the 'who's available' principle, rather than 'who's appropriate'. As *Variety* reported, 'Norman Jewison's second Mirisch film looks like "How To Succeed" which is about to be on the M squad's sked.'[103] John Sturges followed *The Magnificent Seven* with *By Love Possessed*, which could hardly have been less appropriate, but which he was assigned to keep him busy until *The Great Escape*. Jerome Robbins was dismissed from co-directing *West Side Story* with Robert Wise. And *Hawaii* changed directors twice! Not to mention the fact that the film was originally to be directed by Fred Zinneman (who spent months on the payroll before leaving the project).[104] The replaceability of directors on Mirisch productions would have been well-known in Hollywood, adding to the company's reputation as less than an ideal home for wannabe auteurs. Nor did the company seem sensitive to the generic strengths and weaknesses of the directors they contracted. William Wyler was mooted as a possible director of *The Naked Truth* (which became *A Shot in the Dark*) and Anatol Litvak was also named as a contender to direct the same film. Litvak was also touted as a possible director of *The Magnificent Seven*, while Bryan Forbes was suggested as director of Wilder's Sherlock Holmes project.[105]

Family films or prestige products

Third, is the notion of taste. As a family firm the Mirisch Company had a commitment to the family film and indeed the family audience. This meant that certain genres, certain

---

[102] Gladwell, 64–5.
[103] *Variety*, 22.10.64: 2.
[104] *The New York Times* reported "Hawaii" Changes Directors Twice: Hill Is Replaced by Hiller then Takes Over Again', *NYT Encyclopedia of Film*, 4.8.65.
[105] United Artists Collection Addition, Box 5, Folder 12, Wisconsin Historical Society.

ratings and even certain storylines and settings were deemed appropriate, and others were not. One reason for the lack of fit between the Mirisches and the movie brats is the kind of films the Mirisch Company wanted to make. Westerns and war films were skewed towards older, very male, audiences just as the cinema going demographic was changing, but such traditional genres remained those, alongside comedy (far from a movie brat speciality), in which the Mirisch Company remained most prolific. For UA they produced twelve Westerns, twelve war films, fourteen comedies and five musicals (including the Elvis vehicles). None of these coincided with the concerns of the first decade of the movie brats.

Among the sixty-eight films they produced for UA they made no science fiction, fantasy or horror movies – and they studiously avoided the genres that they associated with B movies and those non-prestige productions they had hoped to have left behind at Allied Artists. Walter Mirisch had personally produced sci-fi films including *Flight to Mars*, (1951) and had overseen *Invasion of the Body Snatchers* (1956) just as he had greenlit or produced film noir like *The Big Combo* and *The Phenix City Story*. The Mirisch Company's first and last horror film was *Dracula*, which was made for Universal – after the movie brats had showed the way in which once-disreputable genres could be rebooted. *The Satan Bug*, a sub-Bond knock-off, was among their least engaging films and probably derived, tellingly, from their appetite to acquire an Alistair MacLean novel, albeit a pseudonymous one, despite its generic distance from his war stories which were working so well at the box office.

Their ambitions for their most visible films were that they were, as much as possible, prestige products, with a cultural kudos that almost all their previous films at Allied Artists had inherently lacked. And yet, ironically, some of the exploitation or 'B' films they oversaw at AA, like *Riot in Cell Block 11*, *Invasion of the Body Snatchers* and *The Big Combo* retain a reputation in the canon that surpasses much of their 'quality' output. By contrast, a company like AIP specialized in non-prestige, sensational or 'exploitation' genres (stressing sex and violence). Think of the psychopaths, mobsters, monsters, sharks and psychos depicted in *The Godfather*, *Jaws*, *Star Wars* and *Taxi Driver*. Few if any such human – or animal – monsters appear in Mirisch productions. They remain, for all their cautious licence, either family films or, exceptionally, 'serious' adult films. And of those sixty-eight films, an unusually high number – thirty-three – were set in the past – not necessarily a recommended recipe for currency, though *Bonnie and Clyde* certainly proved it possible.

Indeed, Walter Mirisch is explicit about this in his autobiography, explaining the brothers' decision to leave Allied Artists and set up their own company as a desire 'to continue to produce "A"-quality pictures.... We didn't want to return to producing small pictures again'. Instead, they wanted 'to produce a program of films of consequence'.[106] They had started out by producing Westerns, as Mirisch explained, 'Due to the over-saturation of television Westerns in the 1950s and 1960s, I felt strongly that we had to do more adult subjects for the genre.'[107] Significantly, 'adult' did not mean to the

---

[106] Mirisch, 2008: 84, 85.
[107] Ibid, 91.

Mirisches what it meant to Roger Corman – 'bare breasts and bloodshed'. Thus, 'As with Fort Massacre, Man of the West was an attempt to create a so-called adult Western'.[108]

Mirisch versus Corman

It is thus doubly ironic that Corman, that other progenitor of the American New Wave, through his influence on *Easy Rider*, sold his first script to Allied Artists.[109] Indeed, it was Walter Mirisch, as head of production, who gave Roger Corman his first break by buying that screenplay, *House by the Sea*, for Allied Artists, where it was made into the film *Highway Dragnet* (Juran, 1954). Corman worked as an associate or co-producer on the film. In May 1956 Corman announced that his next film, *The Undead* (Corman, 1957), was also to be made for Walter Mirisch at Allied Artists.[110] In July 1956, however, *Variety* reported that Corman would fully finance the film himself, and it would be distributed by AIP.[111]

In 1957, United Artists took out a full-page ad to announce the initial deal with the Mirisch brothers, declaring that 'With the launching of their new production company, Harold, Walter and Marvin Mirisch bring added stature to the motion picture industry'.[112] The ad noted that 'Commitments have already been made with the distinguished, Oscar-winning producer-director, Billy Wilder and seven top stars . . . Gary Cooper, Tony Curtis, Doris Day, Audrey Hepburn, Joel McCrea, Audie Murphy and Lana Turner'.[113] This is a decidedly establishment, mature, mainstream roster of talent. It doesn't speak to, or seek out, a young audience, but aims to reassure the traditional audience and, particularly, mainstream exhibitors. Words like 'stature' and 'distinguished' would hardly appeal to exhibitors in search of the new teen, drive-in audience.

On the opposite page, in that very same issue, under the headline, 'United Artists No Hive for B's in New Cutback', *Variety* reported that 'United Artists is dropping its schedule of 'B's or marginal pictures to concentrate on strictly A productions, beginning in 1958'.[114] This, of course, may have served to reinforce the Mirisch strategy. Only the previous week, however, the front page of *Variety* had run the headline 'Horror Pix as Global Clicks, Teenagers Key Chillers' BO'. The article began, 'The road to riches is partly paved with gimmicks. Inexpensive exploitation product, including the horroramas and outer-space entries, have done well during 1957 . . . Attack of the Crab Monsters and Not of this Earth were produced by Roger Corman for Allied Artists'.[115] What are *Jaws* and *Star Wars*, after all, if not precisely such horroramas and outer-space entries, albeit stylish seventies reboots of those genres, on inflated budgets? Harold

---

[108] Ibid, 96.
[109] Roger Corman, *How I Made a Hundred Movies in Hollywood and Never Lost a Dime*, 1.
[110] 'Hypnosis Rage Goes On', *Los Angeles Times*, 4.5.56: B9.
[111] 'Inside the Lots', *Variety*, 18.7.56: 4.
[112] *Variety*, 13.11.57: 21.
[113] Ibid.
[114] Ibid, 20.
[115] 'Horror Pix as Global Clicks, Teenagers Key Chillers' BO', *Variety*, 6.11.57: 1–3.

was no stranger to gimmicks, but the brothers' appetite for 'quality' and antipathy to exploitation proved decisive. Meanwhile, many of the movie brat films, most notably *Star Wars* and *Jaws* but also the film that, arguably, opened the door to them both, *Easy Rider*, were heavily influenced by Roger Corman and exploitation cinema. Gilbey quotes Corman's remark, 'I made movies about interplanetary adventures when George Lucas was still in grade school.'[116] Lucas himself later admitted that his ambition for *Star Wars* had been for it to be 'on the same intensity level as a Roger Corman movie, only a hundred times bigger'.[117]

Unions and uniforms

In 1968, *Variety* correspondent, AD Murphy, wrote an editorial for the *New York Times* entitled 'Students: Stay Out of Hollywood' which accused the DGA and the IATSE of 'inbred, protective unionism' causing a 'near-total freeze-out' of young people from the industry.[118] This perhaps explains why *Easy Rider* was filmed under a contract with the National Association of Broadcast Employees and Technicians rather than with the traditional film union, the IATSE, – indeed, *Easy Rider* was the first hit filmed under other than an IATSE agreement.[119] Nystrom suggests that one explanation for the success of Roger Corman and AIP was that none of their films were made under orthodox union contracts. Some, like Brian DePalma, worked 'undercover', others simply had no union card. AIP was essentially non-union.[120]

The Mirisch Company, on the other hand, was unionized and had internalized Hollywood working patterns as well as stylistic and narrative conventions. The three brothers had all worked for Allied Artists, which was an IATSE signatory. When they left the studio to set up their own independent production company they continued working as they had previously, with the established unions and guilds. And as their output deal was with the distributor United Artists, working with the unions was again necessary as UA's cinema outlets were also unionized – the projectionists were members and would refuse to screen non-union productions. Mirisch's final film for UA, *Mr Majestyk*, even had a union organizer and activist as its heroine. Even *The Hallelujah Trail* treats employers and strikers with equal scorn. But if a latent pro-unionism was evident in some films, a blatant patriotism and perceived pro-military bias were equally visible. Thus, Mirisch's history of cooperating with the Pentagon, for all Walter's reluctant arms' length from its production, meant that the very presence of the corporate letterhead and logo seems to have reassured the CIA, which allowed

---

[116] in Ryan Gilbey, *It Don't Worry Me: Nashville, Jaws, Star Wars and Beyond*, Faber and Faber, 2003, x.
[117] Gilbey, 2003: 47.
[118] 'Students: Stay Out of Hollywood', *New York Times*, 18.8.68: section 2, 13. See also 'Youth Locked Out at the Film Gate', *Variety*, 6.1.65: 25.
[119] 'Screen Actors Guild Moves for Withdrawals from Non-Union Swope', *Variety*, 23.10.68: 16 and 'Easy Rider Biz Sparks NABET Use by Coast Indies', *Variety*, 22.10.69: 6.
[120] Nystrom, 2009: 57.

Scorpio to be the first film to shoot at its HQ in Langley, Virginia. The crew filmed in – and was even staying at – the Watergate Hotel on the night of the infamous break-in.

A hierarchy of genres

The Mirisch Company was intent, specifically and strategically, on underlining the division between the B movie and the A movie, between exploitation and prestige product, between their past and their present – just at the precise moment which Fredric Jameson identifies as undergoing 'the effacement of some key boundaries or separations, most notably the erosion of the older distinction between high culture and so-called mass or popular culture'.[121] Having worked in the arena which Jameson refers to as 'shlock and kitsch' and 'B-grade Hollywood films' while at Monogram/Allied Artists, the Mirisch brothers were determined to occupy, safer, if not necessarily higher, ground culturally, hence their association with so many cinematic, literary and theatrical ready-mades, whose reputational capital was already secure. Their productions are reliant on pre-existing cultural goods, previously established talent and topics (adaptations and remakes and films dealing with historically and socially important and recognizable issues and events).

The Mirisches had exchanged Allied Artists for United Artists and exploitation movies for 'quality' pictures. This was, in part, about cinematic taste – the Mirisches wanted to make films about serious subjects for an adult audience. They wanted to join the major league. Walter Mirisch's autobiography is entitled *I Thought We Were Making Movies, Not History*. But arguably, Mirisch's ambition, *was* to make history, in two specific senses. First, as a graduate in history, the past was endlessly fascinating to Walter, and a surprisingly high proportion of their productions were set in the past. The Mirisch Company was a prolific producer of what might be called history films. But second, and more strikingly, once they moved beyond their early Western programmers, there is a seriousness of subject matter, of social issues, in a number of their films – rape (*Town Without Pity*), race (*The Landlord, Halls of Anger, In the Heat of the Night, West Side Story* and *Fiddler on the Roof*), lesbianism (*The Children's Hour*), the legacy of the Holocaust (*Return from the Ashes*), the foundation of Israel (*Cast a Giant Shadow*), the Cold War (*One, Two, Three, The Russians Are Coming, The Russians Are Coming*) and even colonialism (*Hawaii* and *The Hawaiians*). This is evidence of a concern for history – as it was happening. Curiously, however, as this serious tone was exhausted, there was a headlong retreat into the antithesis of seriousness, an almost hysterical strain of more or less madcap comedy, from the middle of the decade with *What Did You Do in the War, Daddy? How to Succeed in Business Without Really Trying, Fitzwilly, The Party, Sinful Davy* and *Some Kind of a Nut*, not to mention *The Pink Panther* series.

---

[121] Fredric Jameson, 'Postmodernism and Consumer Society', in *The Cultural Turn: Selected Writings on the Postmodern, 1983–1998*, Verso, 1998, 2.

Yet, the Mirisch Company was crucial in the transition to that New Hollywood and pioneered many of its on-screen sexual (*Some Like It Hot*, *The Children's Hour*, *The Apartment*), racial (*The Landlord*, *In the Heat of the Night*, *Halls of Anger*) and political (*Cast a Giant Shadow*, *The Russians Are Coming*, *The Russians Are Coming*) themes, as well as its industrial strategies – from the package-unit system of production, to the saturation release of *The Magnificent Seven*, (fifteen years before *Jaws*), the franchises spawned by *Magnificent Seven*, *Pink Panther* and *In the Heat of the Night* (a decade before *The Godfather* or *Star Wars*) its film and TV synergies (*Pink Panther*, *Rat Patrol*), and merchandising (*Pink Panther* again).

Today, much of the Mirisch modus operandi remains default industrial strategy in Hollywood and many of its films rate among American cinema's most popular post-war classics. And yet those films are rarely, if ever, included in accounts of the American New Wave. To examine a company whose films never quite qualified as New Wave through such a lens may seem unorthodox, not to say counter intuitive – but identifying the characteristic industrial and textual strategies of the former may help reveal the necessary conditions of existence for the latter, if only by omission.

Almost close encounters

There were one or two near misses, besides failing to hire Arthur Penn to direct *Two for the Seesaw* and failing to greenlight Laurence Turman's production of *The Graduate*. The Mirisches hired screenwriter William Peter Blatty (on *A Shot in the Dark*) years before he wrote *The Exorcist* and director George Roy Hill before he directed *Butch Cassidy and the Sundance Kid* and *The Sting*. However, the name-recognition movie brats – Scorsese, Spielberg, Lucas and Coppola – never worked for the company at all, though they came close on several occasions.

In 1959, United Artists handed Mirisch the rights to produce three prestige projects UA had developed with Seven Arts – a play, a musical and a bestseller. (One of them, *West Side Story*, has just been remade by Steven Spielberg.) Just three years later, in 1962, a young film school graduate was hired by Seven Arts to develop scripts from the plays and books they had acquired. His name was Francis Coppola. On *The Party*, the technology of Video Assist was developed and used for the first time on a feature film, to monitor Peter Sellers' improvisations, but it wasn't resurrected until Coppola requested it for *Apocalypse Now*. *The Landlord* was the first feature in which film was intentionally underexposed during shooting but processed normally. Gordon Willis repeated this on Coppola's *The Godfather* in 1972. Fred Roos, who went on to produce for Coppola, was the casting director for the Mirisch sitcom *Hey Landlord*.

George Lucas, meanwhile, has acknowledged the inspiration *633 Squadron* provided for the 'trench run' sequence in *Star Wars*.[122] Irvin Kershner worked for the

---

[122] *The Telegraph*, 8.5.14 http://www.telegraph.co.uk/film/star-wars--a-new-hope/movies-influences-george-lucas/

Mirisch Company over a decade before directing *The Empire Strikes Back*. Walter Mirisch acknowledged Lucas' box office pulling power by 'galloping ahead with the release of his western, "The Spikes Gang," to bow pre-Easter with a campaign spurred by young stars, Ron Howard and Charles Martin Smith – who happen to be hotter'n pistols now because of "American Graffiti"'.[123] One of the USC students, Gary Kurtz, who was an intern at Mirisch in 1962, subsequently produced Lucas's *American Graffiti* and both the first and second *Star Wars* films.

Perhaps the closest Mirisch came to working with one of the New Hollywood directors was with Robert Altman. In partnership with producer Ray Wagner (and, subsequently, agent George Litto) Altman developed a Black comedy about First World War flyers, *The Bells of Hell Go Ding a Ling a Ling*, originally as an idea for a TV series – Litto sold the idea of it as a series to Screen Gems briefly but it was then developed as a feature.[124] Altman's friend Brian McKay worked on the storyline and this was then handed to Roald Dahl to work up as a screenplay. At this point, Cary Grant, an admirer of Altman's TV work, became interested in the project. 'After a successful meeting with Grant, Altman, Wagner and Litto approached Mirisch ... in partnership with United Artists for financing.' Altman apparently shot a test sequence of an aerial dogfight for potential investors (the director had been a co-pilot in the Second World War) 'but neither Mirisch nor United Artists would accept him as a suitable director for a big budget Cary Grant vehicle'.[125] Apparently, Altman wanted Edwards' title, *What Did You Do in the War, Daddy?* for the film.[126] Then Grant pulled out and, when Dahl's wife became seriously ill, he too withdrew. Mirisch retained the rights to the project, paying off its creators (according to O'Brien, Altman received $75,000). *The Bells of Hell Go Ding a Ling a Ling* starring Gregory Peck and Ian McKellen, directed by David Miller, was abandoned after five weeks of filming in Switzerland in July 1966 because of the illness of Peck and early snow in the Alps. Altman seems to have briefly re-entered the project in 1970, when it was abortively resurrected, ('"The Bells of Hell Go Ting A-Ling-A-Ling," a seriocomedy to be produced-directed by Robert Altman".[127]) Once again, nothing came of the announcement.

In 1969, Julia Phillips, who went on to produce *The Sting*, *Close Encounters of the Third Kind* (Spielberg, 1977) and *Taxi Driver*, was a young story editor at Paramount, working for an executive named Marvin Birdt. When Birdt was fired, he moved to the Mirisch's New York office and took Phillips with him.[128] Coincidentally, *The Landlord* started shooting in New York at almost exactly the same time, 2 June 1969.[129] According to Phillips, the Mirisch office is

---

[123] *Daily Variety*, 5.2.74: 3.
[124] Daniel O'Brien, *Robert Altman: Hollywood Survivor*, Continuum, 1995, 24.
[125] Ibid, 25.
[126] 'Label Babel: Ad Men Spur Industry in a Hot Race for Lengthy, Exotic Film Titles', *NYT Encyclopaedia of Film*, 6.12.64.
[127] 'Mirisch In Prod'n Lull', *Daily Variety*, 23.2.70: 1.
[128] *Variety*, 29.5.69.
[129] Ibid.

in the funky part of town. Seventh Avenue between 48th and 49th . . . This situation lasts a year and is the most fun I have in a job like this. Mirisch is now run by the younger brothers – Walter and Marvin – of the dynamic Harold, who has now passed from the scene, but they still have a slew of deals with directors: John Sturges, Peter Yates, Pollack and Rydell, Billy Wilder. I actually find a book that Pollack buys . . . Marvin and I last a year at Mirisch. They are now making movies like *The Return of the Return of the Magnificent Seven* and UA isn't so inclined to maintain their overhead. Walter comes to visit one afternoon, asks if I have any hot tips. I tell him everything I know, then he fires me.[130]

She is probably here referring to the second sequel, *Guns of the Magnificent Seven*, which opened in July 1969. Its reception was dampened by the almost simultaneous release of Peckinpah's *The Wild Bunch* (1969), which had a similar plot but was an incomparably better film. Ironically, Peckinpah himself was a Mirisch alumnus, though characteristically he never directed for the company. He had, however, agreed to write and direct on the proposed Mirisch TV series of *The Magnificent Seven*, which was nearly made in the early 1960s. Another 1970s auteur, Walter Hill, was the second assistant director on *The Thomas Crown Affair*.

At just this time (summer 1969) Hal Ashby was making *The Landlord* for the Mirisches in New York, but Phillips doesn't mention it. The only project she mentions in relation to this period is a treatment she pitched for Mirisch to Peter Yates' then manager, David Begelman, which was unceremoniously turned down.[131] Phillips, of course, went on to produce *The Sting* for George Roy Hill (an ex-Mirisch-contracted director), *Taxi Driver* for Scorsese and *Close Encounters of the Third Kind* for Spielberg. By then, Mirisch's contract with UA had ended and they had signed a deal with Universal, just as Spielberg was shooting *Jaws* for the studio. Spielberg's subsequent *1941* is virtually an homage to *The Russians Are Coming, The Russians Are Coming*, which was an adaptation of a Nathaniel Benchley novel. *Jaws* was adapted from a novel by Benchley's son, Peter.

Elmore Leonard wrote *Mr Majestyk*, for Mirisch, in 1974, decades before Soderbergh or Tarantino got the Leonard bug, and novelized it himself subsequently, as his admirer, Tarantino, recently did with *Once Upon a Time in Hollywood*. Ten years later, Scorsese was down to direct an adaptation of Leonard's *La Brava*, to star Dustin Hoffman, for Walter Mirisch. Scorsese bailed out and for a while Coppola wanted to direct. Then Ashby was in the frame. Sadly, perhaps, the film was never made. Leonard's Hollywood-set novel, *Get Shorty,* drew on this experience – and is dedicated to Walter Mirisch, 'one of the good guys'.[132] In the spirit of Tarantino's novel, in a hypothetical Hollywood history, Mirisch might have made Julia Phillips a producer, instead of firing her, and rehired George Roy Hill, and the latter might have directed their huge hit, *The Sting*, for the company and who knows, her subsequent successes, *Taxi Driver* and

[130] Julia Phillips, *You'll Never Eat Lunch in This Town Again*, Faber and Faber, 2002, 94–5.
[131] Ibid, 97.
[132] Mirisch, 2008: xi.

Close Encounters of the Third Kind, could have been Mirisch productions too. (Walter had worked with an award-winning editor, Verna Fields, while she was still a sound editor and must have renewed the acquaintance at Universal where she was a vice president.) But Mirisch's encounters with the movie brats were never quite so close and such Tarantino-esque 'what if-ery' remains just that, an alternative scenario that never happened, an unmade script. Indeed, at Mirisch, as at most other companies in the period, producing like directing remained exclusively white, male professions. In 1976 Walter Mirisch as academy president was MC at an event, calling the occasion one in which 'the academy recognizes the work of young people – the people who will someday take our place'. Groucho Marx, one of the presenters, interrupted, 'No one's going to take my place!'[133] That the Mirisch Company failed to make room for that younger generation may have been a critical mistake. But then nobody is perfect.

---

[133] *Daily Variety*, 24.6.76: 2.

10

Midway

Between blockbusters and television – The Mirisch Company after United Artists

In 1973 UA acquired the domestic distribution rights to all MGM films. According to Balio, 'MGM had the potential of becoming UA's principal supplier of product – another Mirisch, perhaps . . . .' Once Norman Jewison completed his commitments to Mirisch with *Fiddler on the Roof*, however, UA signed a multi-picture contract with him and another with Blake Edwards.[1] Of course, signing such deals meant not only that UA was creating 'another Mirisch' but also that it was rendering the original redundant, an industrial anachronism. With two of its most successful filmmakers now signed up to UA, Mirisch began looking for another home.

In May 1974 *Variety* reported a fire at the Mirisch offices.

> Billy Wilder's office, along with Walter and Marvin Mirisch's were among those totally destroyed in the Goldwyn Studio fire . . . All of Walter Mirisch's files went up in smoke, complete financial records. In Walter's office, his 16mm collection of Mirisch films, dating back to the beginnings at Allied Artists, went. Ironically, the Mirisch Oscar for 'In the Heat of the Night' was recovered in his burned-out office – but it was headless.[2]

The conflagration provided dramatic punctuation for the end of an era. Mirisch's third and final deal with United Artists ended only three months later, on 31 August 1974. The UA consensus seemed to be that the company was itself headless, that Walter and Marvin 'didn't have the background that Harold brought into the deal' and that, after Harold's death in 1968, things were never quite the same.[3] In fact, Harold had already been unwell for some years, having had a series of heart attacks and periods of hospitalization and convalescence from 1961 and his day-to-day involvement in the company had been intermittent at best since the early 1960s. Nevertheless, several of the directors who worked with the company agreed that it was Harold, the dealmaker,

---

[1] Balio, 1987: 325.
[2] *Variety*, 22.5.74: 25.
[3] Herb Schottenfeld, quoted in Balio, 191.

who had been the heart of the company, overseeing distribution, exhibition and advertising, which had, of course, been his background. 'He was the real go-for-broke fellow – a gambler spirit', according to John Sturges. 'Harold was the King. The brains of the outfit,' reported Norman Jewison.[4]

In September 1974, Marvin, Walter and their secretaries moved into a bungalow on the Universal studio lot. It was a considerable comedown from their long-term home at the Samuel Goldwyn Studios. Universal, unlike UA, did not want Mirisch to be a truly independent company under their wing, let alone accommodate autonomous producer-director units within it. The Mirisches were now, essentially, Universal staff producers, albeit ones allowed to retain their customary corporate credit. Ironically, the vice president of Universal in 1974 was the same Jennings Lang whom Walter Wanger had famously shot in 1951 – and may have enjoyed mildly humiliating the brothers, ensuring Wanger's corporate hosts were obliged to deploy Universal's Sensurround process on *Midway*, their first film for the studio. The deal, nevertheless, guaranteed 50 per cent interest in the profits of their productions based on two picture cross-collateralizations.

Those directors and other talent on multiple film deals with Mirisch were released from their previous contacts. All the rest of the Mirisch staff were made redundant, as their new 'landlord', Universal, unlike UA, provided business affairs, legal and accounting services itself. Happily, *Mr Majestyk*, their final UA film, had proved to be a considerable hit, the company's first since *Fiddler*, earning rentals some ten times its $2 million budget. Meanwhile, the outlay on an unmade feature adaptation of Arthur Hailey's *Wheels*, which was to also have been directed by Richard Fleischer, was recouped by selling the rights to Universal, which produced an eight-hour mini series adaptation for TV (NBC, 1978).

Daily Variety, in its obituary on the UA deal, commented that 'For many years, the Mirisch pix provided a healthy chunk, and a larger prestigious share, of the entire UA release schedule. UA's recent 10-year deal with MGM may have anticipated the Mirisch switchover. Total of 23 Oscars have gone to Mirisch features.'[5] The profits and prestige which Mirisch had earned UA were key to the signing of the new contract. The trade paper noted that 'Universal four years ago embarked on a feature policy of signing major indie film units to provide bulk of its product. Last big addition to the stable before the latest announcement was the Richard D. Zanuck-David Brown unit.'[6] This, of course, was the unit behind Universal's next huge hit, *Jaws*.

Relocated at Universal for five of their final six feature films, Mirisch returned to type, literally. First among the characteristic Mirisch strategies of the past was adaptation, followed closely by period settings, bi-media production, series and cycles and, indeed, recycling, multi-picture talent deals and so-called 'runaway' production. Of the company's final six features, five were adaptations, four were set in the past, and though none were strictly in series, two were adapted from plays by Bernard Slade,

---

[4] Lovell, 2008: 189.
[5] 'Mirisches Leave UA After 17 Years for Contract at U', *Daily Variety*, 8.1.74: 1.
[6] 'Mirisches Leave', *Daily Variety*, 8.1.74: 4.

another two from stage adaptations of (oft-filmed) novels and the latter pair were both filmed outside the United States.

The initial production for Universal, *Midway*, was based on military history – the battle had taken place on the eve of Walter's arrival at Harvard. The other four Universal features were based on novels, two already much filmed – *The Prisoner of Zenda* (Quine, 1979) and *Dracula* – plus *Gray Lady Down*, another naval outing and stage plays, Bernard Slade's *Same Time, Next Year* and what was an adaptation of the current stage version of *Dracula*. *The Prisoner of Zenda* was to be the first (but, as it turned out, only) production in a new three-picture deal signed between Sellers, Mirisch and Universal.[7] *Dracula* was the exception that proved the rule for Mirisch. It was their only entry into horror, science fiction or fantasy – genres they otherwise avoided as a vampire avoids garlic and the hours of sunlight. Perhaps only the fact that it was both a literary and a stage adaptation ensured its acceptability. Their final film as a company, *Romantic Comedy* (Hiller, 1983) was once again for United Artists, following a regime change at Universal, and was an adaptation of another of Slade's Broadway plays.

In Porter's terms, this was a period of managed decline for a mature corporation in a rapidly changing market. Porter's diagnosis of businesses in decline commonly attributes such decline to an inability to decide between cost leadership (low-budget production) and product differentiation (quality) strategies. In fact, the Mirisches opted for medium cost, middlebrow productions, literally midway between blockbusters and indie-sensibility films on the one hand or television on the other. Those six final features were all based on pretexts, either literal texts or familiar historical events, all but *Gray Lady Down* well-known ones. This differentiated them as always already familiar 'brands'. Indeed, some of the competitive strategies that Porter identifies in companies entering an industry for the first time could conceivably still apply in this final period of the company's history. These include a continuing balance between quality (often through adaptation) and economy (recycling archive footage, securing subsidies and the savings of runaway production, with lower-budgeted TV movie commissions and, whenever possible, TV industry personnel). The company's heavily trimmed staff budget, due to the change in studio/distributor, prevented the kind of consistency of collaborations or continuity across a portfolio of projects as had been the case in the past, though it did manage two Charlton Heston naval films and two Bernard Slade Broadway adaptations. But there was an increased uncertainty of tone – particularly in *Dracula* (which failed to decide whether to place its tongue firmly in its cheek or its teeth, equally firmly, in the neck) and *Prisoner* (which appeared to assume that every single second of its interminable running time was hysterical) – and a curious indecisiveness between docudrama and melodrama in *Midway*.

Midway begins with a caption. 'The story of the battle that was the turning point of the war in the Pacific told wherever possible with actual film shot during combat. It exemplified the combination of planning, courage, error and pure chance by which

---

[7] 'Sellers Goes Mirisch', *Variety*, 2.6.76: 4.

great events are often decided.' Such considerations also impact on the making of great movies – with their own combination of planning, creativity. error and chance. As Admiral Nimitz puts it during the film, military action is 'governed by the principle of calculated risk'. The same principle governed all Mirisch managerial decisions, not least of which, of course, was the calculation of which projects to develop and ultimately to green light.

John Ford had directed the documentary, *The Battle of Midway*, in 1942 and it seems more than likely that Ford and history buff Walter Mirisch had discussed the battle – and the film – when they worked together on *Horse Soldiers*. Henry Fonda, who co-narrated the documentary, co-stars in the film as Admiral Chester Nimitz. Mirisch mentions the documentary in his autobiography, and having just graduated in History at Wisconsin, he had started his studies at Harvard only a few days after the battle took place. He attributes his inspiration to his first naval film, *Flat Top*, about another aircraft carrier, and to a 1967 non-fiction book about the battle, *Incredible Victory*, by Walter Lord. But he had put the idea aside in the late sixties, while the company produced its cycle of 'British' Second World War films, though it is worth remembering that three of those – *Attack on the Iron Coast*, *Submarine X-1* and *Hell Boats* – were also naval stories. Initially turned down by United Artists, *Midway* was only eventually greenlit, by Universal, because of the casting of Charlton Heston. The resulting film steered a course literally 'midway' between docudrama and melodrama, between historical accuracy and soap operatics, between war movie and TV movie.

Once Donald Sanford's draft screenplay was complete (Sanford had scripted half of the company's six-film Second World War cycle), Mirisch submitted it to UA, but because Fox's *Tora! Tora! Tora!* was then imminent, UA vetoed it once again. Thus, *Midway* was not produced until 1975, the year after the company's parting of the ways with UA, but it certainly proved exceptionally successful for both Mirisch and Universal. On an estimated budget of only $5 million, it made $40 million at the box office.[8] At one level, *Midway* was something of a continuation of Mirisch's prior commitment to history and the epic – hence its assembly of a galaxy of such previous Mirisch stars as Charlton Heston (from *The Hawaiians*), Robert Mitchum (from *Two for the Seesaw*), John Wayne (from *Horse Soldiers* and *Cast a Giant Shadow*), James Coburn (from *The Magnificent Seven*, *The Great Escape* and *What Did You Do in the War, Daddy?*), Cliff Robertson (from *633 Squadron*) and Robert Wagner (from *The Pink Panther*). Ironically, for a 'true story' it was only Heston's agreement to star, in a fictional role added to the actual historical personae of the battle, which convinced Universal to greenlight it.

Midway was the first major American victory of the Second World War and a turning point in the Pacific, so Mirisch conceived of the project as a tribute to the American Bicentennial. The Navy's initial reaction to the script, in December 1974, was positive, the Head of Navy Aviation Periodicals and History wrote to the Navy's chief of information, noting that the film 'could be useful in recruiting efforts and as

---

[8] Mirisch, 2008: 330; See also, Tanine Allison, *Destructive Sublime: World War 11 in American Film and Media*, Rutgers University Press, 2008, 99.

part of the Bicentennial'.⁹ The Navy decided that 'cooperation is both feasible and in the best interests of the service'. Indeed, The Navy 'saw cooperation with Hollywood as inexpensive lobbying'.¹⁰ The Navy even allowed the crew to film on board the *USS Lexington*.

One key to the aesthetic of *Midway*, but also to its economy, was its use of stock footage. Pitching it to Universal, Mirisch 'explained the concept of using actual footage that existed in the naval archives for the action sequences in the film. I knew what existed because I remembered what we had used years before in Flat Top'.¹¹ Mirisch felt that the techniques for transferring 16 mm Kodachrome to 35 mm had improved so much in the intervening years that transitions between colourized archive footage and newly filmed reconstructions would be virtually invisible. *Midway* recycled sequences not only from documentaries made during the war, including *The Battle of Midway* and *The Fighting Lady*, but also from Hollywood movies, including portions of the Pearl Harbour attack from *Tora! Tora! Tora!*, the Doolittle Raid sequence created for *Thirty Seconds Over Tokyo* (Le Roy, 1944), and several scenes from the Toho production, *Hawai Middowei daikaikusen: Taiheiyo no arashi* (Matsubayashi and Grimaldi, 1960), released in the United States under the titles *Storm over the Pacific* and *I Bombed Pearl Harbour*.¹²

The film's opening montage, suitably colourized, came from *Thirty Seconds Over Tokyo*. Shots of the take-off of a B-25 from the USS Hornet, used in *Thirty Seconds Over Tokyo*, were also reused in *Midway*. A sequence of Japanese planes taking off at dawn for the attack on Pearl Harbour filmed for *Tora! Tora! Tora!* appeared several times in *Midway*.¹³ Because the American and Japanese navies had never come within sight of each other, Mirisch was able to rely on reconstructing air-to-sea and air-to-air battles and deployed as much 'Navy combat and gun-camera footage' as he could find.¹⁴ The use of such footage, 'gives you a feeling of validity that I find tremendously dramatic' Mirisch wrote, and it enabled the crew to use 'real, full-size planes, not models'. However, even the authenticity of archive sequences like these was dubious. The crash of an F6F Hellcat, breaking in two, had actually been filmed several months after the battle, in October 1944, and *Midway*'s climactic crash was footage of a Korean-war vintage jet, shot a decade after the events it depicts.

Such stock footage, though sometimes 'authentic' was equally often entirely fictional or anachronistic. It was, however, comparatively cheap and, considering the inflated booking charges imposed on exhibitors for the film, this caused considerable concern in the industry. *Variety* reported that Walter Mirisch had acquired the rights to a Japanese film with strikingly shot action sequences, and then built 'Midway' around those sequences.

⁹ Quoted in Lawrence H. Suid, *Guts & Glory: The Making of the American Military Image in Film*, The University Press of Kentucky, 2002, 301.
¹⁰ Ibid, 301, 402.
¹¹ Mirisch, 2008: 329–30.
¹² Allison, 2008: 99.
¹³ Suid, 2002: 85, 289.
¹⁴ Mirisch, 2008: 301.

'Some exhibitors are complaining that Universal should have alerted them to the use of borrowed footage in "Midway" before it blind-bid the picture. . . . A kicker in the bidding is up to a 5% surcharge to exhibs per week to cover installation and use of Universal's sound system, "Sensurround," a device which acoustically increases the aural effects from the soundtrack.'[15]

Sensurround had first been used on Universal's *Earthquake* (Robson, 1974) which also starred Heston.

If its use of Sensurround made *Midway* cinema-specific (indeed, it became one of the six highest-grossing films of 1976) it was also almost a bi-media production itself, with additional material subsequently shot for and edited into the TV version.[16] Universal negotiated a TV sale with NBC, on the basis that that the film's running time could be extended to fill four hours of primetime, including commercials, over two successive nights. Mirisch agreed in principle and Smight shot several new sequences with Heston's Captain Garth and Susan Sullivan as his girlfriend, a character who does not even appear in the theatrical version, while Mirisch was in Europe on location with *Dracula* and *Prisoner of Zenda*. Such amendments remained a bone of contention between the producer and both studio and network.

Of *Midway*'s success at the box office, and in TV sales, Mirisch claims, 'Of all the films that I have made in my lifetime, it produced the greatest amount of profit.'[17] In 1973, ironically, Arthur Krim had boasted, before its production, that 'I do not know of a single picture in this period which Bob and I vetoed that became a hit for another company.'[18] Mirisch himself testifies that UA had rejected *Midway* in the late 1960s on the grounds that 'there was no longer much interest in World War II for young audiences . . . the time had simply passed for that genre of films'.[19] According to Mirisch, 'This marked the only instance, during the whole period of our relationship with United Artists, that I financed a script apart from our deal with them.'[20] Transamerica's John Beckett and his data analytics, algorithmic approach to greenlighting projects, would probably have agreed with UA. While Transamerica might have echoed the scientific management aspects of Walter's Harvard education, it conflicted with the latter's desire to act on his hunches and allow investment to follow instinct. This, after all, is the distinction depicted in *Midway* itself between Admiral Nimitz on the spot and far off, by-the-book Washington, and it is a conflict in which, subsequently, Nimitz and Mirisch were proved right. There is an oblique reference to the potential anachronism of the subject matter in the script itself. At one point, Heston tells his son, who has professed his love for a Japanese girl, 'Six months after Pearl Harbour, boy, you have one lousy sense of timing.' In earlier Mirisch productions, timing had been one of the

---

[15] *Variety*, 9.6.76: 7.
[16] Mirisch, 2008: 338.
[17] Ibid, 339.
[18] Quoted in Balio, 321.
[19] Mirisch, 328.
[20] Ibid, 328.

touchstones of their protagonists, from Thomas Crown to the mission commanders of the Second World War cycle. By 1976, Mirisch's timing was also beginning to be questioned.

By the mid-1970s Mirisch had dispensed with development, sourcing all its stories from pretexts – pre-existing narratives, presold and road-tested on the page or stage. As Walter Mirisch told *Screen International* 'There's no story department, no studio, we just rent space when we need it.'[21] Nevertheless, for Mirisch, *Midway*'s success meant that, 'having produced a big naval film led agents to consider me a producer with a serious interest in naval subjects'.[22] Certainly, *Gray Lady Down* was another naval film (Mirisch's seventh), but while not sharing *Midway*'s historical origin, it does have a pronounced valedictory quality – following the final voyage of Charlton Heston's submarine commander – 'Funny feeling – taking her home for the last time' he says to his crew, to which they reply, 'We're sure going to miss you sir.' His response, 'Shame they can't overhaul me' evokes not only the actor's and character's age, but also that of his producers. (Heston had played another sea captain on his final voyage in *The Hawaiians*.) The crew watch *Jaws* on board and clearly know it off by heart. *Jaws* had been in pre-production when Walter and Marvin arrived at Universal in 1974. Of course, at Universal, without the commitment to a program of pictures of the kind United Artists had contracted from them, it was now entirely possible that each film could, indeed, be the Mirisches' last (Figure 13).

The first screenplay of *Event 1000*, based on David Lavallee's novel of the same name, had arrived in the Navy Public Affairs Office in 1971, when Frank Rosenberg (then at Avco Embassy Pictures) and ABC Pictures inquired about whether the project might receive Navy assistance. Thus, when, in 1975, Robert Aldrich submitted a script entitled *Gray Lady Down* to the Pentagon, it was noted that this screenplay was 'virtually identical' to Rosenberg's *Event 1000*. In December 1975, Aldrich was

Figure 13 The submarine crew watching *Jaws* in *Grey Lady Down*.

---

[21] *Screen International*, 29.1.77: 7.
[22] Mirisch, 2008: 339.

informed that the Pentagon would provide no assistance to the production.[23] In January 1976 Marvin and Walter Mirisch acquired the screenplay of *Gray Lady Down* which had been brought to them by the William Morris Agency for the Mirisch Company,[24] Rosenberg decided not to pursue his own project but instead to initiate legal proceedings, seeking compensation for the 'loss' of his property. 'Ultimately he received suitable remuneration and a screen credit for his adaptation of the novel.' The Writers Guild resolved the dispute over authorship by determining the credits should read 'Screenplay by James Whittaker and Howard Stackler, adapted by Frank P. Rosenberg.' [25]

Walter Mirisch's relationship with the Department of Defence dated back to *Flat Top* and *The Annapolis Story* in the 1950s and the fact that the company was now based at a major studio, Universal, gave the project even more credibility. The lengths to which the Mirisch Company was willing to go to win the Navy's favour is evidenced by the sending of multiple drafts of the screenplay to be vetted and eventually approved.[26] On 2 July 1976, a revised script was sent to the assistant deputy chief of naval operations (submarine warfare) who confirmed, 'The script overall is very pro-Navy.' Just as the Mirisch Company had acquiesced to the on-set Mexican censors' requests regarding the portrayal of Mexicans in *The Magnificent Seven*, so now Mirisch agreed to make any requested changes to the script and to an on-set Navy Information Office representative who would resolve 'any differences encountered in portraying the U.S. Navy'.[27] It is hard to disentangle industrial pragmatism here from American patriotism.

While *Gray Lady Down* was still in production, Mirisch also produced *Same Time, Next Year* (1978) another Broadway adaptation. However, its narrative structure – a couple meeting in the same hotel room every year from 1951 to 1977 – allows it to revisit the decades of Mirisch's own corporate history to date – with appropriate montages to evoke the periods between each meeting we actually see – 1951, 1955, 1961, 1966, 1971 and 1977 respectively – including evocative stills of Elvis (with whom Mirisch made two films), Martin Luther King (about whom they developed an unmade biopic), *Bonnie and Clyde* (which they beat to the 1967 Oscars), the Berlin Wall (which was erected while *One, Two, Three* was being filmed in Germany) and so on. *Same Time, Next Year* dramatizes the relationship between an adulterous couple who only meet once a year. 'Sometimes it seems to me our lives are completely out of synch', says the Ellen Burstyn character, Doris, at one point. The film cost approximately $5.25 million and earned about $27 million, so it was a considerable success.[28]

---

[23] The producer-director was already associated with such 'anti-military' films as *Attack* (1956), *The Dirty Dozen* (1967) and the controversially anti-Vietnam, *Twilight's Last Gleaming*, then in production.
[24] Suid, 2002: 406–8.
[25] Mirisch, 2008: 340.
[26] Suid, 2002: 409.
[27] Ibid, 410.
[28] Slade's play was adapted again in 1994, in the Hong Kong film *Nian nian you jin ri* [*I Will Wait for You*].

Nevertheless, by the late 1970s, the Mirisches were themselves increasingly out of step with their times, not only in terms of their audience (with, for instance, the cinemagoing demographic now seriously out of sync with the theatre audience, which had made Slade's plays and Langella's *Dracula* into Broadway hits) but also of the most critically and commercially successful filmmakers of their time – all of whom were almost a generation younger than they were. Mirisch followed *Same Time, Next Year* with another adaptation and another comedy, *The Prisoner of Zenda*, but this time they were far less successful, with a painfully unfunny Peter Sellers in several roles. To direct, Mirisch hired and then fired, both at Sellers' request, commercials director, Stan Dragoti, and replaced him with Richard Quine, who had been largely relegated to making TV episodes for over a decade, his feature career apparently over. It was to be his final credit as director. *Zenda* was budgeted at about $10 million and earned approximately the same amount in rentals, meaning that it lost money because of print and marketing costs. By now, meanwhile, Sellers, together with Blake Edwards, had embarked on their successful relaunch of the *Panther* franchise for UA.

Prisoner of Zenda was followed by *Dracula*, which attempted to resuscitate an undead horror perennial. In it, the eponymous vampire explains his resistance to modernity: 'I am of an old family. To live in a new house would be impossible for me.' Much the same seems to have been true of the Mirisch's apparent discomfort at Universal. The studio remained, however, the cinematic home of *Dracula*, having retained the movie rights to the stage play, and even provided a 'house' director, John Badham, who was on contract to the studio, in the wake of his success with *Saturday Night Fever*. But Universal certainly was not a home from home for Mirisch, and *Dracula* proved their final film for the studio, not least perhaps because it was pipped at the box office post by the vampire pastiche, *Love at First Bite*, directed by Sellers' nemesis, Stan Dragoti, that same year. Both *Dracula* and *Prisoner of Zenda* had been based on well-known and, in previous incarnations, well-loved material, while both *Dracula* and Bernard Slade's Romantic Comedy, *Same Time, Next Year*, had been Broadway hits (the latter running for three and a half years). Mirisch hired Frank Langella from the former production and Ellen Burstyn from the latter, to reprise their successful stage roles.

The initial contract with Universal had been for four years but in 1978 the two brothers negotiated an extension for another seven, although the company's once steady rate of production had slowed to a trickle. Reporting that contract extension, *Variety* noted that 'Marvin Mirisch, Mirisch Corp. board chairman, told Variety that the indie producing organization plans to average two features a year. . . . The new seven-year contract, coupled with the initial five-year pact, ties the Mirisch Corp. with Universal for 12 years. Only Alfred Hitchcock has a longer association with the studio.'[29] The promised production rate of two films per year proved unsustainable, though it only amounted to half of the company's average annual output for UA.

In fact, between 1974 and 1982, the Mirisch Corporation produced only six features, while continuing to deploy two specific strategies that Porter identifies as typical of a

---

[29] 'Mirisch Deal', *Variety*, 30.8.78: 3, 27.

mature company, substitution and globalization. By now, Mirisch was a past master at bi-media production, accommodating cinema's 'substitute', television, by making TV movies, but also by ensuring its theatrical features had a viable second life on the small screen. Mirisch deployed what Porter calls 'harvesting', defined as 'taking advantage of whatever residual strengths the business has in order to raise prices or reap benefits of past goodwill.'[30] Thus, *Midway* and *Gray Lady Down* reprised prior Mirisch experience filming on aircraft carriers and on submarines and submersibles respectively.

Meanwhile, in January 1978, less than four years after the Mirisches had left United Artists, Arthur Krim and the other top four executives resigned from UA, frustrated at continual Transamerica interference, and formed Orion Pictures, releasing through Warners. The move was reported in the press as intended 'to provide a home for independent film-makers'. The *New York Times* commented, rather ironically in the circumstances, 'In some ways the relationship of the new company with Warner Bros. will be similar to that of the Mirisch Company with U.A. after Mr Krim and Mr Benjamin took control there in 1951. The smaller company, in effect, acted as a middleman between the stars, directors and producers on the one hand and the distribution and financing and service organization on the other.'[31] In fact, the Mirisch Company was being challenged, if not actually supplanted, by Orion, a rival 'quality' independent. Like the Count, the Mirisches were now homesick for a home which no longer existed.

Mirisch continued to produce films abroad when the subject was appropriate, budgets could be reduced and local subsidies secured, with *Zenda* filmed in Austria and *Dracula* in the UK. In February 1979, *Variety* asked whether American producers get value for money in the UK. Citing the exchange rate as one worrying variable, the emphasis of the article was on 'the British work rate'. John Badham estimated that *Dracula*, based at Shepperton studios, could have been completed in the United States in two-thirds of the time and his assessment of the British crew was 'Charming but leisurely'. With post-production in London, *Dracula* qualified for British Eady Levy subsidy, on top of UK box office receipts, but *Variety* concluded, 'As the U.K. exhibition market continues to shrink by 100 theatres a year, U.S. production here could literally be subject to a law of diminishing returns.'[32]

Mirisch, meanwhile, had convinced Universal to buy the rights to another Bernard Slade play, *Romantic Comedy*, which they did for some $750,000. But in 1981 Universal vacillated about greenlighting the production and, a change of management at United Artists led to a return there. The new president was Norbert Auerbach, whose father had negotiated the deal with Harold Mirisch at Monogram over the rights to *The Little Rascals* in the 1950s. The Mirisch brothers met with Auerbach and in March 1981 they signed a new, five-year contract with UA. Ned Tanen of Universal arranged for the Mirisches to be released from their Universal contract and the rights to *Romantic Comedy* were put into turnaround. The budget for the film was set at $9 million.

---

[30] Porter, 269.
[31] '5 at United Artists Quit Top Posts Plan New Company', *New York Times*, 10.2.78.
[32] 'Dracula' Helmer Badham Raps U.K. Workers' Leisurely Pace', *Variety*, 7.2.79: 66.

However, in May 1981, only two months after their arrival, UA was sold by Transamerica to MGM (hence Tarantino's mistaken attribution of the original distribution of Mirisch movies). Mirisch was thus obliged to move into new offices, not, as had been agreed, at UA, but at MGM Studios, the HQ of UA's new owners. *Romantic Comedy* was filmed in New York and on MGM sound stages and post-production was also completed at MGM. The central couple are a pair of playwrights, diagnosed in the dialogue as 'victims of unsynchronised passion'. As Dudley Moore's character puts it, 'We're about nine years out of synch' to which his co-star, Mary Steenbergen, replies 'Our timing's that bad!' It is, of course, Bernard Slade's dialogue quoted here, not a Mirisch insertion, but the presence of such phrases in the screenplay may at the very least have appealed to the brothers and, indeed, rung ironic bells for them. Twenty-five years earlier, in *Man of the West*, Link says to Doc Tobin, 'Lasso is a ghost town and you're a ghost. You've outlived your kind and you've outlived your time.' Being an anachronism was then a characteristic of the antagonist. But by the 1980s, Mirisch protagonists were out of sync, too, if not with each other, then with their times. *Romantic Comedy* was only finally released by UA in 1983 but was unsuccessful at the box office. Marvin Mirisch received executive producer credits on both *Comedy* and *Dracula*.

By 1982, a combination of frustration with executive indecision and lack of relationships with the new MGM management encouraged Mirisch to return to Universal on a three-year contract. *Variety*'s brief report on the move simply noted that 'The company had been largely inactive in recent years'.[33] Indeed in their Universal period, the Mirisches produced far fewer films than at any other time. While Universal stressed sequels as a cinematic strategy, Mirisch focused exclusively on single feature films. It was, instead, in the two previous decades that a counter intuitive commitment to sequels had been a core company strategy for Mirisch. In 1984 Walter Mirisch contributed an article for *Variety* in which he finally admitted, 'The day of assembly line picture making is a thing of the past – probably never to return. Similarly, theater attendance, on a habitual basis, is probably also a thing of the past.'[34]

The few cinema projects which Mirisch developed at Universal in this final period never came to fruition, but the brothers did produce a number of TV movies, through Universal Television, the first of which was *Desperado*, again scripted by Elmore Leonard, and which span off a handful of four further *Desperado* TV movies. The *Desperado* franchise, though not the weekly episodic series which Walter Mirisch had envisaged, comprised *Desperado* (NBC 1987), *Return of Desperado* (NBC 1988), *Desperado: Avalanche at Devil's Ridge* (NBC 1988), *Desperado: Outlaw Wars* (NBC 1989) and *Desperado: Badlands Justice* (NBC 1989). Universal proved particularly keen on sequels. As Ned Tanen, Universal President from 1976–82 said, 'there is less risk in making a sequel than in almost anything else'.[35] Frank Price, who succeeded Tanen from 1983 to 1986 was even more confident. 'We spend millions of dollars to make something unknown into something that is known. A non-sequel starts from zero. A

---

[33] 'Pix Biz Fingers in Lotsa Pies', *Variety*, 13.1.82: 72.
[34] *Daily Variety*, 11.5.84.
[35] 'Hollywood Sequels Are Just the Ticket', *New York Times*, 18.7.82: section 3: 1.

sequel is a guaranteed reward.'[36] And at Universal, the studio was the law. In *Desperado*, the hero tells Yaphet Kotto's character 'You're not the law.' To which Kotto replies, 'The company is the law in this town. I'm the company.' Meanwhile, if a film had no prequel, then at least a successful pretext – play, novel or famous historical event would do.

Walter Mirisch eventually suspended his deal with Universal, to try to make Elmore Leonard's adaptation of his novel, *La Brava*, first for Cannon (with Scorsese lined up to direct and Hoffman to star) but this came to nothing, as did another Poitier project, which Mirisch took to Columbia under David Puttnam, but which was shelved when Puttnam left the studio. Leonard also adapted a novel, *Wild Card*, for Mirisch, but it too was never produced. Alongside a handful of other made-for-television films, Mirisch also received an executive producer credit for a TV series of *The Magnificent Seven* for CBS, which ran for two seasons. A pilot had been commissioned in 1975, but Mirisch had to wait until 1998 for a series, when Universal made a deal with CBS-TV (1998–2000).[37] A movie remake finally followed (Fuqua, 2016), with Walter once again credited as executive producer.

Just as *Same Time, Next Year* had evoked the very decades of Mirisch's UA heyday (from the 1950s to the 1970s) so *Lily in Winter* was set in 1957, the year the company was founded, and told the story of a white child following his Black maid to her family home in Alabama, while his show business parents prove too absorbed in their busy careers to notice. This is a depiction of the south a decade before *In the Heat of the Night*, but produced more than twenty-five years later, and it has none of the (contained) anger or (charismatic) polish of the Poitier vehicle. It is set at Xmas and is more concerned with healing family fissures than racial ones. The father is absent for a film job in Hollywood, while the mother is busy with a part on Broadway. In the end, both parents turn their new jobs down and the missing boy returns to them unscathed, perhaps wiser about families – if not necessarily about the realities of racial segregation. The moral, that family trumps Hollywood, may have been the writing on the wall. Mirisch meanwhile sweated its assets and exploited such properties as were either readily available – like *Dracula* and *Prisoner of Zenda* – or easily renewable, like the TV movie, *Desperado*, which functioned as a pilot for further outings. Mirisch TV Movies were for both the traditional networks and new broadcasters – for instance, *The Desperado* films and *Trouble Shooters: Trapped Beneath the Earth* (1993) were for NBC, while *Tagget* (1990) and *Lily in Winter* (1994) were for the USA network.

There was, perhaps necessarily, a new clarity about Mirisch's strategy, with exclusively major projects (star-led theatrical and literary adaptations, or historical reconstructions) aimed at the cinema – *Midway, Dracula, Same Time, Next Year, Prisoner of Zenda*, while lower-budgeted productions were made for the small screen – *Desperado, Lily in Winter, A Case For Life* (ABC, 1995), ideally in the form of series, like those spun off from *The Pink Panther* for NBC and ABC. While the feature films were often 'presold' or risk-averse, in the sense that their sources were classics, Broadway hits, or historical events with instant name-recognition (like *The Battle of Midway*).

---

[36] 'The Sequel Becomes the New Bankable Film Star', *New York Times*, 8.7.85: C15.
[37] 'Walter Mirisch, U-TV Will Pilot Seven' For CBS', *Daily Variety*, 24.12.75: 1.

For Mirisch, the resulting film was a fitting tribute both to the Bicentennial and a 'good war', in contrast to Vietnam, which proved so divisive. 'Mirisch thought that Midway rode the wave of nostalgia then in evidence in the United States.'[38] If so, that diagnosis might also explain the greenlighting of such anachronistic projects as *Dracula* and *Prisoner of Zenda* as well as the explicit nostalgia of *Same Time, Next Year* and *Lily in Winter*. Moreover, Mirisch's previous cinematic strategy of dramatizing primarily American social issues became an almost exclusively television tactic – so that *Lily in Winter* depicts segregation in the south, while *A Case for Life* dramatizes the conflict over abortion, telling the story of two sisters with radically opposing views, whose private lives get entangled in the issue. The feature films, on the other hand, became much less topical (indeed four of those six final features were set in the past), more focused on being entertaining and internationally accessible.

As for globalization, Mirisch projects were increasingly selected for their international name-recognition – both in terms of IP and the global fame and familiarity of their casts. But where there was a global marketplace there were also international locations, with the potential budgetary savings which lower local salaries and cheaper facilities still promised, though not always delivered. Both *Prisoner of Zenda* and *Dracula* were shot entirely on location in Europe, though a combination of star behaviour and changing industrial relations respectively may have reduced or indeed negated any such economies.

Mirisch opted for either veteran film or, more often, established TV directors for most of its final feature film projects. Half the directors Mirisch hired, in this period, were either recently promoted from television, like Jack Smight for *Midway* (another veteran of the Army Air Force) and David Greene for *Gray Lady Down*, or had been largely relegated to it, like Richard Quine. Meanwhile, the three Broadway hits were allocated to slightly more elevated, mid-ranking talents – *Same Time, Next Year* was directed by Robert Mulligan, *Dracula* by John Badham and *Romantic Comedy* by Arthur Hiller. Loyalty to long-time collaborators is admirable, but employing the 85-year-old Ralph Winters to co-edit a TV movie in 1994, *Lily in Winter*, which Delbert Mann (who had helmed *Fitzwilly*) was brought out of retirement to direct, was perhaps generous to a fault. The descent from Anthony Mann to Delbert Mann, reveals a great deal about the decline in Mirisch's industry status in the Universal years. *Desperado* (NBC, 1987) was directed by Virgil W. Vogel, *Trouble Shooters: Trapped Beneath the Earth* by Bradford May and *A Case For Life* by Eric Leneuville (the first Black director Mirisch ever employed). By 1996 Walter was seventy-five, while Marvin, at seventy-eight, had already retired. The brothers never hired a female director.

Bridal Wave (Hallmark, 2015) the most recent 'original' film for which Walter Mirisch received an executive producer credit, is a romcom about a nurse having cold feet on the eve of her wedding to the plastic surgeon for whom she works. Plastic surgery, of course, had been touched on in two previous Mirisch productions, the pilot for a *Some Like It Hot* series and the feature, *Return from the Ashes*. In this case it is

---

[38] Suid, 2002: 304.

partly the corporate 'nuptial package' which the couple have booked for their wedding which puts the bride-to-be off the ceremony. When the heroine, Georgie, points out to her fiancé, 'The incredible wedding garden view, where we can watch complete strangers get married from dawn til dusk', she is identifying a virtual assembly line of marriages. Indeed, as her meet-cute new boyfriend, Luke, who lives next door, points out '4 weddings a day, 365 days a year . . . an assembly line for brides'. To which Georgie replies, 'Well, I see four nose jobs a day, that's 1040 noses a year'. The way in which both professional and personal lives have been subsumed into a Taylorized world is all too visible and audible when the mother-in-law to be admits her late husband gave her 'a lifestyle lift'. There are the slightest of echoes of *The Apartment*'s social critique in this Hallmark film.

Indecision about whether to aim for cost leadership or product differentiation, Porter's diagnosis of a declining company, was not entirely the case as far as Mirisch was concerned, as the six feature films in its final years were based on mostly well-known, presold stories and boasted major stars, if not major directors. The company's less expensive output, meanwhile, was aimed at the small screen, without such stars and the biggest television hits were *The Pink Panther* series and the *Desperado* TV movies. Furthermore, the culture of the Mirisch Company meant certain predilections (history, the stage, social issues), genres (the services, Westerns, comedy), talent (from industry rather than film school, past collaborations rather than recent discoveries) and tastes and traditions were followed, but also that one project could still lead to another – if not through sequels, then through relationships as well as strategic priorities, personal preferences and corporate propensities.

11

Conclusion – Cast a giant shadow

> Vin: Reminds me of a fellah back home who fell off a ten-storey building. . . . As he was falling, people on each floor kept hearing him saying, 'So far, so good'.
> *The Magnificent Seven* (1960)

If the final few films the Mirisches produced prove less memorable than many of their predecessors, the cinema of the early twenty-first century remains marked by the impact of Mirisch output, almost half a century after the United Artists deal ended. Indeed, if many of the company's films were, in Tarantino's words, 'entertaining if unmemorable potboilers:', a dozen or more are unforgettable classics.[1] Moreover there are plots, characters, lines of dialogue, scenes, shots and theme tunes to sustain a *Precious Moments* of exclusively Mirisch material. The Mirisch recipe was for repetition and difference, a sequence alternating highly differentiated and distinctive movies with minimally differentiated, standardized ones. Of course, some of those expected to be memorable turned out to be entirely forgettable, or to be remembered for all the wrong reasons, while other, often generic, offerings, made in the expectation that they would be swiftly forgotten, have proved to be uniquely unforgettable. Who today remembers *The Hallelujah Trail* with its self-important intermission, and mirthless comic interludes, or the interminable *Hawaii* and *The Hawaiians*, with much affection? But a much shorter Western, *Man of the West*, dwarfs most others from the era, and a much less garlanded adaptation, *The Landlord,* rivals the best of 1970s cinema.

The Mirisch Company punched above its weight and its films continue to exercise a remarkable grip on and influence over our culture. And this apparent timelessness isn't only at the level of plot, character or indeed title but also includes iconography and dialogue. Even Vin's line, quoted earlier, for instance, is reprised a number of times in *La Haine* (Kassovitz, 1995). The eve of the millennium remake of *The Thomas Crown Affair* (1999), initiated a period of rediscovery of the viability and versatility of Mirisch properties. That same year, Steven Soderbergh's *The Limey* was released and Soderbergh himself has cited Mirisch's *In the Heat of the Night* sequel, *The Organization*, as a key influence

---

[1] Tarantino, 2021: 113.

on the film.² In 2001 Baz Luhrman's *Moulin Rouge* simultaneously reimagined Lautrec's and Huston's Parisian nightclub. Nor was Luhrman a stranger to such reinventions, as his *William Shakespeare's Romeo and Juliet*'s (1996) contemporary setting and urban gang conflict, reprised that of *West Side Story*.

More recently *The Pink Panther* (Levy, 2006) and *Pink Panther 2* (Zwart, 2009) starring Steve Martin, and *The Magnificent Seven* (2016) starring Denzel Washington, are further evidence of an apparently insatiable appetite for remaking Mirisch classics – an entirely appropriate development, given the company's own attitude to and aptitude for adaptations and remakes (of both Warner classics and world cinema). In 2014 Hubert Monteilhet's novel, *Le retour des cendres*, the basis of *Return from the Ashes*, was adapted again, as *Phoenix* (Petzold, 2014). More recently, the huge success of *The Haunting of Hill House* (Netflix, 2018) proved that the Mirisches were right to acquire the novel, if perhaps wrong to let Robert Wise ultimately make it independently, as *The Haunting*, although the film was not a commercial success at the time.

In 2019, Roland Emmerich's remake of Mirisch's *Midway*, or, more accurately, retelling of the story of that battle, with the same title, starring Woody Harrelson, was released. But another film that year was far more explicit about its ancestry. *Once Upon a Time... in Hollywood* (Tarantino, 2019) interweaves its own fiction with pre-existing fictions made in – and historical facts about – Hollywood in 1969. And the movie world it references is precisely that period of the Mirisch's final deal with United Artists. At one point in the film, we hear that the fictional actor, Rick Dalton (played by Leonardo DiCaprio), was considered for the role of Captain Virgil Hilts in *The Great Escape*, a part actually played by Steve McQueen. (McQueen himself is played by Damian Lewis in Tarantino's movie.) The film even includes digitally altered footage from *The Great Escape* in which 'Dalton' rather than McQueen, plays Hilts. This is the dialogue which cues that sequence:

> Jim Stacy: Hey, Rick, I gotta ask you something I heard about. Was it true you almost got the McQueen part in The Great Escape?
> Dalton: Never had an audition, never had a meeting, never met John Sturges, so, no, I don't think you could say I almost got the part. But the story goes, for a brief moment, McQueen almost passed on the movie, and in that brief moment I think I was on a list of four.
> Stacy: You and who?
> Dalton: Me and the three Georges
> Stacy: Which three Georges?
> Dalton: Peppard, Maharis and Chakiris
> Stacy: Oh man, that's got to hurt.
> Dalton: Yeah, well, I didn't get it. McQueen did it. And frankly I never had a chance. (Figure 14)

---

² Mark Gallagher, 'Discerning Independents: Steven Soderbergh', in Geoff King, Claire Molloy and Yannis Tzioumakis (eds), *American Independent Cinema: Indie, Indiewood and Beyond*, Routledge, 2013, 91.

Figure 14 Leonardo DiCaprio as 'Rick Dalton' as *The Great Escape*'s 'Hilts', in *Once Upon a Time . . . in Hollywood*.

According to Tarantino's film, then, 'Dalton' was up against George Peppard (star of Mirisch's *Cannon for Cordoba*, which was filming that very summer, 1969), George Maharis (star of Mirisch's *The Satan Bug*) and George Chakiris (Oscar-winning co-star of Mirisch's *West Side Story* as well as co-star of *633 Squadron*).

Once Upon a Time . . . in Hollywood also references spaghetti Westerns, not only in the fictional Corbucci film that Leonardo DiCaprio's Dalton goes to Europe to perform in, but also in the title of Tarantino's film itself, a riff on Leone's *Once Upon a Time in the West* (Leone, 1968) and *Once Upon a Time in America* (Leone, 1984). And, of course, Leone's spaghetti Westerns themselves featured three of *The Magnificent Seven*'s stars – Eli Wallach in *The Good, The Bad and the Ugly* (1966) James Coburn in *Duck, You Sucker* (1971) and Charles Bronson in *Once Upon a Time in the West* itself. Tarantino's previous film, *The Hateful Eight* (2015), meanwhile, contains an implicit reference to – or echo of – *The Magnificent Seven* in its very title. Furthermore, the writer-director first name-checked *The Great Escape* in *Reservoir Dogs* (1992) when Mr Brown remarks, 'This cat is like Charles Bronson in The Great Escape, he's digging tunnels'.[3] *Once Upon a Time . . . in Hollywood* was so successful at the box office that it proved to be the highest earning movie of its year that was neither a remake, a sequel nor a franchise film. In that sense, if nothing else, it is thus also an ironic echo of the differentiated one-offs that were the exception to the rule of standardized Mirisch productions.

In 2021, Walter Mirisch's hundredth year, Steven Spielberg's new film version of *West Side Story* was released and a new musical adaptation of *Some Like It Hot* was due to open on Broadway. A live action/CGI version of *The Pink Panther* is currently in development, to be directed by *Sonic the Hedgehog*'s Jeff Fowler.[4] Walter Mirisch is listed as an Executive Producer. On 28 May 2020, it was also announced that MGM

---

[3] Tarantino has also acknowledged that the torture scene in *Reservoir Dogs* was influenced by Allied Artists' *The Big Combo*, made while Walter Mirisch was AA's head of production.
[4] *Deadline*, 19.11.2020: 1.

and producers Dan Jinks and Aaron Harnick will remake *Fiddler on the Roof*, with Thomas Kail – known for his work on *Hamilton* (2020) and *Fosse/Verdon (FX, 2019)* directing.[5] In 2022, *Blonde* (Dominik, 2022) a fictional Monroe biopic, based on Joyce Carol Oates' novel, includes the story of the making of *Some Like It Hot*, with actors playing Wilder and Curtis alongside Ana De Armas's Marilyn. The same year, a feature-length documentary, *Sidney*, (Hudlin, 2022) about the life and work of Sidney Poitier, includes a detailed discussion of *In the Heat of the Night*, without mentioning the Mirisch brothers or their company.

The Mirisch Company represents a transitional phase, both industrially and cinematically, in Hollywood history. At their best Mirisch films were transformative, in terms of subject matter and approach. Think, for instance, of how *Man of the West* punctuated the end of one era of the Western and *The Magnificent Seven* initiated another. Or how *Some Like It Hot* proved an elegant apotheosis of – but also epigraph to – studio-era comedy, indeed, in a sense, classical genre cinema itself. And occasionally these films included transgressive representations, of gender (*Some Like It Hot*), of sex and sexuality (*The Children's Hour, Town Without Pity, Kiss Me, Stupid*), of race (*In the Heat of the Night, West Side Story, The Landlord*), of work (*The Apartment*) and even of America itself (*West Side Story* again, *Hawaii* and *The Hawaiians*).

But if Mirisch helped rewrite the rulebook of what could appear on-screen in Hollywood, it also revised the rubric of how Hollywood films were made, deploying franchises, foreign filmmaking, the freeing of frozen funds, freelance crews and casts, co-productions, adaptations, cycles and series, promotional stunts and saturation release strategies.[6] Indeed, the Mirisch Company proved itself transformative in its business structures and strategies as a transnational, transmedia independent, in its pioneering attitudes to IP and the package-unit system of production, all of which in turn accelerated changes in the way Hollywood as a whole operated. The Mirisch Company was thus a bridge between the continuity of production of the studio system (through UA's commitment to four films a year) and the film-by-film, deal by deal modus operandi necessitated by the package-unit system.

The brothers' professional experience before they set up their own company, was of film factories whose production processes approximated Fordist assembly lines as closely as film making could and reinforced the Fordist and Taylorist principles Walter had imbibed at Harvard and implemented at Lockheed, while minimizing overheads and labour costs. Their subsequent career, packaging individual film projects with a minimum permanent staff and almost exclusively freelance labour, epitomized post-Fordism. Mirisch was, then, a transitional company, a halfway house between the studio era's vertical integration and the post-Paramount Decree outsourcing and – albeit relative – independence of their output deal, as an independent producer,

---

[5] https://variety.com/2020/film/news/fiddler-on-the-roof-hamilton-director-mgm-1234619064/
[6] That the company pioneered, or helped pioneer, promotional featurettes, or 'making-ofs' is particularly pertinent to the present writer, since his own introduction to Mirisch was producing a pair of television documentaries about the making of two of the company's classics, *The Magnificent Seven* and *Some Like It Hot*.

with United Artists, and the company survived by combining residual Fordist with emergent post-Fordist strategies. Series and cycle production proved one profitable way of reconciling those two imperatives, just as adaptation, runaway production, subsidies and subsidiaries, were strategies for squaring that cinematic circle.

This then is a company *and* a filmography, as these recent references and remakes reveal, ripe for rediscovery. Even a lesser film, like *The Satan Bug*, set in a laboratory developing biological weapons, and a new virus, felt newly relevant during the pandemic. And that same pandemic made something as quotidian as office work the subject of intense discussion – breathing new life into the already evergreen *The Apartment*. Meanwhile, today's gig economy rewires *Some Like It Hot*, Black Lives Matter re-radicalizes *In the Heat of the Night* and *The Landlord*, and the 'me too' movement reignites *Town Without Pity*, giving both classics and non-classics alike renewed currency.

Finally, it is worth repeating that the 'efficient' film which kick-started the Mirisch Second World War cycle, *633 Squadron*, helped inspire the 'trench run' sequence in *Star Wars*, which was perhaps the movie, more than any other, that launched the franchise film culture so characteristic of today's Hollywood. More recently the same sequence inspired an equally iconic, beneath the radar, between perilous mountain ridges raid in *Top Gun: Maverick* (Kosinski, 2022).[7] For Mirisch, meanwhile, *633* provided not just an iconographic but also an industrial blueprint for an emergent cinema and industry that could, albeit briefly, square the circle of post-Fordist, one-off package-unit production with residual Fordism's continuous mass production and mass consumption cycle. And of course, *Star Wars,* in turn, did much to initiate the blockbuster era that helped bankroll the vertically re-integrated film industry of twenty-first-century Hollywood. By the early 21st century, mainstream adaptations included fantasy fiction like the *Harry Potter* and *Lord of the Rings* franchises. Similarly, sequels and series films, far from being characteristically programme pictures, as had been the case with Mirisch, were often big budget blockbusters, increasingly based not on bestsellers but on Marvel comics and featuring not the recognisably human, decent people of many Mirisch movies, but superheroes. Hollywood cinema seems currently to be on the run from the social realism of the Mirisch era. The Mirisch Company provided a missing link between those two periods, the end of the vertically integrated studio era and the multimedia conglomerates of today and left its corporate fingerprints on all the films it made not just as strategic decisions but also as cinematic choices. For all those reasons, it is well worth remembering. That so many Mirisch films do still hold a special place in our collective memories is evidenced, at least in the UK, by the scheduling of *Some Like it Hot* on Xmas Day 2022 on BBC2, *The Great Escape* on Channel 4 that same day, *The Magnificent Seven* on Boxing Day on BBC2 and West Side Story on New Year's Eve also on BBC2.

---

[7] Of course, in *Top Gun: Maverick,* not only were there no fictional fatalities among the pilots, some of the mountain sequences were CGI. This is a long way, cinematically, from a squadron being 'probably all dead' and stunt sequences despite also including model shots.

Mirisch Company filmography

Fort Massacre (14 May 1958)
Director: Joseph M. Newman; Producer: Walter M. Mirisch; Screenplay: Martin M. Goldsmith; Cast: Joel McCrea, Forrest Tucker, Susan Cabot, John Russell, George N. Neise. 80 min; colour by De Luxe; Cinemascope; presented by The Mirisch Company, Inc; Distributor: United Artists

Man of the West (1 October 1958)
Director: Anthony Mann; Producer: Walter M. Mirisch; Screenplay: Reginald Rose, based on the novel The Border Jumpers by Will C. Brown; Cast: Gary Cooper, Julie London, Lee J. Cobb, Arthur O'Connell, Jack Lord; 100 min; colour by De Luxe; Cinemascope; presented by Ashton Productions, Inc, in association with The Mirisch Company, Inc; Distributor: United Artists

Some Like It Hot (29 March 1959)
Director: Billy Wilder; Producer: Walter M. Mirisch; Screenplay: Billy Wilder and I. A. L. Diamond, suggested by a story by R. Thoeren and M. Logan; Cast: Marilyn Monroe, Tony Curtis, Jack Lemmon, George Raft, Pat O'Brian, Joe E. Brown; 120 min; b&w; Ashton Productions, Inc., presents a Mirisch Company Picture; Distributor: United Artists
Six Academy Award nominations; one Academy Award

The Man in the Net (20 May 1959)
Director: Michael Curtiz, Producer: Walter M. Mirisch; Screenplay: Reginald Rose, based on the novel by Patrick Quentin; Cast: Alan Ladd, Carolyn Jones; 96 min; b&w; presented by The Mirisch Company; Distributor: United Artists

The Gunfight at Dodge City (20 May 1959)
Director: Joseph M. Newman; Producer: Walter M. Mirisch; Screenplay: Martin M. Goldsmith, Daniel B. Ullman; Cast: Joel McCrea, Julie Adams, John McIntire, Nancy Gates; 80 min; colour by De Luxe; Cinemascope; presented by The Mirisch Company, Inc., Distributor: United Artists

The Horse Soldiers (12 June 1959)
Director: John Ford; a Mahin-Rackin Production; Screenplay by John Lee Mahin and Martin Rackin, based on the novel by Harold Sinclair; Cast: John Wayne, William Holden, Constance Towers, Althea Gibson; 119 min; colour by De Luxe; presented by The Mirisch Company, Inc; distributor: United Artists

Cast a Long Shadow (July 1959)
Director: Thomas Carr; Producer: Walter M. Mirisch; Screenplay: Martin M. Goldsmith, John McGreevey; Screen Story: Martin M. Goldsmith, based on the novel by Wayne B. Overholser; Cast: Audie Murphy, Terry Moore, John Dehner; 82 min; b&w; presented by The Mirisch Company, Inc; Distributor: United Artists

The Apartment (15 June 1960)
Director: Billy Wilder; Producer: Billy Wilder; Screenplay: Billy Wilder, I. A. L. Diamond; Cast: Jack Lemmon, Shirley MacLaine, Fred MacMurray; 125 min; b&w; Panavision; presented by The Mirisch Company, Inc; Distributor: United Artists
Ten Academy Award nominations; five Academy Awards, including Best Picture

The Magnificent Seven (23 October 1960)
Director: John Sturges; Producer: John Sturges; Executive Producer: Walter Mirisch; Screenplay: William Roberts, based on the Akira Kurosawa film, Seven Samurai, Toho Company Ltd.; Cast: Yul Brynner, Eli Wallach, Steve McQueen, Charles Bronson, Robert Vaughn, Brad Dexter, James Coburn, Horst Buchholz; 128 min; colour by De Luxe; Panavision; presented by The Mirisch Company; Distributor: United Artists
One Academy Award nomination

By Love Possessed (15 June 1961)
Director: John Sturges; Producer: Walter Mirisch; Screenplay: John Dennis, based on the novel by James Gould Cozzens; Cast: Lana Turner, Efrem Zimbalist Jr, Jason Robards, Jr; 115 min; colour by De Luxe; presented by Mirisch Pictures, Inc., in association with Seven Arts Productions, Inc.; Distributor: United Artists

Town Without Pity (10 October 1961)
Director: Gottfried Reinghardt; Producer: Gottfried Reinhardt; Screenplay: Silvia Reinhardt, Georg(e) Hurdalek; Adaptation: Jan Lustig, based on the novel, The Verdict, by Manfred Gregor; Cast: Kirk Douglas, E. G. Marshall, Robert Blake, Richard Jaeckel, Frank Sutton, Barbara Rutting, Christine Kauffmann; 103 min; presented by The Mirisch Company in Association with Osweg Ltd., Switzerland; Distributor: United Artists
One Academy Award nomination

West Side Story (18 October 1961)
Director: Robert Wise, Jerome Robbins; Producer: Robert Wise; Screenplay: Ernest Lehman, based on the play by Arthur Laurents; Cast: Natalie Wood, Richard Beymer, Russ Tamblyn, Rita Moreno, George Chakiris; 152 min; Technicolour;

Panavision 70 mm; presented by Mirisch Pictures Inc., in association with Seven Arts Productions, Inc.; Distributor: United Artists

Eleven Academy Award nominations; ten Academy Awards, including Best Picture

One, Two, Three (15 December 1961)
Director: Billy Wilder; Producer: Billy Wilder; Screenplay: Billy Wilder and I. A. L. Diamond, based on the play Eins, Zwei, Drei by Ferenc Molnar; Cast: James Cagney, Horst Buchholz, Pamela Tiffin, Arlene Francis; 108 min; b&w; Panavision; presented by The Mirisch Company; Distributor: United Artists

One Academy Award nomination

The Children's Hour (19 December 1961)
Director: William Wyler; Producer: William Wyler; Screenplay: John Michael Hayes, based on the play by Lillian Hellman; Cast: Audrey Hepburn, Shirley MacLaine, James Garner; 107 min; b&w; presented by The Mirisch Company; Distributor: United Artists

Five Academy Award nominations

Follow That Dream (11 April 1962)
Director: Gordon Douglas; Producer: David Weisbart; Screenplay: Charles Lederer, based on the novel, Pioneer Go Home by Richard Powell; Cast: Elvis Presley, Arthur O'Connell, Anne Halm, Joanna Moore; 109 min; colour by De Luxe; Panavision; presented by The Mirisch Company; Distributor: United Artists

Kid Galahad (1 August 1962)
Director: Phil Karlson; Producer: David Weisbart; Screenplay: William Fay; Story: Francis Wallace; Cast: Elvis Presley, Gig Young, Lola Albright, Joan Blackman, Charles Bronson; 95 min; colour by De Luxe; presented by The Mirisch Company; Distributor: United Artists

Two for the See Saw (21 November 1962)
Director: Robert Wise; Producer: Walter Mirisch; Screenplay: Isobel Lennart, based on the play by William Gibson; Cast: Robert Mitchum, Shirley MacLaine; 119 min; b&w; Panavision; presented by Mirisch Pictures and Robert Wise in association with Seven Arts Productions, Inc.; Distributor: United Artists

Two Academy Award nominations

Irma La Douce (5 June 1963)
Director: Billy Wilder; Producer: Billy Wilder; Screenplay: Billy Wilder and I. A. L. Diamond, based on the play by Alexandre Breffort; Cast: Jack Lemmon, Shirley MacLaine; 143 min; Technicolour; Panavision; presented by The Mirisch Company and Edward L. Alperson; Distributor: United Artists

One Academy Award nomination

The Great Escape (4 July 1963)
Director: John Sturges; Producer: John Sturges; Screenplay: James Clavell and W. R. Burnett, based on the book by Paul Brickhill; Cast: Steve McQueen, James Garner, Richard Attenborough, James Donald, Charles Bronson, Donald Pleasance, James Coburn; 172 min; colour by De Luxe; Panavision; presented by The Mirisch Company, Inc.; Distributor: United Artists
One Academy Award nomination

Toys in the Attic (17 July 1963)
Director: George Roy Hill; Producer: Walter Mirisch; Screenplay: James Poe, based on the play by Lillian Hellman; Cast: Dean Martin, Geraldine Page, Yvette Mimieux, Wendy Hiller, Gene Tierney, Nan Martin, Larry Gates; 90 min; b&w' Panavision; presented by The Mirisch Corporation; Distributor: United Artists
One Academy Award nomination

Stolen Hours (2 October 1963)
Director: Daniel M. Petrie; Producer: Denis Holt; Executive Producer: Stuart Millar, Lawrence Turman; Screenplay: Jessamyn West; Cast: Susan Hayward, Michael Craig; Diane Baker, Edward Judd; 100 min; colour by De Luxe; presented by Mirisch Films and Barbican Films; Distributor: United Artists

Kings of the Sun (18 December 1963)
Director: J. Lee Thompson; Producer: Lewis J. Rachmil; Screenplay: Elliott Arnold, James R. Webb, story by Elliott Arnold; Cast: Yul Brynner, George Chakiris, Shirley Anne Field; 108 min; colour by De Luxe; Panavision; presented by The Mirisch Company; Distributor: United Artists

The Pink Panther (28 March 1964)
Director: Blake Edwards; Producer: Blake Edwards; Screenplay: Maurice Richlin, Blake Edwards; Cast: David Niven, Peter Sellers, Robert Wagner, Capucine; 114 min; Technicolour; Technirama; presented by The Mirisch Company
One Academy Award nomination

633 Squadron (22 June 1964)
Director: Walter E. Graumann; Producer: Cecil B. Ford; Executive Producer: Lewis J. Rachmil; Screenplay: James Clavell and Howard Koch, based on the novel by Frederick F. Smith; Cast: Cliff Robertson, George Chakiris, Maria Perschy, Harry Andrews, Donald Houston; 95 min; colour by De Luxe; Panavision; presented by The Mirisch Corporation; Distributor: United Artists

A Shot in the Dark (15 July 1964)
Director: Blake Edwards; Producer: Blake Edwards; Screenplay: Blake Edwards ad William Peter Blatty, based on characters created by Maurice Richlin and Blake Edwards, based on the stage play by Harry Kurnitz, from the play by

Marcel Achard; Cast: Peter Sellers, Elke Sommer, George Sanders, Herbert Lom; 101 min; colour by De Luxe; Panavision; presented by The Mirisch Corporation; Distributor: United Artists

Kiss Me, Stupid (16 December 1964)
Director: Billy Wilder; Producer: Billy Wilder; Screenplay: Billy Wilder and I. A. L. Diamond, based on the play L'Ora della Fantasia by Anna Bonacci; Cast: Dean Martin, Kim Novak, Ray Walston, Felicia Farr; 126 min; b&w; Panavision; presented by The Mirisch Corporation; Distributor: Lopert Pictures Corporation

The Pink Phink (18 December 1964)
Producer: David H. De-Patie, Fritz Freleng; Director: Fritz Freleng, Hawley Pratt; Story: John Dunn; colour by De Luxe; a Mirisch-Geoffrey-DePatie-Freleng Production; Distributor: United Artists
One Academy Award (a complete list of Pink Panther cartoons released to cinemas by United Artists is available in *Pink Panther: The Ultimate Guide to the Coolest Cat in Town!*, Jerry Beck, Dorling Kindersley, 2005)

The Satan Bug (23 March 1965)
Director: John Sturges; Producer: John Sturges; Screenplay: James Clavell and Edward Anhalt, based on the novel by Ian Stuart; Cast: George Maharis, Richard Basehart, Anne Francis, Dana Andrews; 114 min; colour by De Luxe; Panavision; presented by The Mirisch Corporation; Distributor: United Artists

The Pink Blueprint (25 May 1965)
Director: Haley Pratt; Producer: David H. DePatie, Fritz Frelang; Story: John Dunn; colour by De Luxe; a Mirisch-Geoffrey-DePatie-Freleng Production; Distributor: United Artists
One Academy Award nomination

The Hallelujah Trail (23 June 1965)
Director: John Sturges; Producer: John Sturges; Screenplay: John Gay, based on the novel by Bill Gulick; Cast: Burt Lancaster, Lee Remick, Jim Hutton, Pamela Tiffin, Donald Pleasance, Brian Keith; 165 min; Technicolor; Ultra Panavision; presented by The Mirisch Corporation; Distributor: United Artists

A Rage to Live (15 September 1965)
Director: Walter E. Graumann; Producer: Lewis J. Rachmil; Screenplay: John T. Kelley, based on the novel by John O'Hara; Cast: Suzanne Pleshette, Bradford Dillman, Ben Gazzara, Peter Graves; 1012 min; b&w; Panavision; presented by The Mirisch Corporation; Distributor: United Artists
One Academy Award nomination

Return from the Ashes (16 November 1965)
Director: J. Lee Thompson; Producer: J. Lee Thompson; Screenplay: Julius J. Epstein, based on the novel by Hubert Monteilhet; Cast: Maximilian Schell, Samantha Eggar, Ingrid Thulin, Herbert Lom; 105 min; b&w; Panavision; presented by The Mirisch Corporation; Distributor: United Artists

Cast a Giant Shadow (30 March 1966)
Director: Melville Shavelson; Producer: Melville Shavelson; Screenplay: Melville Shavelson, based on the novel by Ted Berkman; Cast: Kirk Douglas, Senta Berger, Angie Dickinson, James Donald, Topol, with special appearances by Frank Sinatra, Yul Brynner, John Wayne; 138 min; colour by De Luxe; presented by The Mirisch Corporation; Distributor: United Artists

The Russians Are Coming, The Russians Are Coming (25 May 1966)
Director: Norman Jewison; Producer: Norman Jewison; Screenplay: William Rose, based on the novel The Off Islanders by Nathaniel Benchley; Cast: Carl Reiner, Eva Marie Saint, Alan Arkin, Brian Keith, Jonathan Winters, Theodore Bikel, John Phillip Law; 126 min; colour by De Luxe; Panavision; presented by The Mirisch Corporation; Distributor: United Artists
Four Academy Award nominations

What Did You Do in the War, Daddy? (29 June 1966)
Director: Blake Edwards; Producer: Blake Edwards; Screenplay: William Peter Blatty; Story: Blake Edwards, Maurice Richlin; Cast: James Coburn, Dick Shawn; 116 min; colour by De Luxe; Panavision; presented by The Mirisch Corporation; Distributor: United Artists

Hawaii (10 October 1966)
Director: George Roy Hill; Producer: Walter Mirisch; Screenplay: Dalton Trumbo and Daniel Taradash, based on the novel by James A. Michener; Cast: Julie Andrews, Max Von Sydow, Richard Harris, Gene Hackman; 189 min; colour by De Luxe; Panavision; presented by The Mirisch Corporation; Distributor: United Artists
Seven Academy Award nominations

The Fortune Cookie (19 October 1966)
Director: Billy Wilder; Producer: Billy Wilder; Screenplay: Billy Wilder and I. A. L. Diamond; Cast: Jack Lemmon, Walter Matthau, Ron Rich, Judi West; 125 min; b&w; presented by The Mirisch Corporation; Distributor: United Artists
Four Academy Award nominations, one Academy Award

The Return of the Seven (19 October 1966)
Director: Burt Kennedy; Producer: Ted Richman; Screenplay: Larry Cohen; Cast: Yul Brynner, Robert Fuller, Julian Mateos, Warren Oates, Claude Akins, Jordan Christopher; 95 min; colour by De Luxe; Panavision; presented by the Mirisch

Productions, Inc in Association with CB Films, S.A. Spain; Distributor: United Artists

How to Succeed in Business Without Really Trying (9 March 1967)
Director: David Swift; Producer: David Swift; Screenplay: David Swift, based on the book by Abe Burrows, Jack Weinstock and Willie Gilbert, based on the novel by Shepherd Mead; cast: Robert Morse, Michele Lee, Rudy Vallee; 121 min; colour by De Luxe; Panavision; presented by The Mirisch Corporation; Distributor: United Artists

In the Heat of the Night (2 August 1967)
Director: Norman Jewison; Producer: Walter Mirisch; Screenplay: Stirling Silliphant, based on the novel by John Ball; Cast: Sidney Poitier, Rod Steiger, Warren Oates, Lee Grant, Larry Gates, Scott Wilson, William Schallert; 109 min; colour by De Luxe; presented by The Mirisch Corporation; Distributor: United Artists
Seven Academy Award nominations; five Academy Awards, including Best Picture

Hour of the Gun (11 October 1967)
Director: John Sturges; Producer: John Sturges; Screenplay: Edward Anhalt; Cast: James Garner, Jason Robards, Robert Ryan, Larry Gates, William Schallert; 101 min; colour by De Luxe; Panavision; presented by The Mirisch Corporation; Distributor: United Artists

Fitzwilly (20 December 1967)
Director: Delbert Mann; Producer: Walter Mirisch; Screenplay: Isobel Lennart, based on the novel, A Garden of Cucumbers by Poyntz Tyler; Cast: Dick Van Dyke, Barbara Feldon, John McGiver, Edith Evans; 102 min; colour by De Luxe; Panavision; presented by The Mirisch Corporation; Distributor: United Artists

Attack on the Iron Coast (March 1968)
Director: Paul Wendkos; Producer: John C. Champion; Screenplay: Herman Hoffman; Story: John C. Champion; Cast: Lloyd Bridges, Andew Keir, Sue Lloyd; 89 min; colour by De Luxe; presented by Mirisch Films; Distributor: United Artists

The Party (4 April 1968)
Director: Blake Edwards; Producer: Blake Edwards; Screenplay: Blake Edwards, Tom Waldman, Frank Waldman; Story: Blake Edwards; Cast: Peter Sellers, Claudine Longet, Marge Champion, Steve Franklen; 95 min; colour by De Luxe; Panavision; presented by The Mirisch Corporation; Distributor: United Artists

Inspector Clouseau (28 May 1968)
Director: Bud Yorkin; Producer: Lewis J. Rachmil; Screenplay: Tom Waldman, Frank Waldman, based on characters created by Maurice Richlin and Blake Edwards; Cast: Alan Arkin, Frank Finlay; 94 min; colour by De Luxe; Panavision; presented by The Mirisch Corporation; Distributor: United Artists

The Thomas Crown Affair (26 June 1968)
Director: Norman Jewison; Producer: Norman Jewison; Screenplay: Allan R. Trustman; Cast: Steve McQueen, Faye Dunaway, Paul Burke; 102 min; colour by De Luxe; presented by The Mirisch Corporation; Distributor: United Artists
One Academy Award nomination

Massacre Harbor (1968)
Director: John Peyser; Producer: Fred Lemoine; Story: John Peyser; Screenplay: Richard H. Landau; Cast: Christopher George, Gary Raymond, Claudine Longet; 81 min; colour by De Luxe; Mirisch-Rich Productions; Distributor: United Artists (repackaged compilation of three Rat Patrol episodes entitled The Last Harbor Raid)

The First Time (April 1969)
Director: James Neilson; Producer: Roger Smith, Allan Carr; Screenplay: Jo Heims, Roger Smith; Story: Bernard Bassey; cast: Jacqueline Bisset, Wes Stern, Rick Kelman, Wink Roberts; 90 min; colour by De Luxe; presented by The Mirisch Production Company; Distributor: United Artists

Sinful Davey (28 May 1969)
Director: John Huston; Producer: William N. Graf; Executive Producer: Walter Mirisch; Screenplay: James R. Webb; Cast: John Hurt, Pamela Franklin, Nigel Davenport, Ronald Fraser, Robert Morley; 95 min; colour by De Luxe; Panavision; presented by The Mirisch Corporation; Distributor: United Artists

Guns of the Magnificent Seven (28 May 1969)
Director: Paul Wendkos; Producer: Vincent M. Fennelly; Screenplay: Herman Hoffman; Cast: George Kennedy, James Whitmore, Monte Markham, Remi Santoni, Bernie Casey, Scott Thomas, Joe Don Baker; 106 min; colour by De Luxe; Panavision; presented by The Mirisch Production Company; Distributor: United Artists

Submarine X-1 (30 July 1969)
Director: William Graham; Producer: John C. Champion; Screenplay: Donald S. Sanford, Guy Elmes; Story: John C. Champion, Edmund North; Cast: James Caan, David Summer; 89 min; colour by De Luxe; presented by Mirisch Films; Distributor: United Artists

Some Kind of a Nut (25 September 1969)
Director: Garson Kanin; Producer: Walter Mirisch; Screenplay: Garson Kanin; Cast: Dick Van Dyke, Angie Dickinson, Rosemary Forsythe; 89 min; colour by De Luxe; presented by The Mirisch Production Company; Distributor: United Artists

The Thousand Plane Raid (October 1969)
Director: Boris Sagal; Producer: Lewis J. Rachmil; Screenplay: Donald S. Sanford; Story: Robert Vincent Wright; Cast: Christopher George, Laraine Stephens, J.D.

Cannon; 94 min; colour by De Luxe; presented by Mirisch Films; Distributor: United Artists

Gaily, Gaily (16 December 1969)
Director: Norman Jewison; Producer: Norman Jewison; Screenplay: Abram S. Ginnes, based on the book by Ben Hecht; Cast: Beau bridges, George Kennedy, Hume Cronyn, Melina Mercouri; 108 min; colour by De Luxe, presented by The Mirisch Production Company; Distributor: United Artists
Three Academy Award nominations

Hell Boats (February 1970)
Director: Paul Wendkos; Producer: Lewis J. Rachmil; Screenplay: Anthony Spinner, Donald Ford, Derek Ford; Story: S.S. Schweitze; cast: James Franciscus, Elizabeth Shepherd; 95 min; colour by De Luxe; presented by Oakmont Productions; Distributor: United Artists

Halls of Anger (March 25, 1970)
Director: Paul Bogart; Producer: Herbert Mirschman; Executive Producer: Walter Mirisch; Screenplay: John Shaner, Al Ramus; Cast: Calvin Lockhart, Janey MacLachlin, Jeff Bridges, James A. Watson Jr; 93 mins. Color by De Luxe, presented by The Mirisch Production Company; Distributor': United Artists

The Last Escape (6 May 1970)
Director: Walter Graumann; Producer: Irving Tamaner; Screenplay: Herman Hoffman; Story: John C. Champion, Barry Trivers; Cast: Stuart Whitman, John Collin; 90 min; colour by De Luxe; presented by Oakmont Productions; Distributor: United Artists

Mosquito Squadron (6 May 1970)
Director: Boris Sagal; Producer: Lewis J. Rachmil; Screenplay: Donald S. Sanford, Joyce Perry; Cast: David McCallum, Suzanne Neve; 90 min; colour by De Luxe; presented by Oakmont Productions; Distributor: United Artists

The Landlord (20 May 1970)
Director: Hal Ashby; Producer: Norman Jewison; Screenplay: Bill Gunn, based on the novel by Kristin Hunter; Cast: Beau Bridges, Lee Grant, Diana Sands, Pearl Bailey; 110 mins; colour by De Luxe; presented by The Mirisch Production Company; Distributor: United Artists

The Hawaiians (17 June 1970)
Director: Tom Gries; Producer: Walter Mirisch; Screenplay: James R. Webb, based on the novel by James A. Michener; Cast: Charlton Heston, Geraldine Chaplin, John Phillip Law, Tina Chen, Mako, Alec McCowen; 134 min; colour by De Luxe; Panavision; presented by The Mirisch Production Company; Distributor: United Artists
One Academy Award nomination

They Call Me MISTER Tibbs (8 July 1970)
Director: Gordon Douglas; Producer: Herbert Hirschmann; Executive Producer: Walter Mirisch; Screenplay: Alan R. Trustman, James R. Webb; Story: Alan R. Trustman, based on characters created by John Ball; Cast: Sidney Poitier, Martin Landau, Barbara McNair, Anthony Zerbe, Norma Crane; 108 min; presented by The Mirisch Production Company; Distributor: United Artists

Cannon for Cordoba (14 October 1970)
Director: Paul Wendkos; Producer: Vincent M. Fennelly; Screenplay: Stephen Kandel; Cast: George Peppard, Giovanna Ralli, Raf Vallone, Peter Duel. 104 min; colour by De Luxe; Panavision; presented by The Mirisch Production Company; Distributor: United Artists

The Private Life of Sherlock Holmes (29 October 1970)
Director: Billy Wilder; Producer: Billy Wilder; Screenplay: Billy Wilder and I. A. L. Diamond, based on the characters created by Arthur Conan Doyle; Cast: Robert Stephens, Colin Welland, Genevieve Page; 125 mins; colour by De Luxe; Panavision; presented by The Mirisch Production Company

The Organization (20 October 1971)
Director: Don Medford; Producer: Walter Mirisch; Screenplay: James R. Webb, based on the characters created by John Ball. Cast: Sidney Poitier, Barbara McNair, Gerald S. O'Loughlin, Allen Garfield, Raul Julia, Ron O'Neal, James A. Watson Jr; 108 min; colour by De Luxe; presented by The Mirisch Production Company; Distributor: United Artists

Fiddler on the Roof (3 November 1971)
Director: Norman Jewison; Producer: Norman Jewison; Screenplay: Joseph Stein, adapted from his stage play; Cast: Topol, Norma Crane, Leonard Frey, Molly Picon; 181 min; colour by De Luxe; Panavision; presented by The Mirisch Production Company; Distributor: United Artists

The Magnificent Seven Ride (1 August 1972)
Director: George McCowan; Producer: William A. Calihan; Screenplay: Arthur Rowe; Cast: Lee Van Cleef, Stefanie Powers, Michael Callan, Mariette Hartley, Luke Askew, Pedro Armendariz Jr; 106 min; colour by De Luxe; presented by The Mirisch Production Company; Distributor: United Artists

Avanti (17 December 1972)
Director: Billy Wilder; Producer: Billy Wilder; Screenplay: Billy Wilder and I. A. L. Diamond, based on the play, A Touch of Spring by Samuel Taylor; Cast: Jack Lemmon, Juliet Mills, Clive Revill; 144 min; colour by De Luxe; presented by The Mirisch Corporation; Distributor: United Artists

Scorpio (19 April 1971)
Director: Michael Winner; Producer: Walter Mirisch; Screenplay: David W. Rintels, Gerald Wilson; Story: David W. Rintels; Cast: Burt Lancaster, Alain Delon, Paul Scofield; 114 min; colour by De Luxe; presented by The Mirisch Corporation; Distributor: United Artists

The Spikes Gang (1 May 1974)
Director: Richard Fleischer; Producer: Walter Mirisch; Screenplay: Irving Ravetch, Harriet Frank Jr, based on the book The Bank Robber by Giles Tippette; cast: Lee Marvin, Gary Grimes, Ron Howard, Charlie Martin Smith; 96 min; colour by De Luxe; presented by The Mirisch Corporation; Distributor: United Artists

Mr Majestyk (17 July 1974)
Director: Richard Fleischer; Producer: Walter Mirisch; Screenplay: Elmore Leonard; Cast: Charles Bronson, Al Lettieri, Linda Cristal, Lee Purcell; 104 min; colour by De Luxe; presented by The Mirisch Corporation; Distributor: United Artists

Midway (18 June 1976)
Director: Jack Smight; Producer: Walter Mirisch; Screenplay: Donald S. Sanford; Cast: Charlton Heston, Henry Fonda, James Coburn, Glenn Ford, Hal Holbrook, Toshiro Mifune, Robert Mitchum, Cliff Robertson, Robert Wagner; 132 min; Technicolor; Panavision; presented by The Mirisch Corporation; Distributor: Universal Studios

Grey Lady Down (10 March 1978)
Director: David Greene; Producer: Walter Mirisch; Screenplay: James Whittaker, Howard Sackler, based on the novel Event 1000 by David Lavallee, adaptation by Frank P. Rosenberg; Cast: Charlton Heston, David Carradine, Stacy Keach, Ned Beatty; 111 min; Technicolor; Panavision; presented by The Mirisch Corporation; Distributor: Universal Studios

Same Time, Next Year (22 November 1978)
Director: Robert Mulligan; Producer: Walter Mirisch, Morton Gottlieb; Screenplay: Bernard Slade, based on his play; Cast: Ellen Burstyn, Alan Alda; 119 min; Technicolor; presented by The Mirisch Corporation; Distributor: Universal Studios
Four Academy Award nominations

The Prisoner of Zenda (25 May 1979)
Director: Richard Quine; Producer: Walter Mirisch; Screenplay: Dick Clement and Ian La Frenais, based on the novel by Anthony Hope, as dramatized by Edward Rose; Cast: Peter Sellers, Lynne Frederick, Lionel Jefferies, Elke Sommer; 108 min; Technicolor; presented by The Mirisch Corporation; Distributor: Universal Studios

Dracula (13 July 1979)
Director: John Badham; Producer: Walter Mirisch; Executive Producer: Marvin Mirisch; Screenplay: W. D. Richter, based on the play by Hamilton Dean and John Balderson, from the novel by Bram Stoker; Cast: Frank Langella, Laurence Olivier, Donald Pleasance; 109 min; Technicolor; Panavision; presented by The Mirisch Corporation; Distributor: Universal Studios

Romantic Comedy (7 October 1983)
Director: Arthur Hiller; Producer: Walter Mirisch, Morton Gottlieb; Executive Producer: Marvin Mirisch; Screenplay: Bernard Slade, based on his play; Cast: Dudley Moore, Mary Steenburgen, Frances Sternhagen; 103 min; colour by De Luxe; presented by The Mirisch Corporation; Distributor: United Artists

Bibliography

Acevedo-Munoz, Ernesto. *West Side Story as Cinema: The Making of an American Masterpiece.* Lawrence, KS: University Press of Kansas, 2013.
Action. 'Breaking Out of the Cutting Room, Hal Ashby'. September/October 1970, 10.
Allison, Tanine. *Destructive Sublime: World War 11 in American Film and Media.* New Brunswick: Rutgers University Press, 2008.
Altman, Rick. *Film/Genre.* London: British Film Institute, 1999.
American Business Consultants. *Red Channels: The Report of Communist Influence in Radio and Television.* New York: Counterattack, 1950.
American Cinematographer. 'The Case for the Cameramen'. February 1949, 66.
American Cinematographer. 'The Pros Show the Students How'. February 1963, 92.
Anderson, Carolyn. 'Film and Literature'. In *Film and the Arts in Symbiosis*, edited by Gary R. Edgerton, 97–132. Westport, CT: Greenwood, 1988.
Balio, Tino. ed. *Hollywood in the Age of Television.* London: Routledge, 1990.
Balio, Tino. *United Artists: The Company That Changed the Film Industry.* Madison, WI: University of Wisconsin Press, 1987 and 2009.
Bazin, Andre. 'La politique des auteur'. *Cahiers du Cinéma*, April 1957, 70.
Bell, Emma. *Reading Management and Organization in Film.* Management, Work and Organizations. London: Palgrave, 2008.
Bennett, James, Niki Strange, Paul Kerr, and Andrea Medrado. *Multiplatforming Public Service Broadcasting: The Economic and Cultural Role of UK TV and Digital Independents.* Royal Holloway, University of London, University of Sussex and London Metropolitan University, 2012.
Bernstein, Irving. *Hollywood at the Crossroads.* Melbourne: AFL, 1957.
Bernstein, Matthew. 'Hollywood's Semi-independent Production'. *Cinema Journal*, 32, no. 3 (1993): 41–54.
Bernstein, Matthew. *Walter Wanger: Hollywood Independent.* Berkeley, CA: University of California Press, 1994 and 2000.
Berson, Misha. *Something's Coming, Something Good: West Side Story and the American Imagination.* Lanham, MD: Applause Theatre and Cinema Books, 2011.
BFI. '10 Great Fish-Out-of-Water Films'. https://www2.bfi.org.uk/news-opinion/news-bfi/lists/10-great-fish-out-water-films.
Biette, Jean-Claude. 'Rewatching *Wichita*'. *Cahiers du Cinéma*, October 1977, 281.
Biskind, Peter. *Easy Riders, Raging Bulls: How the Sex 'n' Drugs 'n' Rock 'n' Roll Generation Saved Hollywood.* London: Bloomsbury, 1998.
Bloore, Peter. 'Re-defining the Independent Film Value Chain'. *UK Film Council*, 2009.
Bordwell, David. *Reinventing Hollywood: How 1940s Filmmakers Changed Movie Storytelling.* Chicago, IL: University of Chicago Press, 2017.
Bordwell, David. *The Way Hollywood Tells It: Story and Style in Modern Movies.* Berkeley, CA: University of California Press, 2006.
Bordwell, David, Janet Staiger, and Kristin Thompson. *The Classical Hollywood Cinema: Film Style & Mode of Production to 1960.* London: Routledge, 1985.

Boxoffice. 'Assembly Line Filming Doomed, Warns Small'. 11 December 1948, 15.
Boxoffice. 'Digest'. 28 September 1946, 5.
Boxoffice. 'Doris Vidor To a Top Post with the Mirisch Company'. 2 October 1961, 16.
Boxoffice. 'Enthusiastic Meeting for Wisconsin TO'. 11 November 1939, 74.
Boxoffice. 'Fine in Milwaukee for Bingo Party'. 4 March 1939, 26.
Boxoffice. 'Hallowe'en Parties for Milwaukee's Youngsters'. 5 November 1938, 52.
Boxoffice. 'Hallowe'en Parties Staged for Kids'. 4 November 1939, 38.
Boxoffice. 'Help To Take Sting Out of Returning to Classes'. 14 September 1940, 85.
Boxoffice. 'Improved Trend for Production'. *Barometer*, 26 March 1962, 16.
Boxoffice. 'Independent Filmmaking Shown Over ABC-TV'. 7 January 1963, 11.
Boxoffice. 'Milwaukee'. 12 August 1939, 62.
Boxoffice. 'Milwaukee'. 1 October 1938, 52.
Boxoffice. 'Milwaukee'. 10 December 1938, 83.
Boxoffice. 'Milwaukee'. 13 January 1940, 44.
Boxoffice. 'Milwaukee'. 15 July 1939, 40.
Boxoffice. 'Milwaukee'. 16 December 1939, 47.
Boxoffice. 'Milwaukee'. 20 April 1940, 40.
Boxoffice. 'Milwaukee'. 22 June 1940, 96.
Boxoffice. 'Milwaukee'. 23 December 1939, 57.
Boxoffice. 'Milwaukee'. 4 November 1939, 36.
Boxoffice. 'Milwaukee, After Announcing It, Abandons Singles Test'. 7 September 1940, no page number.
Boxoffice. 'Milwaukee Country Showmen Hold Parley on Problems'. 11 March 1939, 56.
Boxoffice. 'Mirisch Careers in Horatio Alger Tradition'. 1 October 1962, 9.
Boxoffice. 'Mirisch Gives Up Warner Film Buying'. 3 June 1937, 71.
Boxoffice. 'Mirisch Program of 20 Films Set at cost of $65 Million'. 1 October 1962, 8–9, 16.
Boxoffice. 'Nat'l Screen Names Patz Milwaukee Branch Head'. 27 April 1940, 100.
Boxoffice. 'Public Group Sues Over Withdrawal of "Blockade"'. 24 September 1938, 32.
Boxoffice. 'Valentine Parties Held by Warner-Saxe Houses'. 17 February 1940, 36.
Boxoffice. 'Walter Mirisch, Former Milwaukeean, Now a Monogram Producer, Will Give Localities a Look at His First Monogram Production, Fall Guy, at the Warner in July'. 31 June 1947, 68.
Boxoffice. 'Wisconsin Showmen Play Santa Claus'. 30 December 1939, 35.
Boxoffice. 'Wisconsin Theaters Spread Yule Cheer'. 21 December 1940, 47.
Boxoffice. 11 March 1963, 37.
Boxoffice. 13 March 1962, 16.
Boxoffice. 18 December 1948, 102–3.
Boxoffice. 19 October 1938.
Boxoffice. 23 December 1963, 8.
Boxoffice. 24 September 1938, 58.
Boxoffice. 26 October 1940, 31.
Boxoffice. 29 March 1941, 93.
Boxoffice. 3 July 1948, 78.
Boxoffice. 30 August 1947, 30.
Brookes, Ian. 'The Eye of Power: Postwar Fordism and the Panoptic Corporation in the Apartment'. *Journal of Popular Film and Television*, 37, no. 4 (2009): 150–60.
Buscombe, Edward. 'Walsh and Warner Bros'. In *Raoul Walsh*, edited by Phil Hardy. Edinburgh Film Festival, 1974.

Business Week. 'Fade out for Blockbuster Films'. 20 October 1962, 178.
Cagle, Chris. *Sociology on Film: Postwar Hollywood's Prestige Commodity*. New Brunswick: Rutgers University Press, 2016.
Casper, Drew. *Postwar Hollywood 1946–1962*. Oxford: Blackwell Publishing, 2007.
Cheatwood, Derral. 'The Tarzan Films: An Analysis of Determinants of Maintenance and Change in Conventions'. In *The Studio System*, edited by Janet Staiger, 163–83. New Brunswick: Rutgers University Press, 1995.
Christensen, Jerome. 'Studio Authorship, Warner Bros, and the Fountainhead'. *The Velvet Light Trap*, 57, no. 1 (2006): 17–31.
Christensen, Jerome. 'Studio Identity and Studio Art: MGM, "Mrs. Miniver", and Planning the Postwar Era'. *ELH*, 67, no. 1 (2000): 257–92.
Christensen, Jerome. *America's Corporate Art: The Studio Authorship of Hollywood Motion Pictures*. Redwood City, CA: Stanford University Press, 2012.
Cinema Journal. 'Featurettes'. Summer 2018, 100.
Cohan, Steven. *Hollywood by Hollywood: The Backstudio Picture and the Mystique of Making Movies*. Oxford: Oxford University Press, 2009.
Corman, Roger. *How I Made a Hundred Movies in Hollywood and Never Lost a Dime*. Boston: Da Capo Press, 1998.
Daily Variety. '16 United Artists Mirisch Films Blueprinted to Cost $73,000'. 16 June 1965, 18.
Daily Variety. '3 Mirisch Bros. Set Up Indie Co. For 12 UA Films'. 11 September 1957, 7.
Daily Variety. 'AA's Big Indian Chief Bally on Gold Pays Off'. 10 September 1947, 6.
Daily Variety. 'All 20 Pix For UA; Half Definitely to Be Made In US.; No TV Plans "At Present"'. 21 September 1962, 1.
Daily Variety. 'Allied Artists May Rely 100% on Indie Units'. 18 November 1957, 3.
Daily Variety. 'Allied Artists Recruits 8 Actors as Core of Its First Stock Company'. 15 December 1954, 3.
Daily Variety. 'Allied Enters a Name Class'. 26 May 1954, 1, 29.
Daily Variety. 'Annenberg Loses VS Fox Milwaukee'. 5 February 1941, 6.
Daily Variety. 'Audiences Fragmented'. 23 February 1970, 11.
Daily Variety. 'Avoid Gats and Gams'. 4 June 1958, 1.
Daily Variety. 'Broidy in Speech to Owners Bullish on Films' Future'. 17 October 1953, 9.
Daily Variety. 'Brynner, Mirisch Pledge UA TV Tie'. 1 January 1958, 23.
Daily Variety. 'Casting Their Own UA Horoscope'. 10 December 1958, 4.
Daily Variety. 'Champion Sees War Pix Popularity on The Increase'. 10 August 1967, 3.
Daily Variety. 'Clips From Film Row'. 15 March 1952, 50, 24 and 'Clips from Film Row'. 24 December 1952, 18.
Daily Variety. '"Dracula", Helmer Badham Raps U.K. Workers', Leisurely Pace'. 7 February 1979, 66.
Daily Variety. 'Easy Rider Biz Sparks NABET Use by Coast Indies'. 22 October 1969, 6.
Daily Variety. '"Escape", From Tax Rap, John Sturges', "The Great Escape" Has Been Classified "Wertvoll" (Valuable) by Board of Valuation in West Germany. Rating Gives the Mirisch-UA Release a Special Tax Consideration in All West German Theatres'. 10 October 1963, 4.
Daily Variety. 'Film Resume 1964'. 6.1.65: 56.
Daily Variety. 'Film Reviews'. 22 October 1946, 10.
Daily Variety. 'Films', New Blood'. 1 August 1951, 20.
Daily Variety. '"Gargantua", To Be Mirisch's 9th Pic'. 3 March 1958, 1.

Daily Variety. 'Gidding Winds Plots of 2 Mirisch Films'. 27 July 1960, 4.
Daily Variety. 'Gunfight at Dodge City'. 13 May 1959, 3.
Daily Variety. 'H'wood's Head in the Clouds'. 26 July 1950, 11.
Daily Variety. '"Hawaii", Topping Lists'. *Daily Variety*. 12 February 1960, 2.
Daily Variety. 'Hellman Play Buy, 400G'. 23 March 1960, 4.
Daily Variety. 'Hits Few, Beasts of Burden, Analysis of 1971 Boom-Bust Biz'. 30 November 1972, 5–6.
Daily Variety. 'Home Is Where You Shoot, But O'Seas No Longer Cheap'. 15 June 1960, 3, 16.
Daily Variety. 'Horror Pix as Global Clicks, Teenagers Key Chillers', BO'. 6 November 1957, 1–3.
Daily Variety. 'Inside the Lots'. 18 July 1956, 4.
Daily Variety. 'John Champion Departs Mirisch'. 21 June 1967, 1.
Daily Variety. 'Jungle Telepic Series'. 9 August 1950, 31.
Daily Variety. 'Just for Variety'. 23 February 1970, 11.
Daily Variety. 'Just for Variety'. 29 October 1962, 2.
Daily Variety. 'Just for Variety'. 30 October 1970, 2.
Daily Variety. 'Kingsberg Tees Off RKO Conv'. 27 June 1945, 25.
Daily Variety. 'Korean Situation Cues Circuit War-Pix Buys in Sharp About-Face'. 26 July 1950, 3.
Daily Variety. 'Last Minute Deflection from Plan, Where 69 of M'kee's 72 Cinemas Were to Solo Pix, Snarls Entire Zone'. 28 August 1940, 12.
Daily Variety. 'Lee Rich Calls for All-Industry "Crisis Meeting", to Find Way Out of TV's Red-Ink-Stained Maze'. 13 April 1966, 31, 53.
Daily Variety. 'Lefty Writes a Letter'. 16 August 1944, 13.
Daily Variety. 'Lewis J. Rachmil, Malta Aid Keeps UA Film Ahead'. 23 October 1968, 11.
Daily Variety. 'Lost Audience, Crass vs Class'. 5 December 1956, 1, 86.
Daily Variety. 'M.L. Annenberg's Tower and State, Milwaukee, in Trust Suit Vs Fox'. 23 October 1940, 16.
Daily Variety. 'Majors Originated "Outrageous Wages; Mirisch, Stars A Calculated Risk"'. 10 December 1958, 4.
Daily Variety. 'MCA's Hot Title Sale'. 19 April 1961, 3.
Daily Variety. 'Mirisch Bros. Strike It "Rich", on TV With Sale of All 3 Pilots for '66-'67'. 30 March 1966, 36.
Daily Variety. 'Mirisch Corp. In Agonizing TV "Reappraisal"'. 25 May 1967, 10.
Daily Variety. 'Mirisch Deal'. 30 August 1978, 3, 27.
Daily Variety. 'Mirisch Eyes 25 St Loo Theaters. Also Plans Prod'. 5 March 1947, 3, 18.
Daily Variety. 'Mirisch In Prod'n Lull'. 23 February 1970, 1.
Daily Variety. 'Mirisch Prepping TV Series with Janet Leigh'. 19 June 1964, 1.
Daily Variety. 'Mirisch to WB'. 27 August 1941, 27.
Daily Variety. 'Mirisch-King Bros Deal Cold'. 4 June 1947, 24.
Daily Variety. 'Mirisch-NBC Team on "Wichita", and "Horseman"'. 11 March 1959, 32.
Daily Variety. 'Mirisches Leave UA After 17 Years for Contract at U'. 8 January 1974, 1.
Daily Variety. 'Mirisches Set $10 Mil Theatre, TV, Film Production For 2nd Year'. 11 September 1958, 1.
Daily Variety. 'Mirisch Kings Expansion Set'. 7 May 1947, 9.
Daily Variety. 'Mirisches Takeover'. 12 August 1942, 16.
Daily Variety. 'Mono Sets Record, Ten Different Pix Series at Work'. 28 June 1949, 5.

Daily Variety. 'Mono-AA Execs Hypo Filming with England's ABPC'. 9 July 1952, 5.
Daily Variety. 'More Heat Than Light Shed in Second TV Academy Session on Video Violence'. 18 September 1968, 1, 13.
Daily Variety. 'Mosquito Squadron'. 6 July 1970, 3.
Daily Variety. 'Mosquito', Rachmil Sequel To '633'. 26 March 1968, 1.
Daily Variety. 'Musicalized "Robinson Crusoe" by Sammy Cahn and Jimmy Van Heusen is Now at the Mirisch Film Factory . . .'. 9 November 1960, 2.
Daily Variety. 'NBC-TV Eyes Badge for Mirisch-Rich "Sheriff Who?"'. 17 May 1967, 42.
Daily Variety. 'Perils Of "Rat Patrol"-ing; Computer Spills "Blood"'. 29 March 1967, 13.
Daily Variety. 'Pix Biz Fingers in Lotsa Pies'. 13 January 1982, 72.
Daily Variety. 'Poised Pix Pegged on World War II, Including Champion's 6 For Mirisch-UA'. 10 April 1967, 4.
Daily Variety. 'Presold Material', $3,500,000 Average for the Upcoming 14 Films, All Based on Bestsellers or Stage Hits'. 17 August 1960, 7.
Daily Variety. 'Pros and Cons re Runaway'. 7 December 1960, 11.
Daily Variety. 'Rachmil Promoted to Mirisch V.P.'. 26 May 1966, 1.
Daily Variety. 'Record $285,000 Gross Struck on Limited 3-Day Runs in 37 RKO Houses'. 12 July 1944, 8.
Daily Variety. 'Return to Original Scripts – Presold Theory Less Compelling'. 26 June 1961, 5.
Daily Variety. 'RKO vs. Mirisch "Kong"'. 11 September 1957, 7.
Daily Variety. '"Seven Ride", Shoots in California Previous Three in Mexico and Spain – Comments of Walter Mirisch'. 23 February 1972, 3.
Daily Variety. 'Screen Actors Guild Moves for Withdrawals from Non-Union Swope'. 23 October 1968, 16.
Daily Variety. 'Sellers Goes Mirisch'. 2 June 1976, 4.
Daily Variety. 'Sequel Trend May Bring Return to "Series Films", of 1940 Vogue'. 24 February 1965, 7.
Daily Variety. 'Studio O'Head, What to Do?'. 12 March 1958, 5.
Daily Variety. 'Stu Millar, Turman to Make "Flight", For Mirisch and UA'. 10 January 1962, 1, 4.
Daily Variety. 'Students, Stay Out of Hollywood'. 18 August 1968, no page number.
Daily Variety. 'Submarine X-1'. 27 August 1969, 3.
Daily Variety. 'The Last Escape'. 29 May 1970, 3.
Daily Variety. 'They Call Me Mr Tibbs: Review'. 4 July 1970, no page number.
Daily Variety. 'Today's Producer Must Be More Daring and Creative Than Ever Before'. 11 June 1984, 19.
Daily Variety. 'UA, Random to Co-Plug Hawaii'. 16 September 1959, 1, 4.
Daily Variety. 'UA's $2,700,000 *Seven* is Given Saturation Booking in Switch'. 30 August 1960, 4.
Daily Variety. 'Walter Mirisch, U-TV Will Pilot Seven', For CBS'. *Daily Variety* 24 December 1975, 1.
Daily Variety. 'Wanger Enters 3-Year Deal'. 21 June 1951, 8.
Daily Variety. '"West Side", – The Lead "Story", All-Time Top Film Grosses'. 9 January 1963, 18.
Dassanowsky, Robert. 'Home/Sick: Locating Billy Wilder's Cinematic Austria in "The Apartment", "The Private Life of Sherlock Holmes", and "Fedora"'. *Journal of Austrian Studies* (2013): 1–25.

Derrida, Jacques. 'Declarations of Independence'. *New Political Science*, 7, no. 1 (1986): 7–15.
Diamond, I.A.L. '"Apartment", with View'. *New York Times Encyclopaedia of Film*, 12 June 1960, no page number.
Drucker, Peter. *The Age of Discontinuity*. Oxford: Elsevier, [1969] 2017.
Drucker, Peter. *The Concept of the Corporation*. Abingdon: Taylor & Francis, [1946] 1993.
Drucker, Peter. *The Future of Industrial Man*. London: Routledge, [1942] 1995.
Drucker, Peter. *The Practice of Management*. London: Harper Business, 1954.
Dyer, Geoff. *'Broadsword Calling Danny Boy': On Where Eagles Dare*. London: Penguin, 2018.
Dyer, Richard. *White: Essays on Race and Culture*. London: Routledge, 1997.
Ebert, Roger. 'Review'. *Chicago Sun Times*, 9 May 1969, no page number.
Edwards, Kyle D. 'Corporate Fictions: Film Adaptation and Authorship in the Classical Hollywood Era'. PhD diss., University of Texas at Austin, Austin, TX, 2006.
Edwards, Kyle Dawson. 'Brand-Name Literature: Film Adaptation and Selznick International Pictures' "Rebecca" (1940)'. *Cinema Journal* (2006): 32–58.
Edwards, Kyle Dawson. '"Monogram Means Business": B-film Marketing and Series Filmmaking at Monogram Pictures'. *Film History*, 23, no. 4 (2011): 386–400.
Enacademic.com. 2022. https://enacademic.com/pictures/enwiki/77/Mechanized_P-38_conveyor_lines.jpg.
Factory Management and Maintenance, 'Efficient Production and Cost Control'. 103 no. 12 (December 1945): 109–13.
Factory Management and Maintenance. 'Scientific Management in a Post-War Plan'. 102, no. 9 (September 1944): 96–101.
Factory Management and Maintenance. 'Decentralization in Doing Things for These Industrial Concerns'. 104, no. 12 (December 1946): 144.
Factory Management and Maintenance. 'Measuring Drafting Output'. 102, no. 11 (November 1944): 101.
Factory Management and Maintenance. 'To Get Ready for Lower Unit Costs Take Advantage of Work Simplification Methods, Case of Lockheed Aircraft Corporation'. August 1944, 129.
Feinstein, Herbert, and Jean-Luc Godard. 'An Interview with Jean-Luc Godard'. *Film Quarterly*, 17, no. 3 (1964): 8–10.
Feuer, Jane, Paul Kerr, and Tise Vahimagi, eds. *MTM: 'Quality Television'*. London: BFI, 1984.
Film and Radio Guide. October 1945 – June 1946, 19.
Film Bulletin. 'AA at Low Ebb; Exhibitors Would Welcome Programmers'. 13 December 1954, 37.
Film Bulletin. 'Headliners'. 11 June 1956, 16.
Film Bulletin. 'Huston Deal Closed, Wilder Wyler to Follow'. 31 May 1954, 10.
Film Bulletin. 'Mirisch Brothers, Oscar Monopolists – A Studio Without Walls'. 17 September 1962, 10.
Film Bulletin. 'Mirisch Ups 52 Program, Accent on Quality Pictures'. 3 December 1951, 12.
Film Bulletin. 'New Studio Chief Spurs More Bigger Mono-AA Films'. *Film Bulletin*. 13 August 1951, 12.
Film Bulletin. 'Producer Perlberg Calls for NEW BLOOD'. *Independent Exhibitors Film Bulletin*, 15 May 1961, 12.

Film Bulletin. 'Promotion Pioneering, UA To Plus "Horse Soldiers" via Heavy Title Bout'. 8 June 1959, 16.
Film Bulletin. 'Studio Size-Ups'. 19 December 1951, 18.
Film Bulletin. 'Studio Size-Ups'. 15 January 1951, 14.
Film Bulletin. 'The Allied Artists Story'. 5 March 1956, 17.
Film Bulletin. 'They Made the News'. 11 July 1955, 19.
Film Bulletin. 'They Made the News'. 5 August 1957, 23.
Film Daily. '$85,000,000 Will Be Spent on Indie Production on West Coast During Year'. 26 December 1945, 10.
Film Daily. 'Along the Rialto'. 2 January 1930, 4.
Film Daily. 'Both Tax Absorption and Price Hikes in Milwaukee'. 3 July 1940, 10.
Film Daily. 'Candy Nets Chicago a Sweet "Take"'. 23 January 1941, 4.
Film Daily. 'Coming & Going'. *Film Daily* 26 April 1932, 8.
Film Daily. 'Coming and Going'. 19 April 1948, 2.
Film Daily. 'Coming and Going'. 20 January 1948, 2.
Film Daily. 'Exhibs at RKO Convention'. 20 May 1932, 7.
Film Daily. 'Film Daily Reviews of New Features'. 5 May 1948, 8.
Film Daily. 'Harold Mirisch Rejoins Warners Booking Staff'. 17 July 1931, 2.
Film Daily. 'Harold Mirisch Who Has Been with the Warner Here Left Last Night for St Louis'. 'Along the Rialto'. 13 February 1930, 4.
Film Daily. 'Hollywood Indie List Growing'. 18 November 1946, 24.
Film Daily. 'King Brothers to Make Four Pix for Monogram'. *Film Daily*, 1 June 1945, 2.
Film Daily. 'May Remodel Warner Memphis'. 28 September 1930, 3.
Film Daily. 'New Faces, Getting Full Chance'. 16 October 1967, 20.
Film Daily. 'RKO Met Theater in Three Divisions'. 24 August 1942, 1.
Film Daily. 'Warner-Memphis Turned into a Winner'. 3 December 1930, 1.
Film Daily. 'Waugh at Warner Memphis House'. 1 July 1931, 12.
Film Daily. 'Who's Who in Hollywood'. 7 August 1945, 7.
Film Quarterly. 'Independence with a Vengeance'. Summer 1962, 15. 4, 19.
Film Quarterly. 'The Old Dependables'. 13, no. 1, Autumn 1959, 3.
Film Reference. 'Walter Mirisch – Writer - Films as Producer (Selected List), Publications'. http://www.filmreference.com/Writers-and-Production-Artists-Me-Ni/Mirisch-Walter.html.
Films and Filming. 'Interview with Gordon Gow'. March 1972, 42.
Flynn, Charles and Todd McCarthy, eds. *Kings of the B's: Working Within the Hollywood System.* New York: E. P. Dutton, 1975.
Fuller-Seeley, Kathryn H., ed. *Hollywood in the Neighbourhood: Historical Case Studies of Local Moviegoing.* Berkeley, CA: University of California Press, 2008.
Gabler, Neal. *An Empire of Their Own: How the Jews Invented Hollywood.* London: Random House, 1998.
Gallagher, Mark. 'Discerning Independents: Steven Soderbergh'. In *American Independent Cinema: Indie, Indiewood and Beyond*, edited by Geoff King, Claire Molloy and Yannis Tzioumakis, 83–95. London: Routledge, 2013.
Geraghty, Christine. *Now a Major Motion Picture.* London: Rowman and Littlefield, 2007.
Gilbey, Ryan. *It Don't Worry Me: Nashville, Jaws, Star Wars and Beyond.* London: Faber and Faber, 2003.
Giovacchini, Saverio. 'Postwar Hollywood, 1947–1967'. In *Producing*, edited by Jon Lewis, 63–85. London: I.B. Tauris, 2016.

Gladwell, Malcolm. *Outliers: The Story of Success*. London: Penguin, 2009.
Gleich, Joshua, 'Postwar Hollywood, 1947-1967, Part One: Domestic Location Shooting'. In *Hollywood on Location: An Industry History*, edited by Joshua Gleich and Lawrence Webb, 73-100. New Brunswick: Rutgers University Press, 2019.
Godard, Jean Luc. 'Supermann, Man of the West'. *Cahiers du Cinema*, 92, February 1959.
Godard, Sieving. 'United Artist (sic) Showing Progress in 1970'. *Chicago Defender*, 13 June 1970, 6A, 8A.
Gomery, Douglas. *Shared Pleasures*. Madison, WI: University of Wisconsin Press, 1992.
Gomery, Douglas. *The Coming of Sound*. London: Routledge, 2005.
Gomery, Douglas. *The Hollywood Studio System: A History*. London: BFI, 2005.
Gomery, Douglas and Clara Pafort-Overdun. *Movie History: A Survey*. 2nd edn. New York/London: Routledge, 2011.
Gow, Gordon. 'Interview with the Mirisch Brothers'. *Films and Filming*, March 1972, 40-4.
Guback, Thomas, ed. *The International Film Industry: Western Europe and America Since 1945*. Indianapolis, IN: Indiana University Press, 1969.
Hall, Sheldon. 'Feature Films on British Television in the 1970s'. http://bufvc.ac.uk/articles/feature-films-on-british-television-in-the-1970s/8).
Hamel, Keith J. 'From Advertisement to Entertainment: Early Hollywood Film Trailers'. *Quarterly Review of Film and Video*, 29, no. 3 (2012): 268-78.
Hannan, Brian. *In Theaters Everywhere: A History of the Hollywood Wide Release 1913-2017*. Jefferson, NC: McFarland and Co, 2018.
Hannan, Brian. *The Making of The Magnificent Seven*. Jefferson, NC: McFarland and Company, 2015.
Harris, Mark. *Scenes from a Revolution: The Birth of the New Hollywood*. London: Canongate, 2008.
Harvard. 'Calendar 1942-43'. https://iiif.lib.harvard.edu/manifests/view/drs:423141930$9i)
Harvard. 'Curriculum for Harvard Business School's 'Twelve Month's Course Leading to the Degree of Industrial Administrator: 15 June 1942 to 12 June 1943'. https://iiif.lib.harvard.edu/manifests/view/drs:423141930$1i
Harvard. 'Industrial Management Engineering'. Curriculum. Emailed by Clarissa Yingling, Baker Library Special Collections, Harvard University. 7.10.2019.
Harvard. 'The Graduate School of Business Administration'. *Harvard Business School Course Catalog*, June 1942. https://iiif.lib.harvard.edu/manifests/view/drs:423141930$37i.
Harvard Business School Association. 'Walter Mirisch'. 35, February 1959, 17.
Harvard Business School Bulletin. 'Keeping Up to Date with the Alumni'. Autumn 1943, 155.
Hays, Will H. 'Supervision from Within'. In *The Story of the Films: As Told by Leaders of the Industry*, edited by Joseph P. Kennedy, 29-54. London: AW Shaw, [1927] 2018.
Henderson, Stuart. *The Hollywood Sequel: History and Form 1911-2010*. London: Bloomsbury, 2014.
Hollywood Reporter. 'Almeria – Movie Capital of the World, Says Here'. 15 February 1968, no page number.
Hollywood Reporter. 'IA Backs AFL Film Council on "Runaway Foreign Production"'. 18 February 1949, 4.
Hollywood Reporter. 'Long-Term Deals on Way Out'. 20 January 1953, 1.
Hughes, Howard. 'History of Oakmont Films'. *Cinema Retro*, 10, no. 28 (2014): 42-3.

Huston, John. 'Home is Where the Heart Is – and So Are Films'. *Journal of the Screen Producers Guild*, 10 (3 March 1963): 4.
Independent Exhibitors Film Bulletin. 13 December 1954, 17.
Irving, Ralph. *Factory Management and Maintenance*. 'Rating a Plant's Efficiency'. 103, no. 6 (June 1945): 115–18.
Jameson, Fredric. 'Afterword: Adaptation as a Philosophical Problem'. In *True to the Spirit: Film Adaptation and the Question of Fidelity*, edited by Colin McCabe, Kathleen Murray and Rick Warner, 215–34. Oxford: Oxford University Press, 2011.
Jameson, Fredric. *The Cultural Turn: Selected Writings on the Postmodern, 1983–1998*. London: Verso, 1998.
Jewell, Richard. *Slow Fade to Black: The Decline of RKO Radio Pictures*. Berkeley, CA: University of California Press, 2016.
Jones, Dorothy B. 'Hollywood's International Relations'. *The Quarterly of Film Radio and Television*, 11, no. 4 (1957): 362–74.
Journal of the Producers Guild. 'Why Runaway?'. 6, no. 7 (December 1960): 13–14 and 30.
Katz, Ephraim. *The Film Encyclopaedia*, 3rd edn. New York: Harper Perennial, 1998.
Kerr, Paul, ed. *The Hollywood Film Industry*. London: RKP, 1986.
Kerr, Paul. '"Out of What Past?" Notes on the "B" Film Noir'. *Screen Education*, 32, no. 3 (1979–80): 45–65.
Kerr, Paul. '"A Small, Effective Organization": The Mirisch Company, the Package-Unit System and the Production of Some Like it Hot'. In *Billy Wilder, Movie-Maker: Critical Essays on the Films*, edited by Karen McNally, 117–31. Jefferson, NC: McFarland & Company, 2011.
Kerr, Paul. '"It Seemed Like a Good Idea at the Time": Hollywood, Homology and Hired Guns - the Making of The Magnificent Seven'. In *Reframing Cult Westerns: From the Magnificent Seven to The Hateful Eight*, edited by Lee Broughton, 21–39. New York: Bloomsbury Academic, 2020.
Kerr, Paul. 'A Forgotten Episode in the History of Hollywood Cinema, Television and Seriality: The Case of the Mirisch Company'. In *Exploring Seriality on Screen: Audiovisual Narratives in Film and Television*, edited by Ariane Hudelet and Anne Cremieux, 79–102. Abingdon, VA: Routledge, 2021.
Kerr, Paul. 'Making Film Programmes for the BBC and Channel 4: The Shift From In-house "Producer Unit to Independent Package-Unit" Production'. *Historical Journal for Film, Radio and Television*, 33, no. 3 (2013): 434–53.
Kerr, Paul. 'My Name is Joseph H. Lewis'. *Screen*, 24, no. 4–5 (1983): 48–67.
Kerr, Paul. 'The Last Slave (2007): The Genealogy of a British Television History Programme'. *Historical Journal of Film, Radio and Television*, 29, no. 3 (2009): 381–97.
Kerr, Paul. 'The Magnificent Seven Mirisch Companies: Competitive Strategy and Corporate Authorship'. In *United Artists*, edited by Peter Krämer, Gary Needham, Yannis Tzioumakis and Tino Balio, 112–31. London/New York: Routledge, 2020.
Klein, Amanda Ann. *American Film Cycles: Reframing Genres, Screening Social Problems & Defining Subcultures*. Austin, TX: University of Texas Press, 2011.
Krämer, Peter, and Yannis Tzioumakis. *The Hollywood Renaissance: Revisiting American Cinema's Most Celebrated Era*. London: Bloomsbury Academic, 2018.
Krämer, Peter. *The New Hollywood: From Bonnie and Clyde to Star Wars*. New York: Wallflower, 2005.
Lasky, Jesse. 'Production Problems'. *The Story of the Films*, 99–123.

Lauterbach, Thorsten. 'Clouseau Would Have Been Confounded: Ninth Circuit Throws Out "The Pink Panther" Joint Authorship Claim'. *Journal of Intellectual Property Law & Practice*, 4, no. 6 (2009): 402–3.
Lewis, Jon. 'The Auteur Renaissance 1968–1980'. In *Producing*, edited by Jon Lewis, 86–110. London: IB Tauris, 2016.
Litman, Barry. 'The Economics of the Television Market for Theatrical Movies'. In *The American Movie Industry: The Business of Motion Pictures*, edited by Gorham Kindem, 308–21. Carbondale, IL: Southern Illinois University Press, 1982.
Los Angeles Times. 'Hypnosis Rage Goes On'. 4 May 1956, B9.
Lovell, Glenn. *Escape Artist: The Life and Films of John Sturges*. Madison, WI: University of Wisconsin Press, 2008.
Lyons, James. 'The American Independent Producer and the Film Value Chain'. In *Beyond the Bottom Line: The Producer in Film and Television Studies*, edited by Andrew Spicer, Anthony McKenna and Christopher Meir, 195–212. London: Bloomsbury Academic, 2014.
Maltby, Richard. *Hollywood Cinema*, 2nd edn. Oxford: Blackwell Publishing, [1995] 2003.
Mann, Denise. *Hollywood Independents: The Postwar Talent Takeover*. Minneapolis, MN: University of Minnesota Press, 2008.
Maslon, Laurence. *Some Like it Hot: The Official 50th Anniversary Companion*. London: Pavilion, 2009.
McClain, Stan. 'A History of Aerial Cinematography'. *The Operating Cameraman, The Magazine of the Society of Camera Operators*, 1996. http://www.cinematographers.nl/DoPh4a.html.
McLaughlin, Robert. *Broadway and Hollywood; A History of Economic Interaction*. New York: Arno Press, 1974.
McNary, Dave, and Dave McNary. 'MGM Sets "Fiddler on the Roof" Movie with "Hamilton" Director Thomas Kail'. *Variety*, 28 May 2020. https://variety.com/2020/film/news/fiddler-on-the-roof-hamilton-director-mgm-1234619064/.
McTiernan, John, dir. 2000. The Thomas Crown Affair, DVD.
Menne, Jeff. *Post-Fordist Cinema: Hollywood Auteurs and the Corporate Counterculture*. New York: Columbia University Press, 2019.
Milne, Tom, ed and trans. *Godard on Godard*. New York: Viking Press, 1972.
Mirisch, Harold J. *Correspondence and Bookings, University of Iowa Digital Library Special Collections*. Iowa City.
Mirisch, Harold. 'Why Runaway?'. *Journal of the Producers Guild*, 6, no. 7 (1960): 13–14.
Mirisch, Walter. *I Thought We Were Making Movies, Not History*. Madison, WI: University of Wisconsin Press, 2008.
Mirisch, Walter. 'Make Way for Tomorrow?'. *The Journal of the Producers Guild of America*, 6, no. 7 (1960): 21–2.
Mitchell, Elvis. 2008. 'The Treatment'. *KCRW*. https://www.kcrw.com/culture/shows/the-treatment/walter-mirisch.
Motion Picture Daily. 'AA To Produce Six Films from Novels'. 25 January 1956, 5.
Motion Picture Daily. 'Brass Tack Talk'. 14 December 1938, 12.
Motion Picture Daily. 'Broidy Sets Plans for Two in England'. 9 July 1952, 1.
Motion Picture Daily. 'Gran Named Head of Milwaukee Club'. 17 December 1940, 2.
Motion Picture Daily. 'Harold, Walter Mirisch to Leave AA August 31'. 1 August 1957, 2.
Motion Picture Daily. 'Hollywood Reporter Tradeviews'. 14 September 1955, 3.
Motion Picture Daily. 'Marvin Mirisch Secretary of A.A'. 10 June 1955, 2.

Motion Picture Daily. 'Memphis Take Double Under Warner Wing'. 22 December 1930, 4.
Motion Picture Daily. 'Mirisch Cuts Holdings'. 22 June 1954, 2.
Motion Picture Daily. 'Mirisch to Expand Allied Production'. 7 August 1951, 1.
Motion Picture Daily. 'Mirisch, Seven Arts Set two for United Artists'. 3 April 1959, 2.
Motion Picture Daily. 'Monogram, Allied List 45 Features for The New Season'. 7 September 1951, 1.
Motion Picture Daily. 'Monogram Elects Broidy President'. 15 November 1945, 1.
Motion Picture Daily. 'Monogram Heads Off to Convention'. 25 June 1946, 13.
Motion Picture Daily. 'Name Executives in Warner-Saxe Pool'. 6 October 1936, 4.
Motion Picture Daily. 'News in Brief'. 12 March 1952, 7.
Motion Picture Daily. 'Niesen Personal Appearance Nets Newspaper Publicity'. *Motion Picture Herald*, 1 May 1936, 78.
Motion Picture Daily. 'Plan Radio-TV Drive for AA "Cell Block"'. 24 August 1953, 3.
Motion Picture Daily. '"Re-Tool", AA Studio for New Product'. 26 September 1952, 1, 4.
Motion Picture Daily. 'Realign RKO Circuit, Mirisch Head Buyer'. 24 August 1942, 1.
Motion Picture Daily. 'RKO, Loew in Same Deals in 1943–44'. 11 August 1943, 1, 6.
Motion Picture Daily. '"The Last Escape". Mirisch-UA World War II Yarn is Lensing at Munich's Bavaria-Geiselgasteig Studios and Various Nearby Locations'. 11 September 1968, 15.
Motion Picture Daily. 'Theodora, Security, AA to Make "Combo"'. 24 July 1954, 1.
Motion Picture Daily. 'Wilder, Lemmon Will Tour Europe For "Hot"'. 1 May 1959, 3.
Motion Picture Herald. '10 Autos, $5000 In One Giveaway'. 6 April 1940, 23.
Motion Picture Herald. 'Allied Artists Ready with Big Program'. 9 July 1955, 25.
Motion Picture Herald. '"Book Night" a New Stunt'. 22 July 1939, 18.
Motion Picture Herald. 'First High Court Decision Awaited'. 10 September 1935, 59.
Motion Picture Herald. 'For the Young Audience'. 15 September 1956, 7.
Motion Picture Herald. 'Good Picture Benefits the Entire Industry, Riskin Believes'. 7 December 1946, 35.
Motion Picture Herald. 'Harold Mirisch Takes Over as Milwaukee Booking Manager'. 10 January 1933, 7.
Motion Picture Herald. 'Harvard Receives 25 Film Scripts'. 30 August 1941, 31.
Motion Picture Herald. 'Hollywood Causes Drop at Studios'. 6 December 1947, 33.
Motion Picture Herald. 'Increase in Gross Seen by Branton'. 4 October 1952, 12.
Motion Picture Herald. 'Mirisch Joins RKO'. 19 January 1942, 4.
Motion Picture Herald. 'Mirisch Sends Rogers Congratulatory Message'. 29 March 1941, 64.
Motion Picture Herald. 'Moe Silver Named Assistant Manager of Warners Circuit'. 14 November 1931, 18.
Motion Picture Herald. 'Nat'l Circuit for Mirisch'. 1 April 1947, 1.
Motion Picture Herald. 'New Pre-Designed Theater is Ready'. 18 January 1947, 32.
Motion Picture Herald. 'Production Holds Level With 39 Shooting as Three Are Started'. 15 November 1947, 34.
Motion Picture Herald. 'Sales Personnel Shift in Field, Home Offices'. 16 May 1942, 88.
Motion Picture Herald. 'Says Monogram Star Policy Is "Just the Beginning"'. 28 June 1952, 14.
Motion Picture Herald. 'SEC Report'. 13 October 1945, 16.
Motion Picture Herald. 'Theaters Collecting Thousands for Finns'. 24 February 1940, 25.
Motion Picture Herald. 'This Week, The Camera Reports'. 27 November 1943, 11.

Motion Picture Herald. 'Two Federal Courts Sustain Bank Night'. 18 May 1935, 18.
Motion Picture Herald. 'Warners Acquire Two'. 13 September 1941, 40.
Motion Picture Herald. 'What the Picture Did for Me'. 31 May 1947, 45.
Motion Picture Herald. 'Who Goes to the Movies . . . and Who Doesn't'. 10 August 1957, 21.
Motion Picture Herald. 'Youth Must Be Served'. 23 June 1956, 7.
Motion Picture News. 'Memphis Gathers in 3000 Shekels to Aid Jobless'. 20 December 1930, 15.
Motion Picture News. 'Keep Government Out of Business, Convention Told'. 6 December 1930, 16.
Moving Picture World. 'Baseball'. 11 July 1925, 199.
Murphy, Robert. *Sixties British Cinema.* London: BFI, 1992.
Naremore, James. *Film Adaptation.* New Brunswick: Rutgers University Press, 2000.
New York Times Encyclopaedia of Film. '"Hawaii", Changes Directors Twice, Hill is Replaced by Hiller then Takes Over Again'. 4 August 1965, no page number.
New York Times Encyclopaedia of Film. 'Hollywood Sweeps'. 15 April 1962, no page number.
New York Times Encyclopaedia of Film. 'Label Babel, Ad Men Spur Industry in a Hot Race for Lengthy, Exotic Film Titles'. 6 December 1964, no page number.
New York Times. '5 at United Artists Quit Top Posts Plan New Company'. 10 February 1978, no page number.
New York Times. 'Advertising, A Chip off an Agency Family'. 16 April 1965, 56.
New York Times. '"Apartment" with View'. 12 June 1960, no page number.
New York Times. 'Colleagues Cite Harold Mirisch as Movie Pioneer of the Year'. 24 November 1964, no page number.
New York Times. 'Film Studio Bars Credit to Writer'. 21 September 1956, no page number.
New York Times. 'Films Challenge Censorship Code'. 11 August 1961, 18.
New York Times. 'Flops', Loss-Cutting'. 26 August 1970, 3, 6.
New York Times. 'Hollywood Birthday Mirisch Company'. 30 September 1962, X7.
New York Times. 'Hollywood Paean Producer Praises the West Coast as Best Place to Make Films'. 21 August 1960, X7.
New York Times. 'Hollywood Sees a Rise in Filming'. 8 October 1962, 18.
New York Times. 'Hollywood Sequels Are Just the Ticket'. 18 July 1982, Sect. 3, 1.
New York Times. 'New Film Denied Seal of Approval'. 9 May 1961, 45.
New York Times. 'Round the Hollywood Studios, United Artists Buys RKO Pictures to Bolster Program – A Bit of Horatio Alger in Wonderland – Libel Suit – Other Items'. 5 October 1947, X5.
New York Times. 'Studios Indicate Assembly Line End, Selectivity of Public is Factor in Concentration on Fewer Films of Better Quality'. Thomas M. Pryor, 29 August 1953.
New York Times. 'Studios Indicate Assembly Line End, Selectivity of Public Is factor in Concentration on Fewer Films of Better Quality'. Thomas M. Pryor, 29 August 1953A, no page number.
New York Times. 'The Sequel Becomes the New Bankable Film Star'. 8 July 1985, C15.
New York Times. 'When the Cookie Crumbled'. 7 November 1965, no page number.
New York Times. 'Wilder – And Funnier – Touch'. 24 January 1960, no page number.
Nobody's Perfect. 2001. BBC2.

Nowell, Richard. 'Hollywood Don't Skate: US Production Trends, Industry Analysis, and the Roller Disco Movie'. *New Review of Film and Television Studies*, 11, no. 1 (2013): 73–91.

Nystrom, Derek. *Hard Hats, Rednecks and Macho Men: Class in 1970s American Cinema*. Oxford: Oxford University Press, 2009.

O'Brien, Daniel. *Robert Altman: Hollywood Survivor*. London: Continuum, 1995.

Okuda, Ted. *Grand National, Producers Releasing Corporation, and Screen Guild/Lippert*. Jefferson: McFarland and Co, 1989.

Onosko, Tim. 'Monogram: Its Rise and Fall in the Forties'. *The Velvet Light Trap*, 5 (1972): 5.

Perkins, V.F. *Film as Film*. London: Penguin, 1972.

Personnel Journal, The Magazine of Labor Relations and Personnel Practices. 'Lockheed's Full Testing Program'. September 1942, 21.

Personnel Journal, The Magazine of Labor Relations and Personnel Practices. 'Industrial Relations Research'. July 1944, 22.

Personnel Journal, The Magazine of Labor Relations and Personnel Practices. 'Why Workers Quit'. September 1944, 23.

Personnel Journal, The Magazine of Labor Relations and Personnel Practices. 'Walter's Emergency Administration'. 14, no. 1 (May 1945): 37–40.

Phillips, Julia. *You'll Never Eat Lunch in This Town Again*. London: Faber and Faber, 2002.

Poitier, Sidney. 'A Conversation With Walter Mirisch'. Department of History, University of Wisconsin-Madison, Fall 2008. https://history.wisc.edu/wp-content/uploads/sites/202/2017/05/history_newsletter2008.pdf.

Polan, Dana. *Dreams of Flight: The Great Escape in American Film and Culture*. Berkeley, CA: University of California Press, 2021.

Porter, Michael E. *Competitive Advantage: Creating and Sustaining Superior Performance*. New York: Free Press, 1998.

Porter, Michael E. *Competitive Strategy: Techniques for Analysing Industries and Competitors*. New York: Free Press [1980] 2004.

Powdermaker, Hortense. *Hollywood The Dream Factory: An Anthropologist Looks at the Movie-makers*. Eastford, CT: Martino Fine Books, [1950] 2013.

Production Encyclopedia. 1952 'Lantern'. https://lantern.mediahist.org/catalog/productionencycl1952holl_0616.

Pryor, Thom M. 'Monogram Studio Changes Its Name Stockholders Approve Shift to Allied Artists Pictures, Hear Reports of Earnings Rise'. *New York Times*, 13 November 1953, no page number.

Pryor, Thomas M. 'Film Production Below Forecast, 10% Gain Over '56 Period Attributed to Independents – Big Studios Decline'. *New York Times*, 8 July 1957, no page number.

Quick, J. M., W. J. Shea and R. E. Koehler. 'Motion-Time Standards, A Modern Technique'. *Factory Management and Maintenance*, 103, no. 5 (May 1945): 87–108.

Quinn, Eithne. *A Piece of the Action: Race and Labor in Post-Civil Rights Hollywood*. New York: Columbia University Press, 2020.

Ricketson, Jnr Frank H. *The Management of Motion Picture Theaters*, New York: McGraw Hill, 1938.

Robnik, Drehli. 'Allegories of Post-Fordism in 1970s New Hollywood: Countercultural Combat Films, Conspiracy Thrillers as Genre-Recycling'. In *The Last Great American Picture Show. New Hollywood Cinema in the 1970s*, edited by Thomas Elsaesser,

Alexander Horwath, and Noel King, 333–58. Amsterdam: Amsterdam University Press, 2004.

Rogerson, Ben. 'Wilder's Mensch: United Artists and the Critique of Fordism'. *Arizona Quarterly: A Journal of American Literature, Culture, and Theory*, 70, no. 1 (2014): 53–80.

Rosendorf, Neal Moses. '"Hollywood in Madrid": American Film Producers and the Franco Regime, 1950–1970'. *Historical Journal of Film, Radio and Television*, 27, no. 1 (2007): 77–109.

Sandage, C.H. 'Harvard Studies Air Use by Retailers, Report Will Be of Aid to Buyer, Seller of Radio Time'. *Broadcasting*, 3 May 1943, 18–69.

Sarris, Andrew. *The American Cinema: Directors and Directions, 1929–1968*, New York: EP Dutton, 1968.

Schatz, Thomas. 'The New Hollywood'. In *Film Theory Goes to the Movies: Cultural Analysis of Contemporary Film*, edited by Jim Collins, Hilary Radner and Ava Preacher Collins, 8–36. London: Routledge, 1993.

Schatz, Thomas. *The Genius of the System: Hollywood Filmmaking in the Studio Era*. New York: Pantheon, 1988.

Schein, Edgar H. 'The Culture of Media as Viewed From an Organizational Culture Perspective'. In *International Journal on Media Management*, 5, no. 3 (2003): 171–2.

Schein, Edgar H. *Organizational Culture and Leadership*. San Francisco, CA: Jossey-Bass, 2004.

Segrave, Kerry. *Product Placement in Hollywood Films: A History*. Jefferson, NC: McFarland and Co, 2004.

Showmen's Trade Review. 'Adolescent Appeal Tops "School Hero", Campaign'. 7 December 1946, 16.

Showmen's Trade Review. 'Cocaine to Monogram, Mirisch to Produce Cocaine'. 21 September 1946, 36.

Showmen's Trade Review. 'Drop Plan to End Milwaukee Duals, Mirisch Refuses to Cooperate on Advice of His Attorneys'. 7 September 1940, 4.

Showmen's Trade Review. 'Koret, Princess Pat in Monogram Film Tie-ups'. 7 December 1946, 14.

Showmen's Trade Review. 'Monogram in Fast Pace'. 11 May 1946, 42.

Showmen's Trade Review. 'Monogram Sets National Tie-Ups on "School Hero"'. 7 September 1946, 18.

Showmen's Trade Review. 'Monogram-Koret Tieup'. 12 April 1947, 10.

Showmen's Trade Review. 'New Producers of 1947'. October–December 1947, 122.

Showmen's Trade Review. 'One Starts at Monogram'. 9 November 1946, 40.

Showmen's Trade Review. 'Price "Hikes" Flop in Milwaukee Houses'. 7 December 1940, 6.

Showmen's Trade Review. 'Regional Newsreel'. 7 June 1947, 32.

Sieving, Christopher. *Soul Searching: Black Themed Cinema from the March on Washington to the Rise of Blaxploitation*. Middletown, DE: Wesleyan University Press, 2011.

Singer, Phillip. 'Controversy in Film Contract Construction-That's Show Biz, Booby'. *University of San Fernando Valley Law Review*, 1 (1967): 87.

Spicer, A. H. 'Secret Histories and the Dirty War: The 1970s Second World War Film'. In *Going to War: Film History and the Second World War*. London: Imperial War Museum, 2010. http://eprints.uwe.ac.uk/22267.

Stanfield, Peter. '"Pix Biz Spurts with War Fever": Film and the Public Sphere – Cycles and Topicality'. *Film History: An International Journal*, 25, no. 1–2 (2013): 215–26.

Stanfield, Peter. 'Intent to Speed: Cyclical Production, Topicality, and the 1950s Hot Rod Movie'. *New Review of Film and Television Studies*, 11, no. 1 (2013): 34–55.
Steinhart, Daniel. 'Postwar Hollywood, 1945–1967, Part Two: Foreign Location Shooting'. *Hollywood on Location*, 101–23.
Steinhart, Daniel. '"Paris . . . As You've Never Seen It Before!!!": The Promotion of Hollywood Foreign Productions in the Postwar Era'. *InMedia. The French Journal of Media Studies*, 3 (2013).
Steinhart, Daniel. 'The Making of Hollywood Production: Televising and Visualizing Global Filmmaking in 1960s Promotional Featurettes'. *Cinema Journal*, 57, no. 4 (2018): 96–119.
Steinhart, Daniel. *Runaway Hollywood: Internationalizing Postwar Production and Location Shooting*. Berkeley, CA: University of California Press, 2019.
Stubbs, Jonathan. 'Hollywood's Middle Ages: The Development of Knights of the Round Table and Ivanhoe, 1935–53'. *Exemplaria*, 21, no. 4 (2009): 398–417.
Stubbs, Jonathan. 'The Eady Levy: A Runaway Bribe? Hollywood Production and British Subsidy in the Early 1960s'. *Journal of British Cinema and Television*, 6, no. 1 (2009): 1–20.
Studies in Public Communication. 'Art Films and Eggheads'. 2, Summer 1959, 10.
Suid, Lawrence H. *Guts & Glory: The Making of the American Military Image in Film*. Lexington, KT: University Press of Kentucky, 2002.
Tarantino, Quentin. *Once Upon a Time in Hollywood*. London: Weidenfeld and Nicholson, 2021.
Television Academy. 'Pink Panther, The'. 23 October 2017. http://www.emmytvlegends.org/interviews/shows/pink-panther-the.
Television Business International. 'Amazon to "Reimagine and Develop" MGM Shows After $8.45bn Deal'. https://tbivision.com/2021/05/27/amazon-to-reimagine-develop-mgm-shows-after-8-45bn-deal.
The Exhibitor. 'Exhibitors Must Help Hollywood'. 9 June 1948.
The Exhibitor. 'RKO Executives Meeting at Studio'. 22 September 1943, 20.
The Telegraph. 2016. 'Film'. April 25, 2016. http://www.telegraph.co.uk/film/star-wars--a-new-hope/movies-influences-george-lucas.
Thompson, Kristin, and David Bordwell. *Film History: An Introduction*. London: McGraw Hill, 1994.
Thomson, David. *The New Biographical Dictionary of Film*. London: Little Brown, 2002.
Truffaut, Francois. 'Une certaine tendance du cinéma français'. *Cahiers du Cinéma*, 31 (1957): 15–28.
Truscott, Lucian K. IV. 'Hollywood's Wall Street Connection'. *New York Times Encyclopaedia of Film*, 26 February 1978. https://www.nytimes.com/1978/02/26/archives/hollywoods-wall-street-connection-what-has-become-known-as-the.htm.
Turman, Lawrence. *So You Want to Be a Producer*. New York: Three Rivers Press, 2005.
Tzioumakis, Yannis. *American Independent Cinema*. New Brunswick: Rutgers University Press, 2006.
United Artists Collection. *Wisconsin Center for Film and Theater Research*, Madison. Boxes 1, 4, 5, 7, 24, 25, 42, 47.
Waller, Gregory A. *Moviegoing in America: A Sourcebook of Film Exhibition*. Oxford: Wiley, 2001.
Webb, Lawrence. 'The Auteur Renaissance, 1968–1979'. *Hollywood on Location*, 124–54.
Who's Crying Now? BBC2. 1993.

Williams, Raymond. 'Base and Superstructure in Marxist Cultural Theory'. In *Problems in Materialism and Culture*, 31–49. London: Verso, 1980.

Windrum, Ken. *From El Dorado to Lost Horizons: Traditionalist Films in the Hollywood Renaissance 1967–1972*. Albany, NY: SUNY Press, 2020.

Wood, Tom. *The Bright Side of Billy Wilder, Primarily*. New York: Doubleday, 1970.

Yingling, Clarissa. *Clarissa Yingling Email to the Author, Harvard Baker Library Special Collections*. 26 July 2019.

Zeff, Stephen A. 'The Contribution of the Harvard Business School to Management Control, 1908–1980'. *Journal of Management Accounting Research*, 20, no. s1 (2008): 175–208.

Zinnemann, Fred, John Houseman, Irvin Kershner, Kent Mackenzie, Pauline Kael, and Colin Young. 'Personal Creation in Hollywood: Can It Be Done?' *Film Quarterly*, 15, no. 3 (1962): 16.

Index

3D films   69
20th Century Fox   7, 20, 28, 57, 69, 76, 111, 202
52 War Information Shorts   33
633 Squadron (film, Grauman, 1964)   5, 6, 40, 65, 90, 98, 100, 109, 120, 125, 129, 142, 164, 179, 181–5, 187, 191, 192, 194–200, 203, 228, 229, 247, 254, 267, 269
633 Squadron (novel, Smith)   145, 182

ABC Sunday   82
ABC Sunday Night Movie, The (1964–98)   83
ABC-TV   82, 83, 163, 168, 170, 212
Above Us the Waves (Thomas, 1955)   194
ABPC   202
Absent Without Love   47
Academy Awards   232
Acevedo-Munoz, Ernesto   111
Achard, Marcel   151
adult themes   11, 87, 94, 97, 102, 113
Adventures of Haji Baba (Weis, 1954)   69
advertising   53, 73, 83, 91, 103
Advice and Consent   93
Advice of Counsel   51
Affair in Monte Carlo (Saville, 1952)   68
A films   44, 46, 47, 55, 56, 59, 60, 93, 216
Age of Discontinuity, The (Drucker)   80, 101, 199
Airport (film, Seaton, 1970)   150
Airport (novel, Hailey)   150
Aldrich, Robert   257
allegory   110, 120, 124, 125, 128, 196
Allied Artists. *See* Monogram Pictures Corporation
Allied Exchange Owners convention (1953)   69
All New Pink Panther Show, The (TV series, 1978–9)   158
Along Came Jones (Heisler, 1945)   73
Alperson, Edward   20, 22, 31, 56, 57, 59

Altman, Rick   96
Altman, Robert   117, 238, 248
Amazon   1
American cinemas   78, 97. *See also* Hollywood
candy and popcorn sales in   30–1
industry   34
American Federation of Labor (AFL)   207
American Graffiti (Lucas, 1973)   102, 229, 235, 239, 248
American International Pictures/ AIP   243, 244, 245
Americanism Division of the American Legion   110
The American League for Peace and Democracy   24
American Mirisch Corporation   182
American New Wave   6, 215–17, 241, 244, 247
American Stock Exchange   72
American Zoetrope   212
Anatomy of a Murder   144
Anderson, Christopher   163, 164
Anderson, Ernest   73
Anderson, Sherwood   142, 144
Andrews, Bill   191
Andrews, Julie   204
animated film   97
Annapolis Story, An (Siegel, 1955)   47, 63, 65, 69, 258
Annenberg family   24, 27, 28
anti-communism   110, 210
anti-fascist films   23
anti-racism   110, 112–13
antisemitism   110, 111
anti-trust legislation (1948)   179
Apartment, The (Wilder, 1960)   1, 2, 6, 7, 17, 41, 60, 63, 83, 86, 88, 93, 96, 103, 112, 114, 116, 119, 120, 124, 130–4, 136, 141, 145, 146, 151, 153,

165, 206, 208, 223, 224, 226, 227, 229, 232, 247, 264, 269
Apocalypse Now (Coppola, 1979)   95, 247
Argosy   57
Ariane (*Czinner*, 1931)   74
Arkin, Alan   166, 172
Arkoff   75
Armstrong, Robert   48
Around the World in 80 Days (Anderson, 1956)   149
Arrow in the Dust (Selander, 1954)   73
art cinema   113, 208
artefacts   108
Ashby, Hal   90, 102, 116, 150, 215, 220, 222, 231, 237, 238, 249
Ashdown Productions   164
Ashton, Barry   85
Ashton, Frances   85
Ashton Productions   9, 79, 85
Asphalt Jungle, The (Burnett)   129
assembly-line production   23, 37–9, 55, 76, 78, 90, 97, 133, 155, 177, 179, 180
Associated British Pathe   202
Associated British Pictures Corp (ABPC)   68, 201
atelier theory   106
Attack of the Crab Monsters (Corman, 1957)   75
Attack of the Fifty Foot Woman (Juran, 1958)   75
Attack on the Iron Coast (Wendkos, 1968)   5, 171, 179, 182–3, 185, 187, 189, 191, 193, 195–9, 254
audience tastes   11, 80, 87, 93
Auerbach, Josef   60
Auerbach, Norbert   260
auteur directors   48, 49
auteurs/auteur theory/auteurism   5, 6, 7, 9, 12, 14, 86, 93, 105, 106, 107, 118–19, 231, 232
Autry, Gene   44
Avanti! (Wilder, 1972)   90, 112, 150, 151, 204, 213, 224, 229
aviation films   35

Babe Ruth Story, The (Del Ruth, 1947)   60

backstudio picture phenomenon   116
Badham, John   259, 263
Baker, Herbert   164
Baker Library   33, 137
Balding, David   235
Balio, Tino   1, 10, 11, 15, 18, 80, 84, 87, 163, 166, 251
Ball, John   145
Bancroft, Anne   221
bank nights   24
Barker, Ralph   187, 189
Barretts of Wimpole Street, The (Franklin, 1934)   36
Bart, Peter   102, 234
Battle of Midway, The (Ford, 1942)   32, 33, 254, 255, 262
Battle of the Bulge (Annakin, 1965)   95
Battle Zone (Selander, 1952)   65
Baum, Marty   218
Bavaria Film   203
Bavaria-Geiselgastaig Studios   191
Bazin, André   13, 14, 232
BBC   211
BBS   212
Beach Head (Heisler, 1954)   73
Beckett, John   80, 101, 199, 256
Bedig, Sam   234
Beebe, Ford   52
Beeson, Paul   191
Begelman, David   249
Being There (Ashby, 1979)   222
Belafonte, Harry   111
Belita   47
Bell, Emma   83
Belle of the Yukon (Seiter, 1944)   73
Belson, Jerry   168, 169
Benchley, Nathaniel   249
Ben-Hur (Wyler, 1959)   149
Benjamin, Alan A.   162
Benjamin, Robert   66, 80, 100, 134
Bennett, Joan   62–3, 131
Bernstein, Elmer   109, 110
Bernstein, Irving   207
Bernstein, Leonard   109
Bernstein, Matthew   11, 18, 85
Bernstein, Walter   109, 126
Berson, Misha   111
Best Man, The (Schaffner, 1964)   222

Best Years of Our Lives, The (Wyler, 1946)   58, 109
Bezos, Jeff   1
B films   93, 109, 243
Big Combo, The (Lewis, 1955)   47, 50, 59, 70, 243
Big Raid, The   189
biopics   35, 36
Birdt, Marvin   248
Biskind, Peter   107, 115, 215
Bissell, Whit   234
Black Gold (Karlson, 1947)   47, 60, 61
blacklisting   7, 14, 109, 110, 112, 116
Black Mask Magazine   46
Black Prince, The (*The Warriors*, Levin, 1955)   23, 32, 69, 202
Blockade (Dieterle, 1938)   24
blockbusters   7, 9, 11, 12, 14, 23, 87, 102, 104, 148, 150
Blonde (Dominik, 2022)   268
Bloore, Peter   92
blueprint   184–5
B movies   27, 31, 44, 45, 52, 55, 56, 60, 66, 75, 78, 94, 97, 103, 136, 155, 164, 197, 199, 200
Board of Trade   182
Bogart, Paul   237
Bogdanovich, Peter   238
"Bomba the Jungle Boy" (Rockford)   51
Bomba the Jungle Boy series (Beebe, 1949)   44, 45, 46, 51, 52, 60, 160, 165, 188
   Lord of the Jungle (1955)   69
Bonacci, Anna   151
Bonnie and Clyde (Penn, 1967)   124, 209, 216, 221, 239, 243, 258
book nights   24–6
Border Jumpers, The (Brown)   98, 144, 204
Bordwell, David   17, 48–50, 66
Borehamwood Studios   191
Bout de Souffle, A (Godard, 1960)   221
Bowery Boys series   44, 52, 62, 161
Bowie, Jim   78
Bowie Organization   191
box office   21, 26, 53, 56, 74, 78, 93, 97, 98, 100, 102, 103, 106, 140, 147, 148–51, 177–8, 199

Boxoffice (magazine)   26, 51, 87
Box Office Digest (magazine)   55
Boyle, Robert   89
branding   124, 142
Branton, G. Ralph   62, 71, 72
Breffort, Alexandre   151, 203
Brickhill, Paul   129
Bridal Wave (Hallmark, 2015)   263
Bride and the Beast, The (Weiss, 1958)   75
Bridges, Beau   222
Bridges, Lloyd   185, 196
Brief Encounter (Lean, 1945)   63
British Film Fund Agency   182
British Film Producers Association   182
British films   68, 100, 182
   Second World War   98
Broadway   21, 81, 92, 93, 95, 106, 111, 138, 143, 149, 150, 253
Broadway Melody (Del Ruth, 1936)   35
Broidy, Samuel 'Steve'   43–5, 51, 52, 54, 56, 59, 60, 62, 66, 68–72, 75, 160–1
Bronson, Charles   89, 126, 267
Brookes, Ian   133
Brown, Matt   85
Bryna   86
Bryna Productions   117, 118, 228
Brynner, Yul   74, 126, 162, 175
Buchholz, Horst   126, 175, 203, 204
bureaucracy   37, 40, 41, 124, 133
Burkett, James S.   46
Burnett, W. R.   47, 129
Burrows, George   72
Burstyn, Ellen   258, 259
Buscombe, Edward   105–6
business management theory   86, 118–19
Business Week (magazine)   88
Butch Cassidy and the Sundance Kid (Roy Hill, 1969)   146, 247
B Westerns   61, 75, 151
By Love Possessed (film, Sturges, 1961)   93, 96, 109, 114, 141, 144, 146, 148, 151, 223, 242
By Love Possessed (novel, Cozzens)   144, 145

Caan, James   185, 193
Cagle, Chris   96
Cagney, James   22, 23, 54, 203

Cameron, Rod   61
Cannes   74, 202
Cannon for Cordoba (Wendkos, 1970)   4, 5, 204, 213, 240, 267
Capitol Records   53
Capitol Theater   26, 32
Capra, Frank   57, 71
Captain Blood (Curtiz, 1935)   23
Carr, Thomas   236
Carr, Trem   56, 72
Carrie (DePalma, 1976)   236
Casablanca (Curtiz, 1942)   125
Casanova Brown (Wood, 1944)   73
Cassavetes, John   77
Cast a Giant Shadow (Shavelson, 1966)   33, 110, 112, 114, 118, 139, 174, 204, 215, 228, 246, 247, 254
Cast a Long Shadow (film, Carr, 1959)   85, 90, 93, 112, 135, 136
Cast a Long Shadow (novel)   145
Cavalry Scout (Selander, 1951)   64
CBS   5, 170, 172
censorship   46, 102, 114
Cerf, Bennett   147
Chakiris, George   4, 234, 267
Champion, John C.   61, 187–9, 190
Chapman, Michael   222
Charles, Ray   156, 218
Charlie Chan series   44, 165
Chase, The (Ripley, 1946)   47
Child of the Century, A (Hecht)   149
Children's Hour, The (*The Loudest Whisper*, Wyler, 1961)   6, 23, 35, 49, 96, 108, 109, 114, 140, 141, 208, 223, 224, 228, 246, 247
Christensen, Jerome   80, 106, 107, 115, 123, 124, 125, 134
Churubusco Studios   58
Cinecolor features   61, 63, 69
cinemagoing   21, 30, 53, 78, 103, 188
cinematic cycles   180–1, 186
Cinematograph Films Act   182
cinematography   56
cinephilia   92
Cinerama process   95
Cisco Kid series   44, 52
classical cinema   7, 17–18

Classical Hollywood Cinema, The (Bordwell, Staiger and Thompson)   17, 79
classical studio era   8, 137, 138
Clavell, James   129
Clockwork Orange (Kubrick, 1971)   224
Close Encounters of the Third Kind (Spielberg, 1977)   237, 248, 249
Cobb, Lee J.   109
Coburn, James   89, 126, 163, 254, 267
Coca Cola   54
Coca-colonization   54, 209
Cocaine (*C-Jag*, Woolrich)   46, 47, 49
Cohan, Steven   116
Cohn, Harry   2
Cole, Kenneth R.   39
Collins, Richard   109, 110
colonialism   110
Columbia   7, 127
comedies   25, 61, 94
comic magazines   26
comic strip   52
Coming Home (Ashby, 1978)   222
commissioning   141, 144, 207
Committee of the First Amendment (1947)   110
communism   110
Communist Party   110
Competitive Strategy: Techniques for Analysing Industries and Competitors (Porter)   80
Concept of the Corporation, The (Drucker)   81
confectionery business   28, 29, 49
Connor, J. D.   107, 115, 119, 120, 134
Consolidated Book Publishers   25
Constant Image, The (Davenport)   144
continuous manufacturing cycle   38, 39, 180
continuous production cycle   191
Control of the Motion Picture Industry (Huettig)   106
Conversation, The (Coppola, 1974)   223
Cooper, Gary   73, 74, 85, 109, 164
Coppola, Francis   95, 178, 238, 242, 247, 249
co-productions   7, 68, 70, 78, 85, 88, 89, 98, 118

copyright   44, 45, 51
copyright costs   139
Cordell, Frank   195
Corman, Roger   70, 75, 236, 244, 245
corporate art   106–7
Corporate Art: The Studio Authorship of Hollywood Motion Pictures (Christensen)   106, 107
corporate authorship   106–8, 134–6
corporate capitalism   128
corporate culture   7, 9, 17, 41, 84, 103, 108, 120, 130
corporate strategy   36, 59, 70, 106, 107, 115, 139, 142
cost-cutting   58, 212
cost leadership   84, 94, 99, 100
costs and staffing   40
County Fair (William Beaudine, 1950)   63
Cozzens, James Gould   146
creating customer   81–3
Crime in the Streets (Siegel, 1956)   50, 63, 77
Crosby, Bing   76
Crossfire (Dmytryk, 1947)   58
cultural legitimacy   136
Cummings, Dominic   37
Cuneo Press   25
Curtis, Tony   73, 121, 123, 124, 164, 176
Curtiz, Michael   23, 88, 125, 231, 236, 237
Cyclops, The (Gordon, 1957)   75

Dahl, Raoul   198, 248
Dalton, Rick   3–5, 266
Dam Busters, The (film, Anderson, 1955)   194
Dam Busters, The (novel, Brickhill)   129
Damone, Vic   176
Dark Mirror, The (Siodmak, 1944)   73
Dark Sea Running (Morrill)   234
Dark Victory (Goulding, 1939)   23
Darrell, Emily   42
Das Urteil (*The Verdict*, Gregor)   203
Davenport, Marcia   144
David Copperfield (Cukor, 1935)   35, 137
Davis, Bette   23
Davis, Kristin   220
Davis, Richard Harding   47

'day-and-date' strategy   21
Dead End (Wyler, 1937)   35
Deadline at Dawn (Clurman, 1946)   47
Deagon, Gracie   42
Death Where Is Thy Sting? (*The Bells of Hell Go Ding a Ling a Ling*, 1960s)   118, 183, 186, 198, 248
Declaration of Independents, The (ABC-TV)   82, 83
decline period   84
Decoy (Bernhard, 1946)   48
De Havilland decision (1944)   206
Delon, Alain   204
Del Ruth, Roy   23, 60
Deluxe Laboratories   135
De Mille, Cecil B.   34
demographics   101–4, 188
DePalma, Brian   238, 245
Desperado (TV Movie, Vogel, 1987)   47, 261, 262, 263, 264
Destination Moon (Pichel, 1950)   64
De Windt, Hal   220
Dial Red O (Ullman, 1955)   63
Diamond, I. A. L.   74, 89, 130, 131, 132, 203, 206, 225
Diamond Head (Green, 1962)   5
DiCaprio, Leonardo   3, 267
Directors Guild   2
director-unit system   10
Dirty Dozen, The (Aldrich, 1967)   198
Disembodied, The (Grauman, 1957)   75
Dish Nights   26
division of labour   20
Dmytryk, Edward   70
Doctor Zhivago (1965)   174
documentaries   81, 82
Don't Gamble with Strangers (Beaudine, 1946)   48
dope films   46, 49
Dorchester Productions Inc.   119
double bills   24, 27, 28, 55, 59, 92, 97, 100, 164, 197, 198
Douglas, Gordon   217, 236
Douglas, Kirk   86, 110, 117, 118, 203, 228, 231
Doyle, Conan   149, 203
Dracula (Badham, 1979)   109, 203, 235, 243, 253, 256, 259, 262, 263

'Drafting Controls' (Mirisch) 39
Dragonfly Squadron (Selander, 1954) 65, 187
Dragoti, Stan 259
drive-ins 12, 244
Drucker, Peter 80, 81, 101, 199
Duck, You Sucker (Leone, 1971) 267
Duel in the Jungle (Marshall, 1954) 73
Duke, Patty 221
Dunlop, Scott 46
Dwan, Allan 65
Dyer, Geoff 196
Dyer, Richard 219

Eady, Sir Wilfred 182
Eady Levy 68, 93, 98, 100, 181, 182, 187, 196, 197, 199, 202, 203, 210, 211, 260
Earthquake (Robson, 1974) 256
East Side Kids series, *The* 52, 77
Easy Rider (Hopper, 1969) 104, 212
Easy Riders, Raging Bulls (Biskind) 215, 244, 245
Ebert, Roger 239
Edmondson, Joe 234
Edwards, Blake 7, 61, 88, 95, 102, 149, 187, 204, 231, 237, 251, 259
Edwards, Kyle Dawson 46, 52, 139, 140, 142
efficiency/inefficiency 36, 40, 41, 186
Egy, kettő, három (Molnar) 151, 203
Elmes, Guy 189, 190
Elstree Studios 201, 202
Emmerich, Roland 266
Empire of Their Own, An (Gabler) 2
Empire Strikes Back, The (Kershner, 1980) 235, 248
entry period 84, 95, 96
Evans, Robert 102, 236
Event 1000 (Rosenberg) 257
exhibition and publicity 11–12
Exhibitor, The (magazine) 55
Exodus (novel, Uris) 144
Exodus (film) 93
exploitation cinema 11, 52, 92–4, 103, 136, 151

Faces (Cassavetes, 1968) 223
Factory Management and Maintenance (journal) 38, 42, 179, 199

Fall Guy (Le Borg, 1947) 5, 47–8, 50, 109
family audience 75, 102, 103, 151
family business 42, 65, 84, 87, 89–90, 99, 103
family films 7, 87, 102
Fanfare d'amour (Pottier, 1935) 203
Fanfaren der Liebe (Hoffmann, 1951) 123, 203
Farmer's Daughter, The (Potter, 1947) 58
feature films 83, 142, 164, 177
Federal Defence Tax 27
Ferrer, Jose 66, 109, 211
Fiddler on the Roof (film, Jewison, 1971) 1, 2, 50, 90, 94, 99, 102, 108, 110, 112, 140, 141, 150, 151, 166, 204, 213, 226, 229, 246, 251, 268
Fiddler on the Roof (musical) 142
Fields, Verna 250
Fighting Lady, The (Wyler, 1944) 255
Film as Film (Perkins) 6
Film Bulletin (magazine) 64, 74
Film Daily (newspaper) 29, 50
Film Encyclopaedia (Katz) 2
film industry 85, 132, 156
   history 80
   industrial change by 39
filmmaking 35, 97, 117
   Hollywood 120
   independent 82
Film Quarterly (Journal) 225
film(s)
   business 78, 80, 86, 115, 159, 160
   and fashion 26, 53
   history 2, 5, 9, 23, 116, 134
   noir 47, 48, 50, 59
   pre-selling 54, 81, 91
   production 34, 36, 40, 98
   rights 111, 210
   school generation 242
   series 44, 51–3, 92, 97, 156–9, 167, 173
Films Act
   1960 182
   1966 199
Films and Filming (Magazine) 226
Finnish Relief Fund 27
First National 20
First Texan, The (Haskin, 1956) 32, 78, 118

First Time, The (Neilson, 1969)   102, 152, 204, 206, 223, 224, 227, 230, 239
Fisher, Steve   47, 50
Fitzwilly (Mann, 1967)   109, 112, 116, 145, 152, 155, 187, 215, 241, 246
flashbacks   50, 51, 65, 66
Flat Top (*Eagles of the Fleet*, Selander, 1952)   50, 65
Flat Top (Selander, 1952)   47, 64, 65, 254, 258
Fleischer, Richard   237
Fleming, Ian   194
flexible production   198
Flight to Mars (Selander, 1951)   64, 75, 243
Flynn, Errol   23, 202
Follow That Dream (Douglas, 1962)   90, 112, 145, 239
Fonda, Henry   221
Footlight Parade   23
Forbes, Bryan   242
Ford, Cecil   202
Ford, Derek   190, 191
Ford, Donald   190, 191
Ford, Henry   133
Ford, John   57–8, 88, 89, 96, 231, 232, 236
Fordism   132, 133, 155
Fort Massacre (Newman, 1958)   41, 60, 93, 112, 117, 162–3, 217, 218
Fortune (magazine)   23
Fortune Cookie, The (Wilder, 1966)   90, 113, 119, 134, 153, 215, 217
Fosse/Verdon (FX, 2019)   268
Four Star   163
Fox, Harry   42
Fox, William   34
Fox Wisconsin Theatres   56
franchise films   16, 103, 104, 146, 156
Franciscus, James   3, 185
freelance/freelancing   42, 51, 120, 122–6, 128, 155, 160, 166, 201
French, George   56
French film theory   17
Friedkin, William   70
Friendly Persuasion (Wyler, 1956)   35, 73, 74, 109, 140
From Hell It Came (Milner, 1957)   75

From Here to Eternity (Zinneman, 1953)   146
frozen funds   7, 15, 16, 78, 98
Fugitive, The (Ford, 1947)   58
Fuller, Robert   175
fur fashion   25

Gaily Gaily (film, Jewison, 1969)   8, 32, 35, 83, 95, 99, 100, 112, 114–16, 149, 152, 206, 223, 230, 238, 240
Gaily Gaily (memoirs, Hecht)   143
games   24–6
Gangster, The (Wiles, 1947)   50, 60, 61
gangster films   109, 124
Garden of Cucumber, A (book)   145
Gardner, Ed   42
Garner, James   89
Garrick Theater   22
Gaynor, Mitzi   123
General Federal Studios   116
General Motors   81
General Teleradio Corp   63
Genius of the System, The (Schatz)   14
George, Christopher   168, 185, 192, 204
Get Shorty (Leonard)   249
Getting Straight (Rush, 1970)   235
Ghetto, The (Uris)   144
Gibson, Althea   113
Gibson, William   221
Gift Horse (Bennett, 1952)   194
gimmicks   24–6
Giovacchini, Saverio   11
giveaways   24–6
Gladwell, Malcolm   241, 242
Glashu, Flora   19
Gleich, Joshua   208, 209, 212
globalization   97
Globe Photos   82
Gloria-Film GmbH   203
Glorias   42
Godard, Jean-Luc   209
Godfather, The (Coppola, 1972)   7, 150, 157, 176, 177, 222, 237, 243, 247
Godzilla, King of the Monsters (Morse/Honda, 1956)   11
Goetz, Hayes   65, 73
Goldberg, Fred   147
Goldwyn, Samuel   2, 58, 75, 233

Gone with the Wind (Fleming, 1939) 149
Good, The Bad and the Ugly, The (Leone, 1966) 267
Gordon, Sam 89
Gow, Gordon 226
Graduate, The (film, Nichols, 1967) 133, 209, 216, 221, 226, 239, 247
Graduate, The (novel, Webb) 222
Graham, William 237
Grand National Pictures 31
Grant, Cary 74, 118, 121, 124, 248
Grant, Lee 109
Grauman, Walter 164, 183, 195, 198, 237
Gray Lady Down (Greene, 1976) 119, 180
Grease (Kleiser, 1978) 237
Great Depression 21, 23, 24
Great Escape, The (Sturges, 1963) 1–6, 33, 47, 65, 83, 100, 112, 119, 120, 129–30, 140, 146, 151, 174, 180, 183, 194, 197, 204, 211, 223, 228, 229, 242, 254, 266, 267
Great Escape; The Untold Story, The (TV series, 1988) 129
Greatest Story Ever Told, The (Stevens, 1965) 95
Greene, David 263
Grey Lady Down (Greene, 1978) 253, 257, 258, 260, 263
Greystoke (Hudson, 1984) 107
Gries, Tom 162, 237
guerrilla war 118
Guilty, The (Reinhardt, 1947) 50
Gun Crazy (Lewis, 1950) 59
Gunfight at Dodge City, The (Newman, 1959) 33, 90, 93, 162, 163
Gunfight at the OK Corral (Sturges, 1957) 144, 162
Gunfight (TV series) 163
Gunn, Bill 220
Guns of Navarone, The (Lee Thompson, 1961) 183

Hailey, Arthur 150, 252
Hallelujah Trail, The (film, Sturges, 1966) 5, 17, 60, 95, 115, 245, 265
Hallelujah Trail, The (novel) 145
Hallowe'en 25

Halls of Anger (Bogart, 1970) 102, 110, 206, 218, 219, 220, 224, 230, 239, 240, 247
Hamilton (Kail, 2020) 268
Hannan, Brian 173
Hansberry, Lorraine 111
Hardcore (Schrader, 1979) 222
Harmon, Sidney 70
Harnick, Aaron 268
Harold and Maude (Ashby, 1971) 222
Harvard Business School 33–4
  curriculum 36–7
  on Hollywood 34–6
Harvard Library 35
Harvard University Press 36
harvesting 260
harvest strategy 99, 100
Hateful Eight, The (Tarantino, 2015) 267
Haunting, The (Wise, 1963) 229, 230
Haunting of Hill House, The (Jackson) 230
Haunting of Hill House, The (Netflix series, 2018) 266
Hawaii (novel, Michener) 142, 144, 148, 149, 152, 161
Hawaii (Roy Hill, 1966) 60, 90, 93, 94, 96–8, 102, 109, 110, 112, 119, 140, 141, 146, 147, 149–51, 158, 159, 162, 173–4, 204, 215, 217, 224, 226, 246
  Hawaiians, The (film, Gries, 1970) 90, 97, 99, 110, 147, 158, 159, 162, 171, 197, 204, 215, 246, 254, 257
Hawaiians, The (novel) 149
Hayden, Sterling 64
Hayes, Peter Lind 163
Hays, Will H. 34
Healy, Mary 163
Heaven's Gate (Cimino, 1980) 103
Hecht, Ben 35, 149
Hecht-Lancaster 86
Heermance, Richard 89, 163
Hell Boats (Wendkos, 1970) 33, 179, 182–5, 187, 191, 192, 194, 195, 197, 198, 200, 254
Hellman, Lillian 35, 96, 109, 110, 141
He Looked Like Murder (Woolrich) 50

Henderson, Stuart   156, 157, 166, 172, 174, 177
Henson, Nicky   199
Hepburn, Audrey   74
Heston, Charlton   162, 253, 254, 256, 257
Hey Landlord (TV series, 1966–7)   120, 168, 247
Hiawatha (Neumann, 1952)   44, 47, 69, 75, 143
High School Hero (Dreifuss, 1946)   53, 77
Highway Dragnet (Juran, 1954)   244
Hill, Walter   249
Hiller, Arthur   263
history films   246
Hitchcock, Alfred   57
Hoffman, Dustin   249
Hoffman, Herman   189, 190
Hold Back the Night (Dwan, 1956)   65
Holden, William   76
Hollywood   6, 64, 65, 72, 76, 78, 79, 85, 90, 98, 110, 114, 122, 134, 143, 148, 207
  and assembly lines   54–6
  business strategy in   80
  companies   211
  filmmakers/filmmaking   7, 81, 155
  films   6, 91, 106, 107, 113, 119, 123, 138, 157, 210
  history   1, 9, 105, 157, 201
  parties   28
  post-war   121
  production companies   6, 80, 107
  recession in   174
  Renaissance   216, 238
  sequels and series films   159
  standardization   34–6, 56, 87
  studios   17, 107, 128, 171, 177, 208
  theatre   24, 27, 32
  transformation   103
Hollywood at the Crossroads (Bernstein)   207
Hollywood Film Council   207
Hollywood Goes Independent (ABC-TV)   83
Hollywood on Location (Gleich and Webb)   201, 209
Hollywood Reporter (magazine)   76, 79, 207

Hollywood Special, ABC-TV   82, 83
Hollywood Theater   56
Hollywood The Dream Factory: An Anthropologist Looks at the Moviemakers (Powdermaker)   54
homology   128
Hope, Bob   76
Hopper, Dennis   238
horizontal integration   153, 159, 177
Hornblow, Arthur, Jr.   67
Horse Soldiers, The (Ford, 1959)   13, 17, 35, 74, 93, 113, 224, 232, 254
Hour of the Gun (Sturges, 1967)   90, 140, 162, 215
house style   105–6
House Un-American Activities Committee (HUAC)   109, 110, 210
Houston, Sam   32, 78
Howard, Ron   236, 248
How the West Was Won (Ford/ Hathaway/ Marshall/Thorpe, 1962)   95
How to Succeed in Business Without Really Trying (book, Mead)   130
How to Succeed in Business Without Really Trying (film, Swift, 1967)   41, 83, 86, 90, 112, 115, 119, 134, 136, 141, 148, 152, 187, 215, 246
How to Succeed in Business Without Really Trying (musical)   228–9
Hudson, Rock   148
Huettig, Mae D.   106, 107
Human Jungle, The (Newman, 1954)   73
Husbands (Cassavetes, 1970)   222
Huston, John   66, 68, 70, 71, 74, 109, 110, 115, 143, 150, 201, 202, 210, 211, 231, 236
hyphenate   11, 85, 87, 102, 123

IATSE   207
improvisation   77, 100, 204
Incendiary Blonde (Marshall, 1945)   57
Incredible Victory (Lord)   254
Independent Film Project Value Chain   92
independent films   92, 121, 130
  American   92
  British   92

companies   1, 6, 8, 9, 11, 15, 16, 20, 57, 75, 87, 103, 108, 117, 119, 155, 157, 160, 188, 201, 208
production   1, 6, 8–11, 15, 16, 18, 27, 39, 57, 70, 72, 73, 76, 82, 84, 85, 87, 92, 108
independent Milwaukee theatres   24, 27, 30
Independent Motion Picture Producers Association   66
Indestructible Man (Pollexfen, 1956)   75
indie films   7, 76, 212
Indiewood movies   104
Industrial Management Engineering curriculum   36
Informer, The (Ford, 1935)   35
in-house productions   10, 11, 46, 65, 76, 81, 163, 171
integrated casting   113, 219
intellectual property (IP)   1, 15, 86, 93–5, 99, 136, 140, 151, 167, 177–8, 203–4
International Pictures   73
Interstate Television Corp   62
In the Fog (Davis)   47
In the Heat of the Night (film, Jewison, 1967)   1, 2, 6, 7, 10, 23, 94, 97–9, 108–12, 140, 143, 145, 150, 151, 153, 158, 161, 166, 168, 171, 172, 174, 176, 206, 209, 215, 216, 218, 220–4, 233, 238–40, 247, 262, 265, 268, 269
  Organization, The (Medford, 1971)   99, 134, 158, 171, 176, 223, 230, 265
  They Call Me MISTER Tibbs (Douglas, 1970)   99, 113, 114, 158, 171, 172, 176, 177
In the Heat of the Night (novel, Ball)   142, 145
In the Heat of the Night (TV series)   99
Invasion of the Body Snatchers (Siegel,1956)   47, 63, 75, 109, 110, 209, 243
inventory   36, 45, 64, 139
Irma La Douce (film, Wilder, 1963)   17, 49, 60, 82–3, 98, 112–14, 151, 203, 210, 223, 224, 229
Irma La Douce (musical, 1956)   203

Iron Horseman, The (TV series, 1960)   162
It Happened on Fifth Avenue (Del Ruth, 1947)   60
It's a Mad Mad Mad Mad World (Krämer, 1963)   95
It's A Pleasure (Seiter, 1945)   73
Ivanhoe (Thorpe, 1952)   44, 45, 202
I Wouldn't Be in Your Shoes (Nigh, 1948)   47, 50–1

Jackson, Shirley   229–30
Jameson, Fredric   150, 246
Jaws (Spielberg, 1975)   7, 8, 23, 91, 104, 107, 120, 150, 157, 177, 222, 243–5, 249, 252
Jewison, Norman   7, 8, 88, 95, 96, 102, 116, 149, 169, 216, 217, 218, 220, 232, 237, 242, 251, 252
Jews/Jewish   2, 19, 45, 109–12, 204
Jinks, Dan   268
Johnson, Ben   12, 64
Johnson, Boris   37
Johnson, Clarence L. 'Kelly'   37
Johnston, W. Ray   72
joint production ventures   85, 88
Jolson, Harry   42
Jones, Dorothy   206
Jones, Quincy   169, 218
Journal of the Producers Guild   67, 207, 209
Journal of the Screen Producers Guild (journal)   90, 210
Judgment of Cory, The (Yates)   143
Junior Prom (Dreifuss, 1946)   77
Justice Department   61

Kail, Thomas   268
Kanin, Garson   109, 237
Kanter, Jay   131
Karlson, Phil   24, 56, 237
Katz, Samuel   34
Katzman, Sam   70, 77
Kaufman, Robert   234, 235
Kaye, Danny   123
Keith Theatre   58, 59
Kelly's Heroes (Hutton, 1970)   198
Kenilworth Investment Co   62

Kennedy, George   175
Kennedy, John F.   33
Kennedy, Joseph P.   34
Kershner, Irvin   233, 247
Kid Galahad (Curtiz, 1937)   24, 120, 140
Kid Galahad (Karlson, 1962)   239
Kidnapped (1948)   44, 139
King, Henry   76
King Brothers   46, 47, 51, 59, 61, 70, 72
King Kong (Cooper/Schoedsack, 1933)   48, 229
King Rat (Clavell)   129
Kings of the Sun (Lee Thompson, 1963)   5, 153
Kinney   212
Kintner, Robert   163
Kiss Me, Stupid (Wilder, 1964)   49, 97, 112, 114, 120, 135, 151, 152, 165, 203, 223, 224, 225, 229
Kitty Foyle (Wood, 1940)   28
Klein, Amanda Ann   180-1, 186, 188, 194
Klute (Pakula, 1971)   222
Knight, Arthur   82
Koch, Howard   109, 110, 125
Koerner, Charles   10, 57, 58
Korean War (1950-3)   65-6, 186, 187
Koret, Stephanie   54
Koret Fashions   37, 53-4
Kotto, Yaphet   262
Krämer, Peter   223, 224, 234, 238
Krasne, Philip N.   46
Krim, Arthur   66, 80, 81, 100, 161, 170, 199, 233, 240, 241, 256, 260
Kurnitz, Harry   151, 203
Kurtz, Gary   235, 248
Kwiz Kash   25, 26

La Brava (Leonard)   249, 262
Ladd, Alan   237
Lady Sings the Blues (Furie, 1972)   219
La Haine (Kassovitz, 1995)   265
Lancaster, Burt   86, 231
Landlord, The (film, Ashby, 1970)   17, 51, 83, 90, 100, 102, 103, 109, 110, 112, 116, 120, 143, 145, 150, 169, 206, 209, 218, 222-4, 226, 227, 233, 238-40, 246, 247-9, 265, 274

Landlord, The (novel, Hunter)   149, 219, 220
Lang, Jennings   62, 131, 252
Langella, Frank   259
Lasky, Jesse L.   34, 35, 137, 138
Last Detail, The (Ashby, 1973)   222
Last Escape, The (Grauman, 1970)   100, 153, 179, 183-5, 187, 190, 191, 194-200
Last Harbor Raid, The (TV series, 1967-8)   212
LaVigne, Emile   89
Learning Tree, The (Parks, 1969)   219
Lehman, Ernest   111
Leigh, Janet   1964
Lemmon, Jack   17, 82, 89, 121, 124, 131, 164, 176, 206
Leneuville, Eric   263
Lennart, Isobel   109, 132
Leonard, Elmore   47, 150, 249, 261, 262
Leopard Man (Tourneur, 1943)   47
Le Retourne des cendres (Montheilhet)   151, 203
Lerner, Max   42
Lesser, Sol   52
Lewis, Jon   14, 15
Lewis, Joseph H.   59, 70, 234
liberalism   113-15, 209
Liberty Films   57, 71
L'idiote (Achard)   151, 203
Life (magazine)   166
Lily in Winter (TV movie, Mann, 1994)   262, 263
Limey, The (Soderbergh, 1999)   265
Line Up, The (Siegel, 1958)   209
Lion's Gate   117, 118, 212
Little Caesar (LeRoy, 1931)   22
Little Rascals, The (TV re-release of *Our Gang* series)   260
Litvak, Anatol   242
Liveliest Art, The (Knight)   82
Lloyd, Ted   187
lobby vending machines   30
Lockheed Aircraft Corporation   37-8, 42, 43, 179, 183
Loew, Marcus   34
Loew's. *See* MGM
Lollobrigida, Gina   203

Lonely are the Brave (Miller, 1962)   118, 228
Lonely Crowd, The (Riesman)   130
Lopert Films   114
L'ora della fantasia (*The Dazzling Hour*, Bonacci)   203
Lord of the Rings, The (Jackson, 2001–3)   161, 176
Lorentz, Pare   57
Lorimar   171
Loring, Teala   48
L'orra della fantasia (Bonacci)   151
Love at First Bite (Dragoti, 1979)   235, 259
Love in the Afternoon (Wilder, 1957)   54, 74, 202
Love Story (Hiller, 1970)   220
Lucas, George   178, 238, 242, 245, 247, 248
Luhrman, Baz   266
Lumet, Sidney   77

McCallum, David   185, 195
McCarthyism   110
McCrea, Joel   75, 162, 163
McKay, Brian   248
McKellen, Ian   248
Mackenzie, Aeneas   45
MacLaine, Shirley   17, 89, 221, 223
MacLean, Alistair   183, 243
McNamara, Robert   33
McQueen, Steve   3–5, 89, 105, 126, 175, 223, 266
McQuire, Dorothy   73–4
Maggie and Jiggs in Court (Beaudine, 1948)   52, 54
Magnificent Ambersons, The (Welles, 1942)   5
Magnificent Obsession (Sirk, 1954)   5
Magnificent Seven, The (film, Fuqua, 2016)   173, 266
Magnificent Seven, The (series)   1, 2, 4–6, 10, 157, 161, 163–7, 172, 174, 176, 177, 202–4, 206, 212, 213
  Guns of the Magnificent Seven (Wendkos, 1969)   4, 5, 99, 157, 171, 173, 175, 176, 190, 197, 211, 249

Magnificent Seven, The (film, Sturges, 1960)   58, 65, 91, 93, 94, 97, 99, 109, 110, 112, 119, 120, 124, 126–8, 140, 141, 146, 151, 157, 173, 175, 217, 223, 227–30, 239, 242, 247, 267
Magnificent Seven Ride, The (McCowan, 1972).   99, 157, 171, 172, 173, 175–6, 213
Return of the Seven, The (film, Kennedy, 1966)   157, 164, 168, 171, 173, 175, 176
Magnificent Seven, The (TV series, 1998–9)   249, 262
Maharis, George   4, 267
Mahin, John Lee   35
Mainwaring, Daniel   47
'making-of'   8, 82, 83, 268
Malta Film Facilities   191, 192
Malvern, Paul   46
Man in the Net (Curtiz, 1959)   22, 23, 93, 112, 113, 125, 134, 136, 223, 227, 237
Man in the Net (novel)   145
Mann, Anthony   88, 232, 236
Mann, Delbert   237, 263
Mann, Denise   18, 113, 117, 120–2, 131, 224, 225
Mann, George   42, 96, 106, 130
Man of the West (Mann, 1958)   1, 6, 13, 17, 90, 93, 98, 109, 112, 120, 125, 136, 201, 204, 224, 229, 232, 265, 268
Manuel, Alvin   66
Man Who Would Be King, The (Kipling)   45, 74
Marcus, Allan   234
Marked Man as *Mark of the Whistler, The* (Castle, 1944)   47
marketing   2, 11, 15, 23, 36, 46, 52, 61, 73, 82, 91, 124, 151
Marshall, Garry   168, 169
Martin, Steve   266
Marvin, Lee   229
Marx, Groucho   250
MASH (Altman, 1970)   118, 198
Massacre Harbor (Peyser, 1968)   5, 100, 114, 140, 185, 205, 229
mass consumption   55, 132, 133

Masterson, Bat   162
Mateos, Julian   175
matinee shows   26
Matrix, The (trilogy)   176
maturity period   84
May, Bradford   263
Mayer, Louis B.   2
Mayo, Virginia   75
Maze, The (Cameron Menzies, 1953)   50, 64, 69
Mazurki, Mike   164
'Measuring Drafting Output' (Mirisch and Cole)   39
Medford, Don   237
media culture   108
Melody Ranch   44
Melville, Herman   21, 68
Memphis Warner Theatre   21
Menne, Jeff   80, 86, 107, 117, 118, 134, 225, 227, 228
Menzies, William Cameron   47
merchandizing   7, 10, 53, 54, 60, 88, 92, 247
MGM   1, 7, 20, 45, 52, 103, 125, 127, 202
MGM Television   172
Michener, James A.   97, 144, 147, 148, 161, 162
Midsummer Night's Dream, A (Dieterle/Reinhardt, 1935)   35–6, 137
Midway (Emmerich, 2019)   266
Midway (Smight, 1976)   2, 65, 151, 252, 254–6, 260, 262, 263
Mila 18 (Uris)   144
Milestone, Lewis   119
Milius, John   238, 242
Millar, Stuart   221
Miller, David   118, 248
Milwaukee   22–5, 27–32, 72
Mineo, Sal   77
Ministry of Information and Tourism   211
Miracle Worker, The (Penn, 1962)   93, 221
Mirisch, Harold   2, 8, 10, 19, 21, 43, 44, 52, 53, 63, 64, 66, 68, 71, 72, 74, 77, 78, 85, 87, 91, 92, 98, 100, 102, 103, 108, 117, 131, 139, 145, 159–61, 167, 170, 194, 199, 202, 206, 207, 209, 210, 215, 230, 231, 233, 244, 251, 260
and his brothers Marvin and Walter   31–3
as independent exhibitor   24–8
at Monogram   59–62
at RKO   28, 56–9
The Theatres Candy Co.   29–31
at Warners   19–24
Mirisch, Irving   19–21, 29, 30, 58, 72, 103
Mirisch, Marvin   8, 19, 20, 28, 30–3, 56, 58, 72, 73, 78, 82, 87, 92, 100, 102, 103, 108, 130, 134, 135, 220, 226, 236, 251, 258, 261
Mirisch, Max   19
Mirisch, Walter   1, 3, 5, 6, 8, 9, 14, 19, 20, 31–5, 50, 54, 55, 60, 62–72, 75–8, 86, 87, 89, 91–3, 100–3, 108, 109, 111, 113, 127, 130, 131, 133, 143, 145, 146, 151, 155, 162, 163, 165, 173, 181, 186–8, 194, 202, 207, 209, 210, 213, 217, 224, 225, 226, 232, 235, 236, 243, 244, 246, 248, 249, 251, 254, 258, 261, 262, 263, 267
applying Harvard to Hollywood   179–80
at Harvard   33–4, 80, 85, 137, 139, 155, 159, 160, 189, 195
job in Hollywood   42
at Lockheed   37–8, 155, 159, 160, 183, 189, 192, 195
as management theorist   38–41
at Monogram   43–5
as producer   45–6, 138
search for series   51–3
and Woolrich   46–8
Mirisch Brothers   2, 4, 8, 13, 22, 57, 66, 70, 72, 73, 75–9, 82, 85, 102, 103, 108, 130, 160, 167, 168, 182, 201, 215, 244, 246, 260
corporate working and business strategy   80, 85, 87
management and management theory   83–4
Mirisch Brothers Production Co.   76
Mirisch Company Inc.   1, 4, 9, 19, 20, 23, 24, 28, 35, 36, 37, 39–41, 46, 48,

50–2, 54, 55, 57, 61, 63, 65–8, 70, 74, 76, 78, 79, 82, 88, 89, 90, 106–8, 124, 126–8, 130, 136–40, 180, 199, 206, 207, 215, 220, 221, 231, 232, 234, 236, 238, 239, 242, 243, 245, 246, 247, 248, 250, 260, 264, 265, 268, 269
adaptations of pretexts and contexts 137–40
adaptation strategy and industry trends 145–6
adapting non-literary fiction 142–5
attitude to television 97–8
authorship and genre 12–14
bestselling novels and Broadway hits 148–51
books as props and plot points 152–3
border jumping 204–6
British Second World War films 179
cinematic cycles 180–1
cinematic sequels 171–4
and classical cinema 17–18
contract with United Artists (UA) 84–6, 93, 94, 96–7, 99–102, 145, 162, 211
dual strategy 52, 84, 90, 94, 104
efficiency, artistry and social conscience 90–2
films and allegory 120
films and anti-racism 112–13
films as evidence 115–16
international adaptations 151–2
as Jewish company 110–12
liberalism and/as quality 113–15
and majors as authors 7–8, 116–20
managing creativity 79–81
mini-franchises 161–2
non-American IP 203–4
outsourcing development 140–2
prestige *vs.* programmers 92–4
production outside America 202–3
promotion and adaptation 146–8
rationale for series production 159–61
relaunching TV subsidiary 167–71
reliance on adaptation and quality strategy 94–6, 106
runaway productions 208–10

runback trend 212–13
Second World War cycle 187–9
sequels, series and serials 156–9
sequels and memory 175–7
series, IP and cinema 177–8
shooting international locations 201–2
as social commentators 108–10
social problem film 96
subsidies and subsidiaries 182–3
Tarantino and 3–5
television effect 165–7
TV series 162–5
Mirisch Corporation 9, 79, 97, 99, 134, 147, 173, 204, 228, 235, 259
Mirisch Films Limited 9, 79, 100, 179, 182, 188, 211, 224, 226, 242, 268
Mirisch Pictures 9, 79, 235
Mirisch Productions 9, 79, 99, 215, 223, 242, 243, 250
Mirisch-Rich Productions 3, 168, 169, 204, 211
Mirisch-Rich Television 9, 167
Mitchell, Elvis 108
Mitchum, Robert 254
mobile production 98
Moby Dick (film, Huston, 1956) 66–8, 150
Moby Dick (novel, Melville) 21, 68, 71, 73, 109, 112, 143, 201, 202, 207
mode of film practice 17
Moffat, Ivan 129
Molnar, Ferenc 151
Monnot, Marguerite 203
Monogram Exchange 44, 160
Monogram Midwest Film Company 22, 25, 30, 37, 41
Monogram Pictures Corporation 5, 22, 23, 25, 30, 35, 43–9, 52–6, 59, 63, 64, 66, 68–73, 82, 91, 93, 109, 110, 118, 131, 139, 143, 149, 151, 155, 160–2, 165, 188, 202, 209
failure of quality strategy 75–8
Mirisch (Harold) at 59–62
and narrative forms 50–1
quality and adaptations 73–5
Monogram Productions 66

Monogram Ranch   44
Monroe, Marilyn   123, 124, 167
Monteilhet, Hubert   266
Monteros, Rosenda   175
Montes, Elisa   175
Moore, Dudley   261
Morey, Edward   69
Morris, William   123, 163
Mosquito Squadron (Sagal, 1969)   5, 90, 100, 179, 182–5, 187, 190–2, 194–8, 200
Motion Picture Association   46
Motion Picture Baseball League match   20
Motion Picture Daily (magazine)   46, 55, 76, 206
Motion Picture Herald (trade paper)   29, 77
Motion Picture Theater Operators convention   21
Moulin Productions   22, 66, 67, 71, 73, 109, 143, 201, 202, 211
Moulin Rouge (Huston, 1952)   6, 35, 66–8, 71, 73, 109, 143, 202, 211, 266
movie brats   7, 9, 16, 102, 104, 109, 137, 150, 157, 177, 243
Movie Colony, The (Rosten)   106
Movie History: A Survey (Gomery and Pafort-Overdun)   2
'Movie Kwizzo'   25
Movie Palaces   30
MPH (magazine)   51
Mr Majestyk (Fleischer, 1974)   22, 47, 99, 120, 124, 134, 135, 150, 153, 166, 245, 249, 252
Mrs Miniver (Wyler, 1942)   125
Mr Wong series   44
MTM   171
Mulligan, Robert   263
multinational corporations   153
multi-picture contract   47, 87, 149, 251
Mulvehill, Charles   215
Murch, Walter   242
Mure, Pierre La   66
Murphy, Audie   85
Murphy, Robert   182
The Music Corporation of America (MCA)   121–3, 125, 132

Naked in the Sun (Hugh, 1957)   75
Naremore, James   152, 153
National Brewing Company   54
National Screen Service (NSS)   31–2, 78, 82
Naughty Marietta (Leonard, 1935)   35
Naval Academy   65
Naval Flight School   65
NBC   120, 129, 156, 158, 162, 163, 164, 169, 170
NBC Saturday Night at the Movies (TV show, 1961–78)   83
Ned Kelly (Richardson, 1970)   240
Neilson, James   237
New American Cinema/American Renaissance. *See* New Hollywood
New Biographical Dictionary of Film (Thomson)   2
New Hollywood   6, 7, 8, 107, 117, 118, 130, 178, 198, 201, 209
Newman, Joseph   237
Newman, Paul   221
Newman, Walter   127, 128
New Pink Panther Show, The (TV series, 1993–4)   158
new realist films   50
newsreel   33, 34
New York Times (newspaper)   66, 75, 126, 144, 145, 206, 207, 210, 245, 260
Nichols, Mike   222, 235, 238
Niesen, Gertrude   23
Nigh, William   50
Niven, David   166
Noble, David   133
non-American films   140
non-American IP   203–4
non-profit experiment   234
North, Edmund H.   189
North Star, The (Milestone, 1943)   57
Not of This Earth (Corman, 1957)   75
Nowell, Richard   181, 197

Oakmont Films   79, 100
Oakmont Productions   3, 4, 9, 179, 182, 188, 211
O'Brien, Pat   123
Ocean's Eleven (Soderbergh, 2001)   119

Odlum, Floyd   58
off-shelfing   140, 208
off-shoring   81, 136, 140, 208
O'Hara, John   144–5
Old Hollywood   76
Old Hollywood Studios   132
Once Upon a Time in America (Leone, 1984)   267
Once Upon a Time in Hollywood (Tarantino, 2021)   3–5, 44, 249
Once Upon a Time … in Hollywood (Tarantino, 2019)   266, 267
Once Upon a Time in the West (Leone, 1968)   267
One, Two, Three (Wilder, 1961)   23, 54, 95, 112, 134, 151, 203, 204, 211, 246, 258
One Flew Over the Cuckoo's Nest (Forman, 1975)   223
one-off productions   39, 51, 160, 179
One Way Street (Woolrich)   47
Operation Chariot   193
Operation Crossbow (Anderson, 1965)   195
Operation Jericho   194
Operation Millennium   194
Operation Paperclip   194
Operation Ruthless   194
Operation Source   194
Orchard Films   204
organizational culture   108
Organizational Culture and Leadership (Schein)   108
Organization Man, The (Whyte)   130
Oriental Theatre   24–9, 32
Orion Pictures   260
Oscar   74, 96–8, 99, 147
Our Gang series (*The Little Rascals*)   25, 60
Outliers (Gladwell)   241
outsourcing   81, 88, 140–2
Overend, George   21
overheads   52, 68, 79, 84, 88, 95, 103, 140, 160, 170, 201, 208

P38 Lightning assembly line   37
package-unit system   7, 10–11, 39, 70, 85, 87–9, 119, 123–6, 128, 159, 172, 179, 180, 200

Palme D'Or   74
Palmer, Patrick   232
Panavision   11, 87, 97
Panavision Laboratory   135
Panhandle (Selander, 1948)   61
Pantages Theater   21
Paramount   7, 9, 15, 20, 28, 45, 71, 76, 91, 97, 102, 111, 123
Paramount Decree (1948)   60, 61, 90, 132, 155, 157, 177, 206
Park Plaza Theater   32
Parks, Gordon   219
Party, The (Edwards, 1968)   17, 95, 100, 112, 114–16, 119, 149, 165, 204, 206, 246, 247
Pathe News'   33
Patterson, Dick   176
Peck, Gregory   118, 183, 248
Peckinpah, Sam   63, 77, 164, 238, 249
Pembroke Productions   45
Penn, Arthur   221, 238, 247
Penn, Leo   109
Penn theatre   32
Peppard, George   4, 267
Pepsi Cola   54
Percy, Joyce   190
Perlberg, William   233
Persoff, Nehemiah   123
Personnel Journal   133
Persons, Lindsley   46
Peter Blatty, William   247
Peter Loves Mary (TV series, 1960–1)   89, 163
Petrie, Daniel M.   96
Peyton Place   144
Phenix City Story, The (Karlson, 1955)   47, 50, 82, 209, 243
Phillips, Julia   248, 249
Phoenix (Petzold, 2014)   266
Photoplay (magazine)   53
Picker, Arnold   74, 200
Picker, David   200, 233, 235, 236
Piece of the Action: Race and Labor in Post-Civil Rights Hollywood, A (Quinn)   216
pilot   16, 62, 63, 65, 162–5, 169–72, 176, 177, 192
Pink Panther, The (Edwards, 1964)   1, 2, 6, 10, 83, 94, 97, 99, 112, 116, 141,

146, 151, 156, 157–8, 161, 166, 167, 176, 177, 204, 247, 264
   Inspector Clouseau (Yorkin, 1968)   99, 158, 166, 172, 182
   Shot in the Dark, A (1964)   141, 151, 158, 166, 167, 176, 182, 203
Pink Panther, The (Levy, 2006)   266, 267
Pink Panther 2 (Zwart, 2009)   266
Pink Panther and Sons, The (TV series, 1984–5)   158
Pink Panther Laugh and a Half Hour, The (TV series, 1976- 8)   158
Pink Panther Meets the Ant and the Aardvark, The (TV series, 1971–6)   158
Pink Panther Show, The (TV series, 1969–71)   158
Pink Phink, The (Freleng and Pratt, 1964)   97
Pin Up Girl (Humberstone, 1944)   42
Pioneer Go Home   145
Players-Lasky. See Paramount
Poitier, Sidney   166, 172, 176, 216, 217, 222, 223
Polan, Dana   129, 130
Porter, Michael E.   80, 84, 86, 89, 91–103, 253, 260, 264
Post-Fordist Cinema: Hollywood Auteurs and Corporate Counterculture (Menne)   107
Poverty Row   44, 51, 55, 70, 136, 231
Powdermaker, Hortense   54, 55
precarity   124
Preisser, June   53, 54
'pre-selling the customer'   54
Presley, Elvis   24, 90
presold films   63, 69
pretexts and contexts   15, 26, 33, 36, 51, 108, 137–40
Price, Frank   261
Pride and Prejudice (Leonard, 1940)   35, 137
Pride and the Passion, The (Krämer, 1957)   82
Prime Time Access Rule (1970)   171
'The Principle of Scientific Management' (Taylor)   133
Principles of Management (Beckett)   80, 101

Prisoner of Zenda, The (Cromwell, 1937)   35
Prisoner of Zenda, The (Quine, 1979)   253, 256, 259, 262, 263
Private Life of Sherlock Holmes, The (Wilder, 1970)   115, 142, 174, 182, 197, 203, 213
Proctor and Gamble   163
producer-unit system   10, 46
product differentiation   84, 87, 94, 96, 99
Production Code   46, 49, 236, 241
Production Code Administration   100
Production Encyclopaedia   66
product placements   53–4
profit-sharing   11, 87, 88, 172
programmers   61
promotional featurettes   81–3
promotions   22, 26, 28, 56, 64, 65, 78, 81, 83, 92, 146–8
proprietary product technology   95
Public Enemy (Wellman, 1931)   22
Puttnam, David   262
Pygmalion (Asquith/Howard, 1938)   35, 137

quality cinema   66, 113, 188
Queen of Outer Space (Bernds, 1958)   75
Quine, Richard   259, 263
Quinn, Eithne   216, 217, 218, 220
quota system   202

Rachmil, Lewis   89, 187, 189, 190–2
racial difference   111
racism   176
radio advertising   36, 37
Radio Advertising for Retailers (1945)   36
Raft, George   62, 121, 124
Rage to Live, A (Grauman, 1965)   96, 114, 141, 146–8, 223, 234
Rage to Live, A (novel, O'Hara)   144, 145
Raging Bull (Scorsese, 1980)   215, 222
Rainbow Over the Rockies (Drake, 1947)   55
Raisin in the Sun (Hansberry)   111
Rat Patrol (TV series, 1966–8)   3, 5, 6, 90, 95, 99, 100, 168, 170, 177, 183, 204, 211–12, 247
Readers Digest (magazine)   144

Reading Management and Organization in Film (Bell)   83
Rebel Without a Cause (Ray, 1955)   77
Red Channels   75, 109, 110
Red Light (Del Ruth, 1949)   60
Reeve, Christopher   129
Reinventing Hollywood: How 1940s Filmmakers Changed Movie Storytelling (Bordwell)   18
Relyea, Robert   89
remakes   1, 2, 15, 22, 36, 48, 63, 74, 85, 92, 93, 103, 140, 149, 151, 167
reputational capital   95
Reservoir Dogs (Tarantino, 1992)   267
Return from the Ashes (Thompson, 1965)   5, 90, 110, 112, 114, 151, 174, 182, 203–4, 209, 223, 226, 246, 263, 266
Return from the Ashes (novel)   145
Rey, Alvino   42
Rich, Lee   167–71, 183
Riot in Cell Block 11 (Siegel, 1954)   50, 63, 109, 110, 209, 243
risk aversion   95, 124, 126
Riskin, Robert   55
Ritt, Martin   109
Ritz Hotel   202
RKO   7, 10, 28, 33, 45, 52, 56–9, 76, 78, 194
RKO Albee Theater   56, 189
RKO Theater Circuit   56, 58
roadshows   12, 94, 99, 140, 222
Roar Like a Dove (stage play, 1960)   144
Roar of the Crowd (Beaudine, 1953)   63
Robbins, Jerome   242
Roberts, William   127, 129
Robertson, Cliff   254
Robinson, Edward G., Jr.   22, 121, 124
Robinson Crusoe (Defoe)   143
Robnik, Drehli   198
Rock Around the Clock (Sears, 1956)   77
Rocketship XM (Neumann, 1950)   64
Rockford, Roy   51
Rodeo (Beaudine, 1952)   63
Rogers, Ginger   28
Rogers & Cowan   73
Rogerson, Ben   132
Roll, Gernot   191

Romantic Comedy (Hiller, 1983)   253, 260, 261, 263
Romulus Films   66, 67, 73
Roos, Fred   247
Rose, Reginald   77
Rose Bowl Story, The (Beaudine, 1952)   63
Rosenberg, Frank   257, 258
Rosenberg, John   45
Rosten, Leo   106
Roth, Leon   147, 233, 234
Roth-Kershner Productions   37–8, 233, 234
Roy Hill, George   7, 88, 102, 146–8, 161, 237, 247, 249
Runaway Hollywood (Steinhart)   201
runaway productions   7, 11, 15, 16, 78, 81, 85, 87, 93, 98–9, 103, 126, 201, 207–10, 252
  politics of   210–11
Run Silent, Run Deep (Wise, 1958)   189
rural/outdoor film   44
Russians Are Coming, The Russians Are Coming, The (film, Jewison, 1966)   98, 119, 140, 151, 152, 215, 238, 246, 247, 249
Russians Are Coming, The Russians Are Coming, The (novel)   145
Rydell, Mark   70

Sagal, Boris   187, 190, 198, 237
Saltzman, Philip   190
Salvage (newsreel)   33
Same Time, Next Year (Mulligan, 1978)   140, 148, 253, 258, 259, 262, 263
Same Time, Next Year (play)   142
Samuel Goldwyn Studio   2, 9, 10, 57, 79, 84, 116, 117, 191, 203, 252
Sanford, Donald   189, 190, 254
Sarge Goes to College (Jason, 1947)   54
Sarris, Andrew   7
Satan Bug, The (Sturges, 1965)   4, 5, 95, 129, 143, 183, 243, 267, 269
saturation release   7, 11, 23, 64, 91, 103
saturation technique   7, 11, 12, 23, 64, 91, 103
Saturday Evening Post (magazine)   68, 138

Saturday Matinee Christmas party   25
Saturday Night Fever (Badham, 1977)   259
Scarface (Hawks/Rosson, 1932)   124
Schaefer, George   10, 57
Schary, Dore   58
Schatz, Thomas   14, 15, 23
Schein, Edgar H.   108, 115, 120
Schell, Maximilian   204
Schnee, Charles   96
Schorr, William   164
Schrader, Paul   238
Schweitzer, S. S.   191
science fiction   75, 109
scientific management   36, 38, 39, 80, 85, 90, 133, 139, 179, 180, 193, 194
Scorpio (Winner, 1971)   281
Scorsese, Martin   222, 238, 249
Scott, David   5
Scott, Sir Walter   45
The Screen Actors Guild   123
Screen Producers Guild   14, 67, 232
screen tests   70, 72
Screenwriter, The (magazine)   55
Sea Beast, The (Webb, 1926)   21
Seasons Greetings   30
Second World War   30, 32, 65, 160, 182, 186, 187, 211, 212
Second World War film cycle   10, 11, 40, 61, 99, 100, 119, 142, 171, 179, 180, 183, 187
  calculating probabilities   192–3
  choice of storylines   193–5
  cinematic cycles   180–1
  and corporate self-expression   186–7
  end   197–200
  Mirisch and   187–9
  narrative   184–5
  producing   189–92
  production and reproduction   195–7
  subsidies and subsidiaries   182–3
Security Pictures   70
Segal, Erich   220
Selander, Lesley   61
self-consciously stylized films   50
self-referentiality   121, 122, 130
Sellers, Peter   114, 116, 165, 166, 172, 204, 259

Selznick International Pictures (SIP)   107, 140, 142
semi-documentary genre   209
semi-independent   10, 11, 85
Sensurround   252, 256
sequels   1, 7, 10, 16, 36, 81, 85, 87, 94, 97, 103, 116, 156–60, 167, 177
Sergeants 3 (Sturges, 1962)   129
Seven Arts   144, 149
Seven Samurai (Kurosawa, 1954)   167, 203, 224
Seventeen (magazine)   53
Shadows (Cassavetes, 1959)   77
Shampoo (Ashby, 1975)   222
Shawlee, Joan   164
Sheffield, Johnny   52
Shep Comes Home (Beebe, 1948)   54
Shepherd, Richard   156
Shepperton Studios   202
Sheriff Who? (TV pilot)   169–70
Shot in the Dark, A (Edwards, 1964)   223–3, 247
Showmen's Trade Review (magazine)   52, 60
Show Stoppers (radio show)   53
Shpetner, Stan   205
Sidney (Hudlin, 2022)   268
Siegel, Don   63, 70, 77, 234
Sieving, Christopher   219, 220, 221
Sinatra, Frank   123
Sinful Davey (Huston, 1969)   115, 152, 182, 230, 239, 240, 246
single-bill strategy   61
Skouras, Spyros   21
Skouras Brothers   21
Skouras Brothers Theaters   20
Skunk Works   37
Slade, Bernard   252, 259, 260, 261
Smart Politics (Jason, 1948)   53, 54
Smight, Jack   263
Smith, Frederick E.   181, 186
Smith, John S.   191
social comment film   50
social problem film   96
social realism   50, 96, 109, 113–15, 208
Society of Independent Artists (Salon of Independents)   67

Society of Independent Motion Picture Producers 67
Soderbergh, Steven 265
'solos' 27
Some Kind of a Nut (Kanin, 1969) 102, 109, 112, 115, 136, 215, 227, 241, 246
Some Like It Hot (film, Wilder, 1959) 1, 2, 6, 22, 23, 74, 88, 89, 93, 111, 112, 114, 115, 119–26, 131, 140, 141, 145, 150, 151, 164, 176, 202, 203, 206, 223, 224, 229, 247, 263, 267–9
Some Like It Hot (TV pilot) 164, 177
Sommer, Elke 204
Sondheim, Stephen 111
Song of Bernadette, The (King, 1943) 57
Soul Searching: Black Themed Cinema from the March on Washington to the Rise of Blaxploitation (Sieving) 219
Sounder (Ritt, 1972) 219
Sound Services 44
South Pacific (Logan, 1958) 144
So Well Remembered (Dmytryk, 1947) 58
Spahn Ranch 44
Spartacus (Kubrick, 1960) 110
Spencer, William W. 191
Spicer, A. H. 183
Spielberg, Steven 178, 238, 247, 249, 267
Spikes Gang, The (film, Fleischer, 1974) 4, 5, 17, 51, 102, 211–13, 228, 229, 230, 239, 240, 248
Spikes Gang, The (novel) 149
Spinner, Anthony 191
spin-offs 36, 81, 94, 99, 156, 157, 166, 167, 174, 176, 177
split screen technique 95
sponsorship 37
Stadt ohne mitleid 151
Stage Door (La Cava, 1937) 35
Staiger, Janet 9, 10, 11, 17, 39, 46, 79, 87, 126, 172
Stalag 17 (Wilder, 1953) 71
Stallion, Wild 12
Stalmaster, Lynn 89
Standard American Encyclopaedia 25
standard batch method 38, 39, 180
Standard Theatre Company 23

Stanfield, Peter 181, 186, 187, 188
Star Is Born, A (Wellman, 1937) 35
Stark, Mabel 42
star-replacement strategy 172
Star Wars (Lucas, 1977) 7, 104, 157, 176, 177, 200, 235, 237, 243–5, 247, 248, 269
State Theater, RKO 32
Status Seekers, The (Packard) 130
Steel, Arthur 58
Steiger, Rod 218
Stein, Jules 121, 122
Steinhart, Daniel 82, 83, 212
Stevens, George 57, 71
Stewart, Freddie 53, 54
Stillwater Worsted Mills 42
Sting, The (Roy Hill, 1973) 146, 247, 248, 249
Stolen Hours (Petrie, 1963) 5, 23, 140, 182, 221–2
Storm over the Pacific (Matsubayashi and Grimaldi, 1960) 255
Story of Louis Pasteur, The (Dieterle, 1936) 36
Story of the Films, The (Kennedy) 34, 137
Strange Journey (Tinling, 1946) 55
Stranger, The (Welles, 1946) 73
Straw Dogs (Peckinpah, 1971) 224
Strawn, Arthur 75
Stubbs, Jonathan 182
Studios After the Studios: Post-Classical Hollywood 1970-2010, The (Connor) 107
Studios de Boulogne 202
studio system 14, 76, 104, 153
Studio Vista 153
Sturges, John 4, 88, 95, 96, 102, 120, 126, 127, 129, 130, 133, 146, 164, 175, 181, 227, 231, 237, 242, 252
Sturges, Preston 48
Submarine X-1 (Graham, 1969) 40, 100, 179, 182, 183, 185, 187, 189–91, 193–5, 197, 199, 254
subsidiaries 88, 101, 179, 182–3
subsidies 7, 15, 16, 20, 68, 78, 93, 98, 99, 179, 182–3, 186, 208, 210
substitution and substitutes 97

Sullivan, Barry   47
Sunset Boulevard (Wilder, 1950)   60
Super Bwoing Show, The (TV series)   168
Suspense   47
Susskind, David   111
Swift, David   237

Tagget (TV movie, 1990)   262
Tales of the South Pacific (Michener)   144
Tall Stranger, The (Carr, 1957)   75
Tanen, Ned   261
Taradash, Daniel   110, 146, 147, 161
Tarantino, Quentin   3–5, 249, 265, 267
Tarzan series   52, 165
tax evasion   27
Taxi Driver (Scorsese, 1976)   222, 243, 248, 249
Taylor, Elizabeth   221
Taylor, Frederick   36, 133, 139
Taylor, Jud   129
Taylor, Samuel   151
Taylorism   40, 42, 155
Technicolor   62, 69
Technicolor CinemaScope films   11, 69, 87, 202, 208
Teenage Doll (Corman, 1957)   75
teenage pictures   77
Teenagers series   26
television   30
    audience   83
    and differentiation   97–8
    initiatives into cinema   91
    series   1, 5, 6, 8, 9, 89, 97, 99, 153, 155, 158, 160, 162–5, 171–3, 177–8
    subsidiary   62, 161, 167
Temaner, Irving   187
Temptation (Pichel, 1946)   73
Ten Commandments, The (DeMille, 1956)   149
Ten-O-Win   25
Thaler Candy Company   36
The Theatres Candy Co.   29–32, 49, 72, 78
Theodora Productions   70
These Three (Wyler, 1936)   35
The Teen Agers series   54, 77
They Call Me Mister Tibbs (Douglas, 1970)   216, 219, 223

Thirty Seconds Over Tokyo (Le Roy, 1944)   249, 255
This Is Maggie Mulligan (TV sitcom, 1964)   1964
Thomas Crown Affair, The (Jewison, 1968)   1, 6, 17, 40, 95, 99, 112, 119, 120, 124, 130, 134–6, 141, 149, 151, 197, 201, 223, 226, 227, 233, 238
Thompson, J. Lee   237
Thompson, Kristin   17
Thorpe, Jerry   70
Thousand Plane Raid, The (Sagal, 1969)   33, 38, 40, 179, 184, 185, 187, 189–94, 196, 197, 199, 203
Thulin, Ingrid   204
Tibbs, Virgil   172, 176, 177
ticket prices   21, 26, 27, 99
Time (magazine)   54, 145
time and motion   36, 40, 42
Timeslip (*The Atomic Bomb* in the United States, Hughes, 1955)   75
Tobin, Doc   261
Tom Gries Productions   211
Tom Jones (Richardson, 1963)   230
Tomorrow Is Forever (Pichel, 1946)   73
Top Gun: Maverick (Kosinski, 2022)   269
Tora! Tora! Tora! (Fox, 1970)   229, 254, 255
Torday, Ursula   234
Toulouse-Lautrec   66
Tourneur, Jacques   57
Tower Theatre   24–9
Town Without Pity (Reinhardt, 1961)   17, 49, 60, 96, 109, 110, 114, 118, 151, 152, 203, 208, 211, 223, 224, 226, 246, 269
Toys in the Attic (Roy Hill, 1963)   35, 83, 90, 93, 109, 141, 146, 148, 162, 234
Transamerica (TA)   80, 81, 100, 101, 103, 116, 120, 199, 212, 256, 260, 261
transmedia storytelling   212
transnationalism   202, 204, 212, 213
Trans-Western Pictures   72
Treasure Island (1934)   44, 139
Trilogy Entertainment   172
Trouble Shooters: Trapped Beneath the Earth (May, 1993)   262, 263
True Detective Magazine   49

True Detective Mysteries (CBS, radio series) 49
Truffaut, François 232
Trumbo, Dalton 109, 110, 147, 161, 203
Tull, Patrick 198
Turman, Lawrence 221, 222, 247
TWA 150
Two for the Seesaw (Wise, 1962) 17, 82, 83, 93, 96, 109, 112, 114, 141, 148, 149, 206, 208, 221-4, 226-8, 247, 254
Two for the Seesaw (play) 142
Tyler, Nelson 95
Typee (Melville) 74
Tzioumakis, Yannis 223

UCLA 242
Ullman, Daniel 163, 202
Undead, The (Corman, 1957) 244
United Artists (UA) 1, 2, 3, 7, 9, 15, 22, 37, 76, 79, 80-2, 84-6, 89, 92, 93, 94, 96-103, 107-8, 111, 112, 114-17, 120, 123, 125-8, 134-6, 142, 144, 145, 147, 149-52, 157, 159, 161, 162, 164-6, 170, 174, 177, 181, 183, 186, 187, 197, 200, 202, 208, 211, 243
United Artists Television 211
United Artists: The Company That Changed the Film Industry (Balio) 18
Universal Pictures 1, 7, 11, 57, 91, 107, 109
Universal TV 172
Urbach, Josephine 19
Uris, Leon 144
USC 233, 242

Vacation Days (Dreifuss, 1947) 53, 54
Valentine parties 26
value chain concept 91
Van Cleef, Lee 175
Van Dyke, Dick 102, 152, 155, 168, 227, 241
Vanguard Films 57
Variety (magazine) 27, 28, 42, 52, 53, 59, 62, 64, 70, 76, 77, 85, 88, 91, 100, 101, 113, 145, 148, 149, 156, 160, 162, 164, 165, 167-70, 173, 182, 183, 186-8, 192, 208, 212, 226, 230, 232, 236, 239, 242, 244, 245, 251, 255, 260, 261
Variety Club 56
Vaughan, Robert 126
Vega Aircraft Corp 37, 38
Veiller, Anthony 35
vertical integration 2, 7, 15, 155, 177, 268
Vertigo (Hitchcock, 1958) 125
VFX technology 3
Victor theatre 32
Victory (Cromwell, 1940) 28
Video West Panavision 95
Vidor, Doris 20
virtuosity 65, 137
VistaVision 208
Vogel, Virgil W. 263
voice-over narration 50, 60, 124, 132, 147, 152, 203
von Sydow, Max 204

Wagner, Ray 248
Wagner, Robert 254
Wales, Ken 95
Wallach, Eli 175
Wall Street Crash (1929) 20
Walsh, Raoul 105
Wanger, Walter 10, 18, 24, 25, 67, 72, 130, 131, 252
and Mirisches 62-3
Wanted: Dead or Alive (TV series, 1958-61) 5
War Activities Committee 33
war films 35, 94, 151, 183, 188, 198
Warner, Abe 20
Warner, Harry 2, 20, 23, 34
Warner, Jack 20
Warner, Sam 20
Warner, Sandra 164
Warner Bros. Pictures, Inc. 19, 20, 89
Warner Brothers 7, 10, 19-24, 28, 32, 36, 43, 44, 57, 64, 73, 78, 105, 106, 116, 124, 139
Warner-Saxe Theaters 23
'the Warners- First National' circuit 22
War of the Satellites (Corman, 1958) 75
War Production Board 30

Warren, Charles M.   189
Waye, Anthony   191
Wayne, John   254
Webb, Charles   222
Webb, Clifton   76, 212
Webster, Ferris   89
Welles, Orson   48, 57, 109
Wendkos, Paul   3, 129, 237
West, Jessamyn   73, 75
Westerns   13, 22, 34, 35, 44, 61, 64, 72, 93, 94, 108, 126, 150, 151, 163, 204
West Side Story (Spielberg, 2021)   247, 267
West Side Story (Wise/Robbins, 1961)   1, 2, 5, 7, 77, 90, 93, 94, 96, 98, 102, 108, 110–12, 114, 126, 140, 141, 148, 149, 151, 174, 206, 217, 222, 242, 246, 266, 268
West Side Story (album)   142
Wexler, Haskell   223, 233
What Did You Do in the War, Daddy? (Edwards, 1966)   32, 112, 115, 187, 215, 246, 248, 254
Wheels (Hailey)   150
Wheels (TV series, 1978)   252
Where Eagles Dare (Hutton, 1968)   183, 196
White (Dyer)   219
White Collar (Mills)   130
Whitehead, Joe   42
Whitman, Stuart   185
Who Is Beau Bridges? (ABC-TV)   83
Wichita (Tourneur, 1955)   13, 32, 63, 69
Wichita Town (TV series, 1959–60)   89, 162, 163, 177
Widmark, Richard   234
Wife for a Night (*Moglie per una notte*, Camerini, 1952)   203
Wife Wanted (Karlson, 1946)   48
Wild Bunch, The (Peckinpah, 1969)   249
Wilde, Cornel   70
Wilder, Billy   11, 54, 63, 68, 70, 71, 73, 85, 88, 89, 95, 96, 102, 110, 112, 120, 123, 124, 130–3, 144, 149, 151, 164, 202, 203, 206, 225, 229, 231, 232, 236
Wild Stallion   64
Wiles, Gordon   60

Wilkerson, William 'Billy'   79
William Morris Agency   161, 258
Williams, Raymond   128
William Shakespeare's Romeo and Juliet (Luhrman, 1996)   266
Willis, Gordon   222, 247
Wilson, Michael   74, 109
Windrum, Ken   228, 229
Winesburg Ohio (Anderson)   142, 144
Winner, Michael   237
Winters, Ralph E.   90
Winterset (Santell, 1936)   35
Wisconsin theatre circuit   22
Wise, Robert   57, 88, 111, 189, 221, 222, 230, 231, 237, 242
Woman in the Window, The (Lang, 1944)   73
Women, The (Cukor, 1939)   26
Women in Bondage (Sekely, 1943)   59
Wood, Allen K.   89
Woolrich, Cornell   46–50, 151
work simplification   38, 179, 180
'Work Simplification' programme   41
World Without End (Bernds, 1956)   63, 75
Wright, Robert Vincent   189
Writers Guild of America/West   138, 258
Wuthering Heights (Wyler, 1939)   35, 137
Wyler, William   57, 68, 70, 71, 73, 88, 96, 148, 152, 208, 222, 231, 236, 238, 242

X-Men, The   189

Yates, Peter   249
Yellow Submarine (Dunning, 1968)   197, 198
Yordan, Philip   47, 70
Yorkin, Bud   237
youth audience   102–4

Zanuck-David Brown, Richard D.   236, 252
zeitgeist theory   105–7, 127
Zinnemann, Fred   146–8, 161, 234, 242
Ziv-TV   164
Zukor, Adolph   34
Zweig, Stefan   68

www.ingramcontent.com/pod-product-compliance
Lightning Source LLC
Chambersburg PA
CBHW050617300426
44112CB00012B/1542